DIGITAL
ARCHITECTURE
NOW
>

WITH 872 ILLUSTRATIONS,
700 IN COLOR

DIGITAL ARCHITECTURE NOW

>

A GLOBAL SURVEY OF EMERGING TALENT

NEIL SPILLER

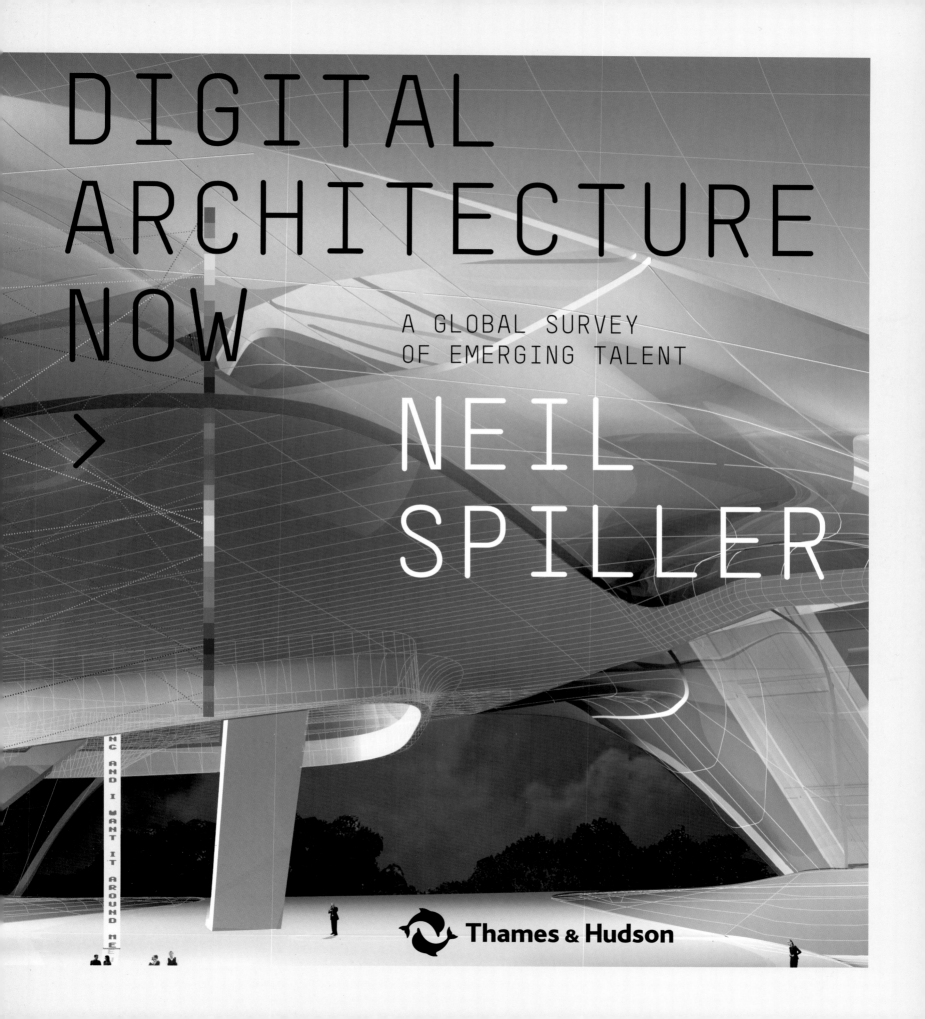

Thames & Hudson

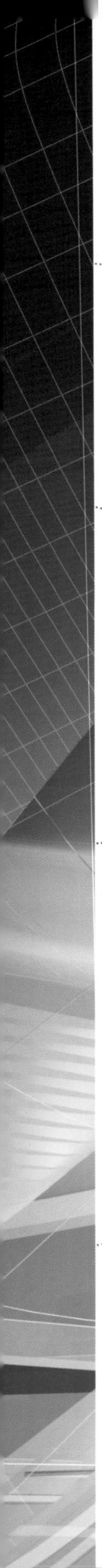

This book is dedicated to my wife, Melissa,
and my lovely sons, Eddie and Tom.

Special thanks to Lucas Dietrich, Cat Glover,
Andrea Belloli and all the architects who gave
their work so happily.

First published in 2009 in hardcover in the United States of America by
Thames & Hudson Inc., 500 Fifth Avenue, New York, New York 10110

thamesandhudsonusa.com

Library of Congress Catalog Card Number 2008900998

ISBN 978-0-500-34247-3

Printed and bound in China by Everbest Printing Co. Ltd.

Book design: Forever Studio

CONTENTS

006   FOREWORD > DIGITAL ARCHITECTURE: THE HISTORY SO FAR

016   AMID* architecture
026   Asymptote Architecture
036   Philip Beesley
050   Preston Scott Cohen
060   Contemporary Architectural Practice (CAP)
070   Hernan Diaz Alonso / Xefirotarch
080   Dennis Dollens / Exodesic
090   Ammar Eloueini / AEDS
100   EMERGENT
110   Evan Douglis Studio
118   Thom Faulders / BEIGE ARCHITECTURE AND DESIGN
128   Mark Goulthorpe / dECOi
140   Greg Lynn FORM
152   Usman Haque / Haque Design + Research
160   Jerry Tate Architects
172   J. Mayer H.
190   Tobias Klein
196   KOL/MAC LLC
212   Arshia Mahmoodi / Void, inc.
218   Marcosandmarjan
228   Stuart Munro
242   Shaun Murray
252   Naga Studio Architects
266   oceanD
276   ORTLOS
284   P-A-T-T-E-R-N-S
294   Qua'Virarch
306   Lindy Roy / ROY Co.
316   Enric Ruiz-Geli / Cloud9
326   servo
336   SIAL
344   sixteen*(makers)
352   Neil Spiller

362   AFTERWORD > PLECTIC ARCHITECTURE: TOWARDS
A THEORY OF THE POST-DIGITAL IN ARCHITECTURE
Massimo Minale, Christian Kerrigan, Lena Andersson,
Glen Tomlin, Melissa Clinch, James Curtis,
Sacha Leong, Martha Markopoulou

386   SOURCES >
388   Biographies
392   Project credits
394   Image credits
395   Glossary
396   Index

FOREWORD

>

DIGITAL ARCHITECTURE:
THE HISTORY SO FAR

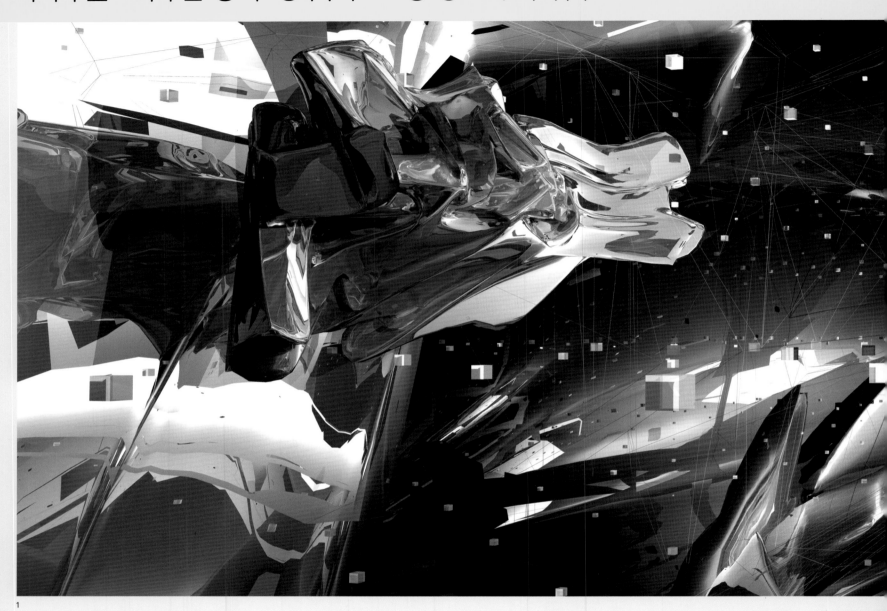

1

This book seeks to be both a succinct introduction to digital architecture and a 'section' through the state of the art. Laid out before you are architectural designers' current preoccupations, fetishes, manifestos and ambitions. I have selected the work shown here because it illustrates the broad, and ever broadening, parameters of what constitutes digital architecture.

During the last ten years, the practice of architecture has changed radically. The commercial availability of complex software and its reliant hardware technologies has created a fast, accurate and globally transferable design culture and community. These changes to the architectural profession will continue; they will not stabilize into some kind of desirable commercial optimum. As architects we are caught in the same running-to-stay-still dance of *Alice in Wonderland*'s Red Queen as we attempt to cope with the changes being brought to us by the virtual world. All of this was predicted a long time ago. What needs to be documented and illustrated is how we came to be where we are, the variety of different approaches enabled by this digital revolution, what architectural practices are producing and what might happen in the immediate future.

This book is about the new generation of architects who are designing digitally. Some aspect of digital production is now embedded in all architects' offices, and there is much more left to be explored and many more ramifications of these technologies to be felt by the profession and its clients.

It is important, initially, to understand the evolution of digital architecture and architects' first responses to digital technology. I myself have been intimately involved with the unfolding of this evolutionary process as a teacher of architects, a theorist, a practitioner of architecture and a cyber-evangelist.

It is often said that times of war are a fecund era for technological advances, and it is true that the blossoming of digital architecture has a prehistory born out of the Second World War. The early advances in computation – particularly the decoding of the Enigma Machine and Alan Turing's work in relation to it – and the evolution of cybernetics – initially provoked in part by a search for the successful prediction of trajectories of moving bodies for ballistic purposes – were both important developments that enabled digital architecture to be developed.

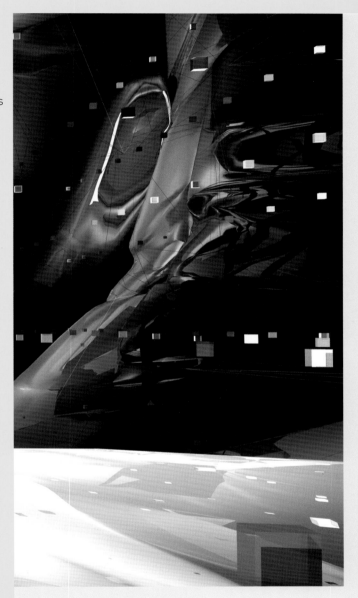

1_Marcos Novak
Eversion information landscapes, 2003

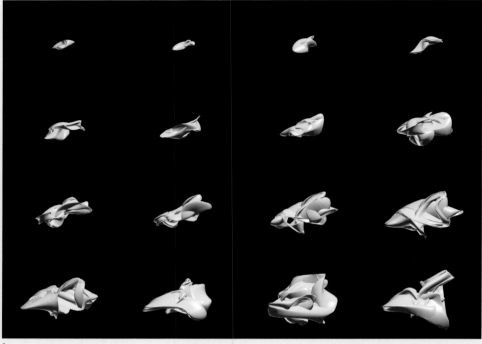

2

3

During the 1950s cybernetic ideas were discussed in avant-garde circles that included architects at the occasional meetings of the Independent Group at the Institute of Contemporary Arts in London. Also in mainland Europe the disaster of the war provoked some Leftist philosophers and artists to search for socialist utopias conditioned by personal perception and a kind of playful transcription of architectural space. The Situationists, as they called themselves, vicariously created one iconic project, whose architect was the artist Constant Niewenhuys. New Babylon was Constant's attempt to create a Situationist city. Its design, which commenced in 1957 and ended in 1973, dealt with 'ambiences' and 'creative play'. Constant occasionally evoked notions of cybernetics and its implied responsiveness – never fully defined – as a technological crutch for his utopian ideas. New Babylon was huge, a kind of meta-skin straddling the Earth.

The fundamental notions that conditioned cybernetics are those of systematic circularity, feedback and control: the governor on a steam engine is a simple cybernetic device. The founding pioneers of cybernetics had little or no contemporaneous affect on the production of architecture. However, during the early 1960s a second generation of cyberneticists – especially Gordon Pask – began to think of architectural design and its numerous interrelations as a cybernetic system. Pask was a second-order cyberneticist who wanted to include the observer, and the observer of the observer, within cybernetic systems. Second-order cybernetics was thus akin to Einsteinian physics and first-order cybernetics to classic physics.

In 1963 Pask was asked to consult on cybernetic systems in relation to a visionary architectural proposal called Fun Palace. Fun Palace was a grand socialist idea, an amusement park for education and play, in London's depressed Lea Valley. It was huge, with a footprint of 8 hectares (20 acres), and its architect was Cedric Price. Price believed that architecture was a service, that it should enable its users to recondition it in relation to their needs and criteria. He also believed that the delaying of spatial decisions in an ever-changing world was vitally important. With Fun Palace, Price wanted to create an architecture similar to a large shipyard, an architecture that wasn't an obstacle to change, enjoyment and delight.

Pask became a crucial member of the Committee for Fun Palace's Cybernetic Theatre. He had always been interested in the theatrical, and indeed the protocols, magic and suspended disbelief of the theatre are all part of cyberneticians' understanding of the world. The Cybernetic Theatre of Fun Palace was intended to have feedback communication between performers and audiences. Meanwhile, Price imbued every system, element and process in Fun Palace with time- and technology-based durations, ideas that are also of much importance to our contemporary digital-architectural condition as Fun Palace was a milestone in architectural history. It is a shame that it was never built, though by now Price would have probably have been campaigning for its demolition, as it would have outlived its usefulness (he had assigned it a lifespan of ten years).

2_Gordon Pask with the Universal Constructor
Diploma Unit 11 installation at the Architectural Association, June 1990
3_Manit Rastogi, Peter Graham and John Frazer
Globally evolving virtual environment, 1994
4_Marcos Novak
Allomorphic forms everting across space from the digital to the analogue, causing cascades of transvergence, 2002

Pask continued to think and speculate on architecture as a second-order cybernetic process and developed his major contribution to cybernetics, known as Conversation Theory. Pask believed that our knowledge of the world is conditioned by the conversation we have with it and with others. In relation to architecture, the process and re-evaluation that a designer adopts is a second-order cybernetic conversation. Once we understand the process we instigate when designing, it follows that we should then ask whether it is possible to create an architecture machine that might then help us to design.

In 1970, the architect Nicholas Negroponte published his team's researches into the creation of such a computational system at the Massachusetts Institute of Technology under the title *The Architecture Machine*. The idea of a machine of this kind has still not been fully realized – the complexities of such an undertaking are highlighted in Negroponte's book – but it is fundamentally about conversation, self-reflection and empathy, all difficult notions to pin down in the binary world of computer programming.

Price's influential involvement with the fledgling field of digital architecture was to manifest itself in another project: Generator. Instigated for the Gilman Paper Company during 1979 on a site in Florida, Generator consisted of simple 4-by-4-metre (13-by-13-foot) structural cubes, each capable of having its sides, bottom and top infilled with a range of panel options. What is remarkable about the proposal is its computational software and its programming intention, which was developed by John and Julia Frazer (who were influenced by Pask's cybernetic ideas). Each cube had embedded chips which told the computer where and in what orientation it was; the computer could then instruct a series of robotic cranes to relocate cubes and built enclosures to meet users' demands. While this in itself was visionary enough, Generator was spatially proactive. If its configuration had not recently been changed, it would dream up new spatial arrangements itself. So it had a sense of its own archaeology and its own 'boredom'. Generator was another critical landmark, again never built, on architecture's slow but definite progress towards embracing the digital.

The 1990s proved to be the era when architects finally embraced the digital in increasing numbers. The decade began quite slowly. By 1990 the more forward-looking members of many disciplines (inspired in part by the science-fiction author William Gibson's 1984 novel *Neuromancer*, which posited a real-time virtual space) started to conceive of such space – dubbed cyberspace by Gibson – as a new arena conditioned by new,

4

ethereal rules. For architects, the publication in 1991 of a collection of essays edited by Michael Benedikt entitled *Cyberspace: First Steps* was the necessary catalyst. The seminal essay in this collection was 'Liquid Architectures in Cyberspace' by the architect Marcos Novak, who had had his own digital epiphany in 1979. In his essay he firmly grounded architectural cyberspace, defining its potential as the province of the avant-garde and relating its idea of flow or liquidity back to previous avant-gardes both within and outside of architectural theoretical discourse.

By the early 1990s, computers had advanced to the stage where debates could be held about whether it was possible to create spatial architecture in the virtual rather than the real world. As the decade progressed, many architects started to experiment with aspects of virtual technology and how it could peek into the real.

My own involvement with cyberspatial architecture commenced around this time. From 1992 on, I encouraged my students at the Bartlett University College London to embrace the potential of cyberspace and design architectures which dwelt entirely or partially within it. I also started to write a book called *Digital Dreams: Architecture and the New Alchemic Technologies*, eventually published in 1998 but finished a few years earlier. The book sought to illustrate the amazing potential of the new technologies for architects, particularly cyberspace, nanotechnology, biotechnology and emergence, and their similarities to the more arcane 'technologies' of alchemy, shamanism and other transmutational systems. *Digital Dreams* trumpeted a transformed future for architects and new ways for architects to operate within the world.

John Frazer further augmented his own progress through his work as well as in his 1995 publication, *An Evolutionary Architecture*. *An Evolutionary Architecture* investigates the fundamental form-generating processes in architecture, paralleling a wider scientific search for a theory of morphogenesis in the natural world. The book proposes the model of nature as the generating force for architectural form. The profligate prototyping and awesome creative power of natural evolution are emulated by creating virtual architectural models that respond to changing environments. Successful developments are encouraged and evolve. Architecture is considered as a form of artificial life, subject, like the natural world, to principles of morphogenesis, genetic coding, replication and selection. The aim of an evolutionary architecture is to achieve in the built environment the symbiotic behaviour and metabolic balance that are characteristic of the natural environment. Frazer's researches

5_Neil Spiller with sixteen* (makers)
Hot Desk: Nanotechnological information surface prototype, 1995
6_Antonio Gaudi et al.
Sagrada Familia, Barcelona, 1884–
7_Antonio Gaudi / Mark Burry et al.
Façade study
8–9_Neil Spiller
Mediatheque, Parker's Piece, Cambridge, 1995. A building designed to 'come alive' when the Turing Test is passed: Plan and Cellular Automata Glider Sculptures

continue today and are very influential on the current generation of digital architects.

Simultaneously with the publication of Frazer's book and Bill Mitchell's 1996 *City of Bits*, which discussed the digital architecture of the great virtual city just over the conceptual horizon, I published (with Martin Pearce) the 'Architects in Cyberspace' edition of *Architectural Design*. It included Novak's, Frazer's and Mitchell's work as well as my own on nanotechnology and architecture.

In the US, prompted by the 'Anyone' conference held in 1991 in Los Angeles and Santa Monica, 'Electrotecture' was being discussed, particularly in relation to an attempt at defining the architectural status of a digital screen. It was this ontological problem and the relishing of the flux between image, surface and architecture that gave birth to the short-lived notion of Hypersurfaces. But technology moves ever more quickly, and cyberspace engulfed architectural theory way beyond the limited notion of the skin and had much greater ramifications for our spatial understanding.

In the last ten years, many architects have been instrumental in exploring some of the emerging terrain engendered by digital architecture. Lars Spuybroek's Fresh H2O building in the Netherlands was an important piece on the way to full-blown responsive architecture. Kas Oosterhuis's attempts to create digital real-time architectures have been influential. Mark Burry's revealing of Antoní Gaudí's second-order geometry has recast the Catalan's place in the pantheon of proto-cyberspatial architects. Burry has been in the vanguard working with parametrics and generative components. Marcos Novak's AlloSpace, AlloSphere, Eversion and Transarchitecture; Greg Lynn's work on Animate Space; and hopefully my own work on Vacillation, Reflexivity, Bioscapes and Surreality have all been important.

Today, parametric design and generative-component design have also developed a whole repertoire of notions about skinning, evolving and fabricating architecture. Some architects have, like Oosterhuis, attempted to construct elements of buildings that have the ability to respond to data streams in real time. Others have recognized that complex, computationally drawn cutting and routing patterns can create minute landscapes and have used them to design furniture and screens. This idea that the old Fordist notions of mass production and limits on the variety of factory-produced goods is no longer valid has allowed architects to posit non-standard geometries or elements in their buildings.

It costs nearly nothing to create ornate works in this vein, and therefore the appropriateness of decoration is manifesting itself as an issue for architectural debate again. This is a challenge to the all-pervading aesthetic of Modernism. The envelopes of buildings can be created from a series of braided surfaces visualized on computers, and, if they are built, machine instructions can be sent straight to the factory to enable full-size fabrication. Others architects still use evolutionary algorithms to generate work, so their proposals are in some sense 'bred'. Information is now ubiquitous. All manner of data can be collected, transmitted and relocated, and this data can be used to create animated surfaces within structures while also forming the fundamental building blocks of buildings. Therefore the old typologies of building have become corrupted and blurred. Without the rapid evolution of the computer and its ways of processing and keeping check on large amounts of data, none of these new projects would be possible.

After the digital revolution, when a lot of architectural babies were thrown out with the bath water, came a period when cyberspace, virtuality, biotechnology and even nanotechnology all had an impact on architecture and the future paradigm of the city. We are still in the midst of this period. Computation technology is a double-edged sword. It promises liberation from laborious work; it promises instant, or near instant, communication. It promises smart interactive materials, surfaces and buildings. However, it can be responsible for surveillance, twenty-four-hour working, a ubiquitous style of place resulting in uniformity of urban design and ecological damage. The task for the current set of architects is to propose architectures that navigate and negotiate between these polarities and vicariously create buildings and cities that are welcoming, enabling, facilitating, liberal, networked and spatially exciting.

At the end of this book, I speculate on a post-digital era in which the digital will be seamlessly dovetailed with contemporary architecture and life. I attempt to illustrate where the new frontiers are and speculate on how architects might address them. One thing is certain. Our world will continue to feel the onslaught of the digital tsunami, and architects must tame its power to create sublime new architectures. In such a context we must finally address the health of our planet. Digital architecture utilized prudently will enable us to do this.

8

9

PROJECTS

>

AMID*
ARCHITECTURE

>

MADRID

The Magic Mountain: Skin aesthetic

Cristina Díaz Moreno and Efrén García Grinda started their partnership in 1997 as cero9, an open collaborative office, located in Madrid, which attempted a real connection between professional practice, research and teaching. cero9 was dissolved in 2003. Shortly thereafter, Moreno and Grinda formed AMID, a more nomadic organization, mainly still based in Spain, based also on today's fast electronic communications, global architectural market and the partners' international teaching commitments. Their work is characterized by curved corners, rounded surfaces and, often, the use of flora and fauna as façade treatments. The architectural language hints at the biological, a language of molars, of blood corpuscles, hair and fur.

While their compositional 'eye' is important to AMID's projects, what is crucial are their attempts to mitigate environmental damage. To this end they use the computer not just to represent architectural forms but to predict and channel energy flows and dissipation throughout their buildings. AMID's architecture can be understood as a variety of interlinked and interdependent fields of energy – virtual, actual, organic and inorganic – that flex over time. Certain set pieces act as environmental lungs and monitors, some are seen to float in water, and others are embedded in complex weaves of hair and tufts of moss-like hillocks.

The Magic Mountain: Ecosystem Mask for Ames Thermal Power Station Ames, Iowa

A power station is situated at the heart of the city of Ames. The proposal was to treat this existing building as a segment of landscape within the city: as a living mountain. The proposal was not merely cosmetic. The architects attempted to mitigate the power station's impact by implementing the instruments and concepts of gardening, species breeding, architecture and ecology. They proposed to cover the fragmented volumes of the power station entirely with a membrane of roses, honeysuckle and lights. This new skin wraps itself around the units at different heights, adapting itself to them, shrouding and unifying them with a silhouette and a single common material. The membrane creeps above the highest parts of the power station and transforms the building into a vertical garden with living walls. In order to facilitate pruning and upkeep by gardeners, a perimeter pathway was cleared between the 'shell' and the power station's walls. The project was intended to attract birds and butterflies.

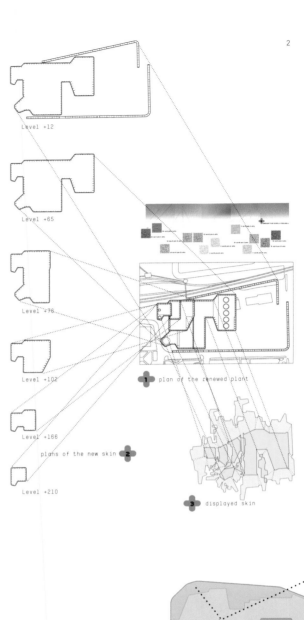

Level +12

Level +65

Level +76

Level +102

Level +166

Level +210

1 plan of the renewed plant

plans of the new skin 2

3 displayed skin

1

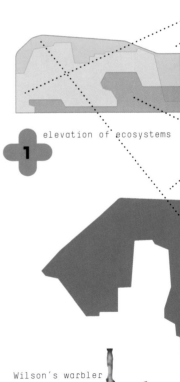

elevation of ecosystems

1

Wilson's warbler

1_Skin study
2_Location plan
3_Exterior view
4_Bird habitat zoning diagram

3

4

southern dogface

glauc

queen

3 butterfly ecosytems

yellow rumped warbler

4 bird families

chestnut-sided warbler

indigo bunting

8th Spanish Architecture Biennale Exhibition
Travelling exhibition

This project is an exhibition installation consisting of thirty-four environments and one space. A system of floating pieces distributed throughout the exhibition illustrates each of the projects. In the half-light of the space, the images, printed on electro-luminescent film, glow around the visitor's head, while the voice of each architect describes the project's most significant aspects. Each of the transparent methacrylate pieces holds a collection of images and allows them to be contemplated from outside and within each pod. The images unfold around the visitor's sight, building up a visual field that aims to reproduce the immersive experience of visiting a building. Thus each building is shown in a small individual exhibition within the context of a larger one. The spaceship-like cocoons are placed in groups along the exhibition rooms, organized according to pragmatic criteria (such as built area, budget and orientation). The final cocoon houses the descriptive material for each project.

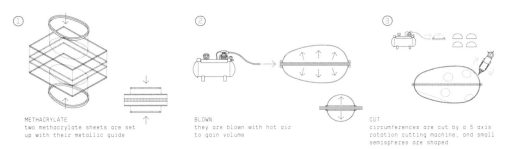

① METHACRYLATE
two methacrylate sheets are set up with their metallic guide

② BLOWN
they are blown with hot air to gain volume

③ CUT
circumferences are cut by a 5 axis rotation cutting machine, and small semispheres are shaped

④ LOCATED
small semispheres are located in the holes

⑤ ELECTROLUMINISCENT
electroluminiscent film with printed images are stuck on

⑥ ADDED
sound, scents and tft screens are added

⑦ PLUGGED
the piece is plugged

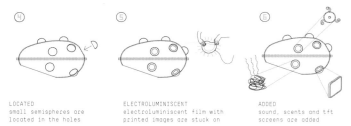

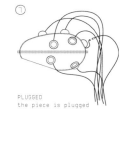

1

2

1_Pod fabrication montage
2_Pod deployment
3_Pod detail
4_Pods installed

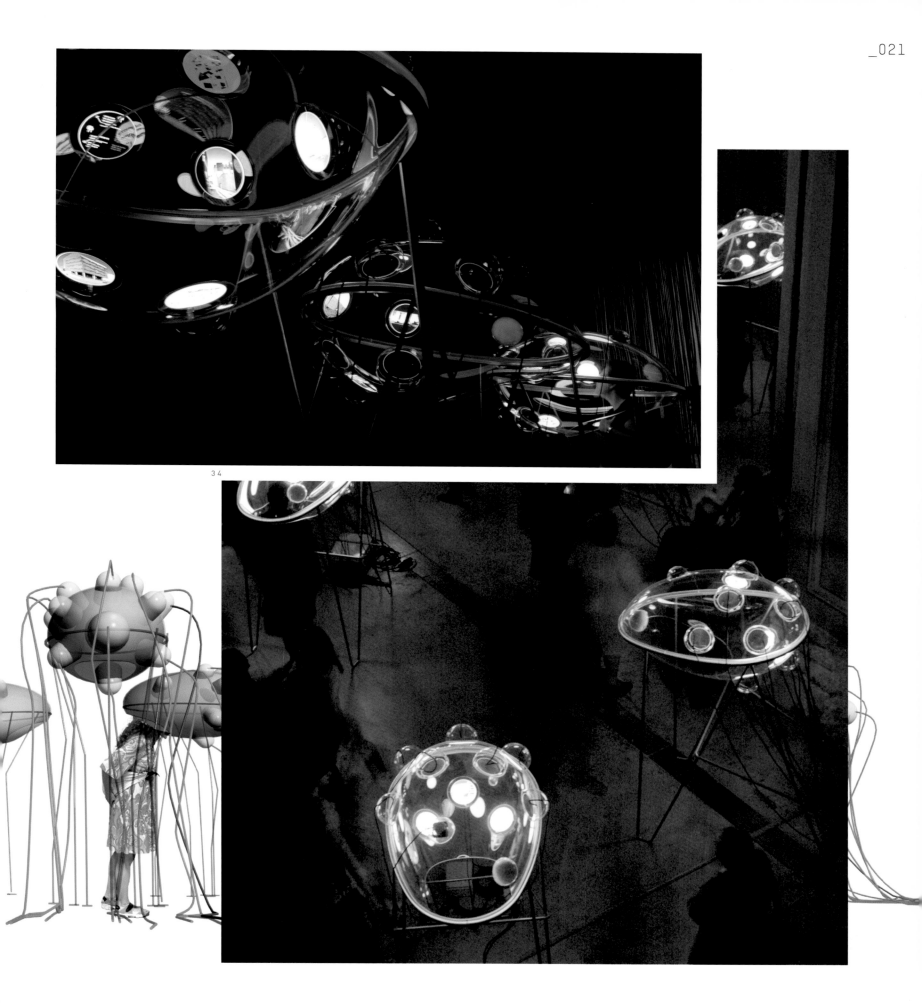

34

Forms of Energy: La Biennale di Venezia
Venice, Italy

Perhaps the contemporary language of architecture can be seen as one in which its visible form is conditioned by the dissipation of energy. A building is a complex thermodynamic system that works through cold or heat, in or out of phase, with differences or homogeneities that change over time.

This project develops systems that regulate processes of energy exchange with the outdoors: dissipation, consumption and capture. Let's imagine a technical system that, through the capture and emission of energy, induces spatial, environmental and visual effects. What we understand as space becomes a set of perceptions linked to environmental effects generated through the management of various forms of energy. Architecture becomes an artificial atmospheric system on a reduced scale, with its unstable equilibriums, transitory states, complex internal relationships and associated visual effects.

Venice is a slowly dying city. Its sweet-water lagoon connected to the sea has been progressively altered by a change in the water's salinity. This project proposed to deploy and install a system of objects throughout the lagoon; each one would work by capturing and emitting energy. The pieces mainly functioned in two ways: reactivating public space through energy and the production of semi-private spaces, and trying to reclaim the lagoon by introducing micro-organisms.

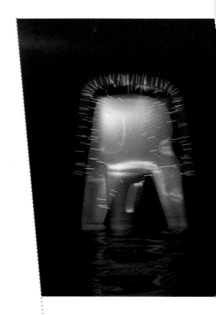

1

trp colectores

trp redes de niebla

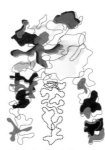

trp trayectorias agua

trp infrarrojos

trp bodas

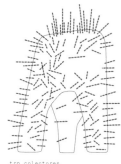

trp microtubos capilares

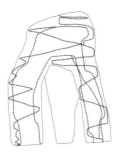

trp uv-a

trp marihuana

1_Skin studies
2_Lagoon vignette
3_Lagoon plan
4_Sectional configurations
5_Exterior perspective

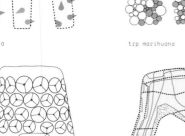

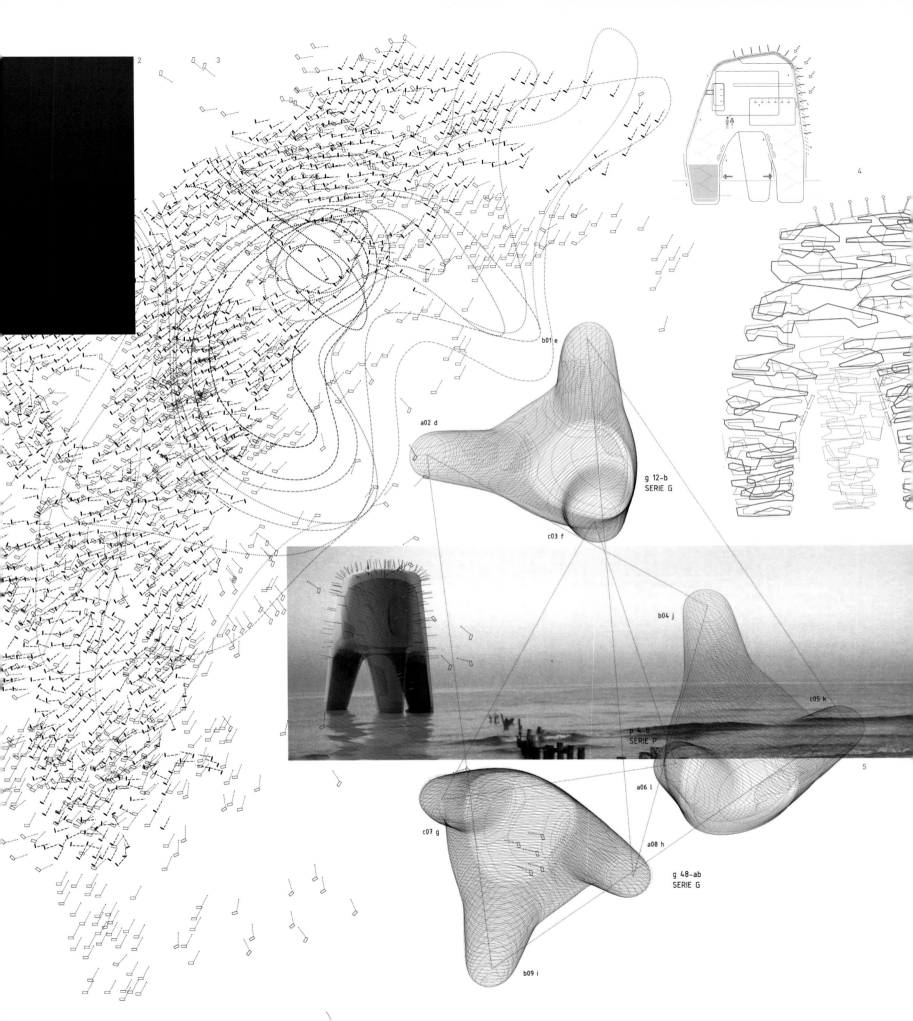

2

3

b01 e

a02 d

g 12-b
SERIE G

c03 f

b04 j

c05 k

p 4-b
SERIE P

a06 l

c07 g

a08 h

g 48-ab
SERIE G

b09 i

4

5

Administrative Building and Town Hall
Lalín, Pontevedra, Spain

The architects wanted to produce a building that encouraged the intersection of roads, people, goods and ideas. Thus the level of public space is elevated 6 metres (20 feet) above ground level, creating a symbolic crossroads. A series of paths connecting the Town Hall with different points in the village stretches upwards, becoming ramps and stairs that converge on the new space. It is hoped that social and intellectual contacts will be fostered through chance encounters.

The structure has been placed at the building's perimeter in order to obtain diaphanous spaces without intermediate pillars. It is a dense woven matrix of steel welded in rigid knots and triangular figures, and forms a structural framework wrapping itself around the building's different wings. The result is a casing of three-dimensional white 'lace' around the entire building. The sun acted as a driver to the structure's final configuration, influencing its density and depth. The most exposed façades avoid excessive direct sunlight in summer. The upper level of the building and the east and west façades have a deeper structure, and in some parts the density of the 'lace' is also greater to optimize passive energy.

> AMID*'s work is both surprising and ecologically valid; their star is bound to rise.

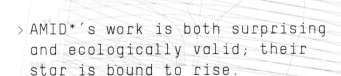

1_Exterior form
2_Plan
3_Rendering showing general structural arrangement
4_General arrangement section / elevation
5_Structural vignette rendering

3

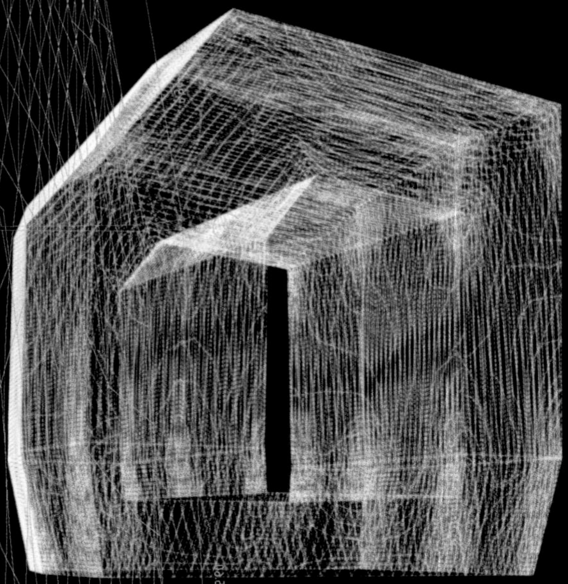

4

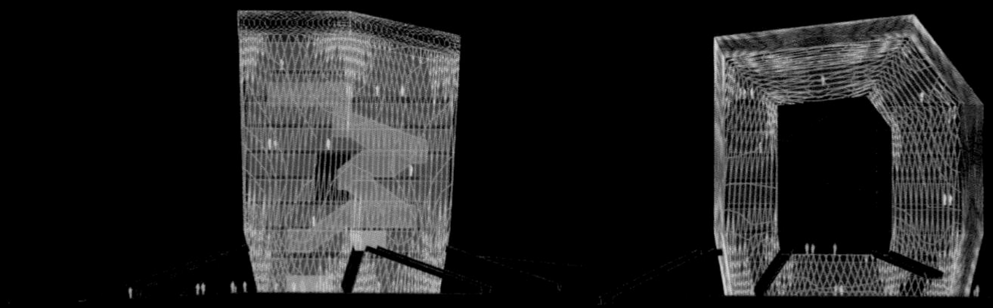

5

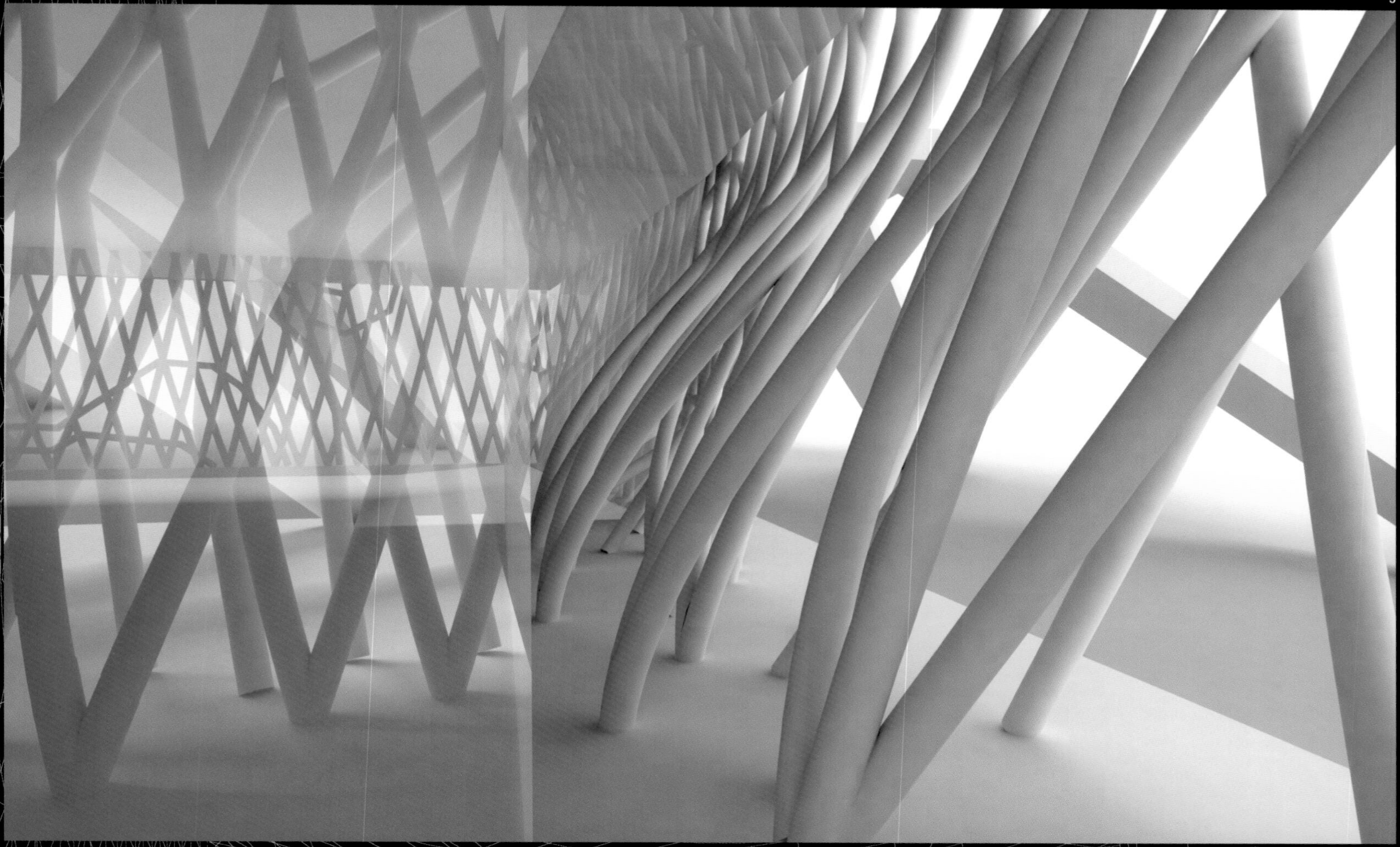

ASYMPTOTE
ARCHITECTURE

>

NEW YORK

Hani Rashid and Lise Anne Couture founded Asymptote Architecture in 1989 and have been the firm's principals since its inception. The practice is based in New York. Rashid and Couture have received international acclaim for their innovative work and contribution to design excellence. Recognized as leading practitioners and academics of their generation, their projects are realized on various scales, including urban plans, buildings, interiors, product design and multi-media installations. In 2004, Rashid and Couture were presented with the Frederick Kiesler Award, one of the most prestigious of prizes, in recognition of their exceptional contributions to the progress and merging of art and architecture. Asymptote has been at the forefront of technological innovation in both the process of generating and developing concepts and in production and execution.

For more than fifteen years, architecture, culture, technology and the city have been dominant themes throughout Asymptote's work. The translation of concepts informed by cultural, technological and social dimensions has provided inspiration to many of the practice's projects and causes them to gravitate towards culturally significant projects such as museum, exhibition and performance spaces but also to rethink the various scales ranging from the urban context to the interior. Asymptote is an established digital-architecture firm and has been a fashion-setter for more than a decade.

Guggenheim Guadalajara: Entrance view

Alessi Flagship Store
New York

1

1–3_Interior views of constructed store

Alessi, an internationally recognized brand, helped set the pace for design in the 1980s with the production of iconic works by critically important postmodern architects ranging from Aldo Rossi to Michael Graves. In subsequent years, a unique and respected image for the company evolved from the creativity and insight of the renowned architect and designer Alessandro Mendini and his strong relationship with Alberto Alessi. Taking a new turn, Alberto Alessi engaged Hani Rashid and Asymptote to develop an entirely novel trajectory for the brand. Asymptote was engaged not only in new product design but also in creating a new graphic identity and flagship store in the heart of SoHo.

Asymptote's approach to the store, product and brand design developed from a search for new languages predicated on mathematically inspired and derived elegance. In a radical shift away from the postmodern staples of historic pastiche, motif, vivid colouration, and iconographic and symbolic form, Asymptote forged an approach that took its cues from fluid and dynamic movement. This approach, intrinsic in new methods and instigated by digital tools and means, privileges a tectonic play of sophisticated geometric solutions in place of symbolic gestures.

Auditorium Beukenhof
Beukenhof, The Netherlands

The Auditorium and Crematorium Beukenhof was a commission prompted by the uplifting and inspiring quality of Asymptote's architecture. The client desired an architecture with a contemporary feel but also an aesthetic of timelessness that would be a graceful addition to its bucolic setting. The interior spaces are imbued with a subtly transforming quality of light that works in concert with the shifting architectural forms. These provide a series of serene backdrops and a fluid spatial and temporal trajectory through the architecture and the events within. On the exterior, the architecture is another landscape element that bridges the adjacent canal. Comprised of an undulating seamed-copper roof and double-curved enclosure, Asymptote's design exploits the Netherlands' rich tradition of brick architecture through a thoroughly contemporary formal expression.

> Asymptote's seamless and sleek output has enabled it to become one of the premier digital practices.

1_Exterior view

1

Budapest Bank Tower
Budapest

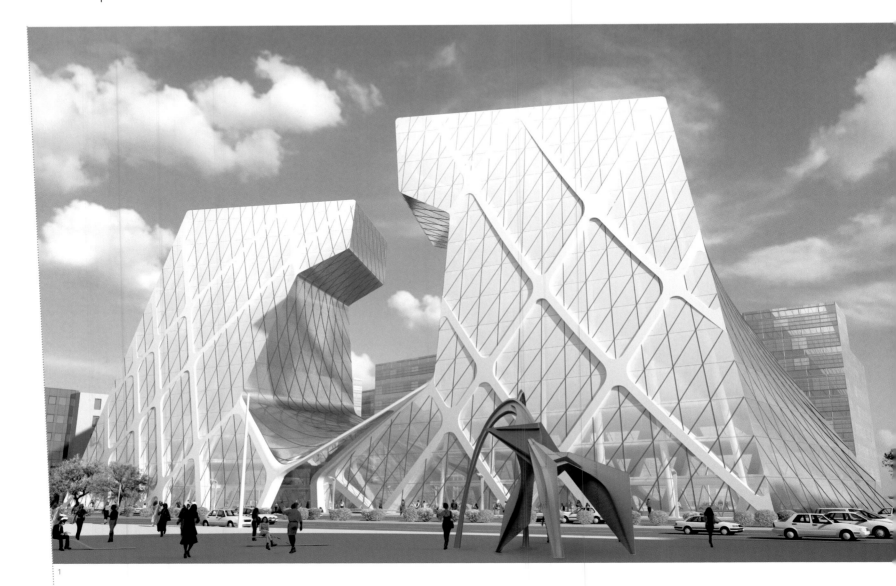

1

1_Exterior view (daytime)
2_Exterior view (night-time)

2

Asymptote's approach for the Budapest Bank Tower project is centred on achieving two twisting, tapering towers rising out of the ground, where the notion of singularity and simultaneity gives way to a strong juxtaposition of forms and void. At the same time a single entity, these spectacular towers turn to address both the historic River Danube and the city centre of Budapest. When seen from multiple vantage points, the two towers will always appear exciting, changing with point of view.

The premise is that such high-profile architecture for the twenty-first century should achieve a supreme and sophisticated elegance in which tectonic expression is born out of an intelligent approach to design. This elegance is achieved not only in aesthetic terms but also in terms of functionality, efficiency and viability.

Through innovative and technologically advanced approaches to the integration and implementation of building systems, structure, vertical transportation and environmental sustainability, a sophisticated formal expression is achieved. The overall massing builds on an innovative structural strategy and is a response to the optimization of both programmatic requirements and light and air. The base of the towers artfully negotiates and accommodates the asymmetrical site at the entrance level, while from the top of the atrium space the towers rise around a spectacular central void.

Carlos Miele
Flagship Store
New York

Asymptote's design for the Carlos Miele flagship store was conceived as a bright, open space utilizing a neutral palette of white and shades of pale green / green-blue and grey, all serving to foreground Miele's colourful clothing designs. The interior space consists of two-tone high-gloss epoxy flooring with embedded neon and halogen lighting set beneath tempered-glass rings. The curved formed-steel hanging displays cantilevered from the walls sit above lacquered bent-plywood display units. At the storefront window, display areas as well as the circular changing-room area are backlit using diffusion film, plexiglass and fluorescent lighting. The ceiling, which is a contoured surface, is formed from a high-gloss stretched-PVC-based material.

The centrepiece of the store is a large floor-to-ceiling sculptural form that traverses the entire interior. This 'altar' element, used for both seating and display, is fabricated from lacquer-finished bent plywood over a rib-and-gusset substructure that was laser-cut directly from CAD drawings and fabricated offsite. For both the design and the fabrication of the curved forms and surfaces, computer-generated drawings and digital procedures were instrumental. Additionally, two Asymptote video installations featuring digital art have been integrated into the architecture.

1-3_Interior of store

1

23

PHILIP
BEESLEY
>

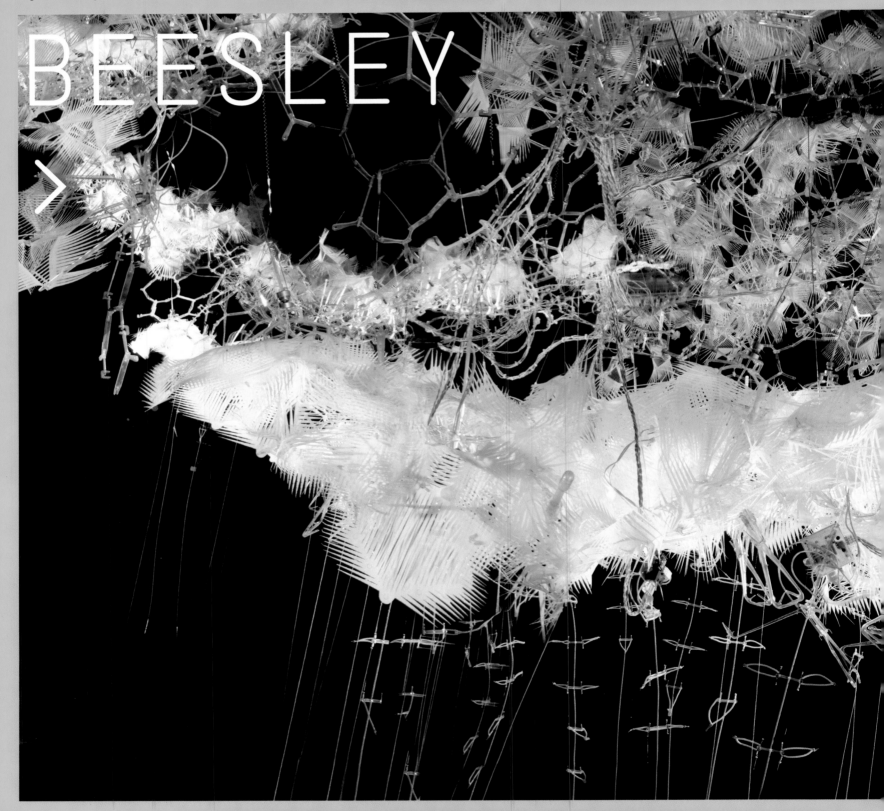

The Canadian academic, architect and artist Philip Beesley creates architecture that concentrates on vital, seething qualities built up from intensive repetition of miniature parts. His early landscape-based work employed flexible draping that sought to create a subtle skin for the land. Other examples tend towards porous, ephemeral spaces in which living functions are implied.

These projects are an extension of the ordinary industrial practice of reinforcing landscapes using geo-textiles. Here digital synthesis has moved from conception through modelling and rendering to new automated manufacturing using rapid prototyping coupled with activation based on sensing and actuator arrays. At the same time, the projects tend to question psychological boundaries. These large-scale field structures offer immersion, an expansion rendering our physical bodies porous and offering wide-flung dispersal of identity. Thus they relate to a long tradition of mysticism.

TORONTO

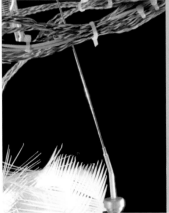

Beesley's current work has an ethereal quality; it moves almost as slowly as a plant, changing its micro-orientation with the nuance of intent of a Venus flytrap. But not for Beesley the final snap shut. His work is an ongoing quest for a composite architecture, an architecture of delicate parts, trembling, ever so subtly, in their ecstatic inhalation of the world and its minute constitutions and micro-climates.

To make these fragile pieces, paradoxically, he uses large machines that laser-cut and depose beautiful and natural-seeming elements, which he places and interlinks with the care of a twenty-first-century demiurge.

Implant Matrix

Cybele
University of
Waterloo, Canada

Cybele is a self-assembling structural framework made of extremely delicate laser-cut components connected and oriented by powerful rare-earth magnets. A barbed cellulose membrane covers the structure; through flex and movement in the system, it knits itself together. The sculpture was installed at the University of Waterloo in 2005.

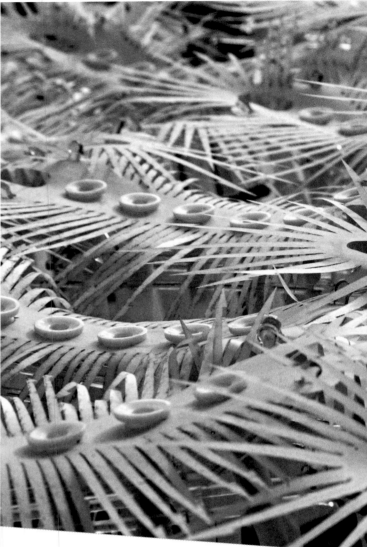

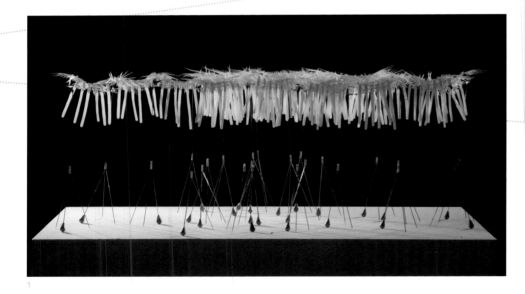

1_Elevation showing laser-cut canopy and magnets
2_Canopy detail
3_View below canopy
4_Detail within canopy

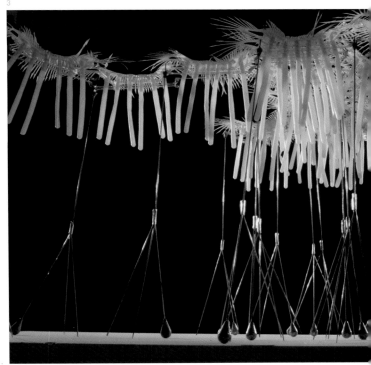

Implant Matrix
InterAccess Media
Arts Centre,
Toronto

Implant Matrix is an interactive geo-textile that could be used for reinforcing landscapes and buildings of the future. The matrix – fabricated by laser-cutting direct from digital models – is capable of mechanical empathy. A network of mechanisms reacts to human occupants as erotic prey. The structure responds to the human presence with subtle grasping and sucking motions, ingesting organic materials and incorporating them into a new hybrid entity.

Implant Matrix is composed of interlinking filtering 'pores' within a polymer structural system. Primitive interactive controls employ distributed microprocessors with capacitance sensors and shape-memory alloy-wire actuators.

Implant Matrix was installed at the InterAccess Media Arts Centre in Toronto in 2006.

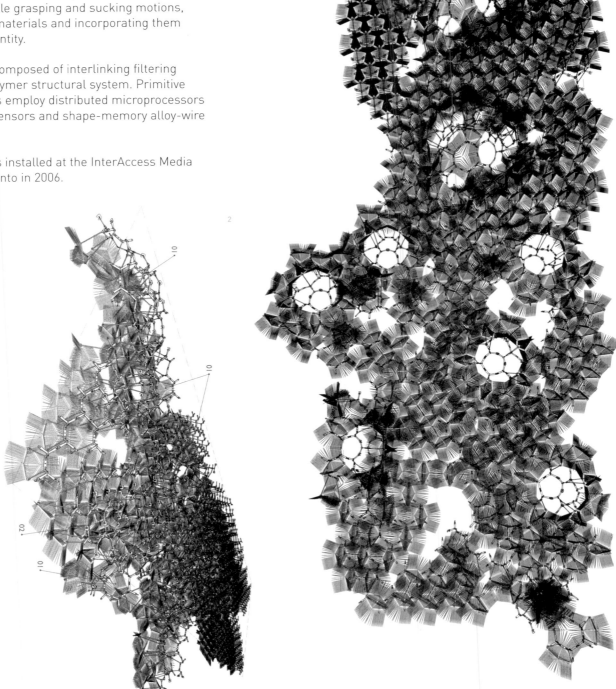

1-2_Plans
3_Component details
4_Canopy
5_Under canopy
6_Exterior detail
7_Detail view

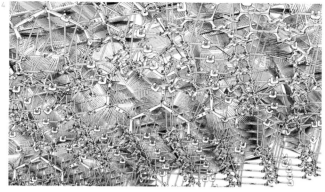

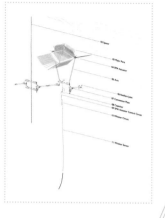

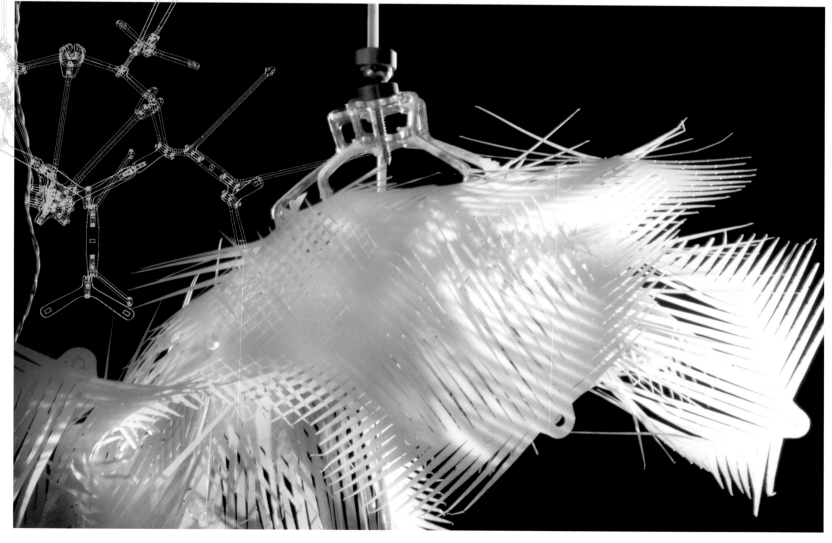

Orgone Reef
Travelling
architectural
installation

Orgone Reef is a hybrid geo-textile equipped with layers of miniature valves and clamping mechanisms that slowly digest and convert surrounding material into a fertile living wall. A minimal amount of raw material is expanded to form a porous network. The array is organized into a cohesive structure using shifting patterns of non-repeating geometry. The work was installed at the Royal British Architects Pavilion at Birmingham and the Building Centre in London in 2004.

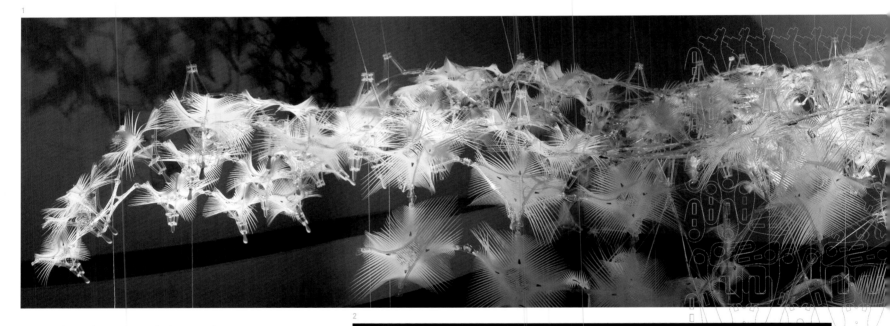

> Beesley's creations have a quivering eroticism seldom seen within the architectural profession.

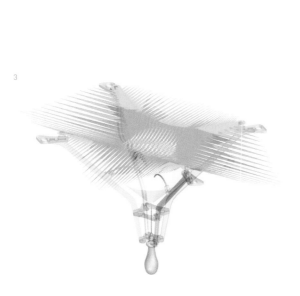

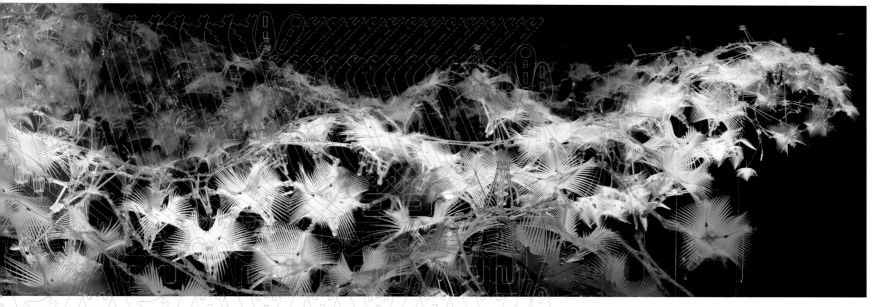

1_General arrangement view
2_Reflected canopy
3_Component detail
4_Detail of heads
5_Laser-cutting patterns

Orpheus Filter
Travelling
installation

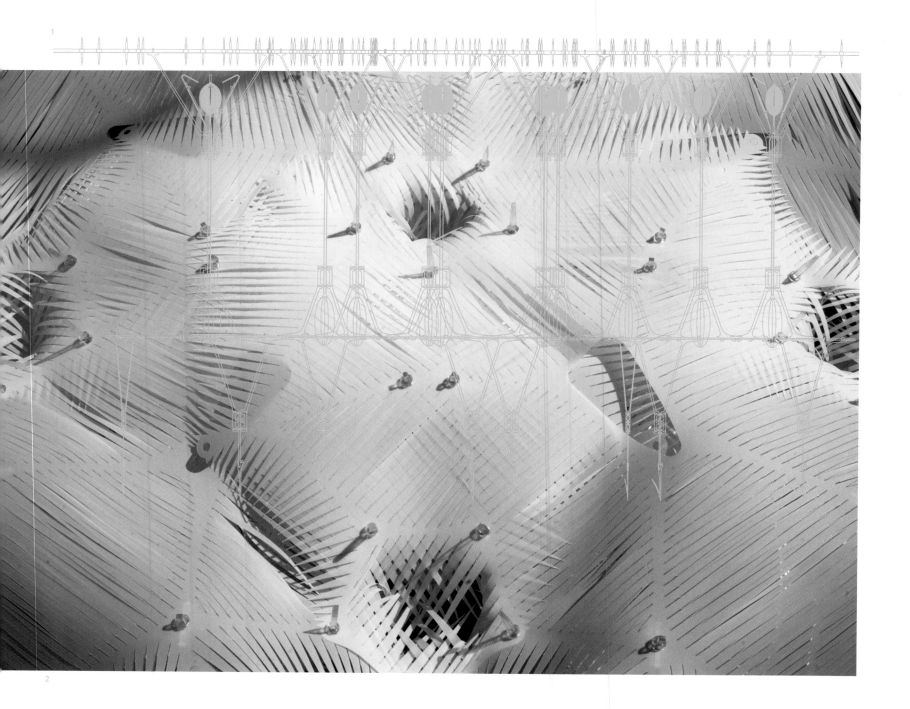

1_Layout drawing
2_Canopy plan
3_Module configuration
4_'Whisker' sensor detail

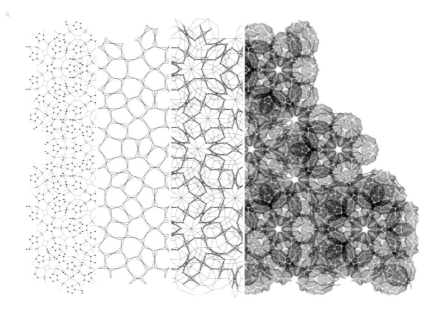

Orpheus Filter is an artificial reef designed to collect and digest organic material. The work attempts to create an immersive experience of a volatile, fertile earth, offering dissociation and absorption and resulting in waves of hybrid behaviour. The structure employs reflexive functions involving arrays of sensors and actuators operating valves and 'whisker' sensors. The work was developed in association with the Media Lab at the Massachusetts Institute of Technology in Cambridge, Massachusetts and the Daniel Langlois Foundation for Art and Technology in Montreal.

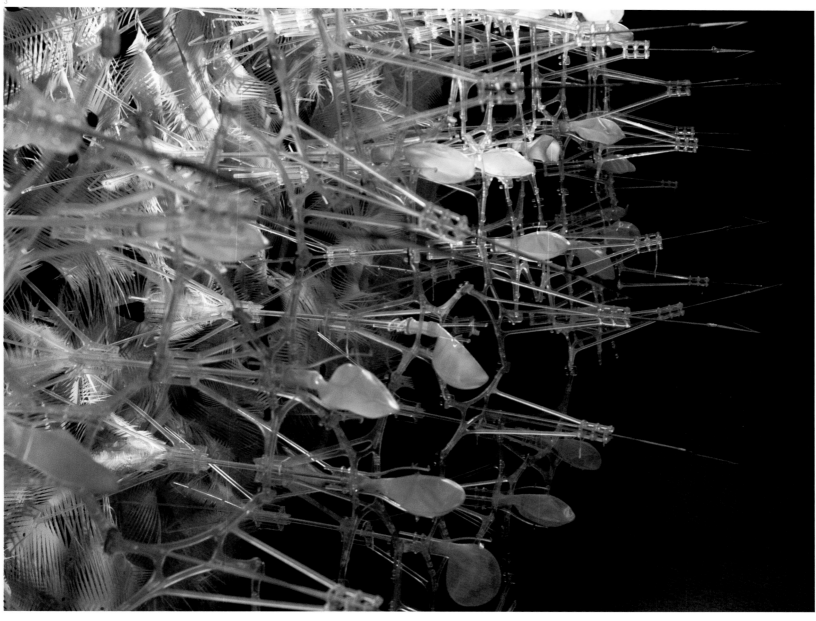

Reflexive Membranes
Cambridge, Ontario, Canada

Reflexive Membranes is an extended sculpture series
of porous interlinking matrices manufactured by
computer-controlled rapid-prototyping equipment
and activated by arrays of sensors and actuators.
These lightweight structures are made of an aggregate
of smaller impulse-based reactions and a 'neural'
network of microprocessor-controlled responses.
The integration of arrayed microprocessing and
activation systems into the structural lattices creates
a physically responsive, adaptive and self-organizing
sculpture system.

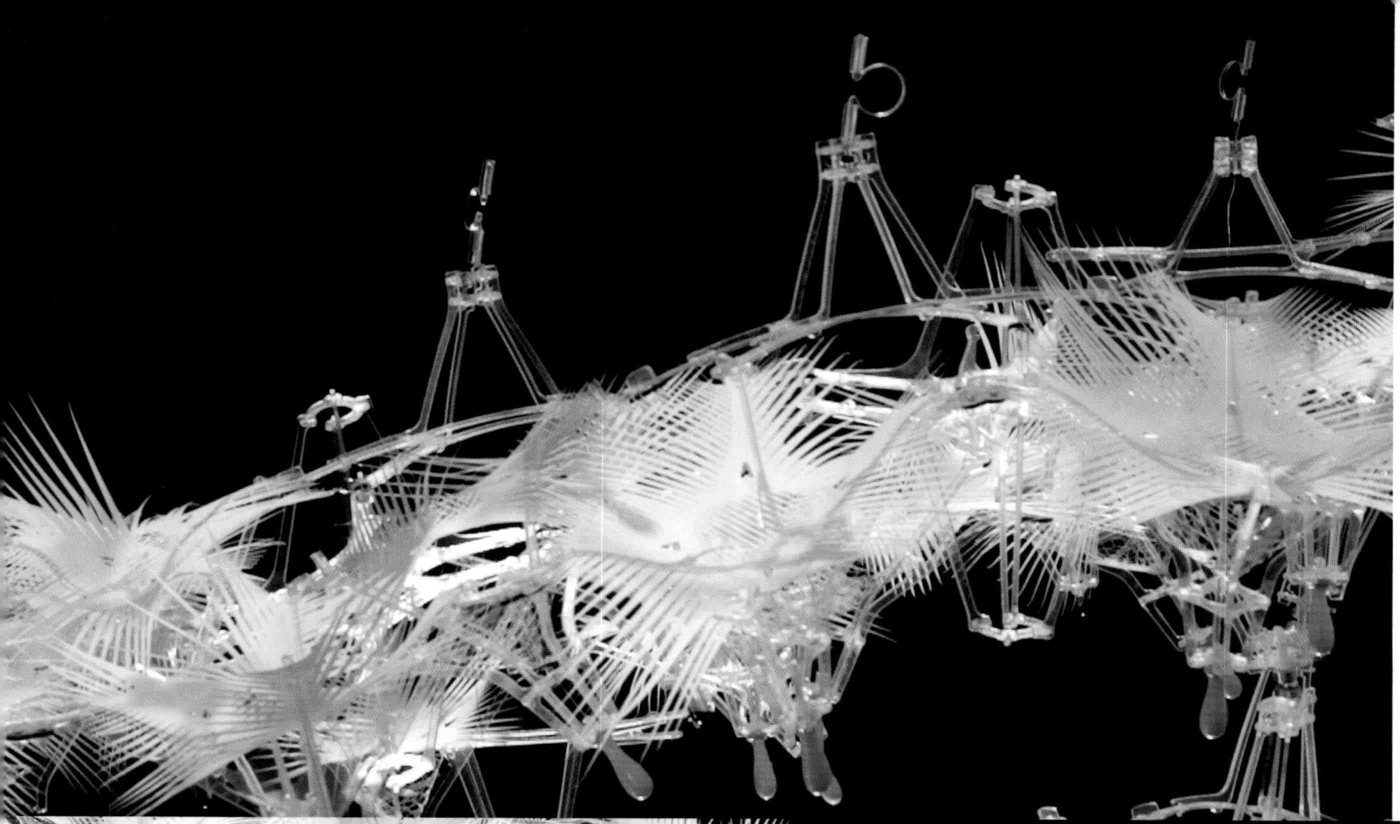

2

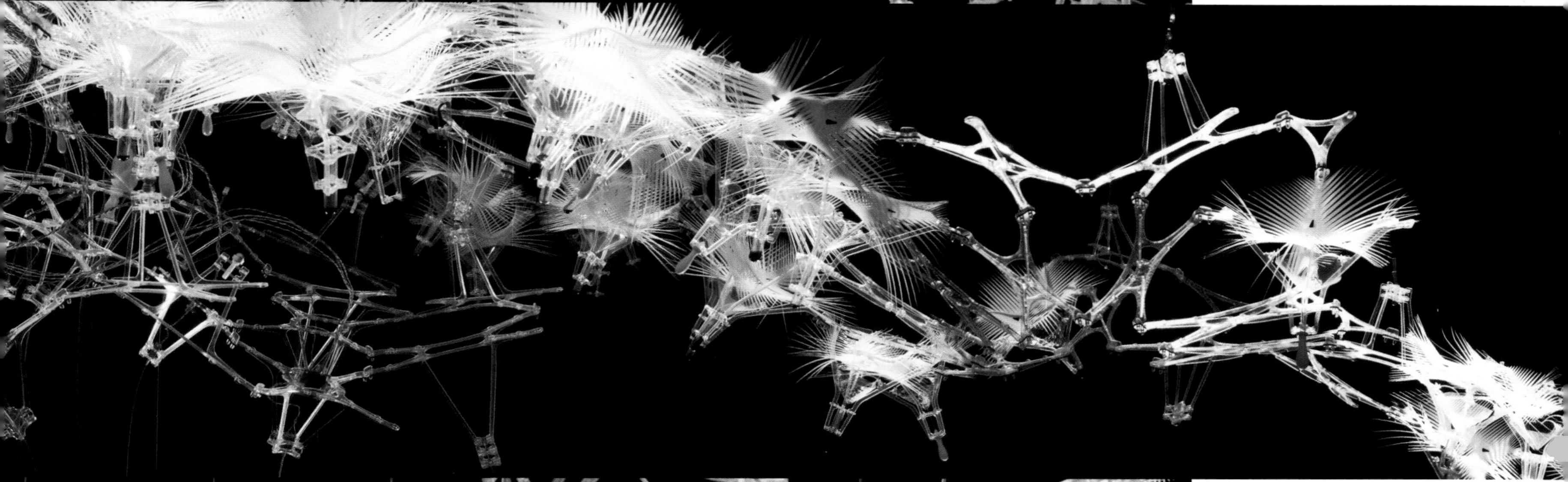

3

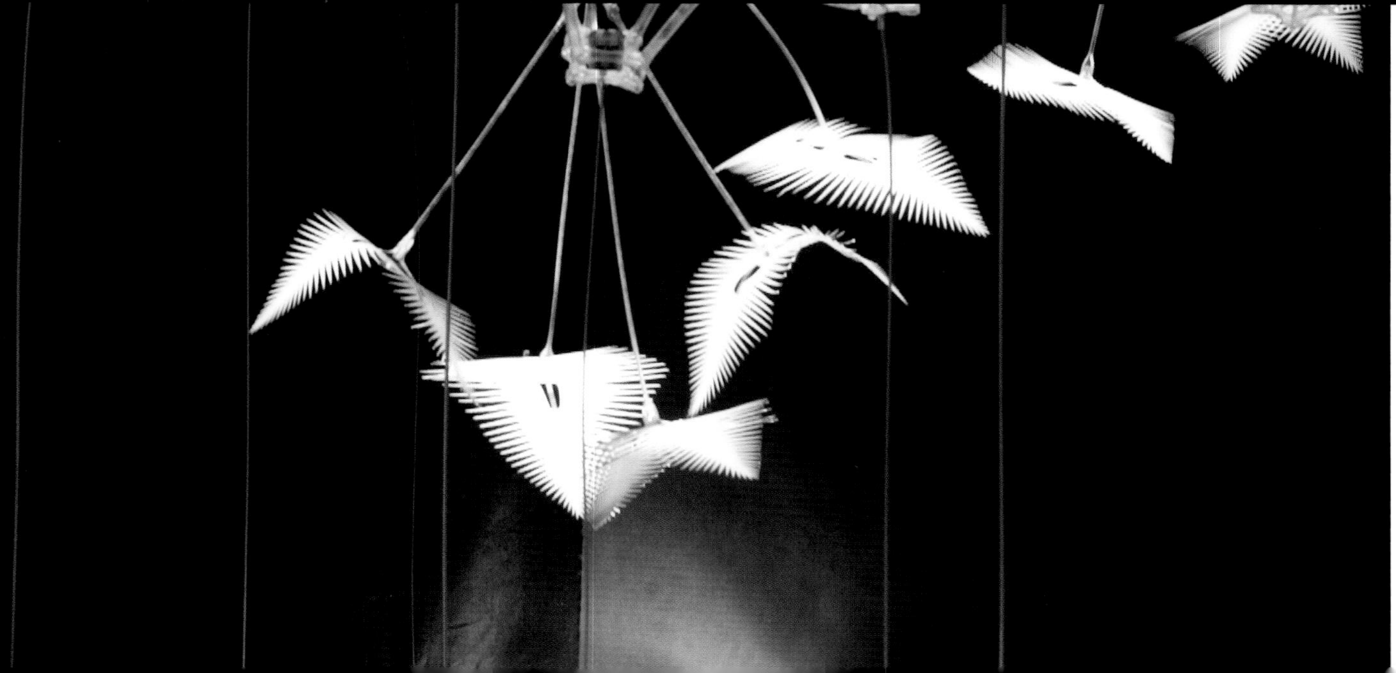

1_General arrangement section
2_Detail view
3_General arrangement views

PRESTON SCOTT COHEN

CAMBRIDGE, MASSACHUSETTS

The architecture of Preston Scott Cohen is recognized for its innovative geometry and its new approach to integrating buildings with their environments. The work of his firm, Preston Scott Cohen, Inc. in Cambridge, Massachusetts, encompasses projects that range in scale from houses to educational and cultural institutions. Recent commissions have ranged from educational facilities in China to residences in California.

The practice's work always has a strong sectional rationale. Often these sections rejoice in the artful collision of differing arrangements. This compositional methodology can also be used in plan, a tactic that gives Cohen's work a characteristic parti of great intensity, both graphic and spatial. Cohen, unlike so many of his North American colleagues, has never thrown the constructional-praxis baby out with the bath water, remaining ready to accept and prosper from the new.

Taiyuan Museum of Art

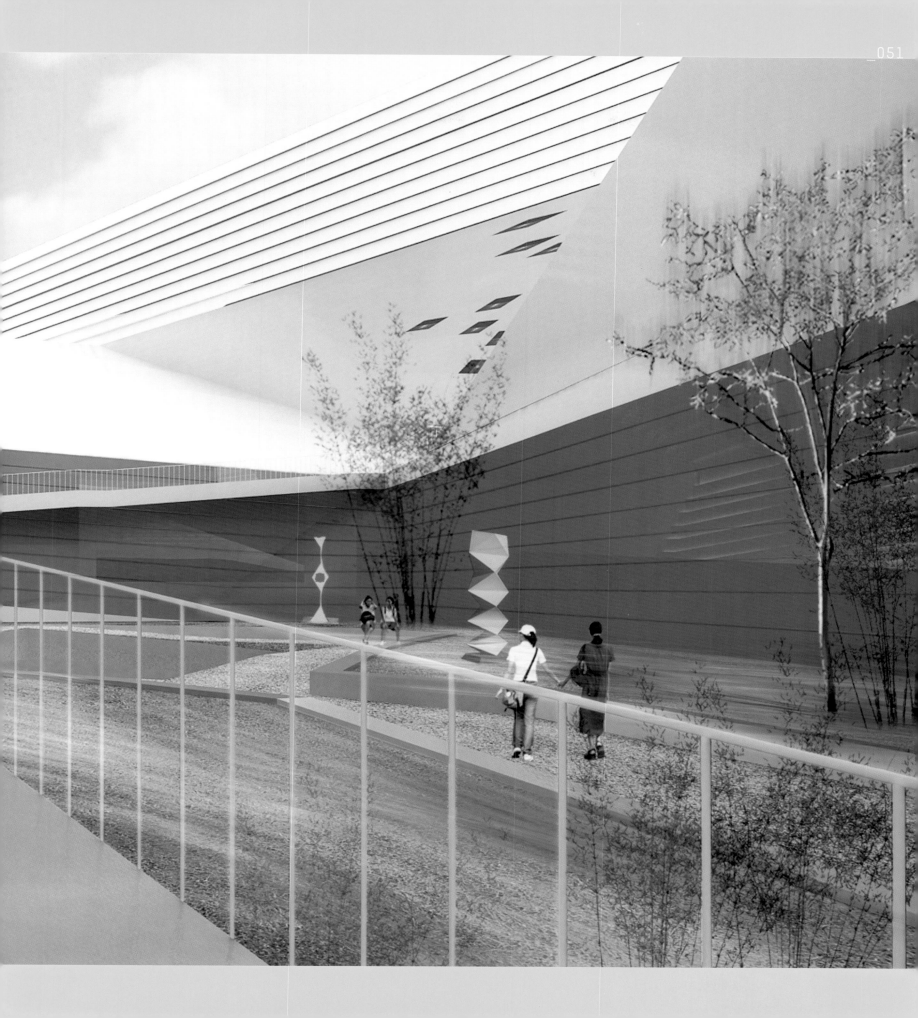

Nanjing University Student Centre
Nanjing, China

The main student centre for the new Nanjing University campus is both a singular, iconic symbol of student activity and a complex building serving more than twenty thousand students and housing 15,000 square metres (162,000 square feet) of programme. The project achieves a rigorous formal complexity by working within standard local means of production. The sweeping roof that twists and turns over the main public areas of the building is formed by twelve adjoining hyperbolic paraboloids. Using parametric modelling software, each part of these twelve segments was, in turn, rationalized into a set of concrete beams which vary in length but share a common section. Like a buoy in the ocean, a tower holding the main student offices rises through this sculptural roof. A fire stair was pushed to the exterior of the tower, producing a distinct formal gesture and providing terraced open spaces for the tower programme.

25 M   50 M   1

2

3

1_Plan and exterior view
2_Aerial view
3_Exterior view from street

Tel Aviv
Museum of Art
Tel Aviv, Israel

Subtly twisting geometric forms, based on hyperbolic parabolas, unify this building with its context and bring natural light into its deepest recesses. The kinetic figures of the exterior volume and the interior 'light fall' at once determine, and are determined by, the disparate angles between the rectangular galleries and the angled site boundaries. Extending towards the sky, seamless curves guide visitors into the architecture galleries, Israeli art galleries, auditorium, library, special exhibitions and other programmes. Walking from gallery to gallery, gazing through the lens of the central space, visitors are able to discern relationships among all interior and exterior spaces.

Among the accomplishments of the scheme is the resolution of a duality: the need for two points of entry and the need to create itineraries for two separate exhibition areas: the architecture galleries and the Israeli art galleries. Stairs and ramps spiral around the light well and link the sets of galleries to one another and to activities below. Regardless of how one arrives, tours commence from the same point.

The Tel Aviv Museum relates to a tradition of the new that exists within Israeli architectural culture. The multiple vocabularies of Eric Mendelsohn and Bauhaus Modernism are resynthesized in a language that is both internationalist and progressive.

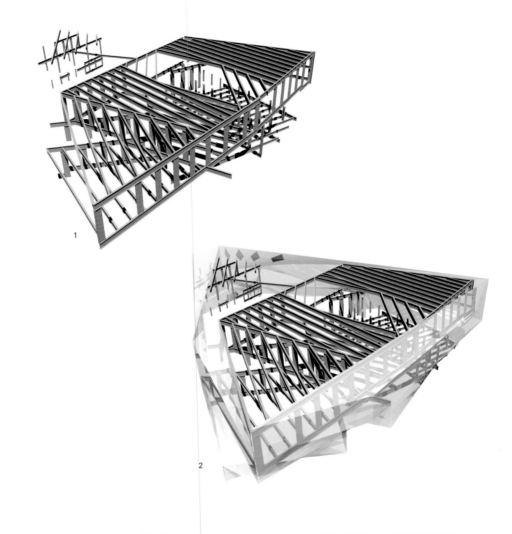

1

2

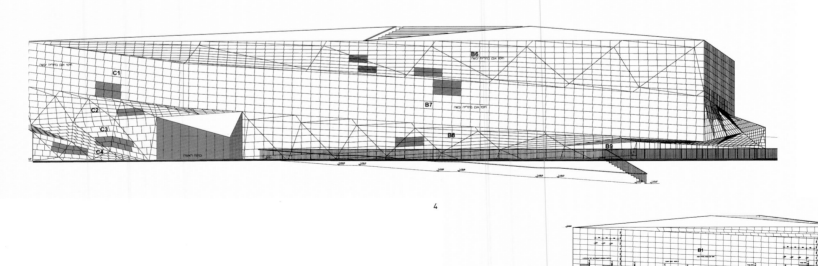

3

4

5   6   7

1_Structural system
2_cladding and structure
3-4_General arrangement sections
5-6_Exterior views
7_Interior view

Taiyuan Museum of Art
Cambridge, Massachusetts

> Cohen's projects exhibit topological twists, turns, dents and punctures that are honed by programme.

The building's form follows the geometric equivalent of a knot: a self-intersecting loop. The knot weaves together two dynamic trajectories of movement, outside and inside. It ties the space of the surrounding cultural island together with the museum programme deep within and establishes the form for the circulation. The exterior promenade, beginning at the western edge of the site, winds its way up and through a sculpture courtyard, emerges above the main entrance to the museum on the southern façade, and descends again to the entrance. The interior sequence is like a bow tie; one side is a promenade that loops around the courtyard, and the other begins in the monumental atrium, ascending a series of discontinuous ramps and escalators via a continuous linear space that terminates above the entrance. The main lift core offers the alternative sequence: a descent from top to bottom via ramps and escalators. This reversal provides the visitor with the opportunity to experience the most comprehensive overview of the museum sequence.

The project exhibits opposing characteristics inside and outside. The outside is heavy, like eroded stone, while the inside is smooth, especially by night. The spatial effect recalls the incoherent perspectives of traditional Chinese landscape paintings. The curved and angled forms of the museum produce unanticipated spatial layers, sequences of light and shade, continuities and discontinuities.

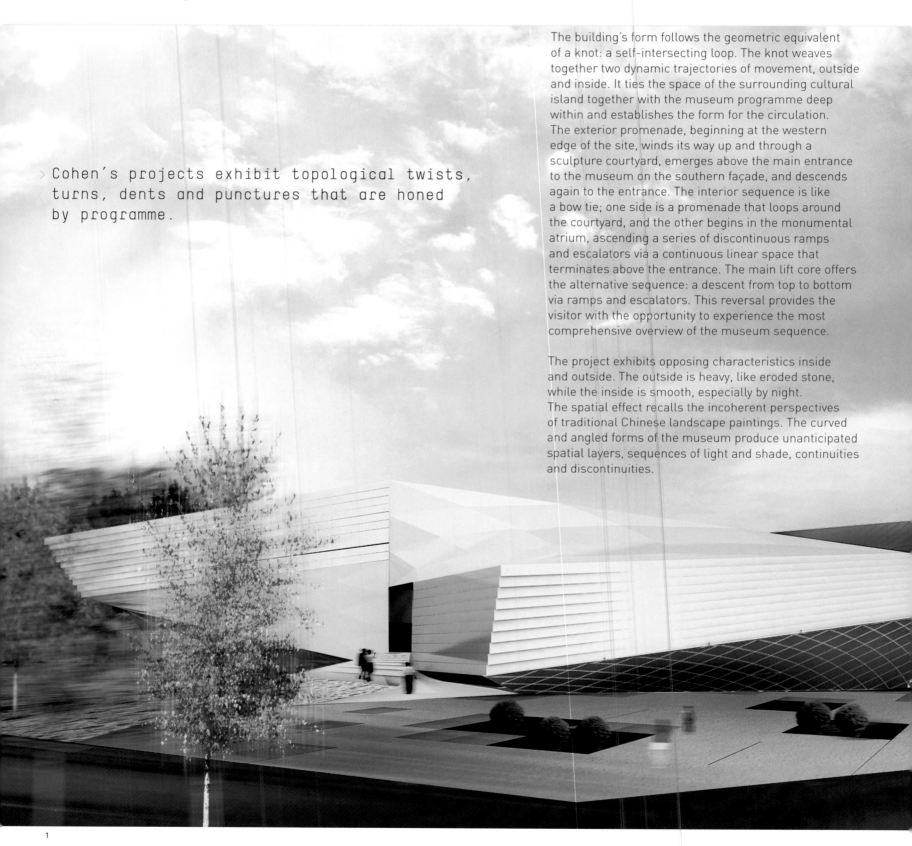

1

1_Entrance view

2
3

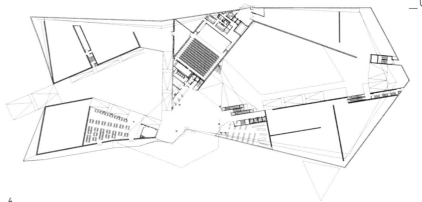

4

5

2-3_Primary circulation routes
4_Plan
5_Aerial view showing immediate context

CONTEMPORARY
ARCHITECTURAL
PRACTICE
(CAP)

>

NEW YORK

Contemporary Architecture Practice is located in SoHo, New York. Its directors, Ali Rahim and Hina Jamelle, have established an award-winning profile in futuristic work using cutting-edge digital-design and production techniques. A book about CAP entitled *Catalytic Formations* was released in 2006. CAP's portfolio includes master plans and residential, commercial and product-design projects ranging from a redesign of Main Street in Houston, Texas to a series of furnishings and light fixtures for the largest American lighting company.

CAP's work is breathtakingly elegant and dazzles with its harmonious complexity. This articulation of form is often created by parametric digital-design techniques. The practice has done much to show the various digital techniques and processes that building designers might bring to bear on their own work.

Residential Tower in Dubai:
View along road

Migrating Coastlines: Residential Tower Dubai

This forty-five-storey, 180-metre- (600-foot-) tall residential high-rise fosters feedback among the city, building and residents in an effort to engender cultural and economic exchange. Dubai serves as an economic attractor and haven for foreign nationals hedging political unrest at home and seeking investment opportunities abroad. Sheikh Zayed Road connects Dubai and Abu Dhabi, securing migratory paths to and from major urban destinations in the region.

The project captures the dynamics of its site in several ways: spatially, organizationally and by means of its system of enclosure. Its envelope provides two contiguous buildings that transform and lose their individual identities, fusing into a hyphenated formation. This transformative envelope allows the project's internal spatial possibilities to favour variation, breaking down the typologically based norms that govern the repetitive production of condominiums around the world. Parameters that define individual units include ceiling heights, room sizes and circulation pathways, not just room numbers. This definition invites a new criteria for the sale of property: volume rather than area.

> CAP is a very influential firm defining its practice by stunning designs and inspiring publications.

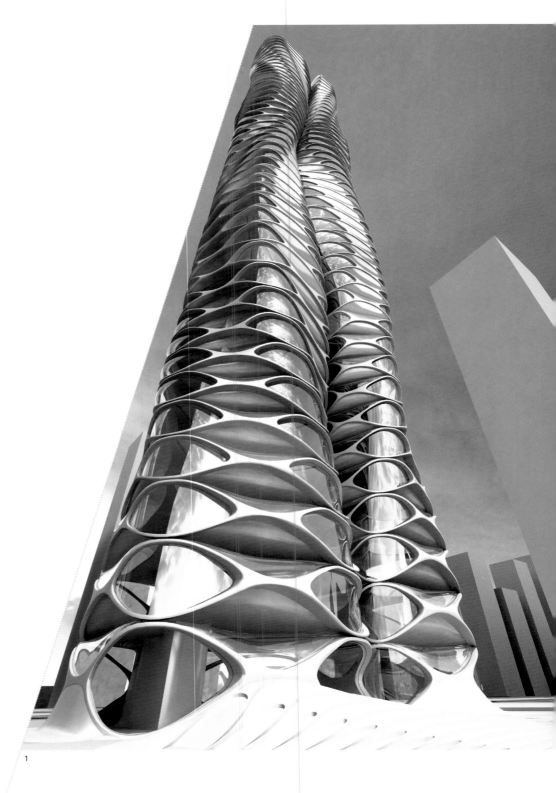

1

1_Exterior perspective from ground
2_Interior

2

Commercial High-Rise
Dubai

This thirty-five-storey, 150-metre- (500-foot-) tall commercial high-rise is located in Dubai's commercial marina district, which is part of a larger ongoing land-reclamation project. Within the high-rise itself, the differentiated spaces reorganize the hierarchical structure of the standard company office. The sectional variation does not permit offices to run contiguously around the perimeter with support staff towards the centre of each floor. Through formational variation, the project escapes a single type of spatial hierarchy and relationship, thus fostering dynamic relations between the formation and the company's employees. The intention is to increase the potential for social and political negotiation.

1

2

1_Context perspective
2_Fenestration patterning
3_Skin composition

Reebok Flagship Store
Shanghai

A flagship store for Reebok responds to the brand strategy launched by the company in late 2003: 'Wear the Vector: Outperform'. The goal for the concept store was to translate the Reebok brand into three dimensions.

The three brand attributes that were developed into the architectural proposal were the vector, performance and authenticity. The vector has direction and force, and is animated over time, capturing its full potential. The vector transforms the architecture, freezing motion through the interior space. The façade, section, floor pattern and lighting are all created by, and respond to, the vector. The architectural experience of inhabiting the vector, along with the performative nature of the store, is invigorated by the dynamic environment of Xin Tian Di in Shanghai. Key surfaces perform as combined circulation, display areas, lighting and seating. The design can respond to many of Reebok's seasonal and event-driven needs; merchandise display areas allow guests to sit and watch sporting or other marketing / entertainment events. At other times these can become the areas where customers try on shoes or simply enjoy the destination while shopping.

1–4_Interior views of shop

Residence for a Fashion Designer
London

A weekend home for a fashion designer explores different event-based temporal cycles ranging from relaxing to corporate entertaining, including preview shows of the designer's seasonal collections. The public areas have surfaces designed for maximum programmatic use, allowing for many different activities to occur: eating, lying down, sitting, viewing, reading and so on. As one traverses the spaces, surfaces are gradually transformed, becoming more precise and so reducing the number of activities that can take place on them. The least performative surface is only used for sitting and sleeping.

The structure of the house has two parts: concrete and aluminium semi-monocoque shell construction. The aluminium structure and sheathing rest on the concrete and are bolted in place with expansion joints.

1

2

1_Sweeping stair detail
2–3_Exterior façade perspectives

3

HERNAN DIAZ ALONSO/ XEFIROTARCH

> LOS ANGELES

Founded by Hernan Diaz Alonso, Xefirotarch is based in Los Angeles. One of the more wayward practices, its work has a recognizable, highly wrought, alien-seeming aesthetic inspired by biological mutation. Alonso describes the process of creation as akin to painting and the sensation of smearing and pulling material into figure and form.

Indeed the members of the practice are cinema fans, and one can see in their images great attention to light source and point of view. So there is a theatrical element to Xefirotarch's production, and much of the work, although highly polished aesthetically, has the magnetism of the strange, the uncanny and the wolfish. This combination of charms – sweet and sour as well as architecturally dextrous – makes Xefirotarch one of the important emerging practices at this time. There is a joyful idiosyncrasy and extravagance about their descriptions of their projects that seems not to subscribe to the often staid language of architectural presentation.

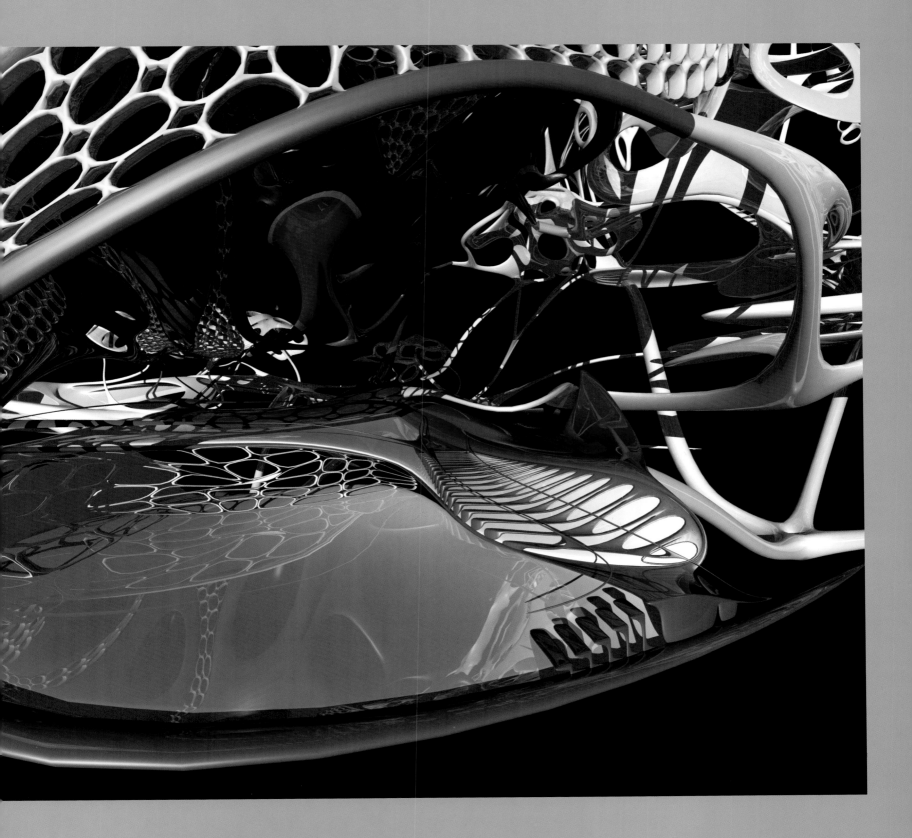

Art Hotel: Interior view

BCA Competition Boston, Massachusetts

Epiphyte (ep·i·phyte) n.
def: A plant, such as a tropical orchid or a staghorn fern, that grows on another plant upon which it depends for mechanical support but not for nutrients.

Architecture is never displayed innocently. Any encounter with the work is framed by multiple determining contexts – political, sensual, spatial – that productively contaminate the moment of reception. This proposal presumes and consumes this critical insight in its proposition for an architecture that will house (and be housed by) the city and its flows.

Instead of repeating the ultimately false presumption of normative architecture to a neutral palette – a blank spatial canvas on which works will be encountered – here the architecture acknowledges its own iconic status within the city as a centripetal gatherer of works and establishes a unique context for their presentation and representation.

Like epiphytic plants, this form is conjoined with the city and its site but is self-sustaining in its capacity to focus public flow and creative intensities. It extends unexpectedly across the urban grid, allowing for several access points, perspectives and experiences. It multiplies individual itineraries from interior to exterior, multiplying in turn visitors' positions in the space and the exhibitions. The architecture's highly charged perspective becomes an invitation to visitors to trust their instincts and enjoy the works they encounter. The project presumes that the visitor's reception is a critical component of any work's completion.

> Diaz Alonso creates outstandingly sensual architectures combining the grotesque and the sublime.

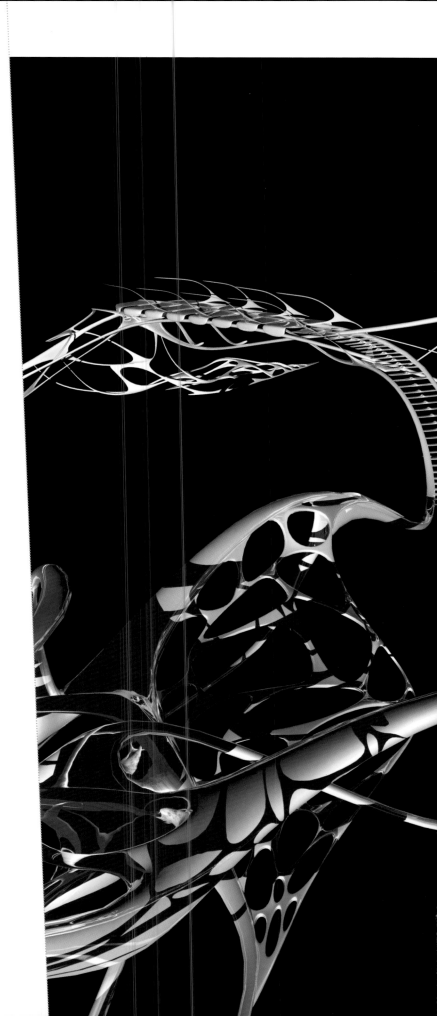

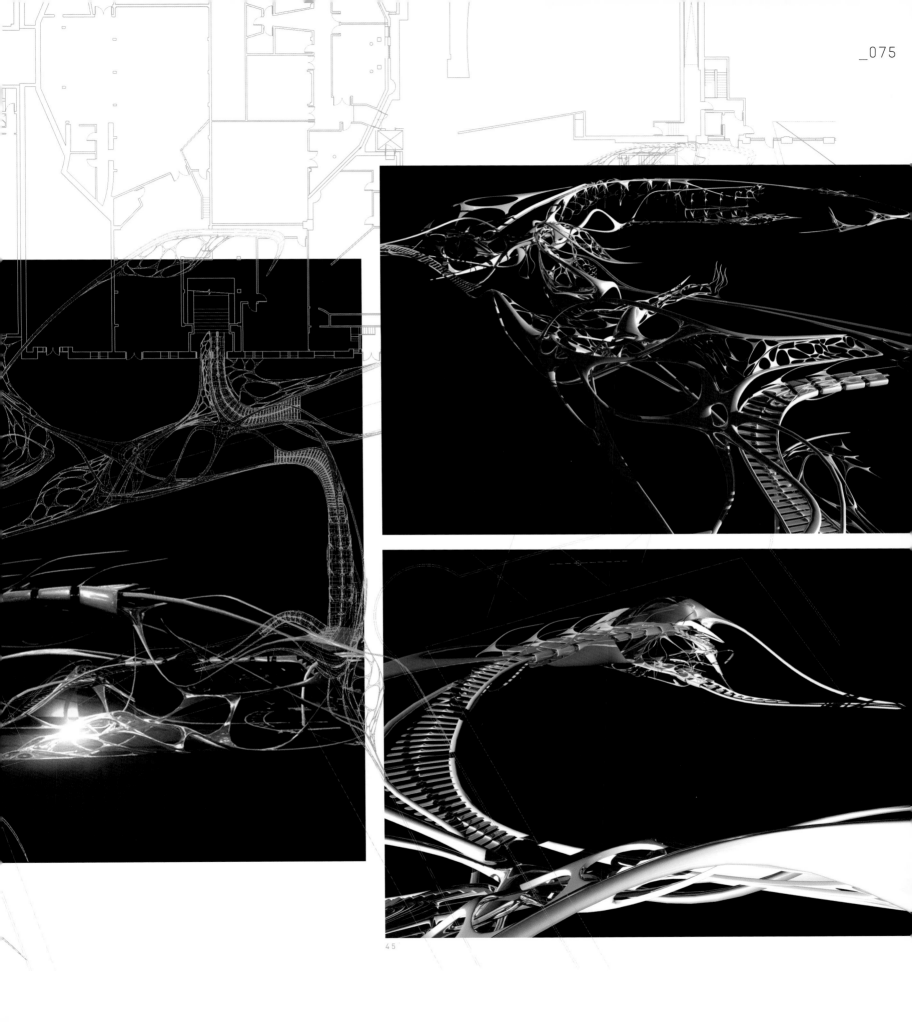

Busan Metropolitan City
Busan, South Korea

The project occurs in Busan Bay and is given shape
by a series of flows. It creates a new spatial continuity
by exploring the possibilities of interiority as a dynamic
field that can be occupied as a network of parts.
This proposal offers incremental transformations
of units rather than an object: a 'world' to dive into
rather than a building on its own. The project is a
multi-purpose arena for both recreational and cultural
activities. Planned as the 'jewel in the crown' of the
scheme, the building / landscape / island occupies
the centre of the bay, taking in 360-degree views of
the waterfront area, with a capacity of six thousand.
The primary auditorium seats that many people, and
although this number is massive, the flattened hierarchy
prevents it from being immediately apparent. Although
the pursuit of affect is primary, the performance
of the architecture as a multi-purpose arena is not
hampered but rather improved upon and intensified.
The concert hall is organized and navigated on the basis
of directional vectors and the distribution of densities
rather than nodes. This is indicative of the concert
hall as a new whole: porous, immense, a field space.
Circulation vectors subvert the solid state. External
as well as internal circulation follows the geometry.
Stairs, lifts and ramps are located at areas of
confluence, interference and turbulence. The move
from object to field is critical to understanding the
relationship the architecture will have to the content
of the music it will house.

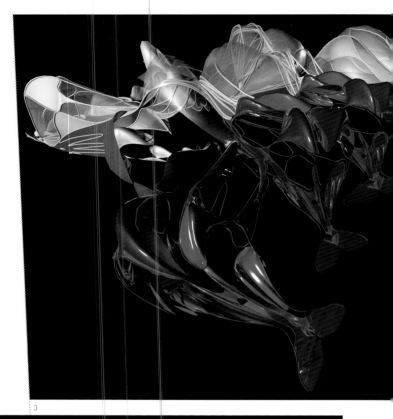

2

3

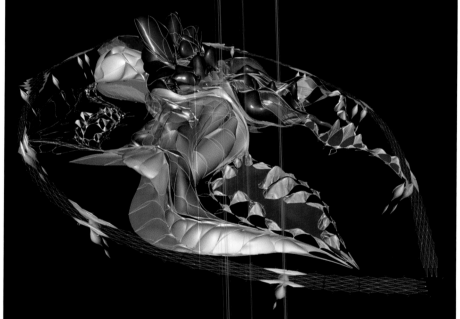

1

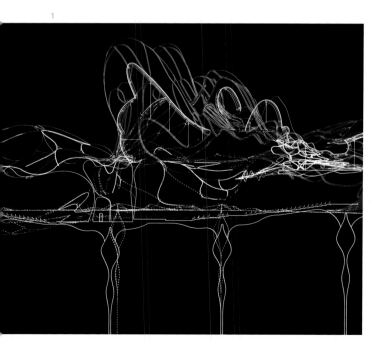

1_Conceptual section
2_Aerial view
3_Elevation
4_Interior skins and ceiling

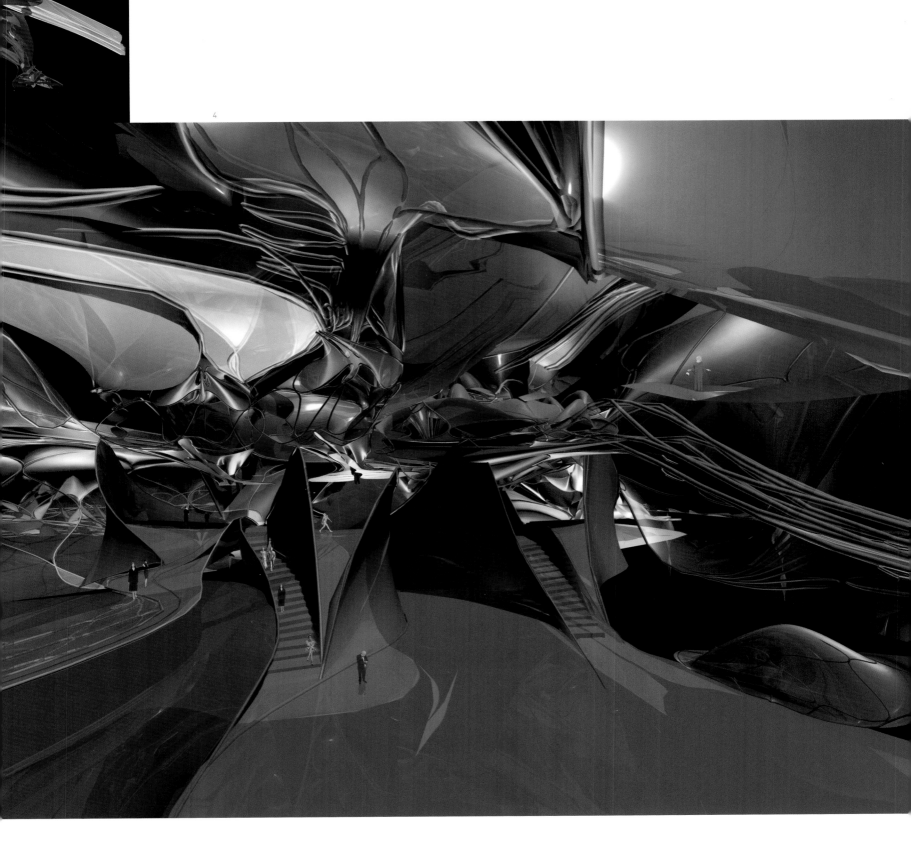

Maison Seroussi:
'Seingemer'
Paris

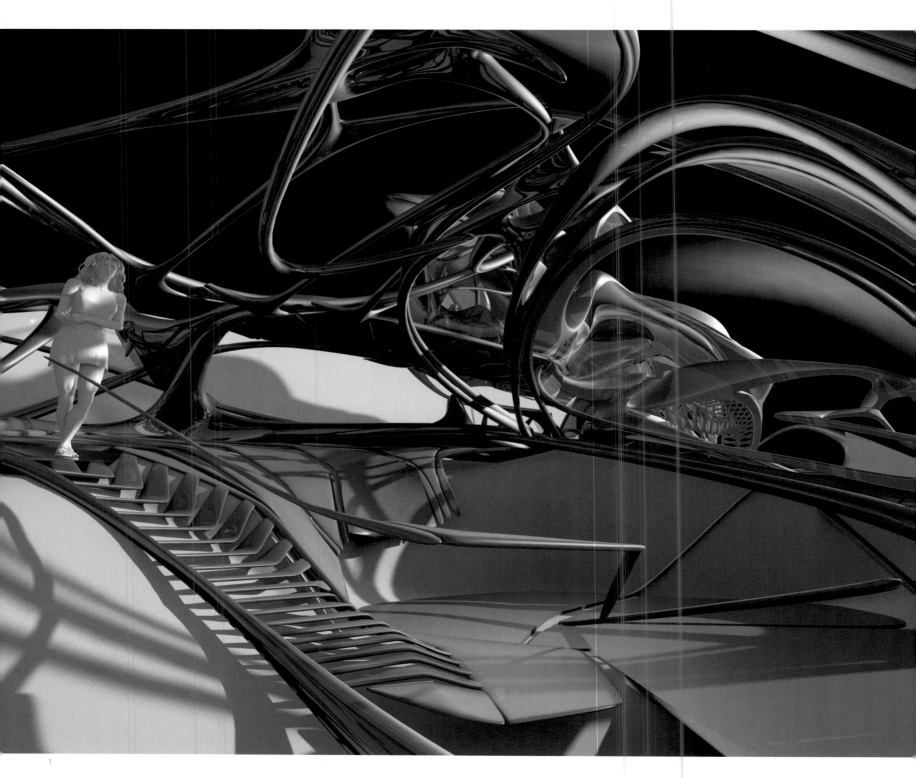

1

The house has taken advantage of the site by extending and branching the programmatic elements, expanding the notion of enclosure to transform it into one of nesting. As in a Möbius strip, where there is no outer or inner side, the programme elements stem both outwards and inwards to engage with the site's topography.

The body of the house is comprised of an open structure that connects all parts: a central mass that holds the main activities (bedrooms, baths, kitchen, main gallery) and three pods that are not fully enclosed and which serve as small galleries, an artist's workshop, landscape features, etc. (These pods could be considered as a future extension to the house.) There are three entrances: street access located in the south corner of the property and two garden entries (from within the property). The ground level houses the main exhibition and working area, along with the kitchen and the garden terraces, while the second level holds the main bedroom and guestroom / office (with corresponding bathroom) and an extended elevated terrace.

1_Interior view
2_Exterior view
3_General arrangement plan

DENNIS DOLLENS/

LOS ANGELES
BARCELONA
SANTA FE

EXODESIC

\>

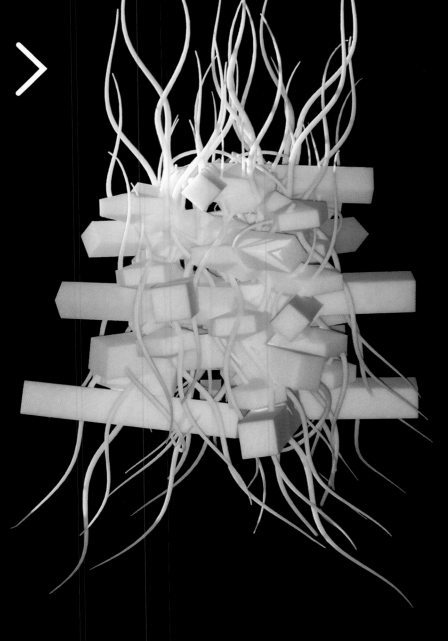
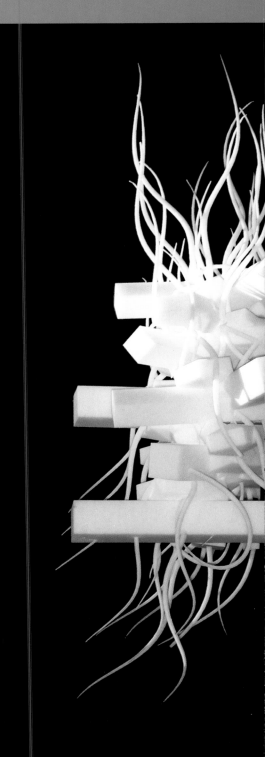

Dennis Dollens and his studio, Exodesic, have evolved a design practice integrating phenotypical data and imagery from nature into architecture. Usually plants, sometimes shells and skeletons, are studied, and then digitally generated simulations are made and synthesized with Dollens's aesthetic prejudices. Exodesic's works have both a highly artistic and a highly technical emphasis, resulting in a method for visualizing design that uses software, animation and digital fabrication techniques, as well as handmade models and experimental materials. Because of the practice's heavy use of Xfrog-plant simulations in the initial design phase, it is only a small stretch to say that most of their work is digitally grown and then developed in various other drawing and rendering programs.

Dollens's studio practice currently includes writing and lecturing as well as teaching Digital Biomimetics for Architecture at various universities. These writing, teaching and speaking activities underpin the design practice on a theoretical level by linking biology with architecture. This all leads to forms that emerge from digital systems but are based on, and embedded within, geometries, orientations and organizations found in biological growth. The practice's work has its own aesthetic that often seems to jar against the more artful work of its peers, and in the long run this can only be a good thing. Dollens is expanding the architectural lexicon away from the fashionable and the aesthetically highly coded.

Digitally Grown Botanic Tower #3:
Housing and servicing modules

Digitally Grown Botanic Tower for Barcelona #2
Barcelona

The generation of the Botanic Tower is linked to earlier experiments that extrapolated environmental information such as solar orientation and air-flow dynamics from flowers producing tall stalks with spiralling blooms – nature's botanical skyscrapers. This project also began an investigation into panels that could be used to incorporate aspects of nature into the building skin. For the skin / panels, the practice used the model of scales (based on the pangolin) as well as the shells of almonds, looking to the seed pod's structure as an inner and outer skin connected with a truss-like system of fibre struts.

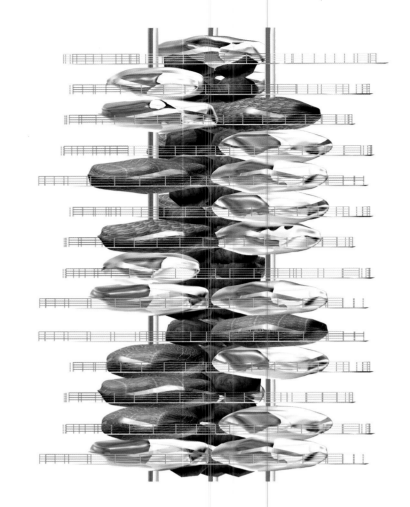

2

3

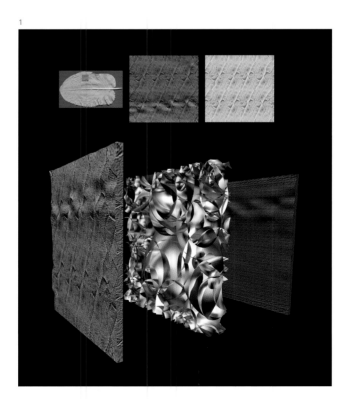

1_Skin composition
2_Botanic Tower elevation
3_Photomontage on site
4_Botanic Tower elevation juxtaposed with its natural inspiration

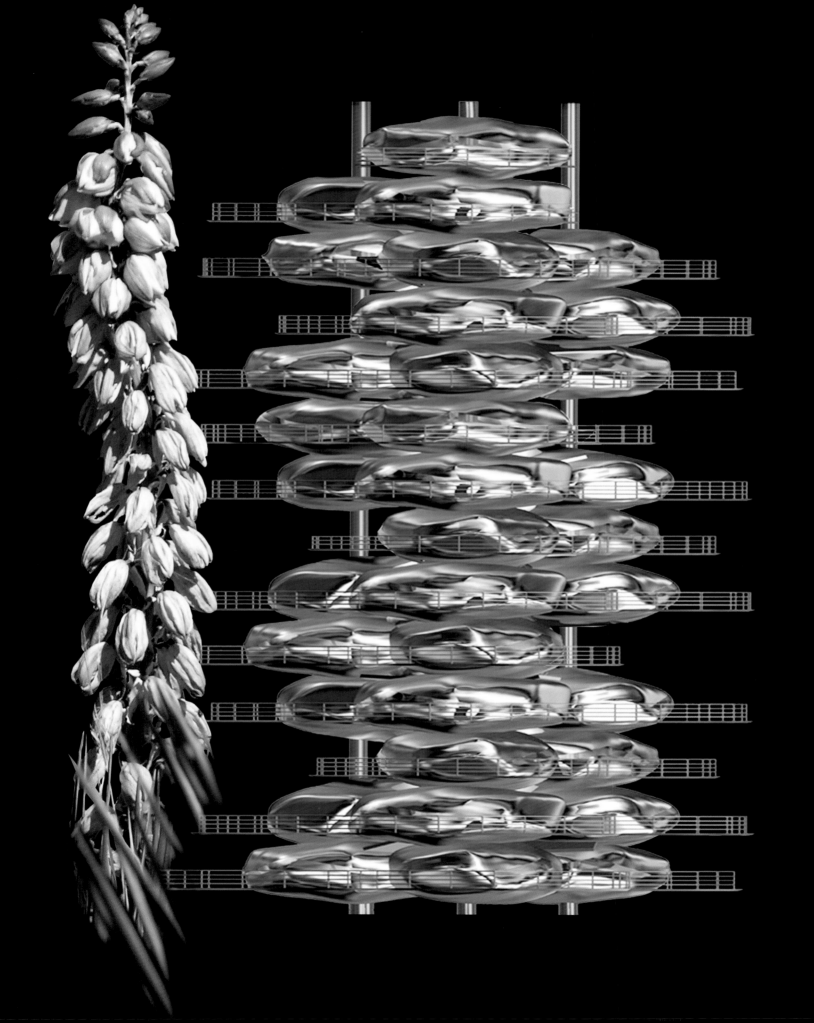

Digitally Grown Botanic Tower #3 (Arizona/Arcosanti): Homage to Arcosanti
Arcosanti, Arizona

In the summer of 2006, Dollens spent ten days at Arcosanti, Paolo Soleri's laboratory for urbanism in the Arizona desert, studying Soleri's use of a fragile and beautiful mesa site, attempting to understand his artistic, social, civil and ecological vision, and researching his earlier work in the site's excellent archive. Dollens came to think that Soleri's vision could also seed emerging biomimetic practice in digital-botanic or digital-environmental visualization for experimental architecture.

In the time Dollens spent at Arcosanti, he explored the nearby mesas and canyons, documenting plants, lava and lichens. During those excursions he took a small motion-computing tablet with him and made what might be called field drawings – not of existing conditions or buildings but of new digital growths suggested by those conditions, plants and lichens. These drawings are compatible with both Soleri's philosophy and the use of digital growth by Dollens's studio.

> Dollens is inspired by growth and form in the natural world.

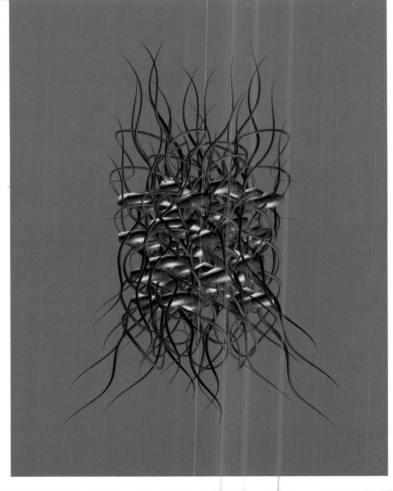

  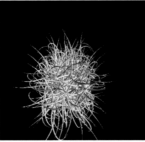 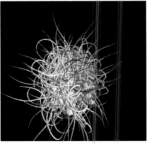 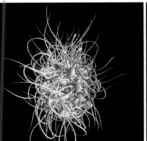 

1_Growth possibilities
2_Possibilities of form
3_Close view

Exodesic/Digitally Grown Trusses, Connectors and Towers (Part 1)

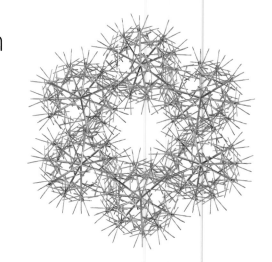

This is a series of structural components based on principles of computational plant growth in which branching is re-programmed, looping and interlocking with other branches in order to achieve a balance between structural tension and compression. This series investigates and produces architectural components based on leaves as walls / ceilings / canopies; trees as columns, beams and trusses; and seeds as material connectors and habitable spaces. Solar orientation, air flow and view distribution are design aspects extrapolated from these ongoing studies looking specifically at branching and blooming flower stalks.

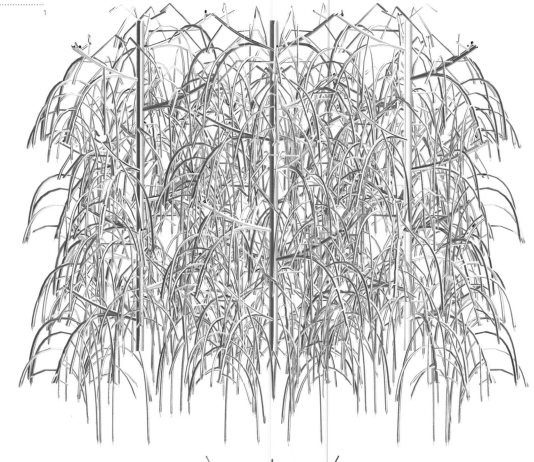

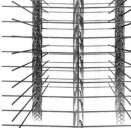

1_Nodes, connections and networks
2_Digitally grown trusses

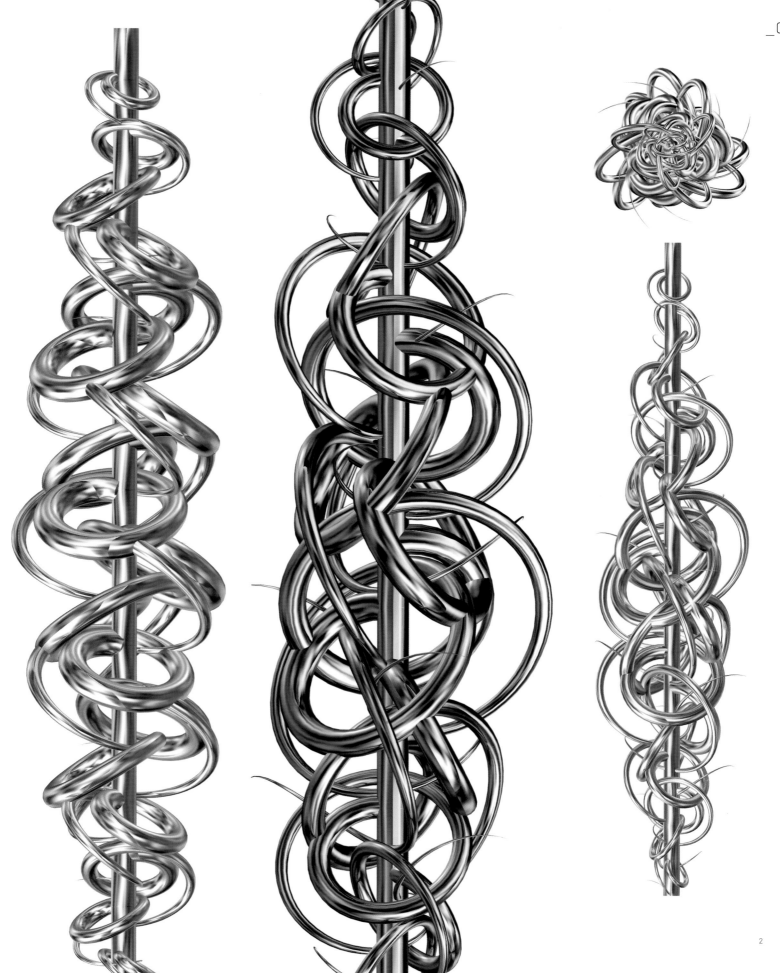

3

4

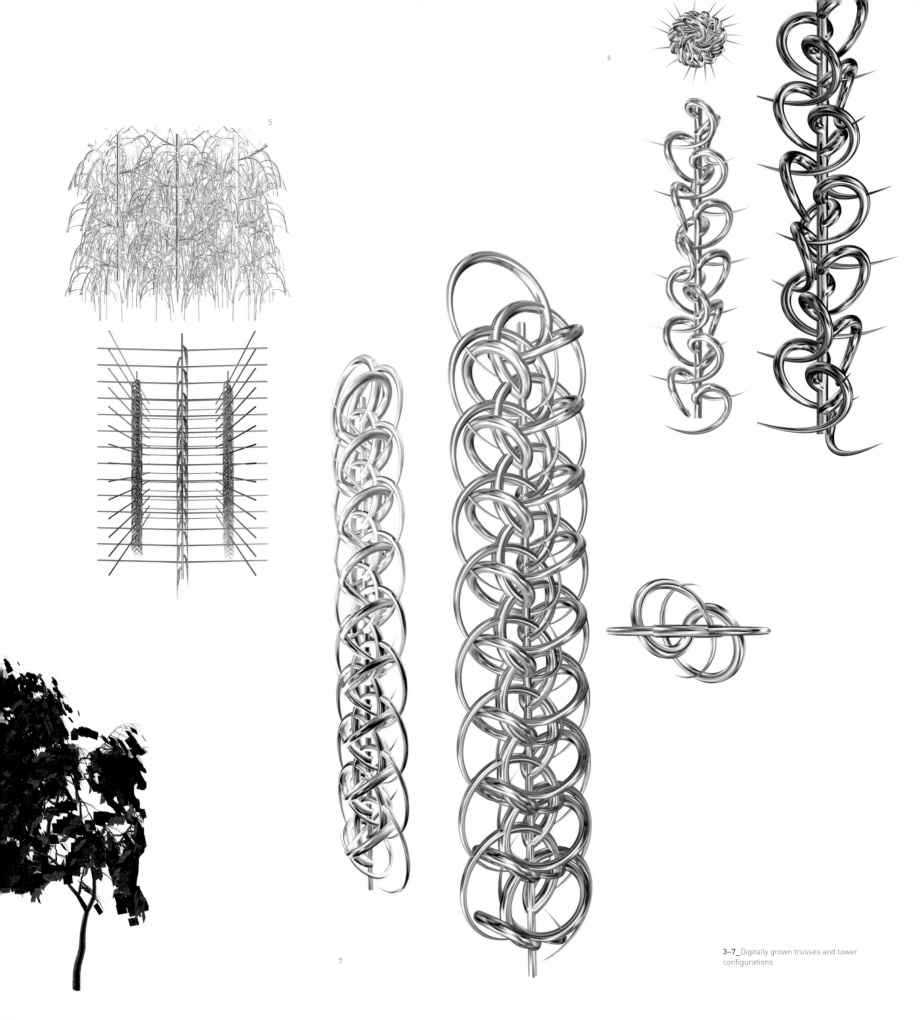

5

6

7

3–7_ Digitally grown trusses and tower configurations

AMMAR ELOUEINI/ AEDS

>

PARIS
NEW ORLEANS

The work of AEDS often combines numerous architectural preoccupations: the double-curved and facetted surface, computer-aided manufacture, triangular tessellating geometries, the one-off event of a performance, the reflective qualities of non-natural materials, and the use of light and projection. Each project seems to have, almost as a badge of honour, a plan of its digital cutting patterns – a show of economic use of material, perhaps, or an establishment of the work's couture credentials. A two-dimensional and pragmatic diagram of what once translated into three or four dimensions becomes an extravagant surface cutting through air or billowing in an unfelt breeze. AEDS's work is small-scale, often related to couture, fashion and the theatre, and intimately anthropocentric. Works actively engage, cosset or attract the human form. To AEDS the dance of architectural space is always vital, always subject to environment and context, with sun, light, material and facetted incision all grist for the practice's mill.

Polycarbonate transparency

CoReFab#71
Paris

1

Ammar Eloueini was the recipient of a grant from VIA in 2006–7. The Paris-based organization annually awards a limited number of grants for the purpose of developing and manufacturing furniture prototypes.

CoReFab #71 is a chair design created utilizing computerized digital-animation technology and realized through deposition-printing technology. VIA has sponsored the fabrication of three CoReFab#71 chair designs.

CoReFab#71 is one chair within a series of infinite possibilities, the result of a computer-designed form layered with varying patterns, animated and then slowed down moment by moment or frame by frame. This frame or moment of computer-animated form is then manufactured through 3-D print technology.

3-D printing, primarily used for creating design-industry models, is here being engaged to create a full-scale piece of furniture. This is the first time that the technique has been initialized for use as a full-scale form from a digital-animated computer design.

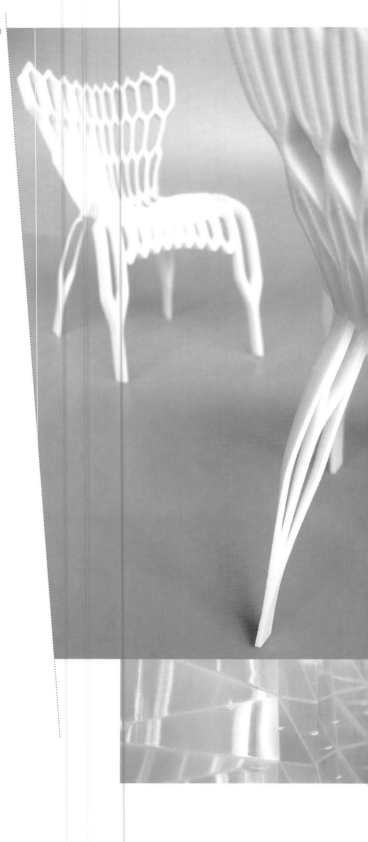

3

1_Seat detail
2_Back view of chair
3_Front view of chair
4–5_Facetted polycarbonate partitions within shop

2

Pleats Please,
Issey Miyake,
Galeries
Lafayette
Berlin

The Pleats Please space in Berlin was the first in a series of retail spaces for the Japanese fashion designer Issey Miyake. The space is in the Galeries Lafayette building designed by Jean Nouvel in 1991–5. The intention was to make the space into a unique environment reflecting Miyake's personality and approach to fashion design while retaining a focus on the clothes. All of the design components relied heavily on the use of computer numerically controlled machines. As the components were fabricated in Chicago and then shipped to and assembled in Berlin, ease of shipping and assembly presented a challenge.

The primary design consists of a wall made of two overlapping pieces. This wall creates both a fitting room and a storage area. Two materials, aluminium and polycarbonate, were used. Thin aluminium plates were cut using water-jet techniques. The aluminium serves as the structure supporting the wall along with polycarbonate panels, the racking system and table structure. Polycarbonate was used to create the organic surface and table top. The surface was modelled on the computer, unfolded using 3-D software, then fabricated using router CNC machines. The polycarbonate panels were assembled using zip-ties. The lightweight polycarbonate material and zip-tie fastening created a system that is both easy to transport and quick to assemble.

45

Me Boutique,
Issey Miyake
Paris

The me-line boutique is a study in minimalism. All white, the boutique's feature elements are a lacquered, reflective floor and ceiling with recessed light fixtures. This unique lighting method prevents direct spot lighting, creating an even, ambient light environment. The forthcoming fitting rooms, digitally designed and using 3-D print technology, will be an ornamental installation within the aesthetically pure Me Boutique space.

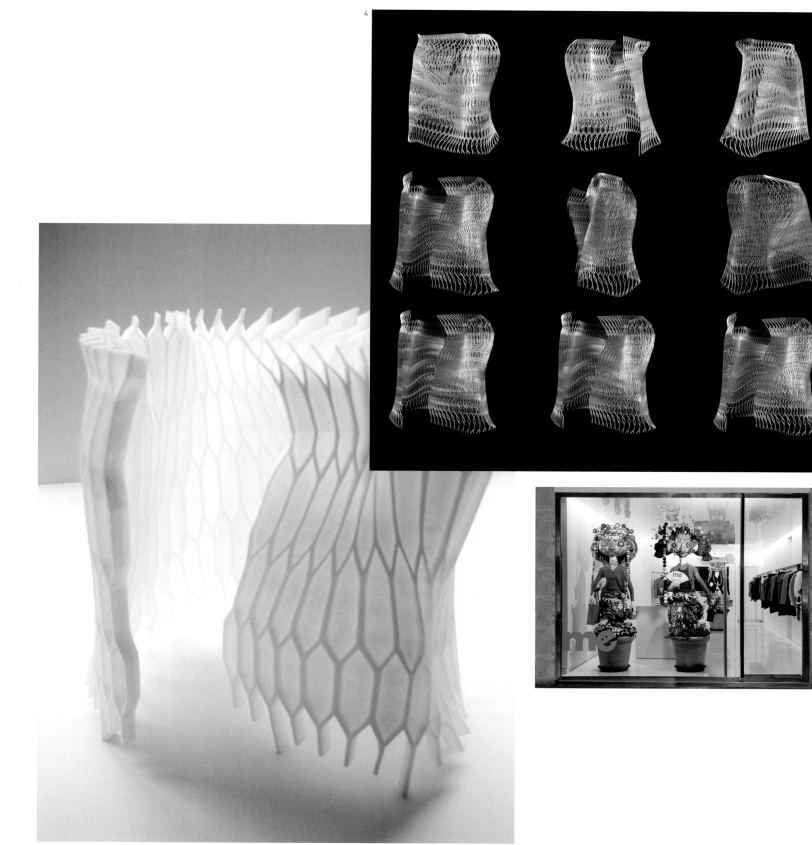

4

5

3

1–2_Interior of shop
3–4_Configuration of interior partitions
5_View into shop

California
Set Design
Performed in
France, Germany
and the US

California is a dance piece developed by the choreographer John Jasperse and performed by his company. As opposed to creating a backdrop or immobile form for the stage, the set was designed as a morphing structure that permitted the dancers to engage directly with it.

A surface-form was created that allowed for flexibility. Creating the set as something that would change geometrically and spatially as an element of the performance allowed easier manipulation as a surface as opposed to a structure. The performers' movements were emulated and adopted through the set. The objective was to see how the dancers affected space – not only how the set could be reconfigured by the dancers but how the set could affect the dance.

The design was modelled from a complex computer-generated geometric surface. Using a basic fabric-pattern layout, the design was unfolded into segments that could work as individual pieces and together form the surface. The primary material was polycarbonate, which maintains translucency and reflectivity, so the piece absorbed and diffused light. Zip-ties secured the pieces, thus allowing for flexibility and ease of construction. This set can be created in hours, and then broken down and packed into boxes to be recreated elsewhere.

1

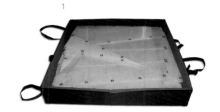

2

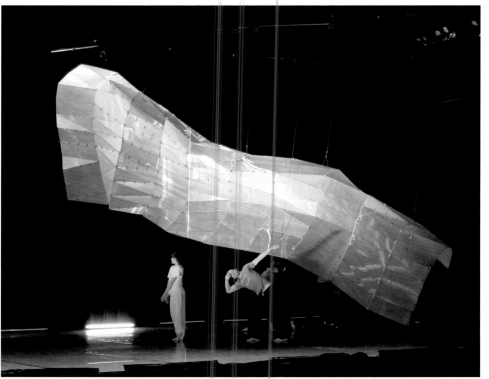

3

1–6_Polycarbonate facetted adaptable stage set
7_Fabrication drawing

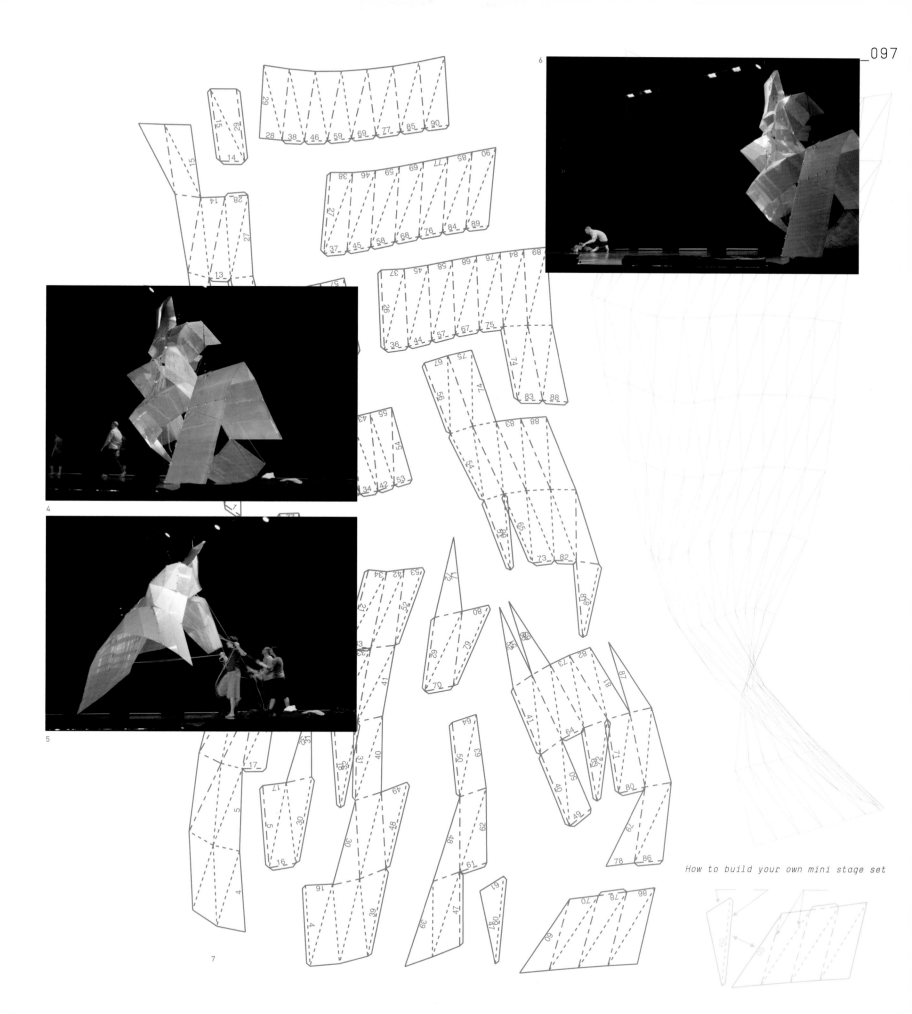

How to build your own mini stage set

MU Chair

The MU Chair was designed and modelled out of a single polycarbonate panel. The lightweight structure of the polycarbonate makes it an interesting material for furniture design. The panel is cut / scored by computer numerically controlled machines. The chair is designed for extreme economy and ease of fabrication and assembly. Once the panel is machined, it can be folded, connected with zip-ties and fully assembled within minutes. The zip-ties can be cut and removed for storage purposes and are easily replaced. The chair is meant for mass production, and the polycarbonate is 100 per cent recycled.

> Eloueini has a quiet confidence and a preoccupation with translucency.

1

1–4_Chair, details and composition

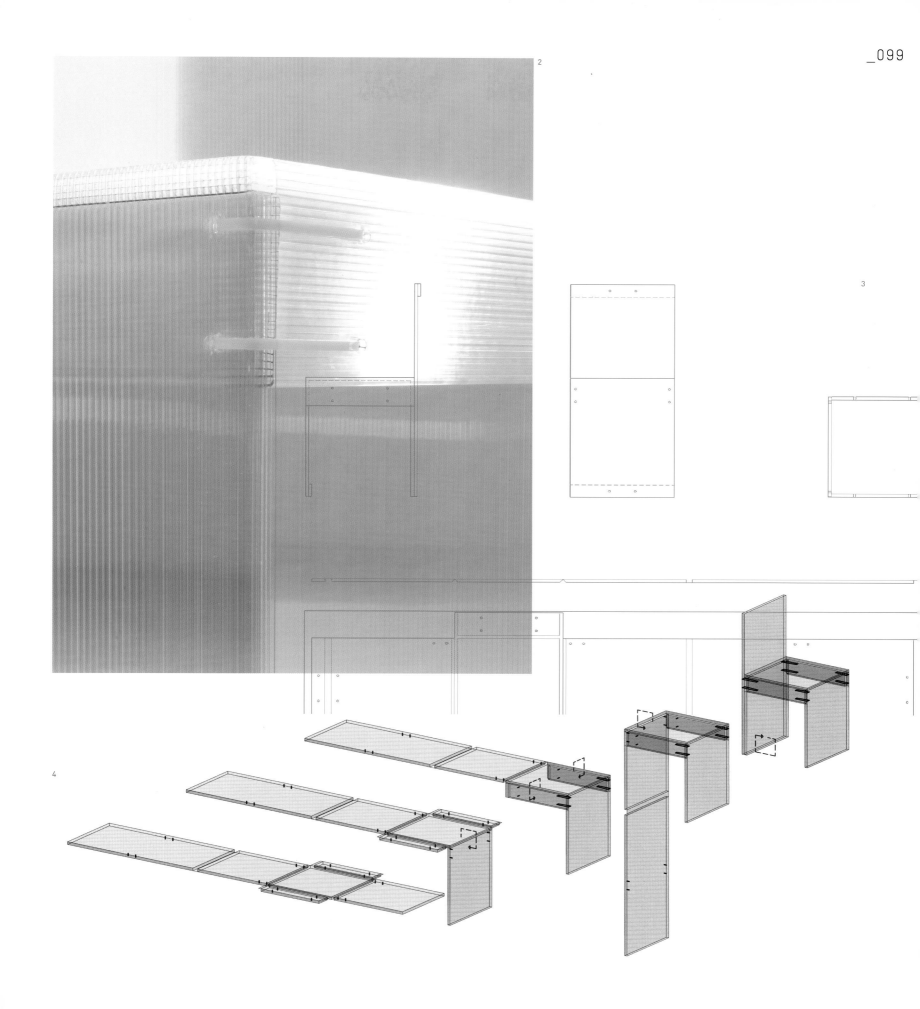

2

3

4

EMERGENT

>

Founded by Tom Wiscombe in Los Angeles in 1999, EMERGENT is dedicated to researching issues of globalism, technology and materiality through built form. EMERGENT is a platform for experimentation, utilizing technologies, techniques and approaches from fields outside architecture, including materials science, aerospace engineering and digital animation.

Key to the practice's work is the phenomenon of emergence, which offers insight into the way apparently isolated bodies, particles or systems exhibit group behaviour in coherent but unexpected patterns. The animated beauty of emergent organizations, as in swarms or hives, points to a range of architectural potentials in which components are always linked and exchanging information, and, above all, where wholes exceed the sums of their parts.

Wiscombe worked as a chief designer and as Wolf Prix's right-hand man at Coop Himmelb(l)au for ten years. EMERGENT's work still advocates Himmelb(l)au's splintered shard to connect with the disparate forces and vectors of the City. However, it takes a calmer, perhaps more considered approach. Compositional disjuncture is controlled and articulated, expedient and considered. EMERGENT's work evokes a beached starship or the orthogonal delicately collided with the organic. Computers, of course, can predict difficult junctions and details, and therefore the artful collision is now seldom fraught with on-site approximation in fabrication. Digital techniques enable this type of architecture to survive, even to be economical.

LOS ANGELES

Paris Courthouse: Aerial perspective

Cell House
Los Angeles

This house is primarily organized by cellular tectonics and structural performance rather than programme or function in the modern sense. Walls become obsolete in their dual function of dividing space and resolving loads in favour of a vivid, multi-directional system of forces and behaviours. Floor plates, structural frame and building envelope are not understood as independent systems but rather as emergent behaviours resulting from variation and adaptation in a three-dimensional cellular pattern. This pattern grows and spreads out, evolving towards local performance based on local conditions without breaking its genetic logic. The micro-cells of the glass envelope branch and thicken towards the interior of the house, resolving lateral loads in floor-plate diaphragms. A feedback loop between force flow and material distribution is created in which maximum effect is created with a minimum of material. Effect is, however, not limited to the technical but includes the atmospheric as well.

1

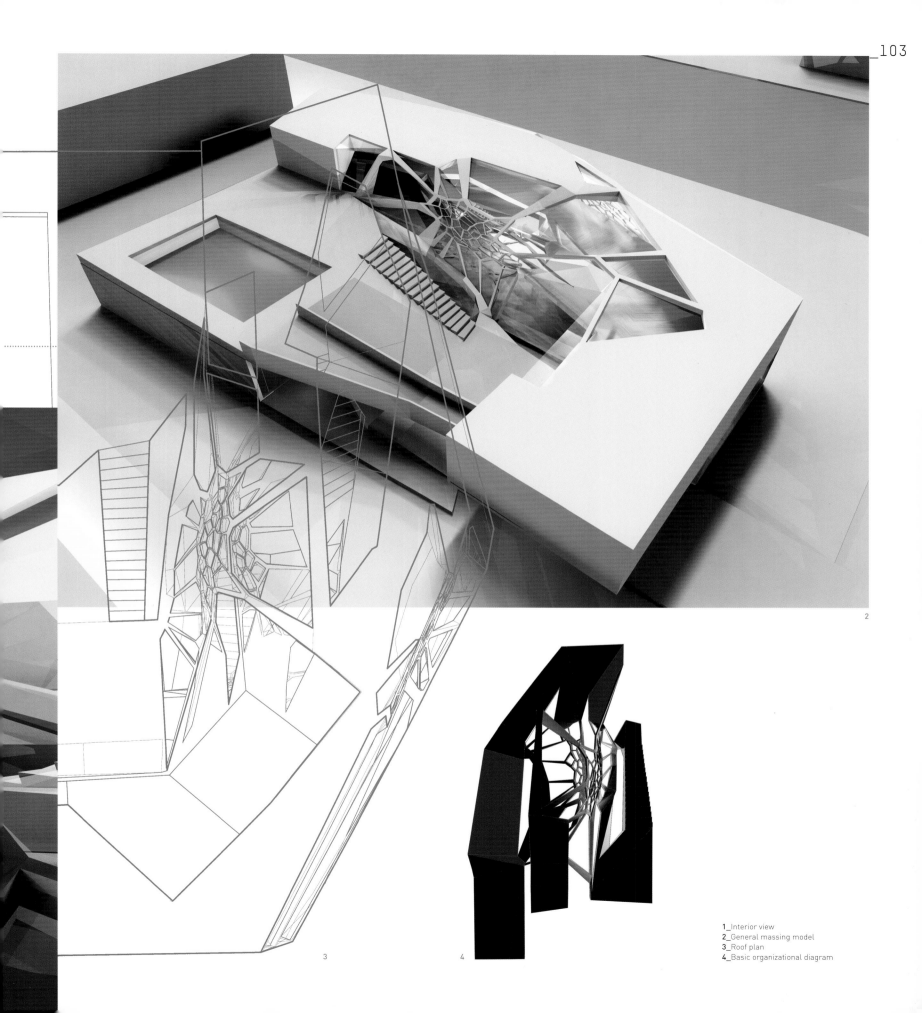

2

3 4

1_Interior view
2_General massing model
3_Roof plan
4_Basic organizational diagram

Paris Courthouse (TGI)
Paris

This project is part of an urban plan for the Left Bank, intended to contain both the Paris Courthouse and an adjacent mixed-use development. The site contains a landmark warehouse building by Eugène Freyssinet (which was to be reused) and is directly opposite the Bibliothèque Nationale to the north.

Due to the extremely tight available site footprint (80 per cent was already inhabited by Freyssinet's warehouse, EMERGENT proposed to float a new building volume above it to create a composite of new and old. The new slab reflects the old building in dimension but is rotated in plan to align with the Bibliothèque Nationale. Spatially, this transformation relates processes of justice to knowledge and culture. A Grand Lobby to the north-west links the new and old buildings vertically and creates an interface with the city.

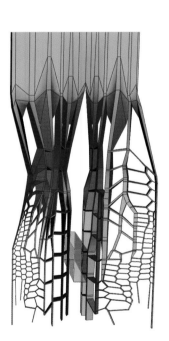

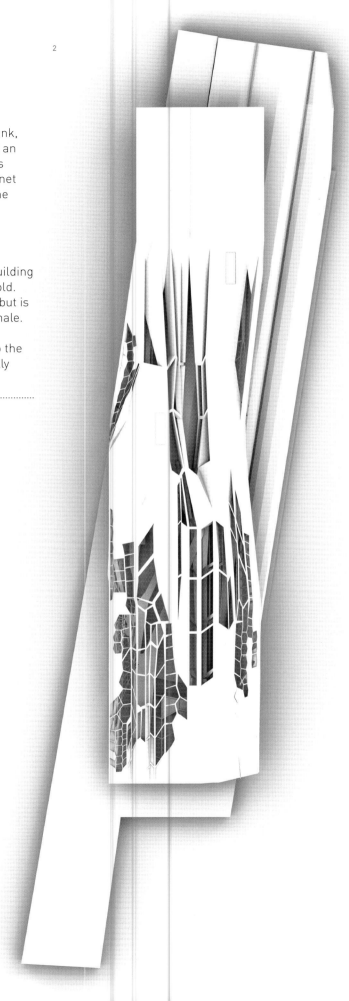

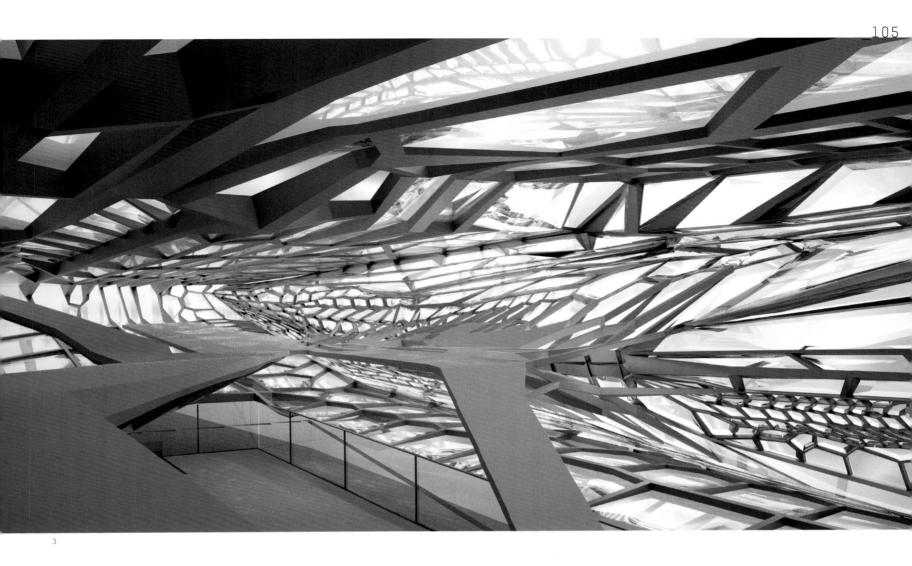

3

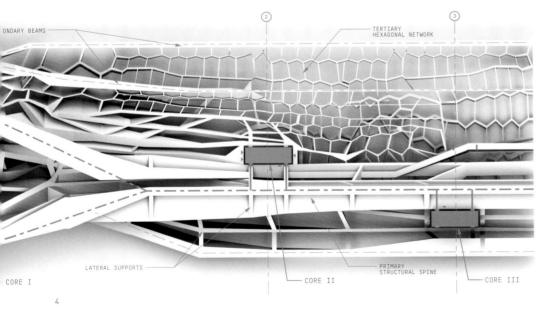

ONDARY BEAMS

TERTIARY
HEXAGONAL NETWORK

LATERAL SUPPORTS

PRIMARY
STRUCTURAL SPINE

CORE I

CORE II

CORE III

4

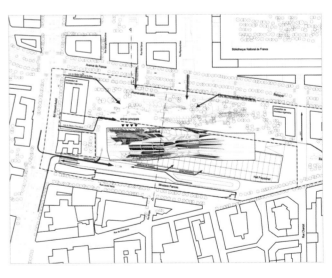

5

1_Virtual generation models
2_Roof plan
3_Interior space
4_Circulation and structural section
5_Location plan

6_External view

Stockholm City Library
Stockholm

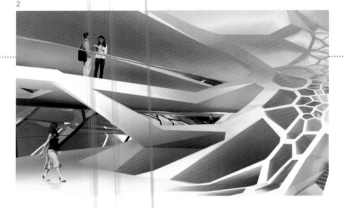

> EMERGENT exhibits structural acrobatics that enable the practice to construct audacious architecture.

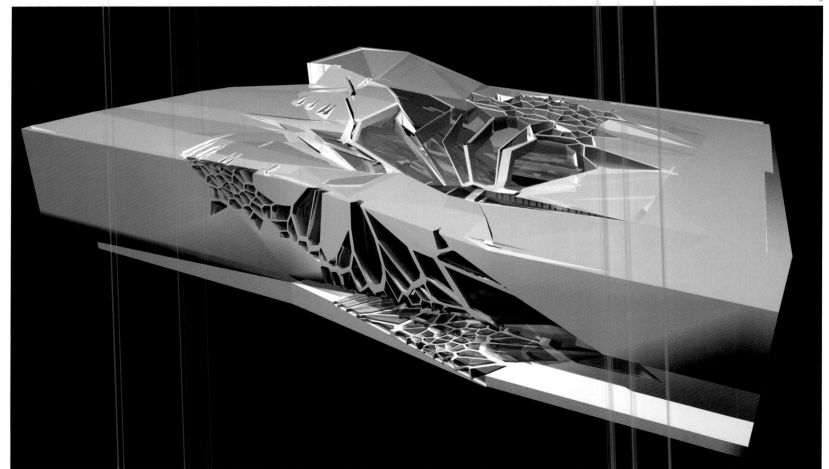

The Library of the Future will be defined by its ability to collect and organize information but also by its ability to network disciplines and people in urban settings. This design is a linking mechanism on an urban scale. It links visually to an existing building in terms of height and width, and materially via an underground passageway. The new building also connects to the steep profile of Observatory Hill via a bridge-like construction. This connection allows library visitors to access the historic Stockholm Observatory directly. Between the new building and the hillside is a Garden Plaza which allows visitors space in which to relax away from the busy street.

The main entrance of the building reflects new urban conditions in the area, and is therefore directed towards Odenplan Plaza and the shopping and public-transit links found there. It cantilevers out to the street to create an inviting space where people can meet and orient themselves before proceeding inside.

The building can be broken down into a Cellular Shell, a Structural Hive and a Circulation Net linking the two. The Structural Hive transmits and resolves vertical and horizontal forces but also serves as an organizational mechanism, sprouting layers of stairs and bridges connecting levels. Hive cells vary in scale from Reading Cells to Study Clusters to other micro-programmes.

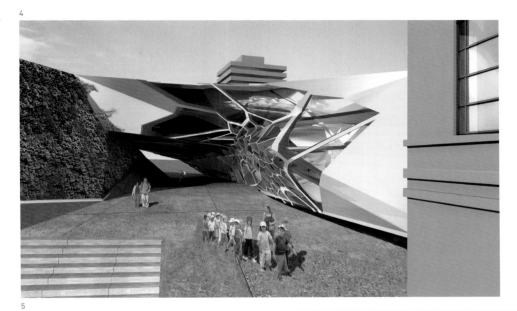

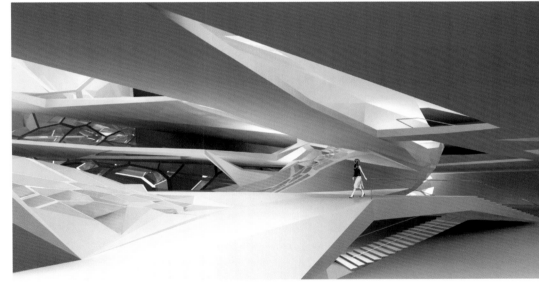

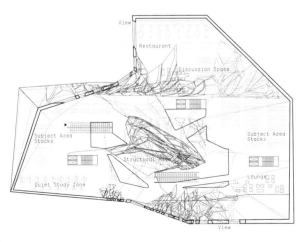

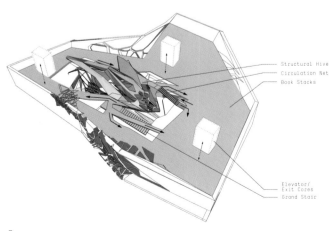

1_Streetscape
2_Interior
3_Massing model
4_Entrance canopy
5_Interior
6–7_Plans

EVAN DOUGLIS STUDIO

> \>

Evan Douglis is the principal of Evan Douglis Studio, an architecture and interdisciplinary design firm committed to innovation. Established in 1990 and currently practising from New York, the firm's unique, cutting-edge research into self-generative systems, membrane technology, contemporary fabrication techniques and multi-media installations as applied to a range of diverse projects has elicited international acclaim. The emphasis of this multi-task research and design lab is on synthesizing a broad-based ecology of theoretical and pragmatic concerns en route to discovering new paradigms of haptic interaction.

As yet the practice has not been given the large commission it surely deserves to indulge its preoccupations. These not only include aesthetic concerns and foibles but also a collaborative, thinly corporately structured and technologically experimental working method. The Evan Douglis Studio's aesthetic is one of sleek yet blobby forms that have the well-tended shine of fetish outfits. This wet-look surface often undulates with sensuous ripples, each of which is unique and skilfully composed. Colours are striking, surfaces fecund and the feel smooth.

NEW YORK

Helioscopes: Virtual model wireframe

Auto-Braids / Auto-Breeding - Jean Prouvé Display-scape Columbia University, New York

Inspired by the French architect Jean Prouvé's commitment to the most advanced technology of his time and his legendary contributions to the development of modular systems, this exhibition installation set out to reinterpret his conceptual directives from a new perspective. Celebrating the opportunities afforded by high-end 3-D modelling software and five-axis rapid prototyping milling, a series of interlocking modular elements was produced for assembly as an exhibition 'display-scape'. Offered as one continuous surface and capable of varying spatial configurations due to changing programmatic and contextual requirements, this topological terrain represented a universal meta-stage for a collection of artefacts.

Through the rigorous and changing assignment of destination, sequence and proximity, an endless scenario of conceptual affiliations was achieved. Intended to function as a curatorial game board, this membrane and its matrix of landing sites offered a range of recombinatory flexibility ideal for any collection of objects undergoing continuous change.

The simultaneous pursuit of curatorial and topological 'multiplicity' inherent in *Auto-Braids / Auto-Breeding* represents an architectural aspiration beyond the limits of the gallery. It concerns the development and application of 'biological mimesis' as a paradigm for architectural production.

3

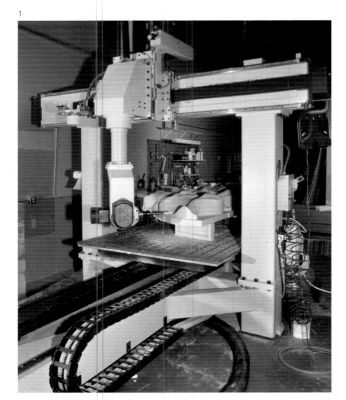

1

2

1_Fabrication machinery
2–3_Exhibition installation
4_Detail of surface

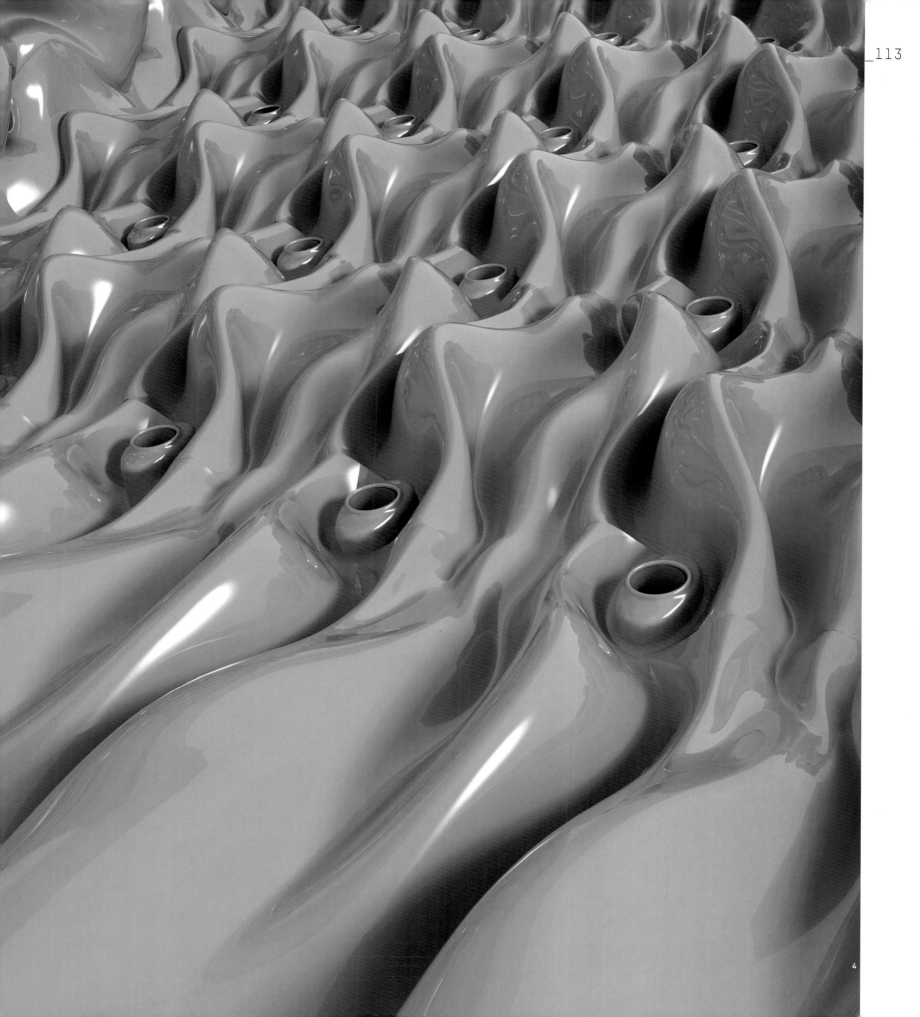

Helioscopes –
Media-scape Installation
Orléans, France

The ideologies of fashion extend into the critical practices of architecture. Based on the premise of commodifiable desire, Japanese 'love hotels' represent a service industry dedicated to providing the consumer with an unlimited menu of domestic interiors. Masquerading as an architect, the system endlessly recycles flat parodies of postmodernism while promising illicit 'newlyweds' the ideal 'dream interior': a seamless exploitation of fantasy in which the recombinant caricatures of architecture are sold as the ultimate utopian accessory.

In the dream-context of recombinant technology and biologically mimetic surfaces for the future of architecture, Helioscopes represents an alternative model of production seamlessly obedient to modern strategies. Situated somewhere between a search for topological indeterminacy and an oneiric vehicle of desire, this fleet of media-scape stalactites represents an entirely new synthetic ecology. Each of the helical tails contains a single vision-orifice through which an endless itinerary of fantasy settings is available to the consumer. Outfitted with the most recent advances in membrane and information-display technology, this new wired flesh serves to highlight the endless algorithms of difference found in everyday life.

1_Helioscope during fabrication
2-3_Machined surfaces

REptile –
Haku Japanese Restaurant
New York

1

2

3

> Douglis has an aesthetic sense unmatched by many
> of his peers.

In appreciation of a legacy of Japanese mythology surrounding the sacredness and virtuosity of reptiles, a restaurant interior was resurfaced with an animate skin capable of emoting a range of visceral and associative responses for the curious spectator. Applying a strategy of biological mimesis in which the divine attributes of a natural system are reinterpreted within the performative logic and effects of its artificial counterpart, a custom lightweight mass-produced tile system was created that exhibited a range of emergent properties synonymous with these venerable creatures. Highlighting its amphibious attributes, the range of surface complexity inherent within its skin, as well its ingenious ability to conform to multiple surroundings, the surface of the modular system reinterpreted these topological and behavioural qualities as an emergent system aimed at producing a range of illusory effects. From an operative standpoint, this was achieved by superimposing within the animation software two independent meshes (pyramidal vs smooth) fluctuating at different frequencies in order to create a variety of productive-interference patterns. Through the use of controlled chance an extensive menu of surface effects emerged, offering an increase of options for the discerning eye. The changing scale and rotation of the matrix of pyramids worked to redirect the light and shadow in such a way that a greater depth of field was perceived. Appropriated as a changing animate surface seen from a variety of perspectives throughout the restaurant, a kaleidoscope of cinematic effects dedicated to the continuous dissolution of memory and the power of recall rewards the consumer.

4

5

1–3_Machined surfaces
4_Interior of restaurant
5_Restaurant façade

THOM FAULDERS/BEIGE ARCHITECTURE AND DESIGN

>

SAN FRANCISCO

Thom Faulders is the founder of BEIGE ARCHITECTURE AND DESIGN, a research-based practice established in 1998 in the San Francisco Bay area. Engaging a wide array of theoretical and built projects, Faulders fluidly blends the discipline of architecture with the design of temporary environments, experimental exhibitions and furniture prototypes. Working at a variety of scales, his recent projects have focused on the innovative use of hybrid materials and emergent systems that stimulate user interaction with architecture. With an eye for a diverse range of newly developing technologies – from innovative products that allow for individual customization to the organization of complex networks – his studio seeks to feature architecture's role as a materially and spatially responsive environment.

Faulders often deploys patterned configurations and complex arrangements of self-similar architectural components. The resulting tectonic language creates an invented methodology wherein bottom-up anomalies result in surprising outcomes that seemingly elude finality. Of note is his development of surfaces (both static and dynamic) that change in response to an occupant's presence in space – either visually through the accumulation of optical effects or in real time through material dynamics. At the core of Faulders's applied research and practice is the push of mutable dynamics beyond design processes and into the realized state of built architecture.

AirSpace: Detail

AirSpace
Tokyo

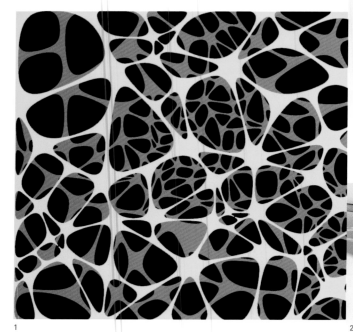

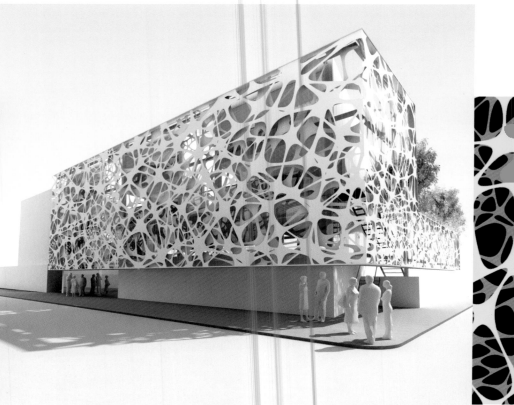

The project creates an exterior building skin for a new four-storey multi-family dwelling unit with photography studios. Located in the Kitamagome Ota-ku district, the site was previously occupied by the owner's family residence uniquely wrapped by a layer of dense vegetation. Since the entire site is to be razed to accommodate construction for the new, larger development, the design invents an architectural system that performs with attributes similar to those of the demolished green strip and creates an atmospheric space of activity. Conceived as a thin, interstitial environment, the articulated densities of the new open-cell mesh are layered in response to the inner workings of the building's programme. AirSpace is a zone in which the artificial blends with nature: sunlight is refracted along its metallic surfaces; rainwater is channelled away from exterior walkways via capillary action; interior views are shielded behind its variegated and foliage-like cover.

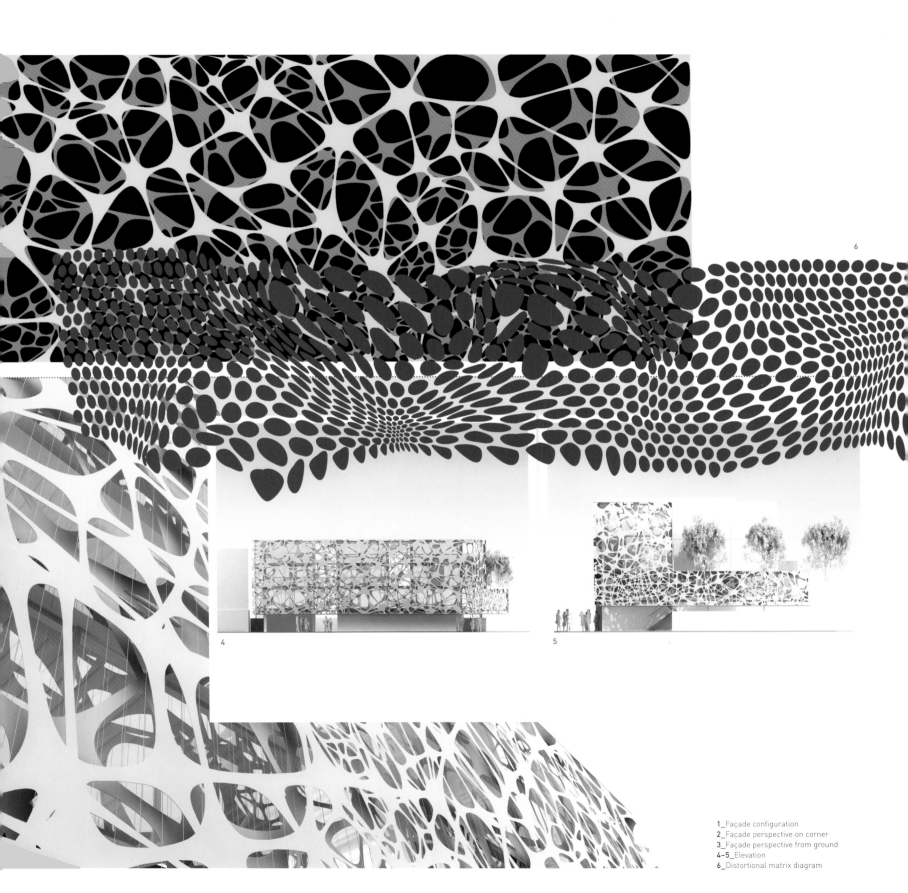

1_Façade configuration
2_Façade perspective on corner
3_Façade perspective from ground
4–5_Elevation
6_Distortional matrix diagram

Chromogenic Dwelling
San Francisco

In this competition proposal for multi-family dwelling units with street-level mixed use, a strategy was invented for situating large buildings that maximize property potentials in smaller neighbourhoods by utilizing an electronic version of camouflage. Unlike most camouflage strategies, which match context through representational mimicry, the opposite tactic was proposed: radically blanketing an object with bold patterns to disguise it, thus rendering it difficult to discern as overall perceptual patterns are disrupted. Known as Disruptive Patterning System camouflage (DPS), larger forms dissolve into a broad visual 'noise' of indefinable geometries.

To create its DPS skin, the Chromogenic Dwelling uses electrochromic glass to create a real-time changing texture of visible solids and voids. In response to climate, light effects and privacy requirements, the building's occupants electronically switch the thermal glass to an opaque, transparent or translucent exterior surface. What emerges is a cumulative building image constantly on the move, a virtual fragmentation of the building's mass.

> Thom Faulders's work is original, phenomenal and perfectly judged.

1

2

3

5

4

1–2_Perspectives at corner
3_Exterior
4–5_Structural system

MOCA@LBC
Sonoma, California

The proposed new Museum of Contemporary Art at the Luther Burbank Center in Sonoma, California is parallel to a motorway and provides an opportunity for the façade to serve as a visual icon for the institution. Responding to a driver's perspective from the road, the building's surface data of text, colour and openings emerges legibly only to recede completely when viewed from a different position. Using redundant layers of metal tubes, the façade's surfaces pulsate with changing visual hot spots. The tubular skin can be sculpted to create varying surface depths, and, due to geometric laws of tubular stacking, it is everywhere unique. As an intelligent skin, the exposed west side of the building provides its own shade to reduce solar gain. The entire building is raised above a linear strip of glass that perfectly aligns sight lines from visitors in the interior courtyard to views of automobiles beyond. The effect is of a building lightly hovering on vectors of movement.

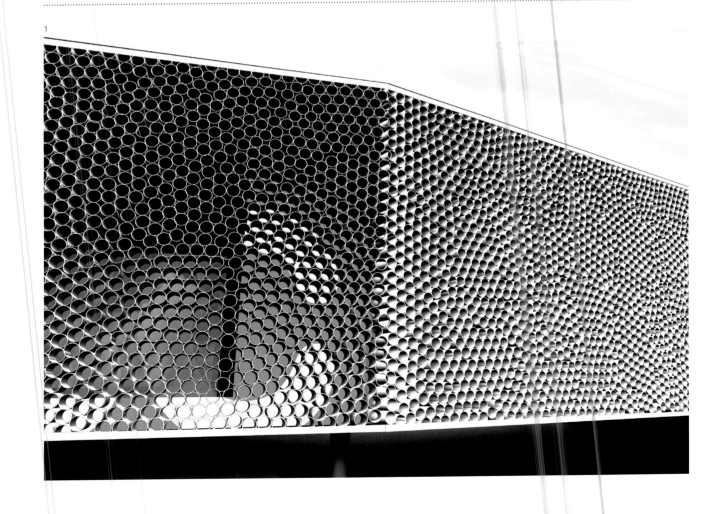

1

1_Tubular skin elevation
2-3_Elevations
4_Tubular skin perspective

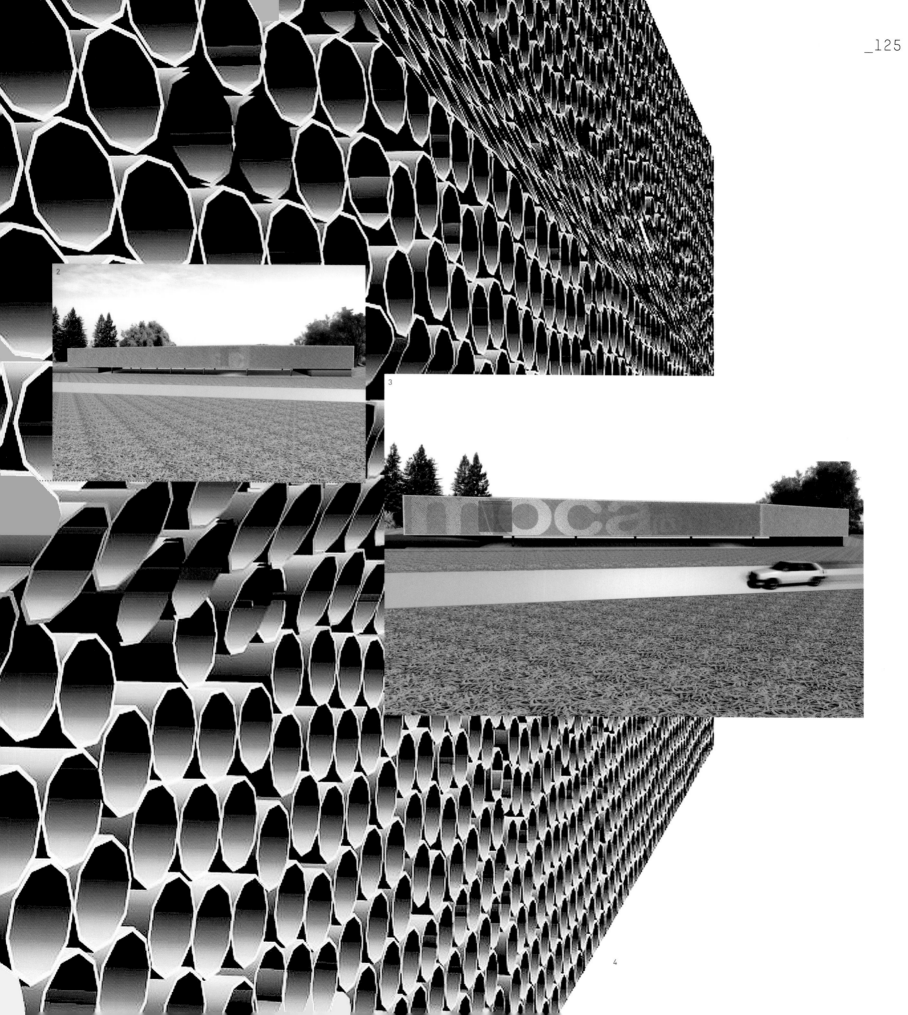

Mute Room
San Francisco

Custom-designed for the 'Rooms for Listening' exhibition held at the California College of the Arts and Crafts in Oakland, California in 2001, Mute Room invites visitors to recline on a wave of spongy foam that fills an entire gallery. A hilly lump beneath the foam's surface is analogous to an overgrown larynx and operates as a fixed sound baffle to enhance acoustical clarity. Just as musical notes 'decay' in the air before dissipating, this surface has a transitory quality; impressions linger until fully erased by the slow-acting foam.

Many people will have experienced the 'intelligent' material of memory foam in the form of earplugs that expand to fill the cavity of the ear, often used to dampen the sound of aeroplane engines, construction drills or over-amplified sound systems. In Mute Room, the sticky foam functions more like a giant hearing aid. Its texture and pink colour are suggestive of orthopaedic devices like insoles, bandages or neck braces, and are uncannily reminiscent of the human body. The room's colour palette of fleshy oranges and pinks is what one sees when one's eyes are closed and light is filtered through one's lids. The room was designed as an environment that would recede so that a sonic experience could come to the fore. Its absorbent textures and warm, soothing colours give the visitor the impression of being suspended in a boundless haze as floor becomes wall becomes colloidal space – the perfect 'room for listening'.

1

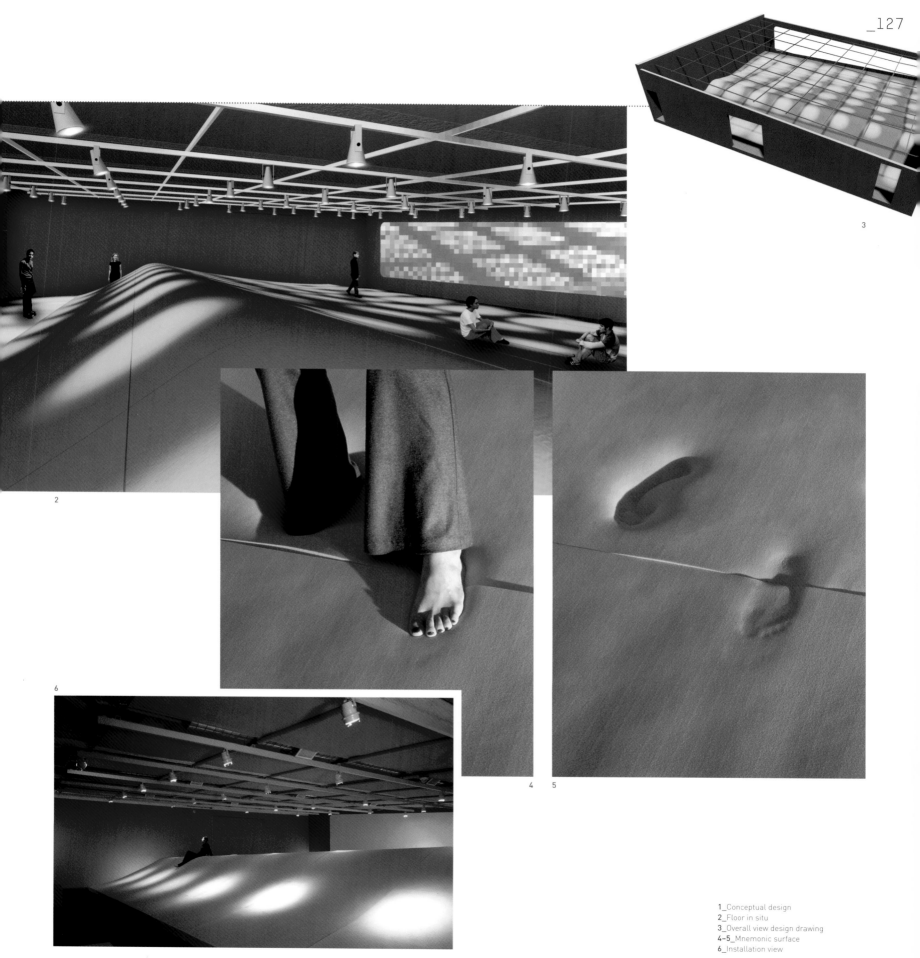

1_Conceptual design
2_Floor in situ
3_Overall view design drawing
4–5_Mnemonic surface
6_Installation view

MARK GOULTHORPE
/
DECOI
>

Educated in England and the US, Mark Goulthorpe worked for four years with Richard Meier in New York and Paris. Later he worked with Foster & Partners in London.

In 1991 Goulthorpe established the dECOi atelier to undertake a series of architectural competitions, largely theoretically biased. These resulted in numerous accolades around the world, quickly enabling a reputation for thoughtful and elegant design work suggestive of new possibilities for architecture and architectural praxis.

dECOi's portfolio ranges from pure design and artwork through interior design to architecture and urbanism, and at every scale the work has received acclaim. The studio has been awarded numerous commissions for artworks / sculptures, and has taken on a small but significant number of architectural projects which have begun to give the group a distinct professional outline. The practice has developed carefully and consistently, focusing on a small number of high-quality international projects. This approach has been reinforced by numerous publications, international lectures and conferences, and frequent guest professorships, including a design unit at the Architectural Association in London and at the École Speciale in Paris.

Goulthorpe's practice is committed to an architectural perfectionism that can see projects beautifully finished and rigorously prototyped.

HypoSurface: Behind skin

BOSTON
PARIS

HypoSurface

1

> Goulthorpe's place in architectural history
> is assured due to his tenacity and commitment.

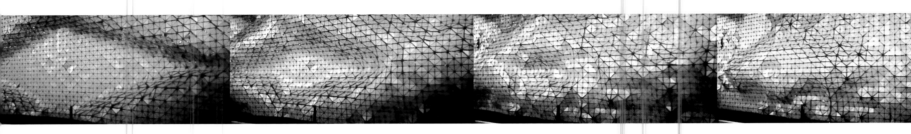

HypoSurface is a dynamically responsive surface
capable of high-speed 'liquid' deformation: it is
an info-form device, deploying digital bus systems
across an array of mechanical actuators to deform a
facetted metallic surface. Beyond the interdisciplinary
technical sophistication of the project, it has been the
user interfaces that have required the greatest design
thought. The sound- and movement-interactivity
systems have been devised to offer both quantitative
and qualitative responsiveness. The basic choreographic
logic is one of constant transformation, such that any
given response is always evolving over time, impelling
continual engagement.

Within an architecture of time, the architect's role
is displaced to establishing rule-sets that offer
sophisticated but differentiated content. This elusive
second-order system is an 'invisible skeleton' that
orchestrates intuitive engagement by others, devising
the possibility of (an) architecture that only comes
into being through the agency of (other) people.
HypoSurface can therefore be seen as a leitmotif
for the shifting role of architects as people acclimate
to a digital (relational) medium.

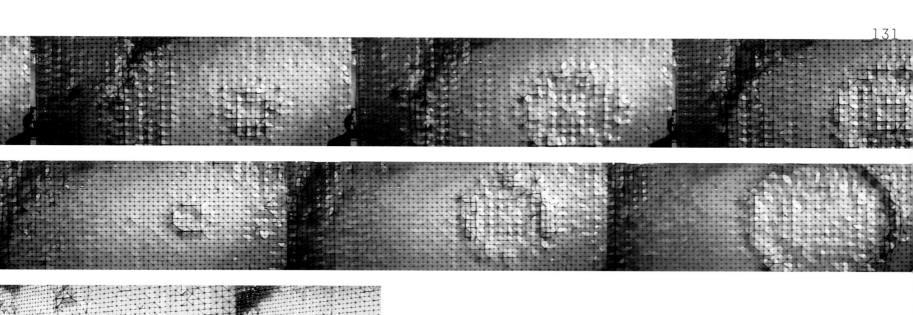

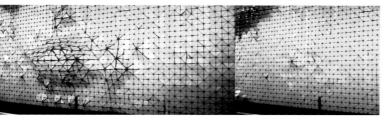

1_Stills from animation show surface movement
2_Detail showing surface articulation
3_Sectional view showing pistons and skin

Miran Galerie
Paris

The Miran Galerie seeks to establish a space that relishes the new constructional opportunities of non-standard digital design and fabrication techniques. The envelope of the fashion showroom swells outwards to offer a sense of spatial expansiveness, stretched taut against existing obstacles. The form 'heaves' into a fully three-dimensional articulation, with the hanging presentation element deformed to give a sense of reciprocal force between it and the outer shell. The final form is articulated as a series of planar 'cuts'. At root, this permits a nuanced aesthetic of striation to be evaluated against the fabrication cost, which offers an extreme elegance of description: a flexible design protocol translated directly into machine code to offer a new material / formal intensity at low cost.

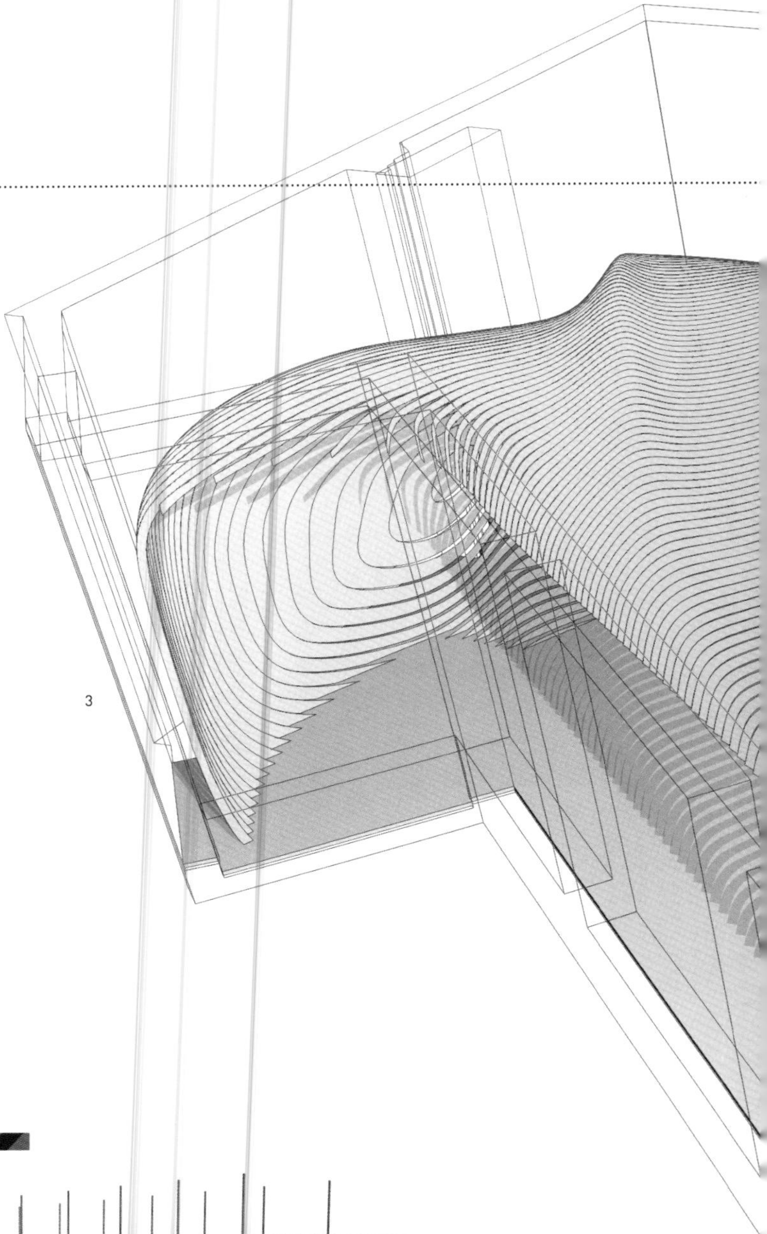

3

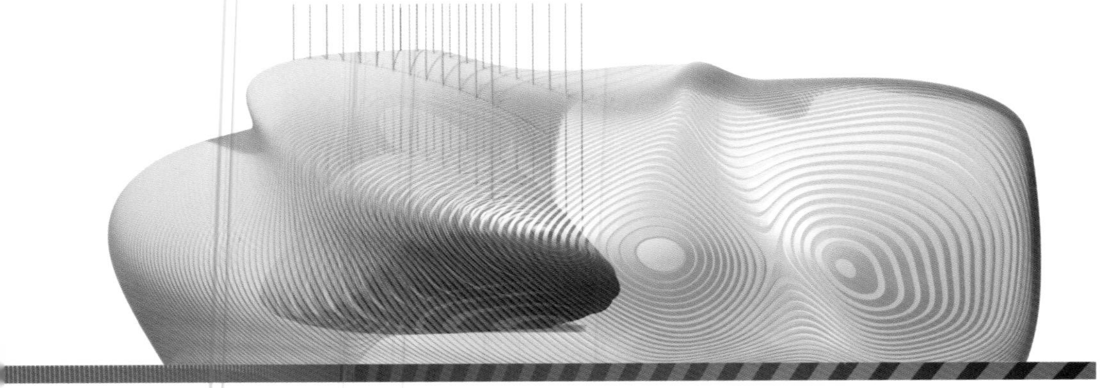

1

2

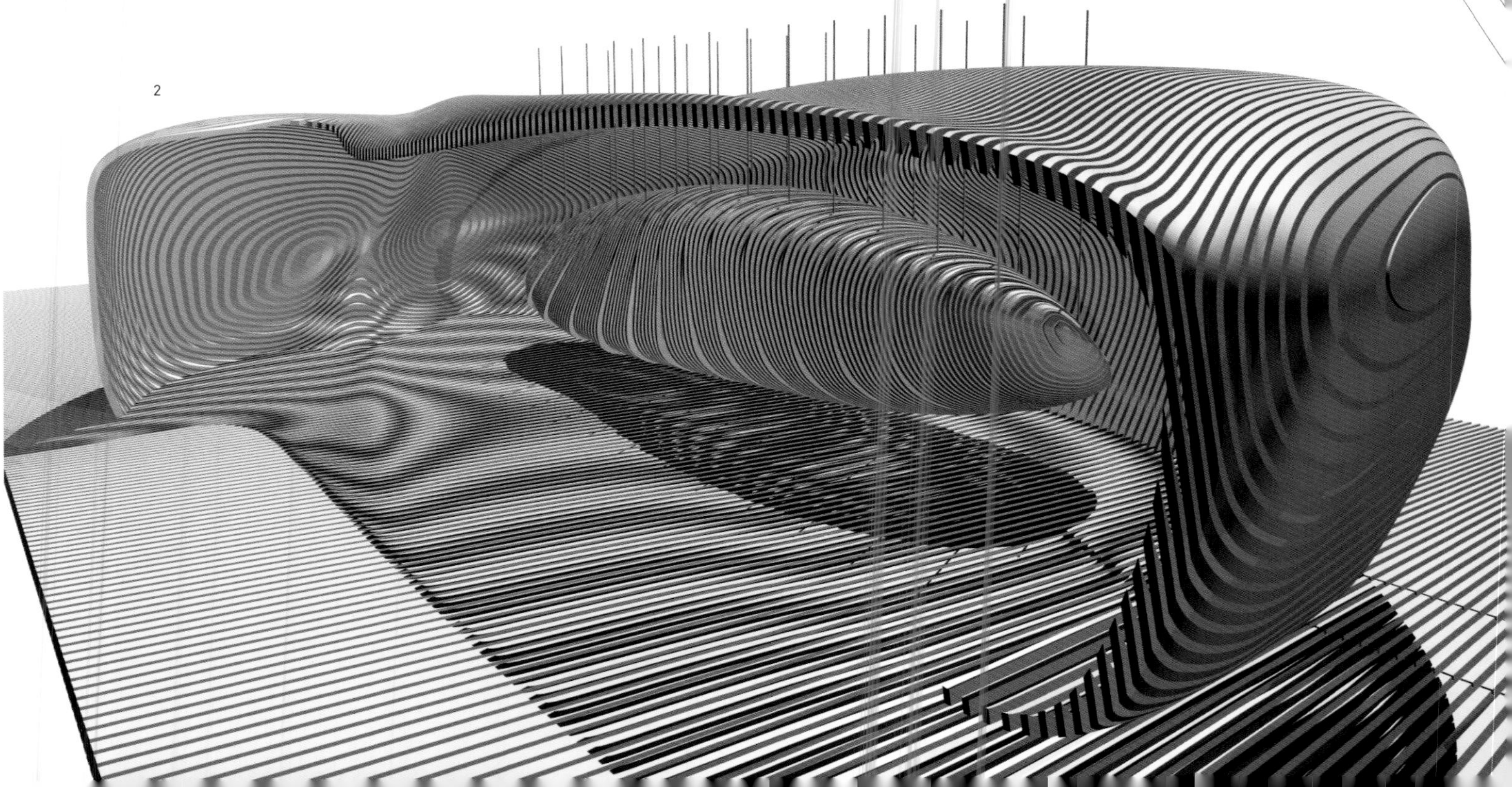

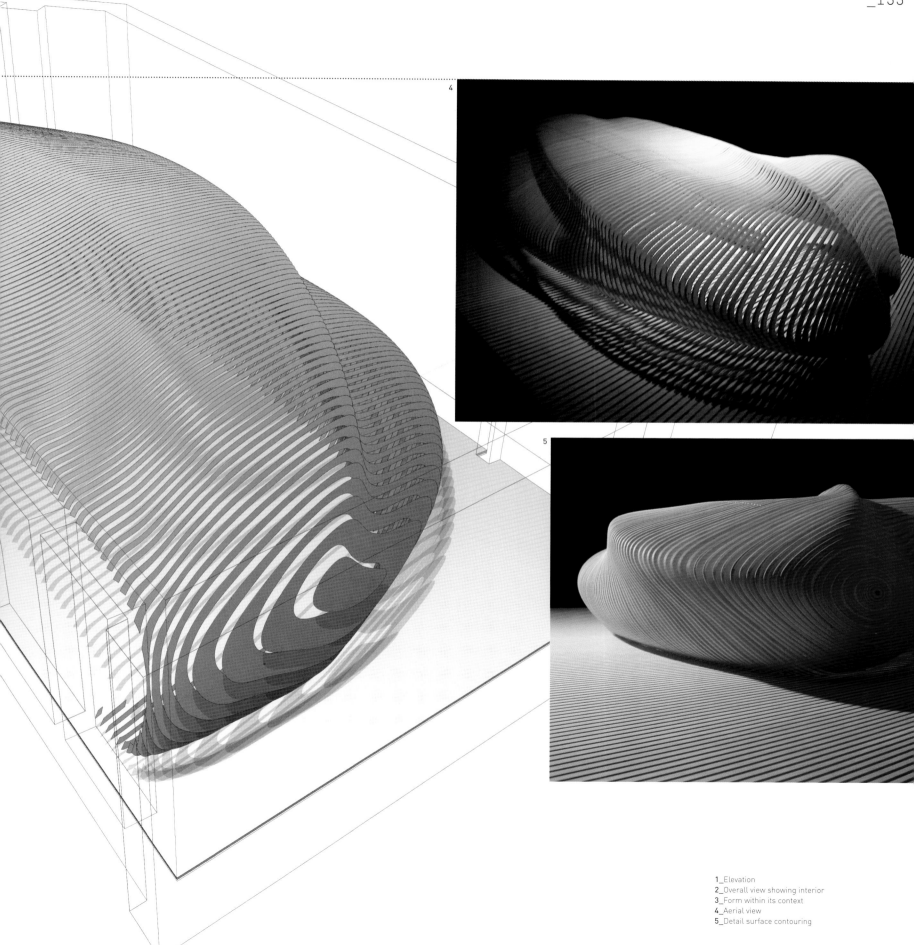

1_Elevation
2_Overall view showing interior
3_Form within its context
4_Aerial view
5_Detail surface contouring

MV² Apartments
New York

The MV² project proposes a floating box above
an existing building to house lofts for two male
partners that share a level of guest bedrooms.
The basic organization presses a single stair along
one longitudinal wall, penetrating a lift shaft up to
a semi-outdoor frontal zone, thereby maximizing
the light and space on the narrow lot.

The existing building has a double façade – an historic
iron-clad warehouse frontage and a second (recent)
façade that replicates the historic Maison de Verre
by Pierre Chareau. Just as the Maison de Verre
epitomizes the transition from an artisanal to a
mechanical paradigm by introducing a fastidious yet
resolutely industrial logic to domestic space, so the
MV² design looks to deploy a seamlessly plastic digital
logic to interior spaces / surfaces, with a few planar
industrial elements as counterpoint. There is an even
deeper affinity in that the Maison de Verre seems
spatially and materially animated by a social tension
that divides male and female spaces. In keeping with
this concept, dECOi introduced a parametric 'solar
element' as a force linking all three MV² levels with
light. This force also 'grips' the entire aesthetic, even
the façade, imparting a disturbance to the otherwise
effortlessly streamlined digital surfaces.

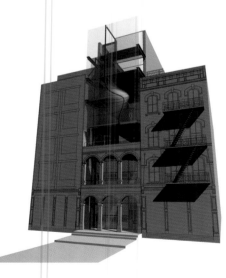

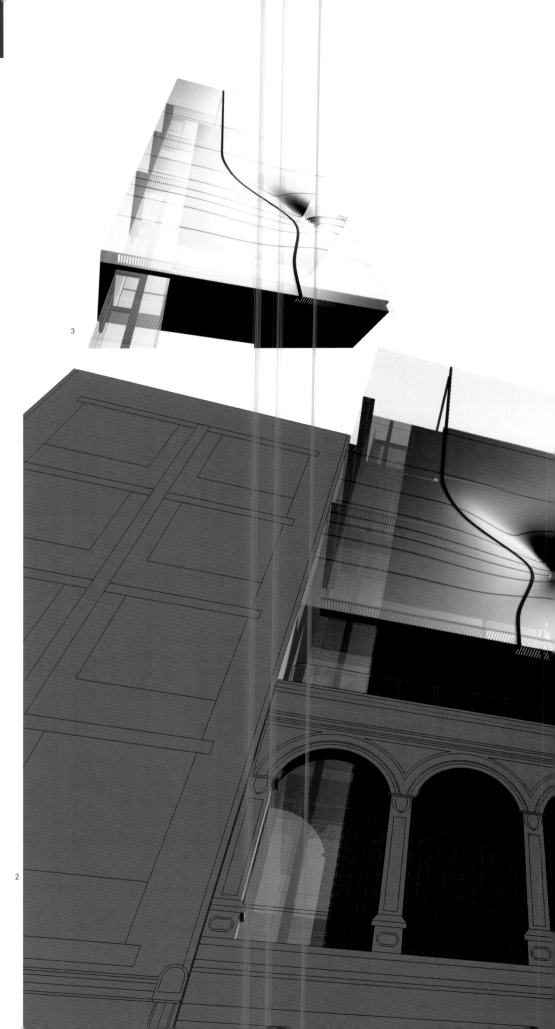

1_Façade context
2_Perspective from street level
3_Façade perspective
4_Section
5_General arrangement sectional / elevation
6_Façade

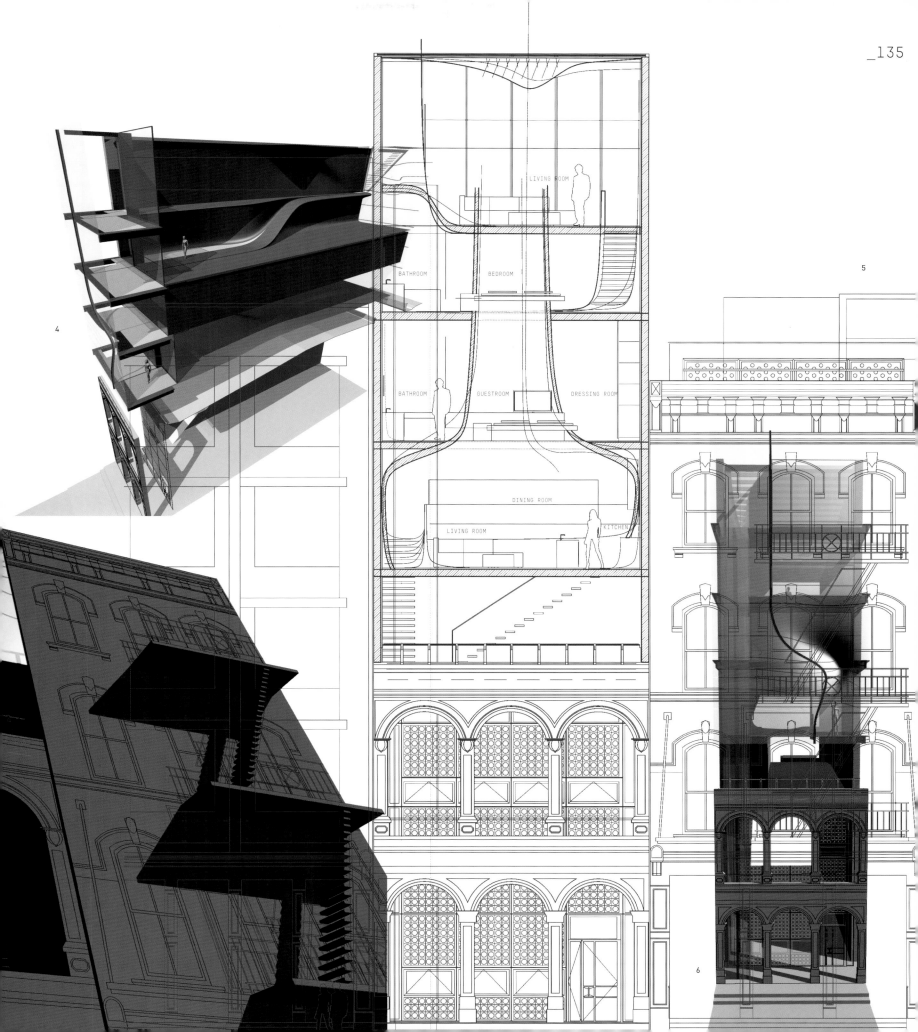

4

5

BATHROOM   BEDROOM   LIVING ROOM

BATHROOM   GUESTROOM   DRESSING ROOM

DINING ROOM

LIVING ROOM   KITCHEN

6

Paramorph 2: Bankside Towertop Penthouse London

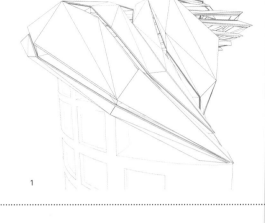
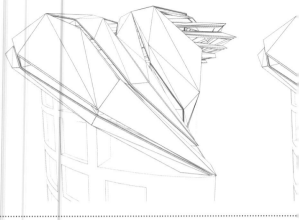

1

The spiralling 'paramorphic' form of the Bankside penthouse embeds legal and technical constraints into a generative protocol such that the three-dimensional structure-surface elements 'grow' according to relational laws. Planar glass quadrilaterals form constrained light / view 'ribbons' around which fibreglass / insulation legs self-organize to meet thermal and structural codes. The gambit of the project is that it might establish new design protocols as profligate parametric tools and that this will force a radical streamlining of fabrication protocols as industrial logics of separatism (materials, functions, trades) collapse into the 'seamless' logic of composites. Here, material is distributed spatially with a radical efficiency that belies its extravagant form: the surface is the structure, is the waterproofing, is the aesthetic – a post-design, post-industrial logic.

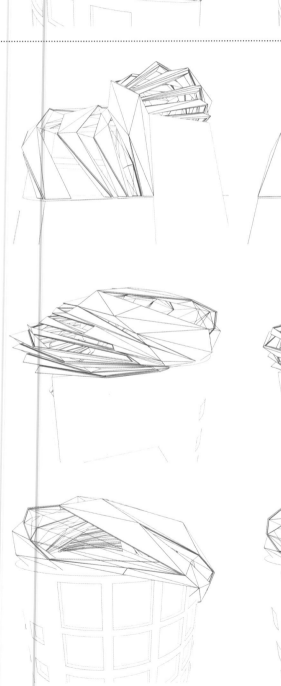

1_Algorithmic formal configurations

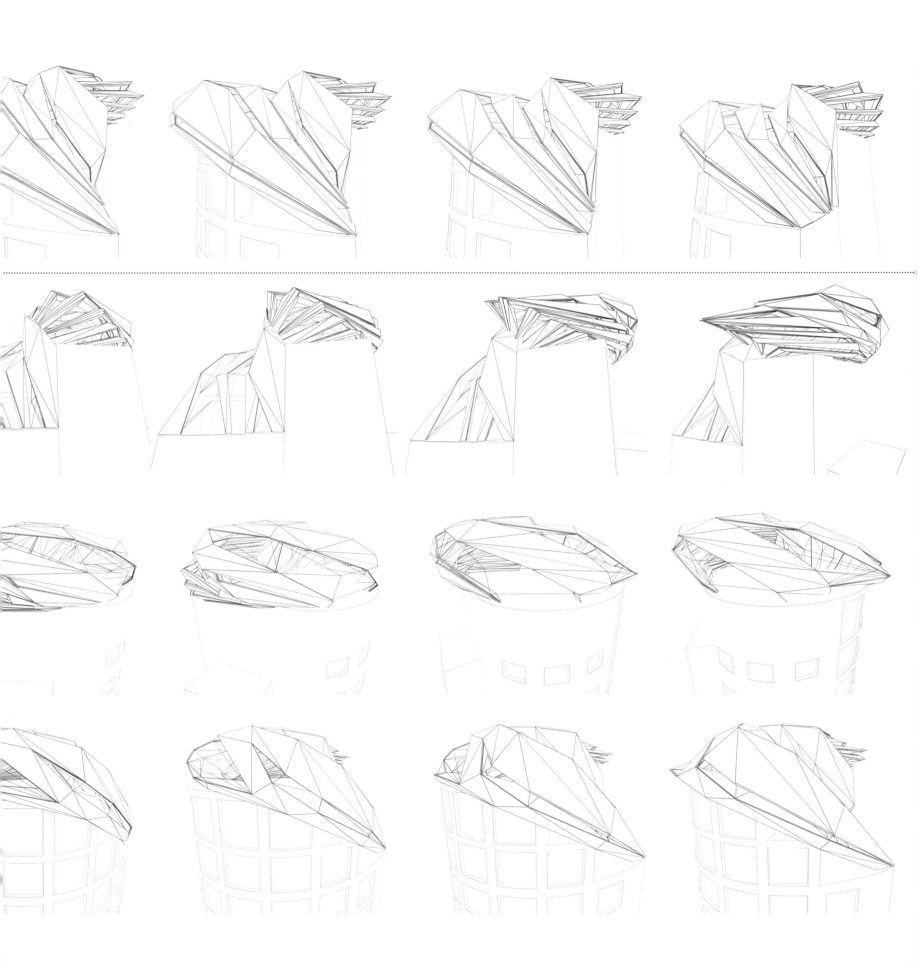

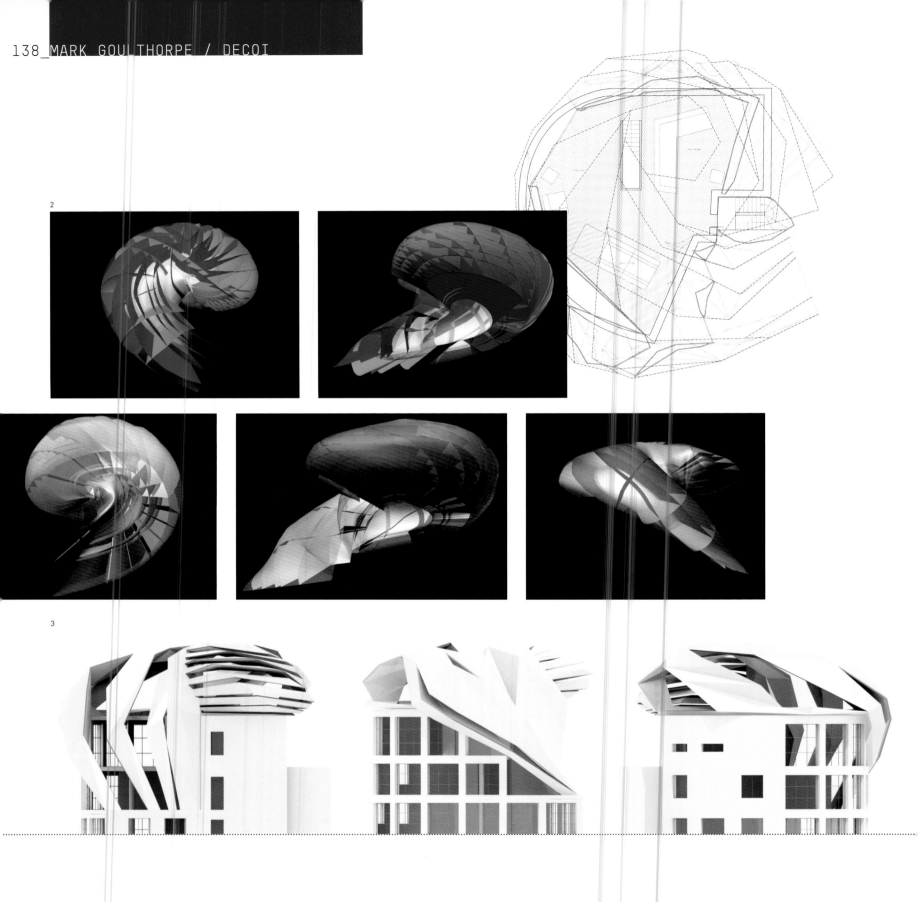

2

3

2_Geometric flow-of-space renderings
3_Elevations
4_General arrangement plans
5_Skin and plane deployment

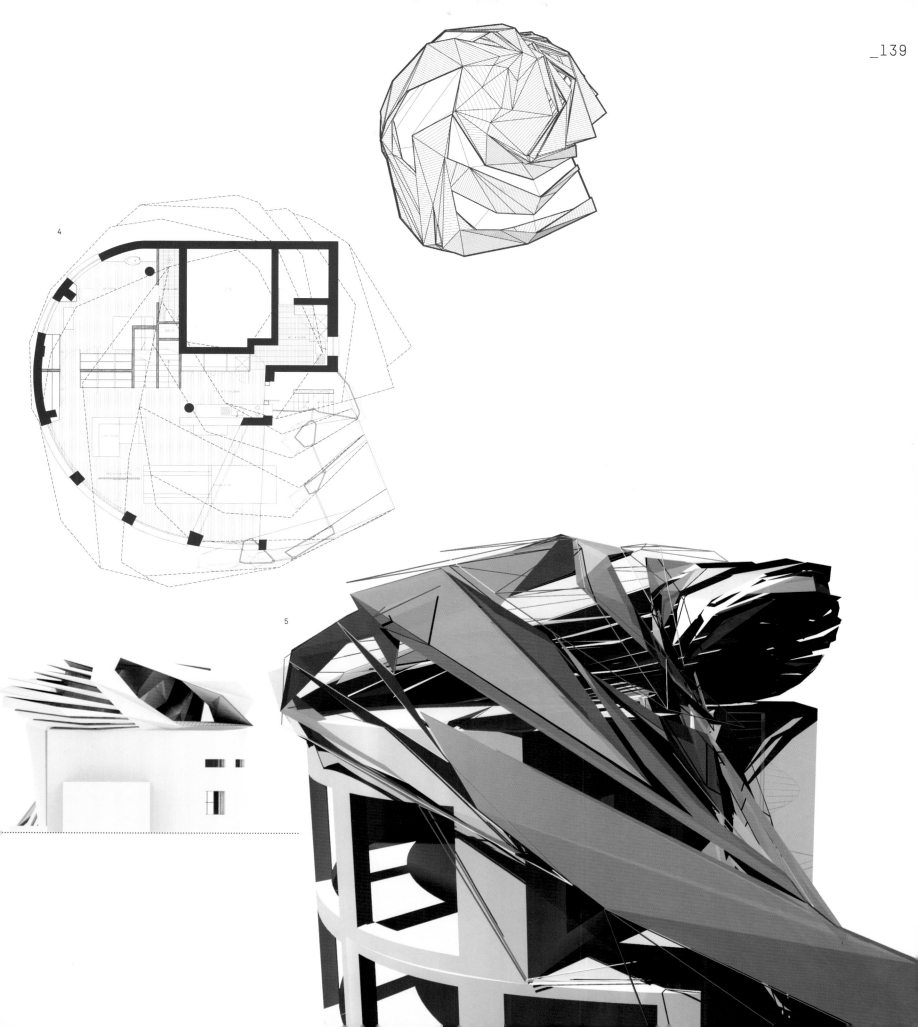

4

5

GREG LYNN FORM

LOS ANGELES

Greg Lynn FORM has been an influential force in the digital design of architecture since the mid-1990s. Lynn has a rare combination of degrees for an architect including one in Philosophy. His book *Animate Form* (1998) is an important milestone in the literature concerning cyberspace and architecture.

The practice's architectural designs have been disseminated with considerable impact worldwide. The work is characterized by its dynamic formal qualities. Recently, much of it has rejoiced in the multiple and the nested. Each element is subtly different from its peers. One can see this aesthetic imperative from the early work to the current output, although it is becoming more biologically analogous, consisting of filigree membranes. Lynn is a fine pedagogue and a revered teacher, and it is clear that he and his practice will continue to help define the near future for digital architecture.

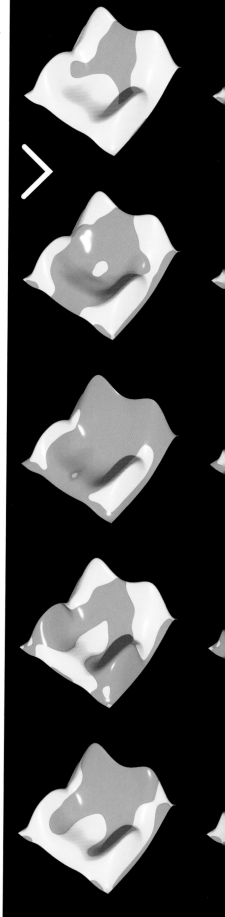

Vitra Ravioli Chair: Configuration renderings

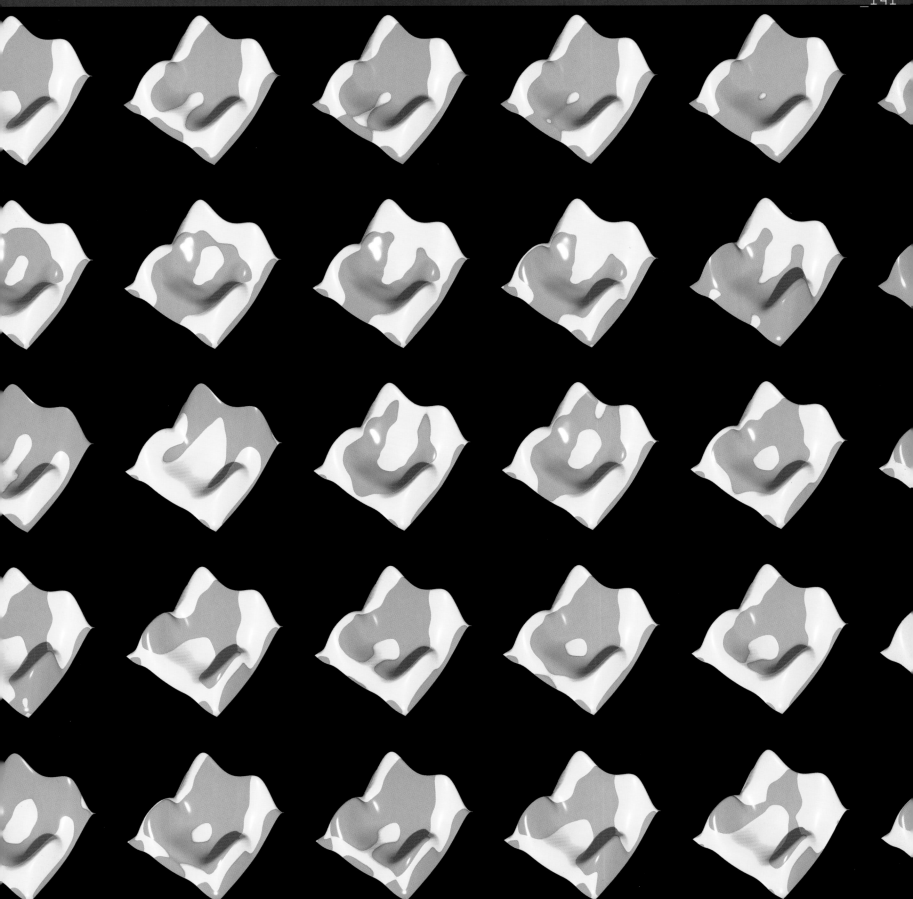

5900 Wilshire Blvd Restaurant and Trellis Pavilion
Los Angeles

This project is situated in a prominent location within the Miracle Mile district of Los Angeles. The glazing of the tower is divided by a series of vertical precast-concrete elements that give the structure a monolithic character. The pavilion seeks to offset this by employing stainless-steel-clad columns set on the same grid as those of the existing structure but branching outwards as they move upwards. This network of columns supports a lattice roof that varies in depth; the variation allows for mottled shading during the day and suggests the experience of being under a tree canopy with moving clouds, shadows and changing light. The roof lattice supports a network of computer-controlled colour- and intensity-changing lights that make for a dynamic but subtle show on the boulevard after dark. This roof spans the main entry staircase of the building, framing a gateway to it from the street.

The restaurant building is designed in harmony with the columns and is composed of gently tapering, curved, drum-shaped volumes clad in stainless steel. These undulating, sensuous exterior volumes form dramatic interior spaces with grand, cathedral-like vaulted ceilings. There are two entries at each end of the building, one of which opens onto the newly landscaped forecourt of the tower. The restaurant is the main component of the pavilion and consists of three connected zones: an indoor seating and kitchen-service area, and a covered outdoor seating area located under the lattice canopy.

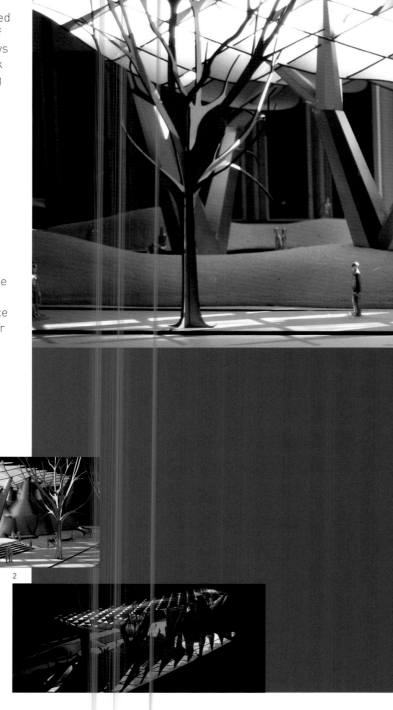

1

2

1_Beneath canopy
2_Roof structure
3_Perspective view
4_Entrance from street

3

4

BLOB WALL©

BLOB WALL©, a collaboration between Greg Lynn and
PANELITE, is an innovative redefinition of architecture's
most basic building unit – the brick – in lightweight,
plastic, colourful, modular elements custom-shaped
using computer numerically controlled technology.
BLOB WALL© is a free-standing, indoor / outdoor
wall system built of low-density, recyclable, impact-
resistant polymer. The blob unit, or 'brick', is a trilobed
hollow shape that is mass-produced through rotational
moulding. Each wall is assembled from individually
robotically cut hollow bricks that interlock precisely.
In addition to stock designs, custom configurations are
available for specific shapes, sizes, room arrangements,
partitions and colour schemes. BLOB WALL© is
intended to recover the voluptuous shapes, chiaroscuro
and grotto-like textures of Renaissance and Baroque
architecture in gradients of vivid colour. The stock
designs are 'S'-, 'L'-, 'I'- and 'U'-shaped walls, as well
as a Dome and a Tree House. There are stock colour
schemes, each made up of seven different colours.

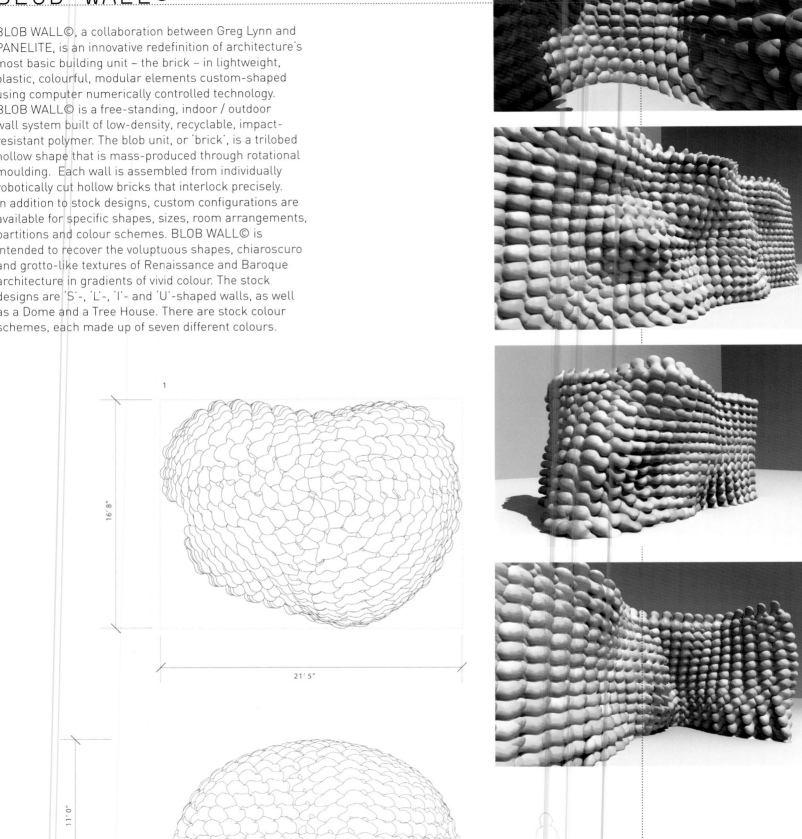

1

16' 8"

21' 5"

11' 0"

2

1_Possible articulation, plan and elevation
2_Possible articulation model
3-4_BLOB WALL© deployed

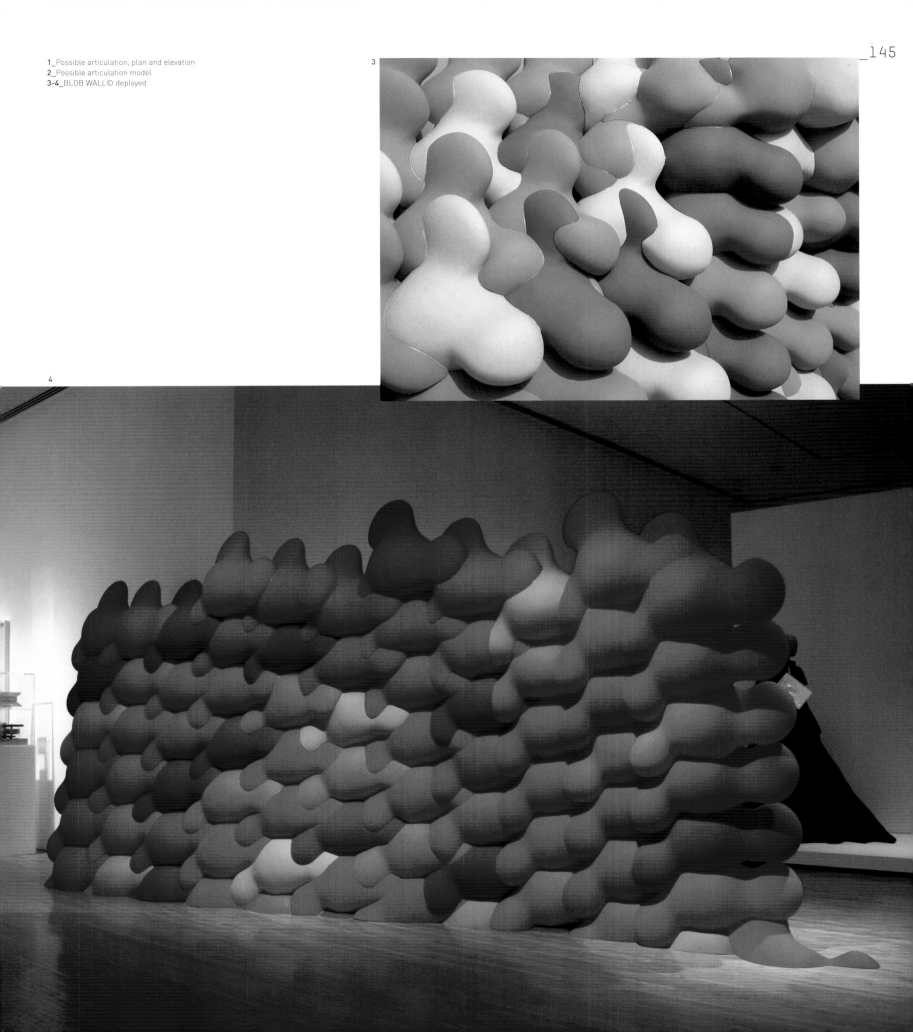

Flatware

> Lynn is the godfather of
much of the work in this book,
and he is still very active
in defining new approaches
to architecture.

The design of flatware is most often a study in typology and variation. Standard utensils such as spoons are used as the basis for series of functional and cultural variations that range from the typologies of fork and knife to more exotic items for specialized practices.

The design of this flatware set proceeded from a primitive beginning: a bundle of ties and a handle with webbing. The design of the individual elements in the set proceeded through the use of software invented for the animated-film industry. The 'primitive' was designed for specific functions and then mutated, blended and evolved into the various functions of fork, spoon, knife and all elements in between. The combined use of dynamic-modelling software with a design element that contained all the potential but none of the familiarity of the specialized functions led to the creation of elements that are at once familiar and individually specialized yet related as a family.

1

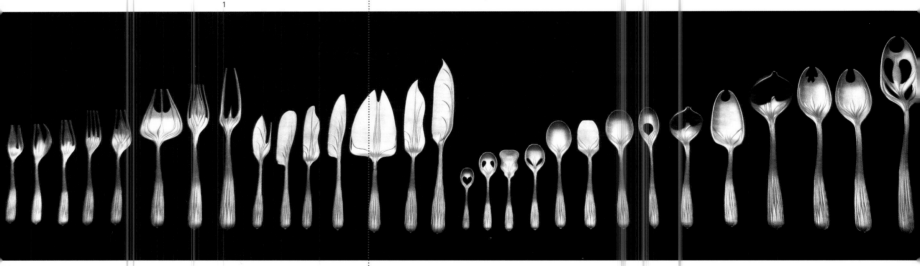

The set was originally designed in sintered ceramic material that proved to be too brittle for daily use. The final set is manufactured as an edition in which each piece is built using a computer-controlled 3-D printer that builds the pieces in micro-layers of sintered tool steel and bronze. The finished parts are then silver-plated directly from the printing machine. No tools or polishing are used.

1_Taxonomy of cutlery suite
2_Detail of cutlery

Slavin House
Venice, California

The Modern house – the California house in particular – was driven by desires for dematerialization and extension. Today we prefer dense luminescence to lightness and rich encumbrances to endless emptiness. This house folds inside and outside rooms into a singular porous environment that occupies the entire triangular site. A one-storey-high truss defines the mass of the house, composed of two continuous extruded and radially bent steel tubes, braided and looped through one another, that function simultaneously as horizontal and vertical members, beams and pilotis. The integrated structure allows a 30-metre- (100-foot-) long ground-floor living area to be partially enclosed and yet blended with outdoor spaces and light courts that perforate the upper level and connect the landscape with the sky. These glowing wells both separate the upper floor's bedrooms, study and children's area from each other and link them with the lower zone as well as the roof as they fold upwards along the curved structural radii. Each element does more than one thing at a time: material and surface continuities make volumes both voids and solids; continuous fillets and radial tangents enable the curvilinear basket structure to support and create hollow courts. This flowing continuity engenders a new kind of porous domestic space that folds together indoor and outdoor spaces; structural frame; void light wells; solid figures; translucent, bounding envelope and undulating ground plane.

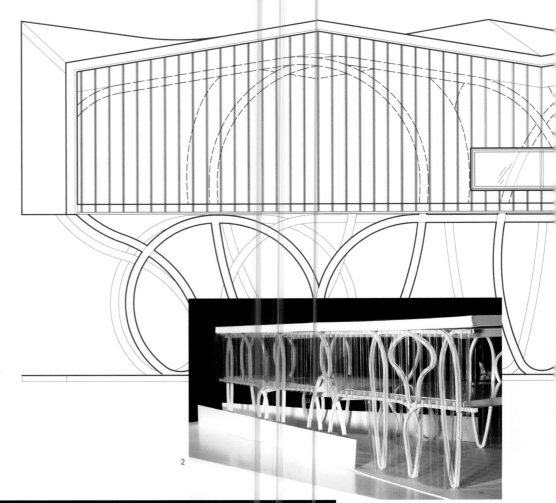

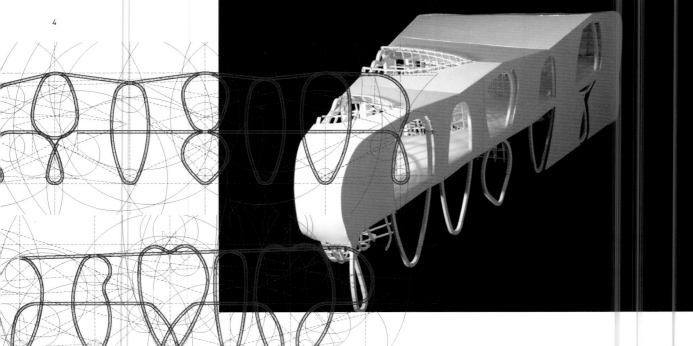

1_Elevation
2_Model shot
3_Overall model view
4_Rotational structural form
5_Sectional model showing structure

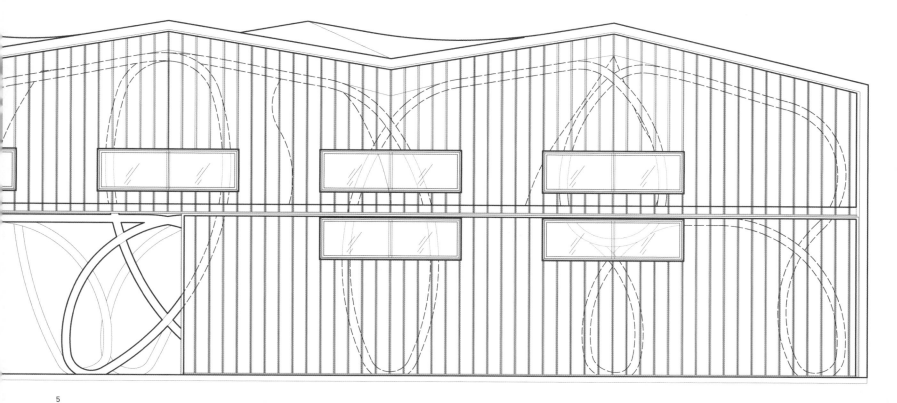

5

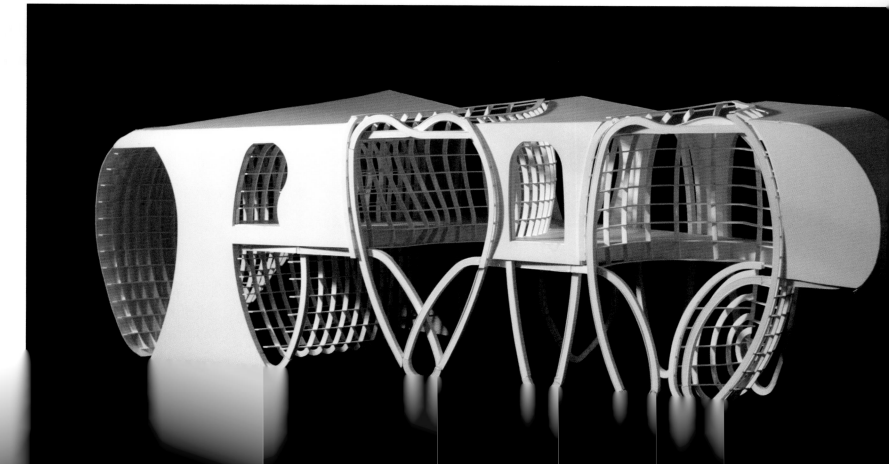

Vitra Ravioli Chair

The Ravioli is a comfortable chair for everyday use. The design was realized using digital ergonomic data and geometry. Prototypes and models were fabricated in Lynn's office using computer numerically controlled routers and rapid-prototype prints, allowing for an organic development of the chair's forms, shapes and materials, as well as its comfort and functionality.

This seamless process from digital medium to prototype was highly compatible with the digital manufacturing processes of toolmaking and 3-D knitting, which was used in the final production of the chair. Using the possibilities afforded by computer simulation, a basic square was expanded to a three-dimensional figure in order to unite all of the required elements in one surface – footprint, seat bucket, armrest and backrest. Ravioli thus represents a contemporary interpretation of a classic upholstered chair.

The finished chair consists of two firmly connected half-shells made of different materials. The upholstered seat with its three-dimensional knit cover rests on a solid plastic base. Functioning like a cloak, the cover allows for a series of set variations. Two different patterns, also designed by Lynn using a digitally controlled process, are available in several colour combinations.

1

3.5

2.5

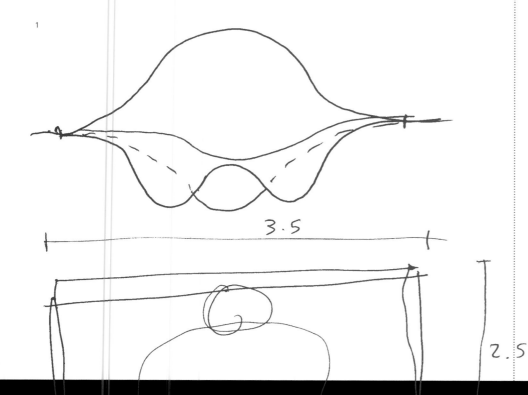

2

1_Conceptual sketch
2_Chair models
3–6_Prototypes

3

4

5

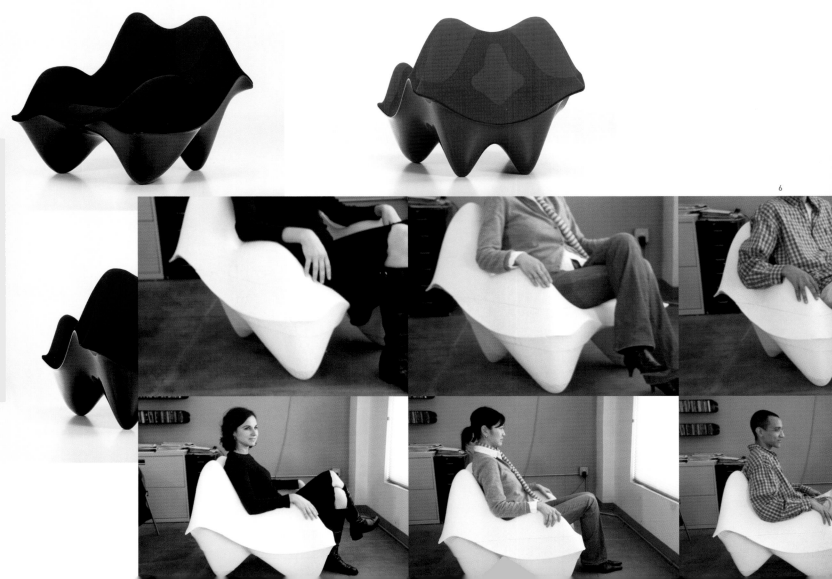

6

USMAN HAQUE/
HAQUE DESIGN
+ RESEARCH >

Open Burble deployed

Haque Design + Research specializes in interactive architecture systems. Architecture is no longer considered as something static and immutable; instead it is seen as dynamic, responsive and conversant. Haque's projects explore some of this territory.

Haque's work is predicated on an understanding of second-order cybernetics. It is often very subtle and dependent on observers, their perception and their movement. Often it is interested in the emergent dynamics of groups of simultaneous users / viewers. This is where it takes on aspects of its own, unrelated to designerly preconditioned or programmed hubris. Haque's systems forge space while responding to conditions on the ground at a particular moment in time. He also artfully flits between digital space analogues and actual spaces, using one to condition the other. Haque's spaces are not drowned in the fashionable digital aesthetics of aerials, cables and twitching armatures but utilize essentially blank devices that come alive in use (mobile phones, for instance).

LONDON

Floatables

Mechanical Systems
air purification
Helmholtz coil
buoyancy control
Faraday mesh shield
blur/thermal barrier

Electrical Systems
ground scan camouflage
solar cells
microwave barrier
802.11 scrambler
digital acoustic
cancellation

1

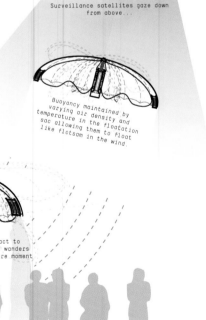

Powered by sunlight, wind and excess
inducted mains electricity, mobile
phone signals and wireless network EMF.

Surveillance satellites gaze down
from above...

Buoyancy maintained by
varying air density and
temperature in the floatation
sac allowing them to float
like flotsam in the wind.

Adaptive camouflage surface

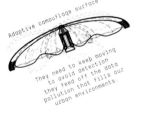

They need to keep moving
to avoid detection
they feed off the data
pollution that fills our
urban environments.

They expand and contract to
change altitude...if one wanders
along near you, grab a rare moment
of solitude.

The myth of public space is that it is
a space open to all...public space has
always implied limited access - limited
to particular members of a community,
particular citizenships, particular
genders or particular income groups.

On the other hand, in a data-saturated
environment, how do you find privacy?

2

The aim of the floatable jellyfish-like vessels that drift around cities is to create ephemeral zones of privacy: an absence of phone calls, emails, sounds, smells and thermal patterns left behind by others. Through various electrical systems, the vessels are also able to prevent access by GPS devices, television broadcasts, wireless networks and other microwave emissions. Finally, by creating a 'blurry barrier' and ground-plane camouflage pattern, they provide shielding from the unembarrassed gaze of security cameras and surveillance satellites.

Floating around urban environments, in the tradition of architecture that tries to break free from the confines of gravity, the vessels provide fleeting moments of private visual, auditory and olfactory space – occupants can wander in at will when they happen to catch sight of one nearby. The absences created are left to be filled with people's own sounds, alpha-waves, smells and laughter.

The vessels are powered mainly by sunlight and wind but are supplemented by inducted electricity from mobile phones and 802.11 networks (a type of wireless network). Buoyancy is achieved by heating or cooling air in a floatation sac, much like hot-air balloons. The entire structure, weighing 4.1 kilograms (9 pounds), can collapse or expand to alter surface area in response to wind speed and altitude. The vessels have no particular destinations and drift like flotsam. However, they must keep moving because to be discovered by the authorities means almost certain destruction.

1_Section
2_Conceptual drawing

Open Burble

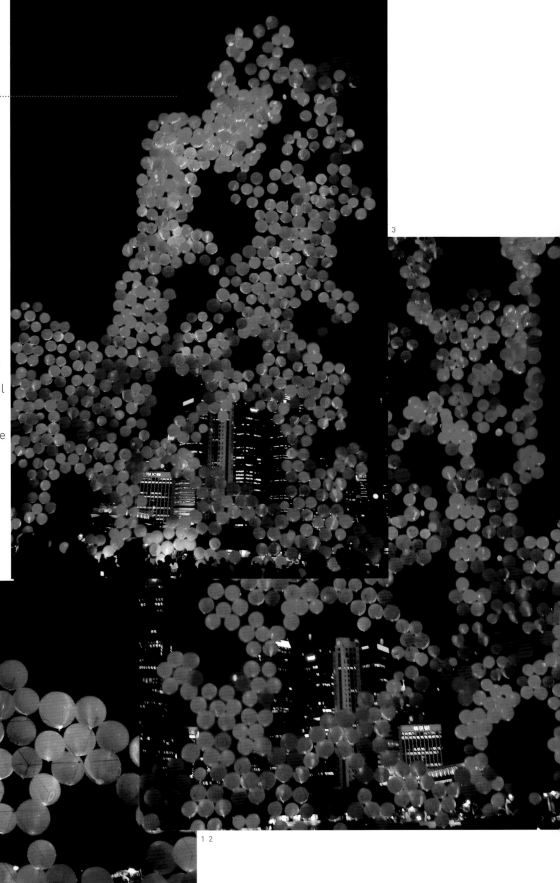

Participants divide into groups in order to assemble approximately 140 hexagonal 'clouds' into a complete Burble, built to such a scale that, when inflated with helium, it soars upwards like a plume of smoke. Just as the participants are the composers of the Burble's tall form, so too are they its controllers. They hold onto it using handles with which they may position the Burble as they like. They may curve it in on themselves or pull it in a straight line – the form is a combination of the group's desires and the impact of wind currents varying throughout the Burble's height.

The Burble moves, rustles, tangles, folds in on itself and creates turbulence as the wind catches it like a sail. Suddenly, the entire construction ignites with colour, sparkling in the evening sky. As people on the ground shake and pump the handle bars of the Burble, they see their movements echoed as colours through the entire system. They can discern their own individual fragments, perhaps even identifying design choices they have made. Their individual contributions become an integral part of a spectacular, ephemeral experience many times their size.

1–3_Open Burble event

Sky Ear

1

> Haque's productions always evolve environments that utilize observers and their perceptual feedback.

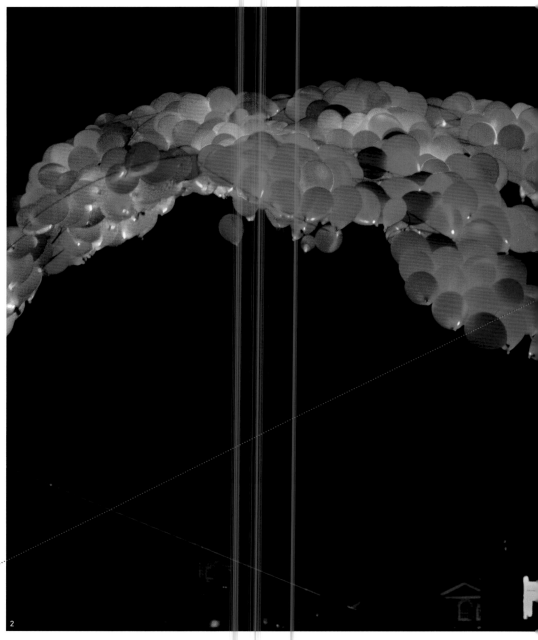

2

Sky Ear is a non-rigid carbon-fibre 'cloud' 30 metres (98 feet) in diameter, embedded with a thousand glowing helium balloons and several dozen mobile phones. The balloons contain miniature sensor circuits that respond to electromagnetic fields, particularly those of mobile phones. When activated, the sensor circuits co-ordinate to cause ultra-bright coloured LEDs to illuminate. The cloud glows and flickers as it floats across the sky at heights up to 100 metres (330 feet).

As people using phones at ground level call into the cloud, they are able to listen to natural electromagnetic sounds of the sky. Their mobile-phone calls change the local hertzian topography; the disturbances in the electromagnetic fields inside the cloud alter its glow patterns. Feedback within the sensor network creates ripples of light reminiscent of thunderclaps and lightning flashes.

Sky Ear shows both how natural, invisible electromagnetism pervades our environment and how our mobile-phone calls and text messages delicately affect electromagnetic fields.

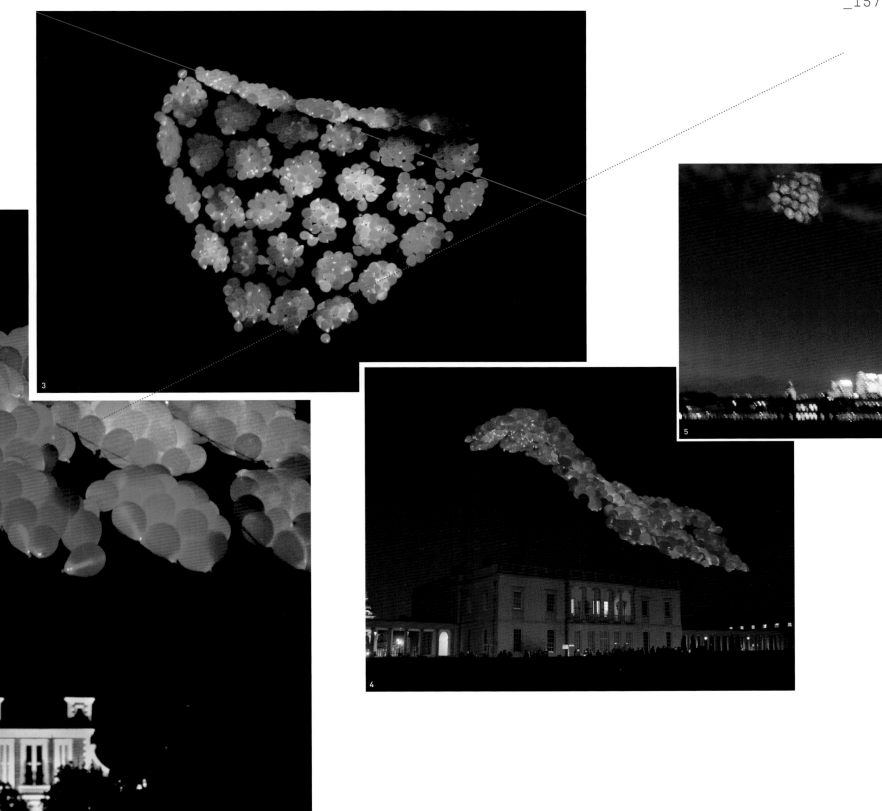

1_Sky Ear in fabrication prior to launch
2–5_Sky Ear deployed in Greenwich Park,
South London

Evolving Sonic Environment

Drawing on the work of Gordon Pask, Donald Hebb and Andrew Adamatzky, the Evolving Sonic Environment, developed together with the psychologist Robert Davis, is an architectural experiment to investigate how one might construct an interactive environment that builds up an internal representation of its occupants through a network of autonomous but communicative sensors. The 'society' of sonic devices functions like simple neurons, though using acoustic rather than electrical coupling. Both respond to and create high-frequency sound, cascade during high activity, alter their thresholds during periods of low activity and become apparently 'bored' by repetitive inputs.

In order for external observers to get a glimpse into the room's changing states (and in order to 'observe' the room's 'observation') there are two possible points of entry. The most straightforward method is to enter the room and listen to the units 'talking' with each other through high frequencies. However, entering the room affects the communication paths of the devices and therefore alters its internal state. An alternative method of experiencing the changing states of the room analogizes the process of EEG recordings of the brain: audio from the population, shifted down ten octaves in real time to comfortable human hearing range, is provided outside the room. This includes visualizations of the sound as well as one of movement as sensed by a camera.

1–5_Shots of inhabited installation

4

JERRY TATE
ARCHITECTS ›

Dubai Waterfront Hotel: Internal structure

LONDON

Jerry Tate Architects believes that the strategic and appropriate use of technology can provide answers to the problems that our built environment faces for both today and tomorrow. At an urban scale, new forms of dynamic-simulation software allow us to harness the urban flows of programme pattern and circulation within the virtual environment. Through this we can generate spatial models to promote community interaction, flexibility and transport optimization. At the building scale, the practice believes that the integration of appropriate construction technologies can produce buildings which address the issues of sustainability in its widest context, from social responsibility to carbon emissions and energy use, and, eventually, recycling of building components themselves.

Tate himself is a catholic designer, conversant with a variety of design approaches and techniques. Originally his work was concerned with a moving mechanical armature that created numerous, perceptually changing windows within and around his architectural proposals. Latterly, he has flirted with seamless, slick, pseudo-biological American forms. Whatever design-language protocols he is using, Tate has a wonderful eye for architectural composition. He is at his best when he lets rip, entertains and runs with an extraordinary idea with a sense of digital theatricality, using his cyberspatial tools to ascertain its parameter and provide its material tailoring.

Dubai Waterfront Hotel
Dubai

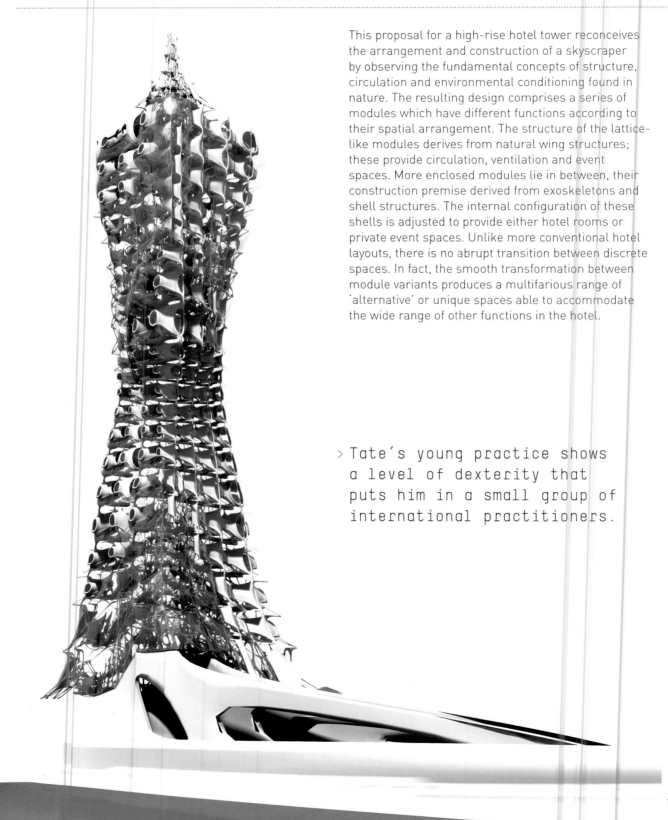

This proposal for a high-rise hotel tower reconceives the arrangement and construction of a skyscraper by observing the fundamental concepts of structure, circulation and environmental conditioning found in nature. The resulting design comprises a series of modules which have different functions according to their spatial arrangement. The structure of the lattice-like modules derives from natural wing structures; these provide circulation, ventilation and event spaces. More enclosed modules lie in between, their construction premise derived from exoskeletons and shell structures. The internal configuration of these shells is adjusted to provide either hotel rooms or private event spaces. Unlike more conventional hotel layouts, there is no abrupt transition between discrete spaces. In fact, the smooth transformation between module variants produces a multifarious range of 'alternative' or unique spaces able to accommodate the wide range of other functions in the hotel.

> Tate's young practice shows a level of dexterity that puts him in a small group of international practitioners.

1_Overall perspective view
2_View of tower head

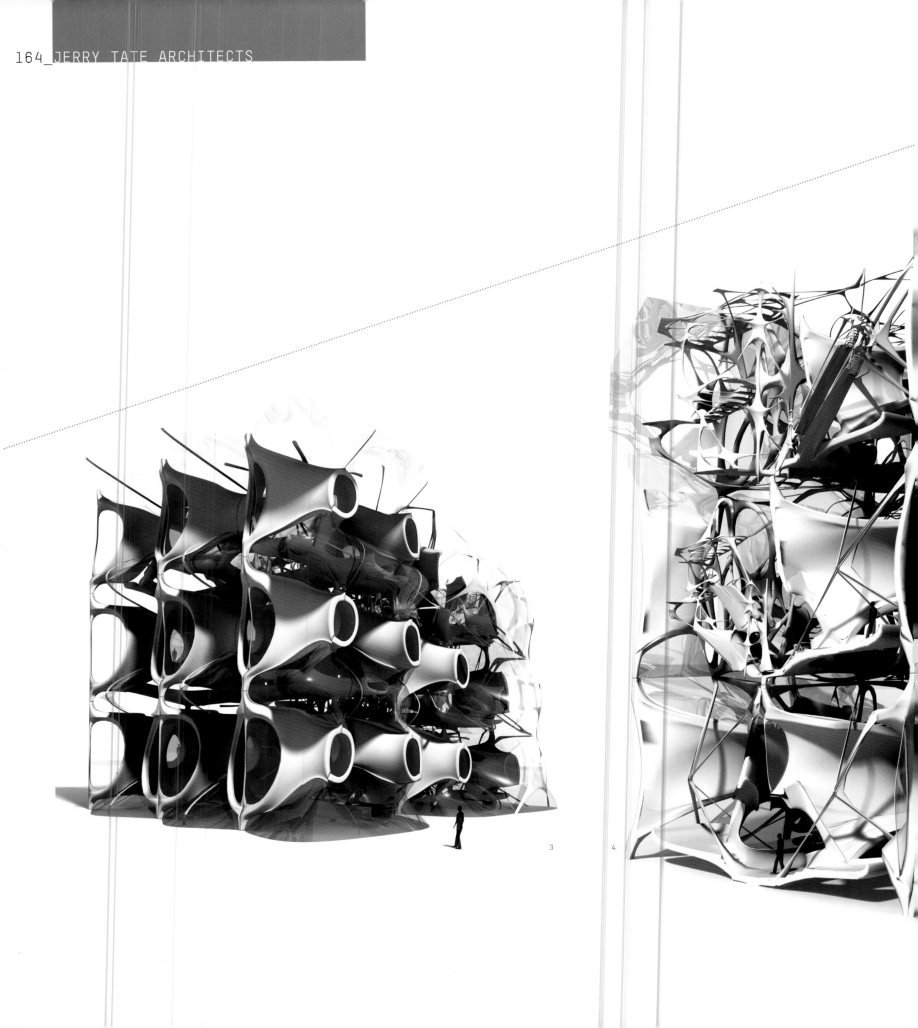

3
4

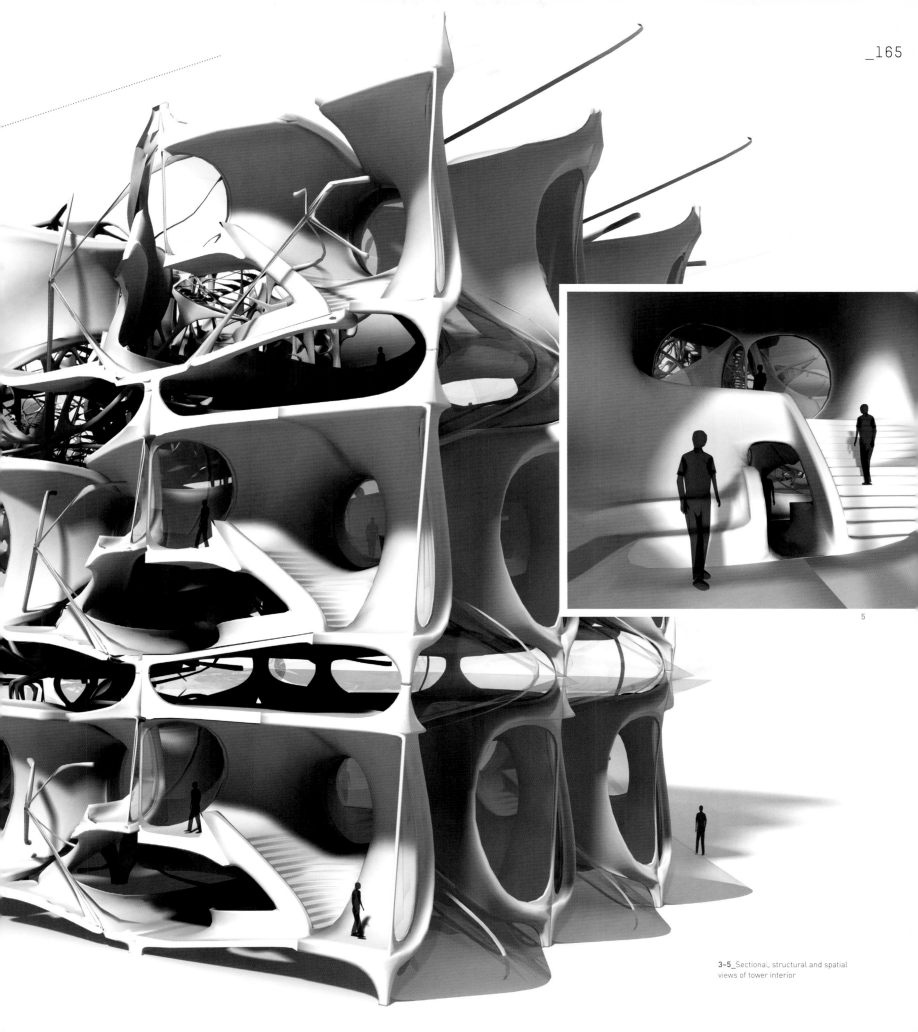

3–5_Sectional, structural and spatial views of tower interior

5

New Orleans Neighborhood Community Center and Hurricane Shelter
New Orleans, Louisiana

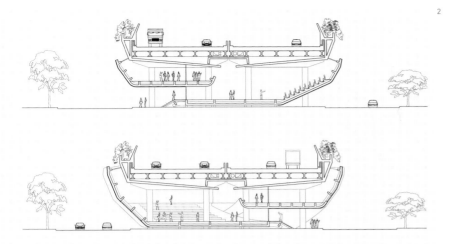

The aim of this project is to reclaim the unused ground in central New Orleans beneath the I-10 elevated interstate highway. Elements of the scheme combine to provide an emergency hurricane facility beneath the safety of the raised concrete deck. Through noise and fume mitigation and the addition of facilities for the improvement of New Orleans, the project seeks to repair the urban scar created by the Interstate cutting through the city.

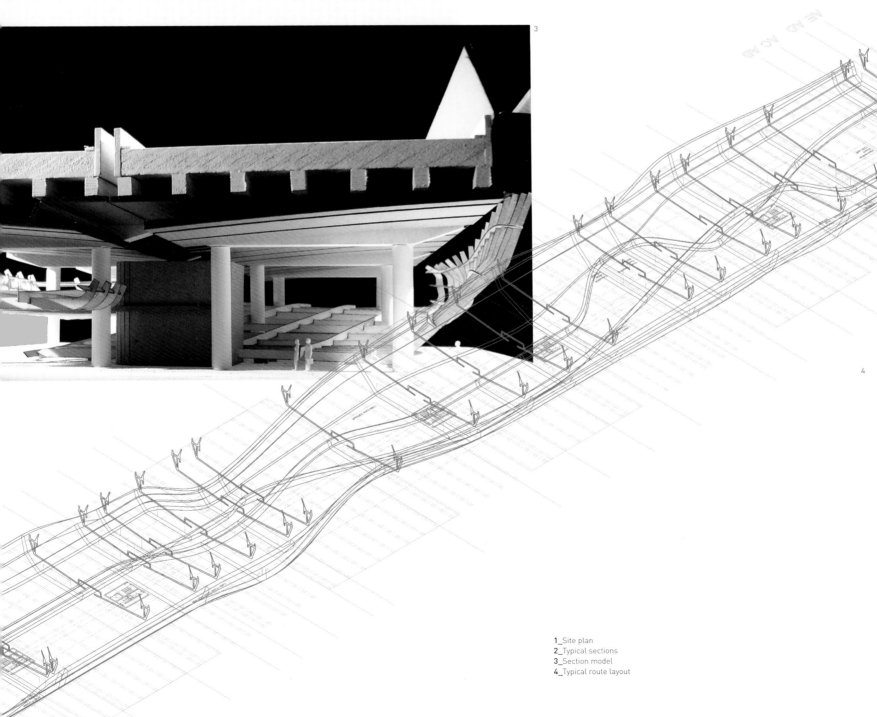

1_Site plan
2_Typical sections
3_Section model
4_Typical route layout

Sorrento Bathing Platform
Sorrento, Italy

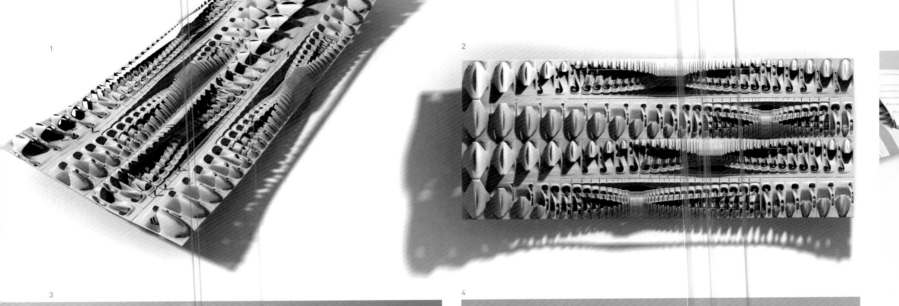

This is a modern reinterpretation of Victorian bathing:
a platform inspired by programmatic studies of bathing
areas in Sorrento. These areas were mapped to produce
a dynamic field; then, from this map, the spatial
relationships were derived. The smooth transition from
shops and restaurants to individual paddling pools
and areas for swimming produces spaces of surprise
and delight in the interstitial conditions. The interface
between the open air and the datum of sea level is thus
enriched beyond present-day possibilities.

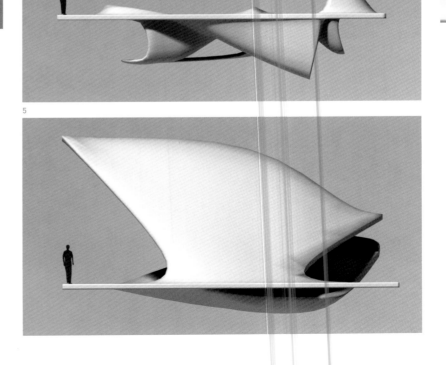

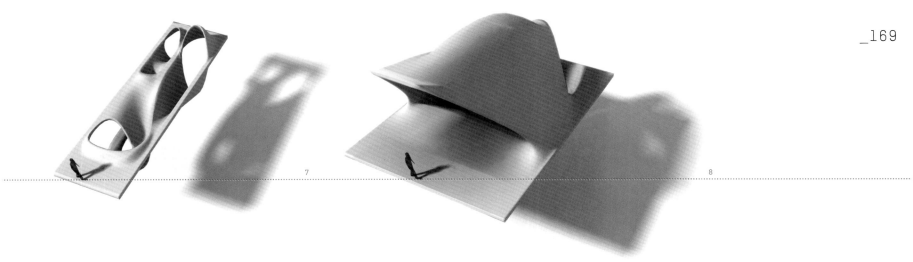

7

8

9

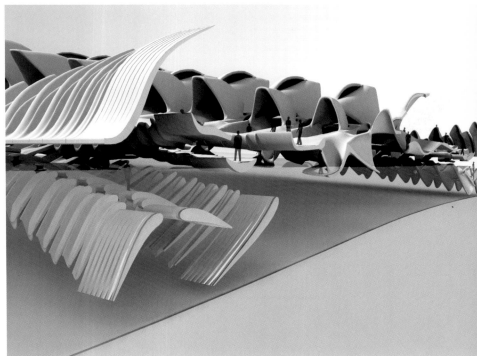

10

1–2_Overall plan
3_Section
4–5_Detail sections
6–8_Modular arrangements
9–10_Interior views

Swiss-Army Wall Project
Hammersmith, London

The complete remodelling of a standard Victorian terraced house in London included a clever way of handling the increased amount of 'stuff' that families accrue while staying true to the feel of the original structure. An innovative 'Swiss-Army' wall was designed to house the client's extensive and varied possessions as well as providing functions for the room itself. These included, variously, a home cinema, hi-fi system, computer, drinks cabinet, fireplace, display area for sculpture, plan-chest (for paperwork), and CD, video and book storage. The concept was that all would be accessible for day-to-day use but could be easily shut away as required.

1

2

1_Wall-unit perspective view
2_Wall-unit general arrangement elevation
3_House plan
4_Built

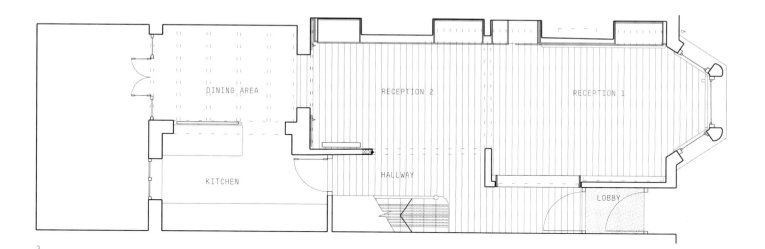

DINING AREA

RECEPTION 2

RECEPTION 1

KITCHEN

HALLWAY

LOBBY

3

4

J. MAYER H.

> BERLIN

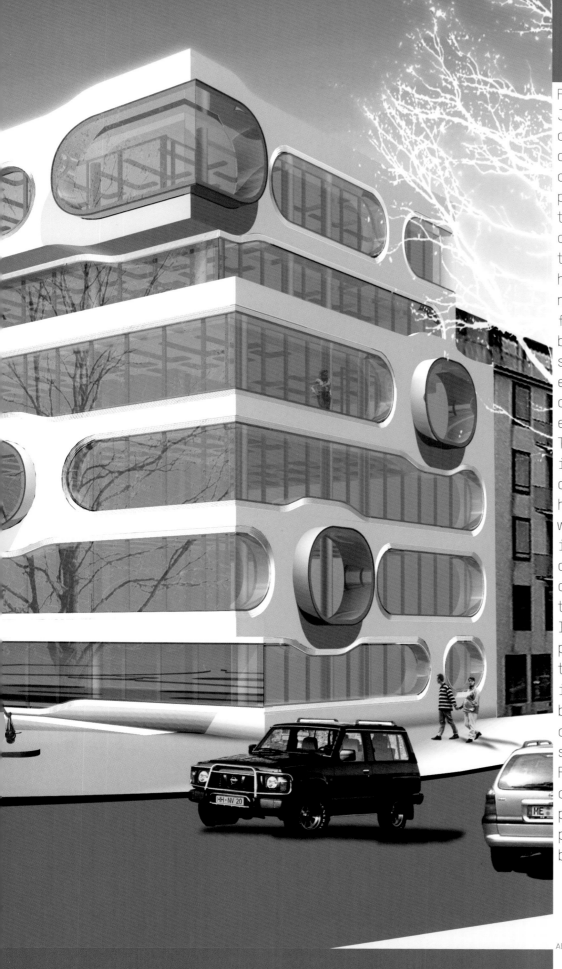

Founded in 1996 in Berlin, J. Mayer H. focuses on works at the intersection of architecture, communication and new technology. From urban-planning schemes and buildings to installation work and objects with new materials, the relationship between the human body, technology and nature form the background for the firm's work. The studio builds often and at a large scale. The projects, while exhibiting Germanic exactitude, create hybridized spaces or experimental ethereal façades. The practice really comes into its own when it finds a little elbow room away from hard-nosed commercial concerns, when it can blur outside with inside, when it is cosseted by an exhibition hall, or when it can playfully experiment with technologies and ambiences. In an era when notions of purity of structure have been taken over by Baroque excess, it is good to see J. Mayer H. being fully explicit about the compositional importance of structure and its reading. For Mayer himself, the computer and its numerous architectural processes and techniques are purely expedient parts of building and ambience creation.

ADA1: View from park

Seasonscape –
Ascona Lakefront Pier
Ascona, Switzerland

1

4

2

3

The design floats on the lakefront of Ascona, doubling the surface of the seaside promenade as well as creating new infrastructure for tourism. This new surface – an artificial landmass – is a pontoon-scape that oscillates at water level and houses a ferry terminal with various tourist programmes. The structural concept resembles a human spine. All pontoons are connected by compressible rubber points and anchored to the bottom of the lake. Surface formations can be modified for different seasons as well as temporal / functional needs. A lightly structured flexible skin covers the pontoons and houses the upper programmatic layer.

1_Context
2–3_Perspective vignettes
4_Site plan

BMW Event and Delivery Centre Munich

The competition entry for the BMW Event and Delivery Centre proposes a building that is both a large event space and the central activator of the vast BMW complex. Situated between the BMW tower and the Olympic Park, the Centre fuses multiple forms of leisure, entertainment, economics and sport.

To emphasize the building's role as a social condenser (facilitating the mixing and meeting of people), large ramps extend outwards into the public spaces of the adjacent structures. This vast, blob-like building also contains a public roofscape with skylights that allow visitors to view events taking place both inside and outside the building.

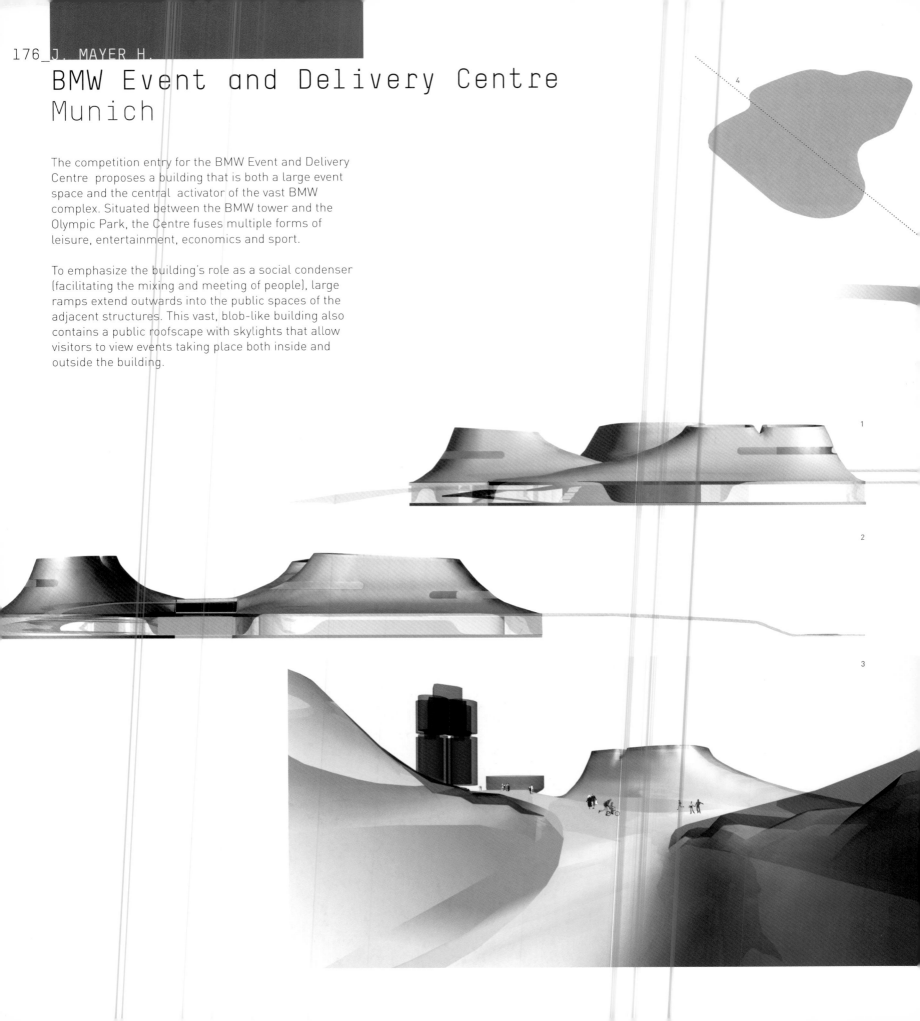

1–2_Elevations
3_Approach view
4–6_Build-up of footprint,
terraform and skin
7_Interior view
8_Context plan

Danfoss Universe, Master Plan – Curiosity.Centre/Food.Factory Nordborg, Denmark

Danfoss Universe is a science park embedded in the agricultural landscape of Nordborg next to the founder's home and Danfoss headquarters. It opened in May 2005 and is being enlarged due to its success. The master plan for Danfoss Universe Phase 2 includes an exhibition building (Curiosity.Centre) and a restaurant (Food.Factory), which will extend the use of the park into the winter months by providing enclosed spaces for exhibitions and experiments.

The new buildings rise up and provide spaces which articulate the fusion of outdoor landscape and indoor exhibition. This active ground modulates according to programme and location. The building's endpoints blur the line between it and the park by offering inside-out spaces as display areas and projection surfaces related to the temporary exhibitions within. Silhouettes as groupings of land formations define the unique new skyline.

1

2

15.90

Exhibition I

3

1_Structure
2_General arrangement plan
3_Conceptual section
4_Formal massing model

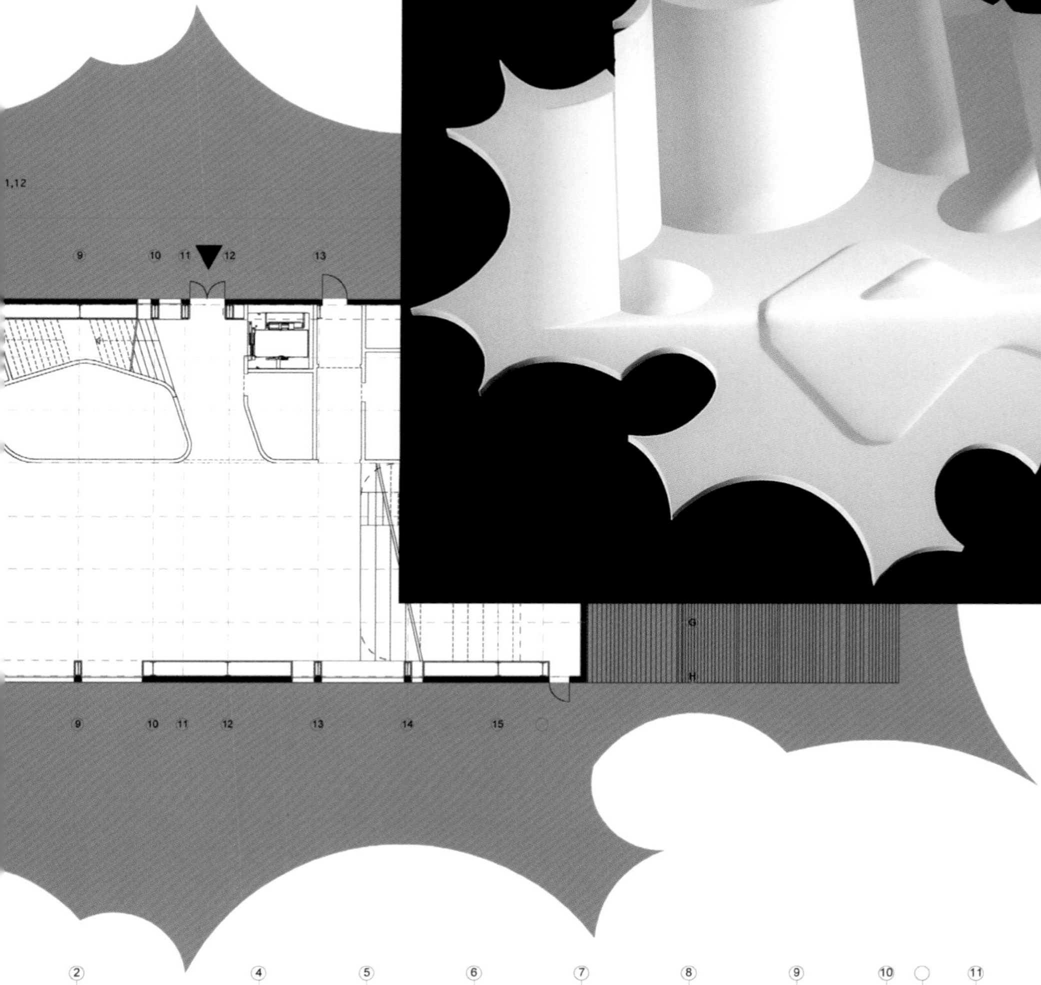

1,12

9   10   11   12   13

9   10 11   12   13   14   15

G
H

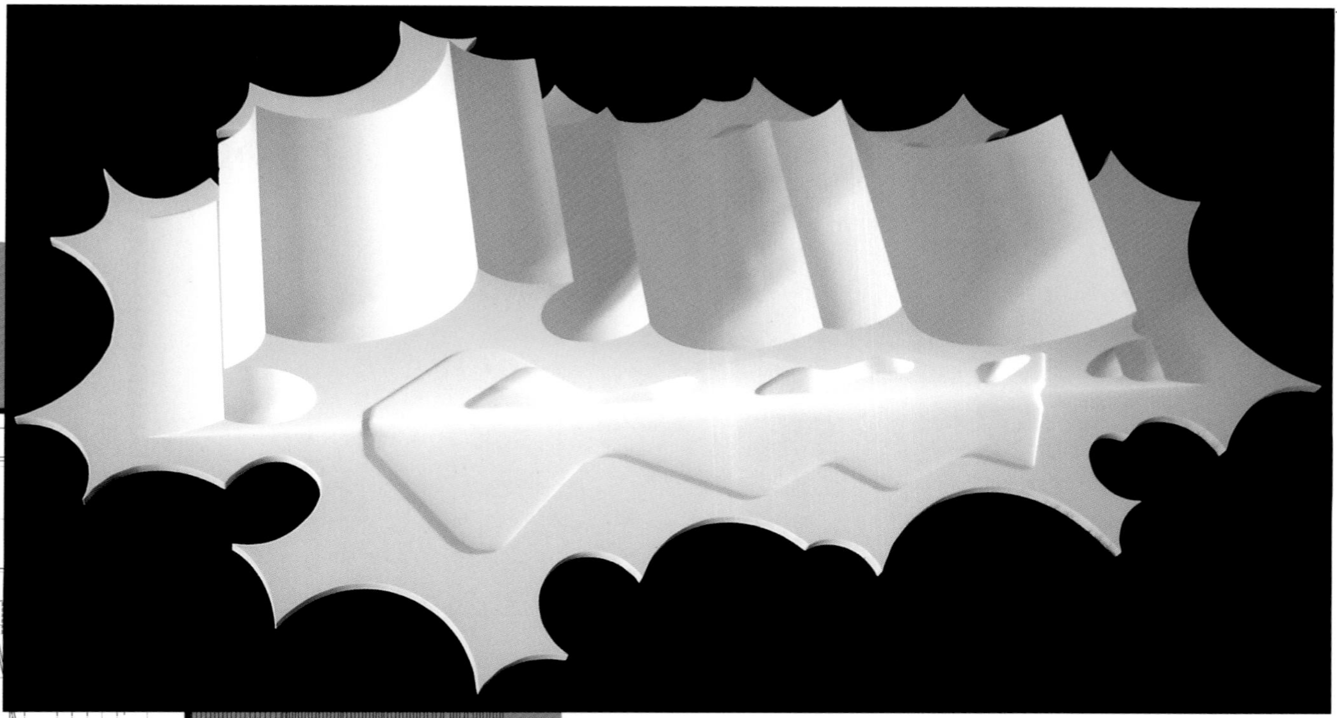

4

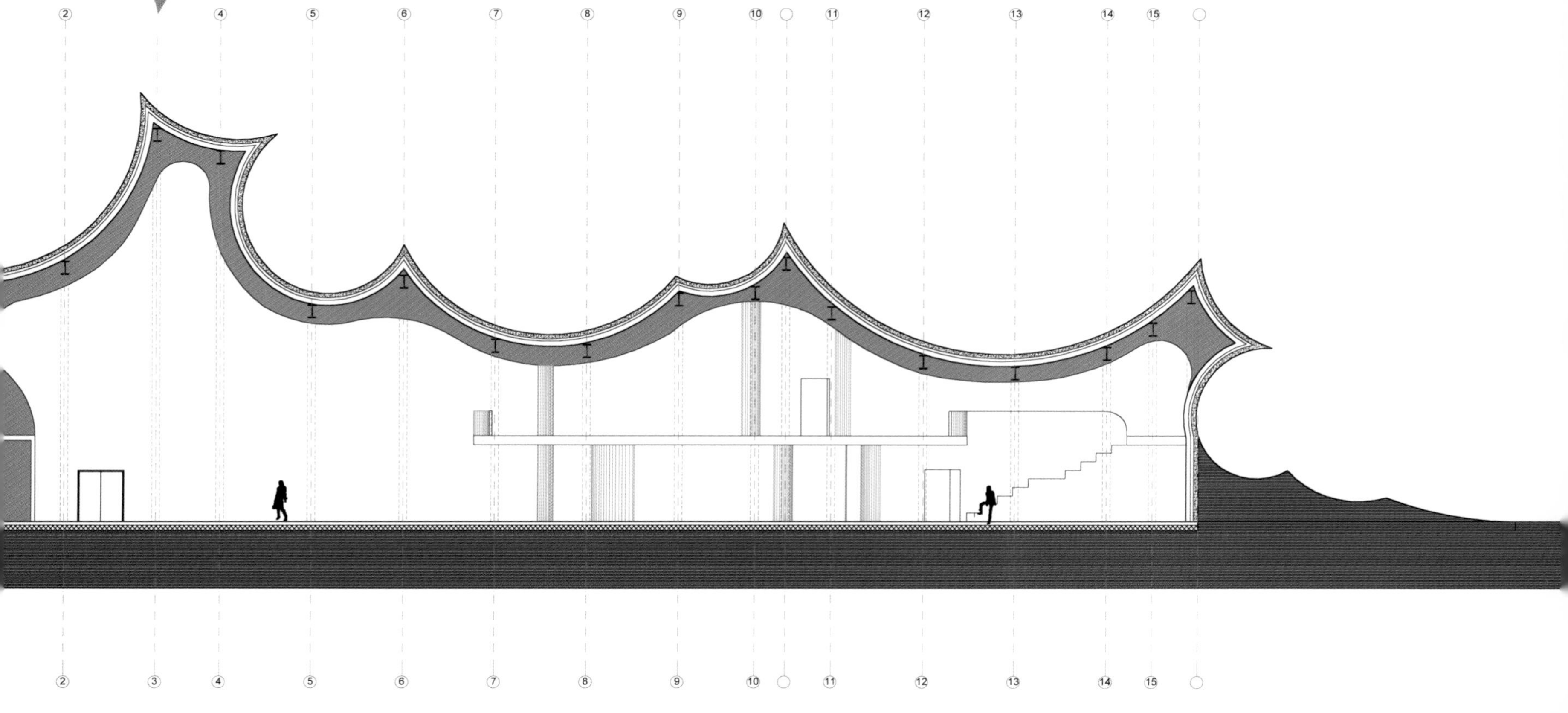

② ④ ⑤ ⑥ ⑦ ⑧ ⑨ ⑩ ⑪ ⑫ ⑬ ⑭ ⑮

② ③ ④ ⑤ ⑥ ⑦ ⑧ ⑨ ⑩ ⑪ ⑫ ⑬ ⑭ ⑮

5

6

7

8

5_Location plan
6–7_Perspectives
8_Ground mediation elevations

New National Library
of the Czech Republic
Prague

1

> J. Mayer H. combines astonishingly
frequent output with a questioning
approach to space.

3

2

1_Façade perspective
2_Perspective from rear
3_Interior view

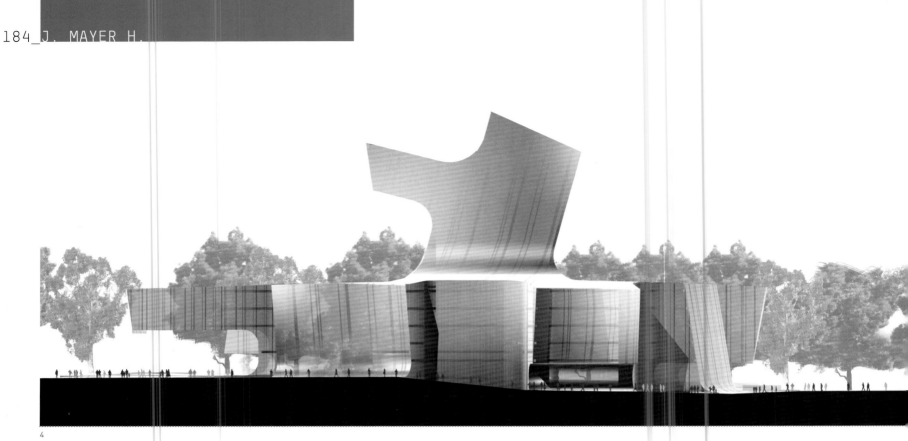

4

The building occupies the centre of the site, reaching out to its edges with branches that relate to the proportion of the buildings in the neighbourhood. The streetscape is therefore defined by similar open and closed dimensions. Large cantilevers interlock the building with the urban landscape, providing entry areas and protected open-air zones. Two public entrances allow a pedestrian connection and good public accessibility from the subway and by foot through the park. Administrative entrance, delivery entrance and entry to the parking garage are along the double-lane one-way street leading from Milady Horákové Avenue to Badeviko Street.

The New National Library building is intended to be seen as a knot in the twenty-first-century network of information and communication. It is meant to function as a built manifesto interconnecting artefacts and virtual libraries on site as well as via the Internet. Branches of the building reach out into the urban context to melt it together with the landscape and public spaces. One branch moves up to overlook the city.

The building's programme is defined in three categories: Archive, Public and Work / Study. The Archive provides the foundation and grows into the tower. The Public spaces define the ground floor and the top of the tower. The Work / Study floors house administration and the open-stack library as a system of shelves and tables organized in a radiating ring around the core of the National Archive.

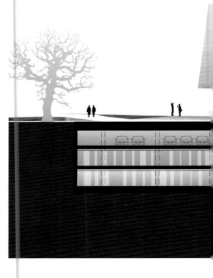

4–5_Elevations
6_Section

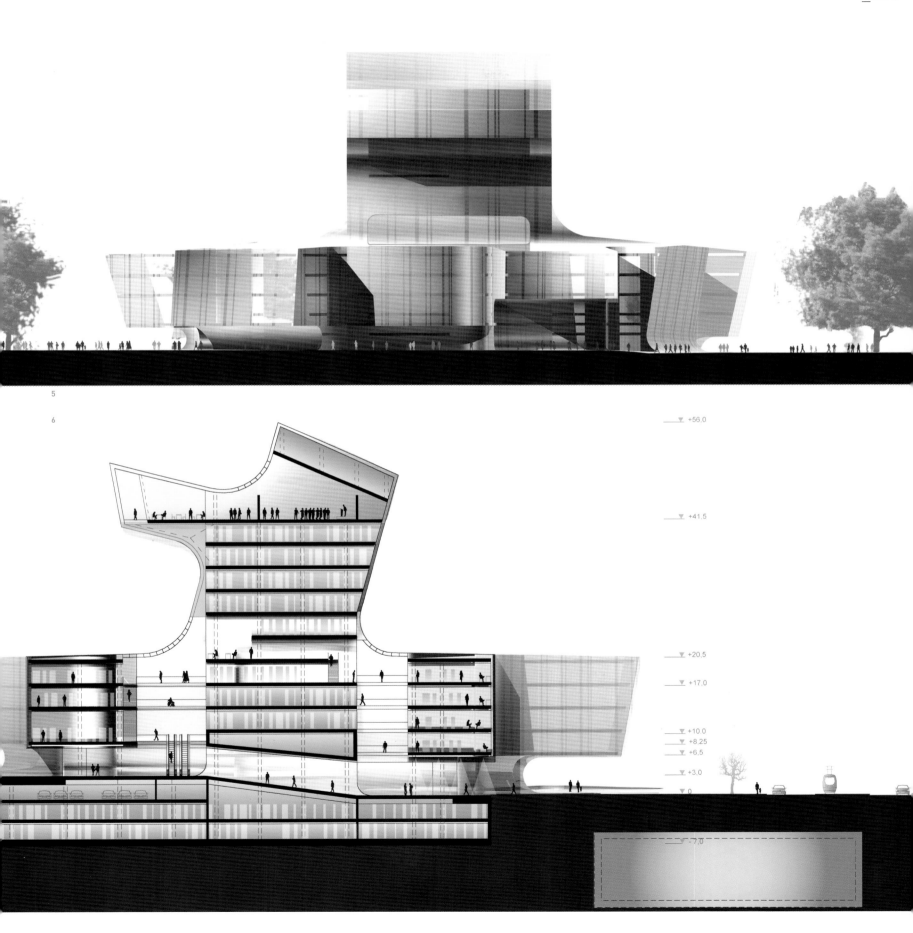

5

6

+56,0

+41,5

+20,5

+17,0

+10,0
+8,25
+6,5

+3,0

0

-7,0

Metropol Parasol
Seville

Metropol Parasol is a place of identification intended to articulate Seville's role as one of Spain's most fascinating cultural destinations. The project explores the potential of the Plaza de la Encarnación to become the new urban centre. Its role as a unique space within the dense fabric of the medieval inner city allows for a great variety of activities such as leisure and commerce. A highly developed infrastructure helps to activate the square, making it an attractive destination for tourists and locals alike.

As the dominating architectural element, the Parasol is the main sign of identity within the proposal. With the Parasol, the plaza combines everyday life with a new programme and new technology. Conceived as a light structure, the Parasol grows out of the historical excavation site into a contemporary landmark. The columns become prominent points of access to the museum below as well as to the plaza above, connecting elements and defining a unique relationship between the historical and the contemporary. Accessibility to one parasol provides visitors with a spectacular view of the city and its monuments. Spanning the bus corridor, the structure emphazises the spatial continuity of the plaza, a concept that is emphasized by the use of homogeneous tiling across the entire site.

3

12

4

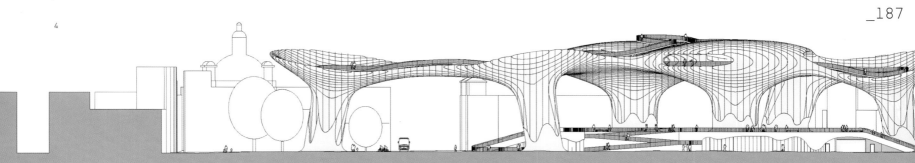

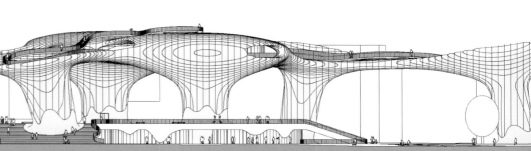

5

1_Site at commencement of building
2_Section
3_Site construction aerial view
4_Elevations
5_Model

6

7

8

9

6_Structural model
7_Roofscape
8_Under canopy
9_Overall view

TOBIAS KLEIN

LONDON

>

Synthetic Syncretism: Façade detail

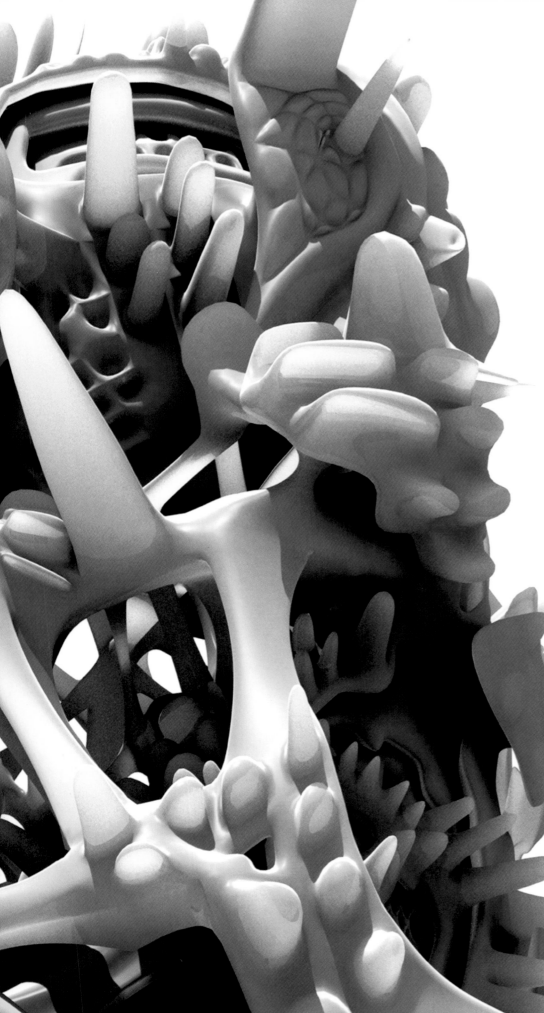

Tobias Klein's architecture attempts to combine the virtual with the actual to create a cybrid reality. His work resonates with a Gaudí-like intensity. No reserve here, just a fecund growth of bony forms. His architecture is half-reliquary and half-cy-Baroque billowing form. The work also has the quality of the hand-made forms of African mud huts.

The cy-Baroque is here to stay; deposition-printing material is the new stucco, the printers are getting bigger and bigger, and the types of materials that can be introduced into them are increasing. Klein shows us a vision of how far the Baroque in architecture might go if aided and abetted by computers and their amazing 3-D printing peripherals. His work also, like Gaudí's, resonates with the precursors of biotechnical architectures. Will it become possible to grow real bones with which to make architecture? Will it be possible in the relatively near future to create walls of arms, eyes and mandibles and activate them digitally? Or, conversely, what else might we want to 3-D / 4-D scan to make our architecture out of: soup tins, paintbrushes or your mother's brooches?

Synthetic Syncretism
Havana

1

The Synthetic Syncretism project is about the
hybridization and synthesis of different religions
and cultures as well as spatial concepts and design
techniques. The design's narrative is based on
the hybrid Cuban religion of Santería (a mixture of
Catholicism and the beliefs of the African Yoruba tribe).

The Christóbal Colón necropolis, Havana's main
cemetery, does not have sufficient burial space. Hence
the proposal for a processional route through the city
culminating in ceremonial funerals at sea. Inside an
existing cross-shaped courtyard, Klein proposes to place
a series of Santerían relics and utensils condensed
from the virtual to the actual. These utensils are
skeletal and visceral at the same time. Cybrid objects,
3-D modelled and printed in order to perfectly fit animal
bones found on the site, and 3-D scanned into virtuality,
then remoulded into actuality, provide the architectural
language. Although digitally driven, the project does not
succumb to the pervasive allure of parametric digital
Modernism.

The project provides an impeccable example of the
creative synthesis of contemporary CAD techniques
and CAD / CAM technologies with site-specific design
narratives, intuitive non-linear design processes
and historical references. It shows the architect as
a creator-craftsman finally having the chance to
overcome the fifteenth- and sixteenth-century schism
between intellectual and manual labour, as well as
the nineteenth-century gulf between (automatic)
mechanization and (poetic) creation.

2

3

1_Initial deposition-printed cybrid object
2-3_Interiors
4_Street elevation episode

4

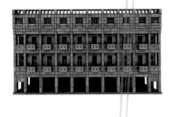

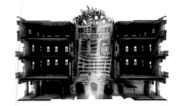

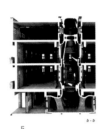

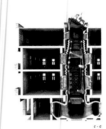

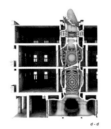

5

b - b

c - c

d - d

a - a

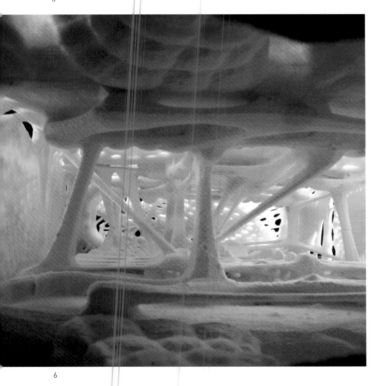

6

7

5_Context of gap site
6_Interior
7_Façade model
8_Façade configuration

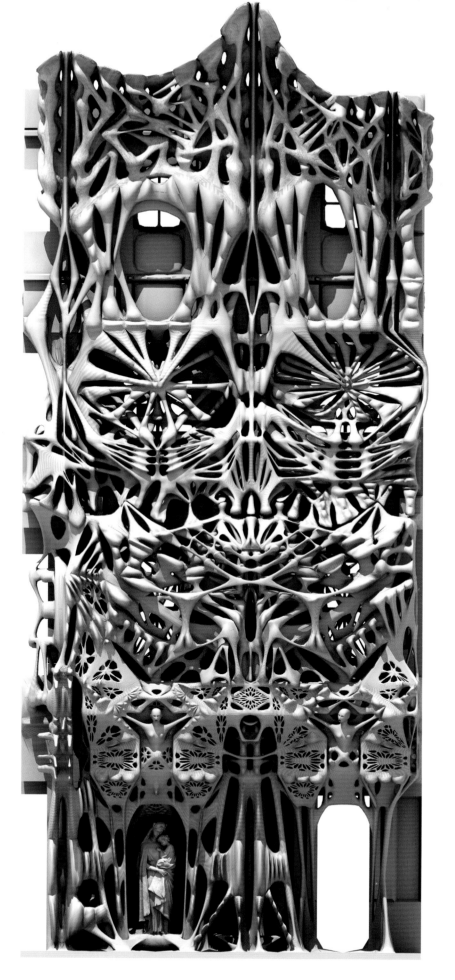

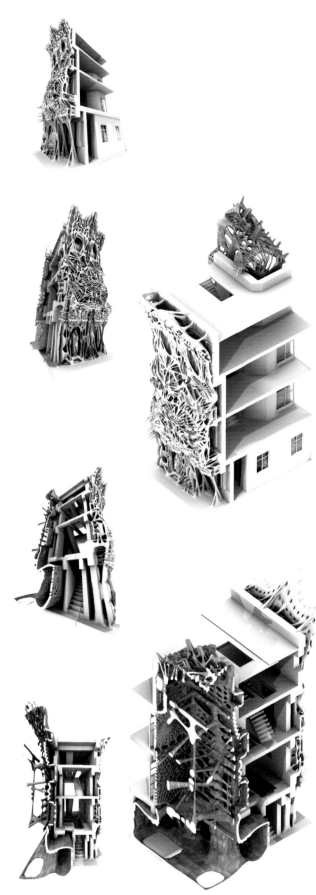

KOL/MAC
LLC NEW YORK

>

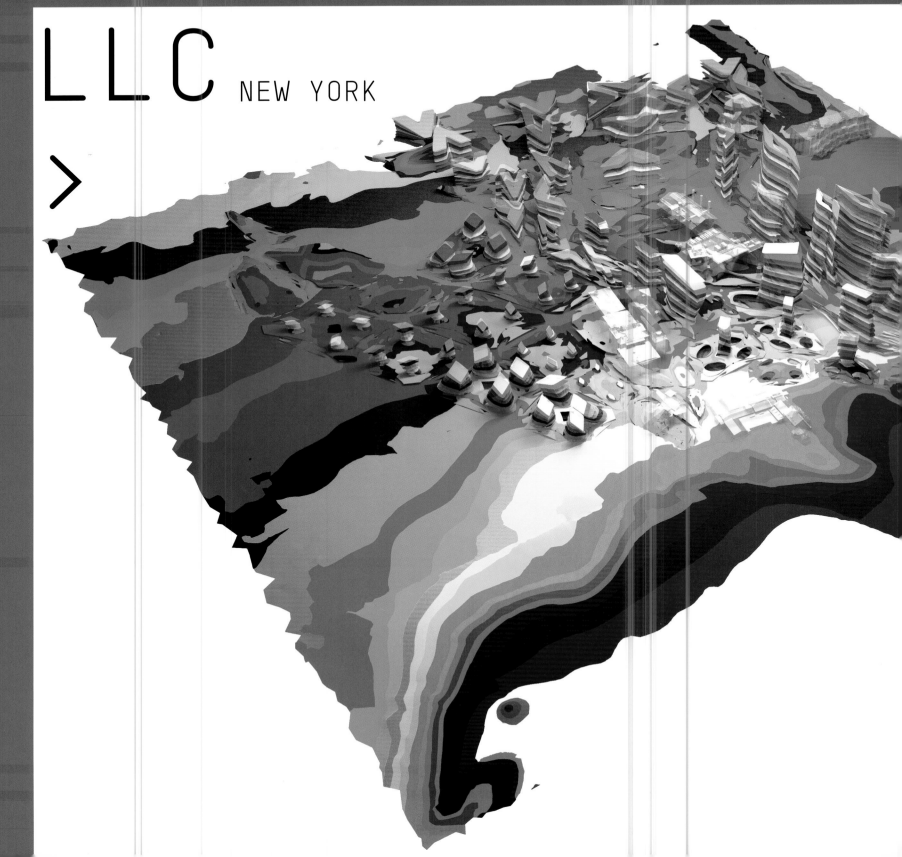

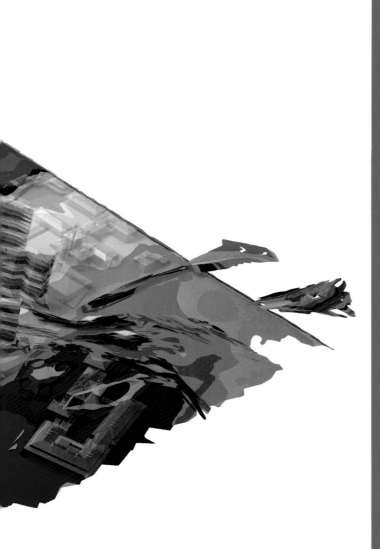

KOL/MAC LLC believes in adding value through design excellence to the everyday experience of the individual, to contemporary urban culture, and to clients' goals and investments. While always forward-looking and progressive, the firm is equally sensitive to the programmatic, situational and socio-economic conditions defining each project. This corporate philosophy has produced some of the most audacious projects and objects.

KOL/MAC's aesthetic is one of synthesis. Forms merge into other forms; the boundaries between them are indeterminate. Ground planes sweep up and into their buildings, and the mutable topology of their work repeats at all scales from wall to floor, lot to lot, tower to tower, city subdivision to city subdivision. This is not to say that their work is self-similar from project to project. Its genetics are the same, but its nature, context and scale cause beautiful mutations. KOL/MAC's architectural lexicon is a second-order emergent phenomenon edited by the compositional 'eye' of its principals.

Urban Redevelopment of Former
Brewery: Topological model

Urban Redevelopment of Former Brewery Copenhagen

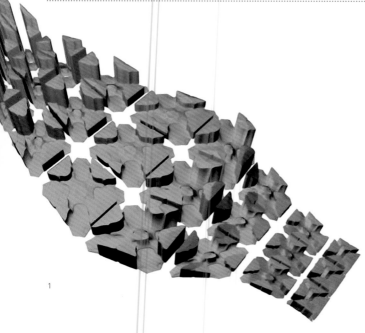

1

A favourite tool of urban ecology is satellite imaging, which maps surfaces with regard to terrain, heat, vegetation and other qualities. Ecological pathologies are diagnosed based on the continuum of urban surface. One of the operative devices ecologists use is the 'patch': a continuous urban surface defined by some degree of homogeneity that makes it discrete from its neighbouring patches. It can be said, then, that an ecological understanding of the city is topological in nature.

This is where the approach exemplified by this project comes into play. The minimal surface and its form / performance interplay are evaluated against the backdrop of an urban eco-logic. The site is constituted of multiple patches, three of which are continuations from neighbouring ones. This project links the site into the neighbouring patches by adopting their urban form and scale to adapt and transform it into a new identity.

1_Topological morphology
2_Perspective view

2

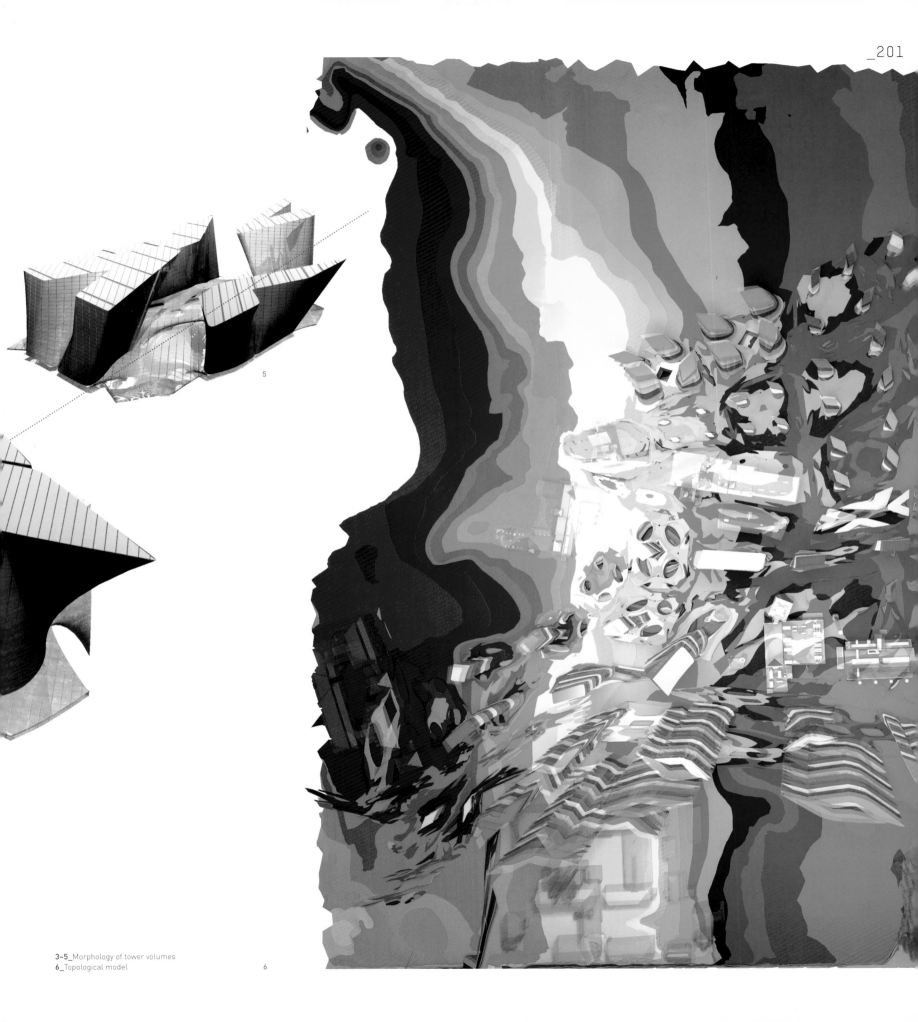

3–5_Morphology of tower volumes
6_Topological model

5

6

Mixed-Use High-Rise and Highway Infrastructure Beijing

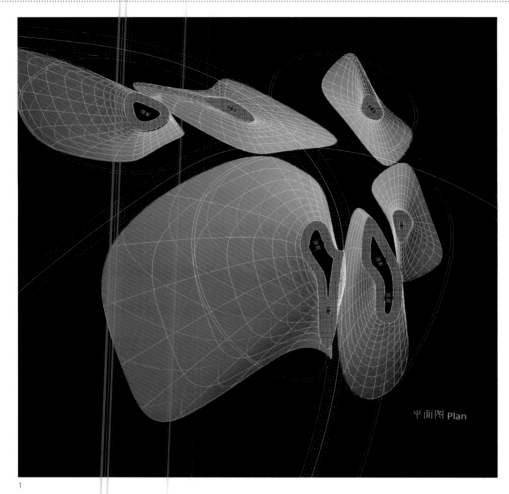

平面图 Plan

1

Unlike other building complexes, this one affords instant access, linked as it is to both fast and slow road networks, with an expansive roof allowing for helicopter landings. Its abundant roof garden is a 'smart' urban park that filters the air while being elevated above the city's smog.

The project demonstrates an alternative model to the side-by-side proliferation of large-scale buildings and transportation infrastructures that lacks the presence of productive urban spaces. Here the connection between infrastructure and building is constitutional, not a mere link. Through an emergent-adaptive logic, families of towers cluster together and settle into situational associations with interchange nodes. Together the inter-cluster and cluster-to-node relations form a new system that outperforms the sum of its parts.

The skins of the individual office towers play an instrumental role in this merging. These are three-dimensional surfaces of more than one category. At the bottom, they graft onto the urban surface, performing to varying degrees as skylights, parking or parks. At the top, they grow towards each other to form a continuous large-scale roof garden. The core / atrium in each tower allows the city to percolate up onto the roof.

2

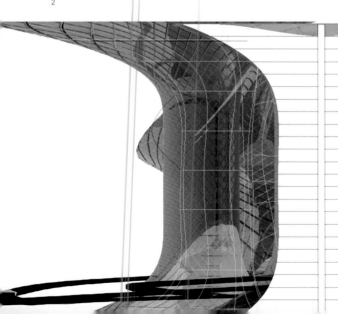
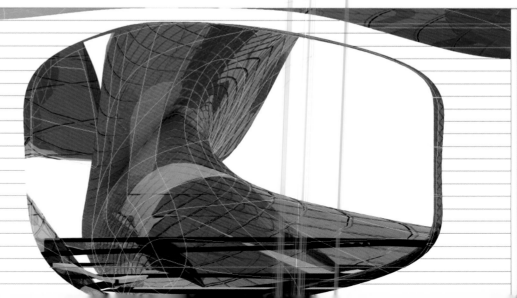

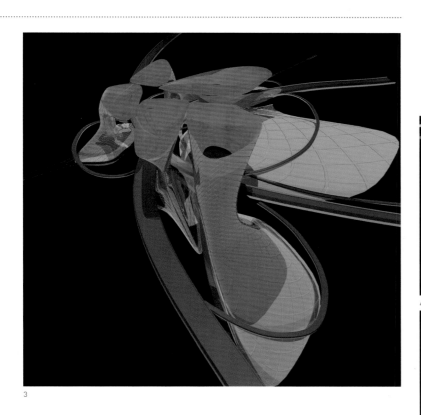

3

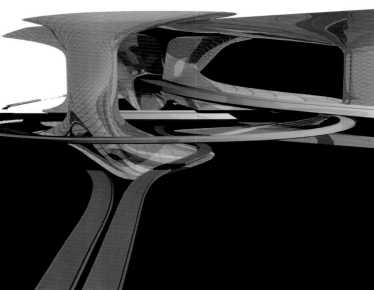

4

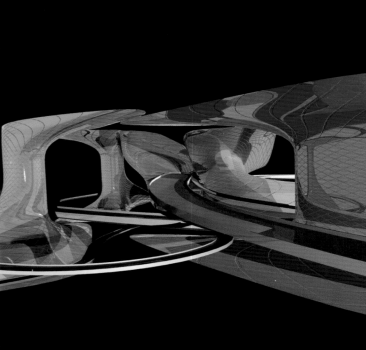

5

1_Plan morphology
2_Sectional articulation
3–5_Virtual model views

MUTEN Galataport/
Coastal Urban Development
Istanbul

1

An aerial view of the site shows that the entire area is a single 'patch' defined by large-scale single-purpose structures, hard edges and impermeable surfaces. According to what we know about patch dynamics, this is a worst-case scenario. In patches with these characteristics, environmental pathologies multiply. In fact, at a macro-scale a similar scenario is being played out, with the encroachment of the urban surface onto the natural one.

In keeping with the patch paradigm, the MUTEN Galataport project starts out by considering the entire urban surface as a continuum. There are no discrete separations between horizontal, vertical and inclined surfaces. Instead, the surface is differentiated as needed. Minimal surface geometry and topology are favoured over building typology. The design's geometry produces a permeable complex surface with the potential to positively affect the flow of water and wind as well as the absorption of solar energy.

Structurally, the minimal surface is highly economical in that it affords strength through curvature and form instead of thickness of material. The breakdown of the surface into many small patch-entities is additionally advantageous to the seismic engineering of the site. It is envisioned that there will be correspondences between topology and ecology patches, each variation combining building, nature and infrastructure to varying degrees.

2

1_Overall view
2_Experimental drawing
3–7_Terraform morphologies

3

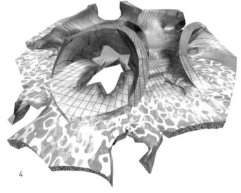

4

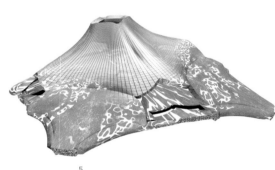

5

6

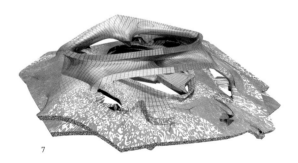

7

Museum Campus Comprising an Archaeological Research Institute, Visitors' Centre, Offices and Parks
Cairo/Giza

The project consists of five programmatic clusters interconnected through four large parks and more than twenty small courtyards that together constitute the open-air space system. The project's core is occupied by the permanent exhibition with its six thematic paths. There are three major entrances into the complex, two for the public approaching from the Cairo–Alexandria Expressway and one for staff entering from the housing complex.

The project explores the archaeological museum from the point of view of a distributed-system paradigm. It extends the notion of hypertext – as proposed in the competition brief in reference to the permanent exhibition – to the entire museum complex, thereby creating an adaptable system of connectivity open to change and growth over time. Different kinds of units interact with each other and the landscape to form a continuous environment. This strategy is by its nature 'open' to change and growth.

The project utilizes sand in many forms. The building walls are concrete panels cast onto the landscape. Sand-filled synthetic blankets help to stabilize the dunes. In strategic places, sand is calcified in place to form hard walls and surfaces.

1

> Their topographic terraformation and metamorphosis
have influenced a thousand young practices.

1_Overall view

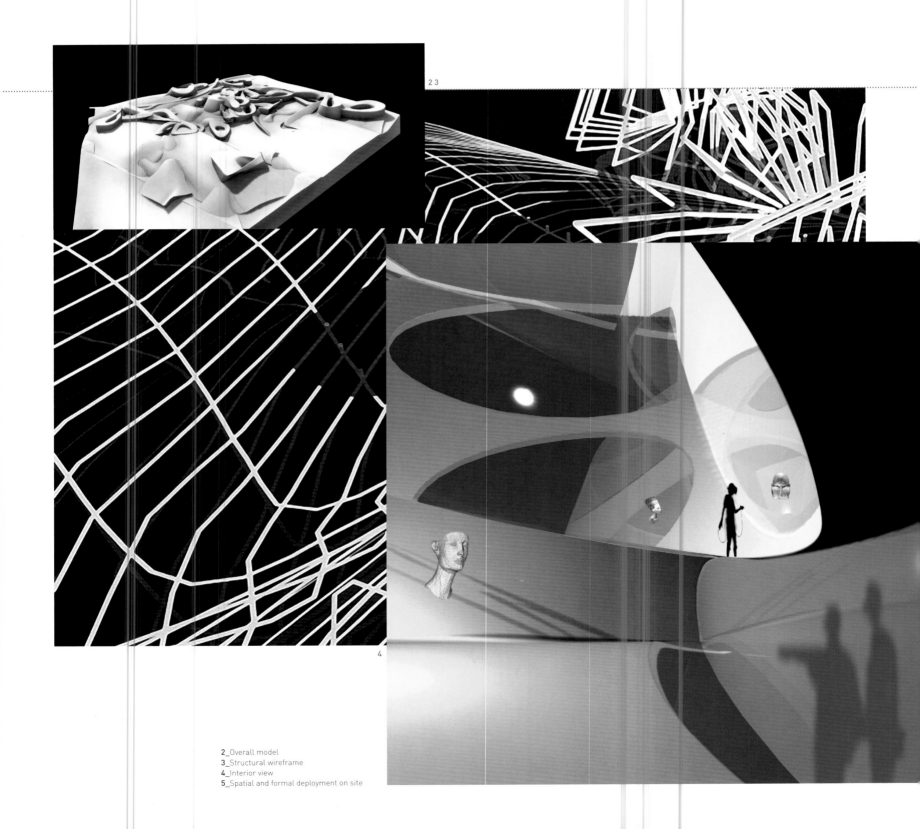

2_Overall model
3_Structural wireframe
4_Interior view
5_Spatial and formal deployment on site

5

Fifty-Storey Office Building and Shopping Centre Istanbul

The project is a mixed-use high-rise building with retail spaces and landscaping in the base and office / residential units above. The tower's extraordinary features are a three-dimensional spatial relationship between its base and the ground, as well as a smart exterior skin. Both features adapt to a specific context. While the building's base produces seamless transitions to the surrounding urban surface, the skin changes to respond with economy and elegance to building geometry, structure and orientation.

The tower is conceived with a unique identity that is designed to stand out in the skyline. Unlike previous generations of unique tower designs, this one is capable of adaptation to specific conditions of both site and programme which affect its final form. This concept provides an opportunity for repeated applications of the tower in different locations. Such a roll-out strategy of similar but different versions is unprecedented in that it combines a potential for branding with sensitivity to local context.

The tower's smart skin is composed of variable scales. Its façade elements perform ecological functions such as air purification due to their large, curved surface area. They change in scale based on their location in relation to the tower's local geometries. Smaller scales and greater densities are found in areas requiring an increase in structural strength.

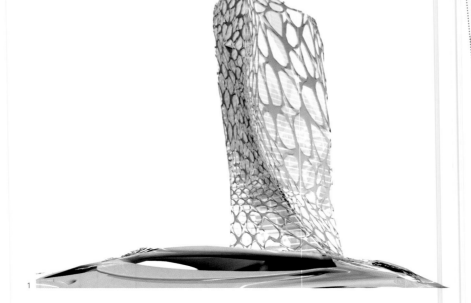

1_Overall tower view
2_Perspective from ground

1

2

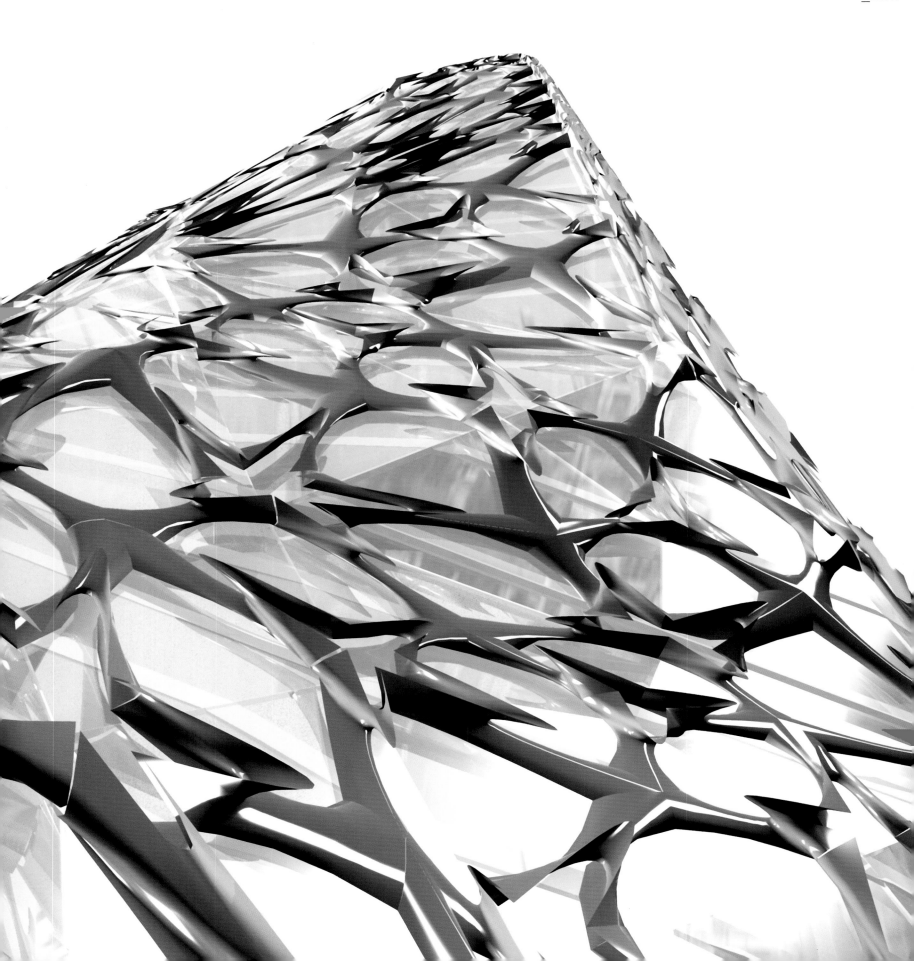

ARSHIA MAHMOODI/

VOID, INC.

>

LOS ANGELES

Arshia Mahmoodi has had two practices: null.lab (now defunct) and Void, inc. Both have had an interest in the multi-disciplinarity of television and dramatic productions. Mahmoodi has seen these practices, despite having a leaning towards building-scale environments, as distinguishing themselves by synthesizing behavioural qualities (ranging from those of materials and structures to human intelligence) into unified productions. Void, inc. uses the term 'weave' to describe its complex assembling of functional classifications, statistics, materiality and architectonic space. The aesthetic of their work changes from project to project. It has been metallic and fragmented, it has been topologically woven, and it has been extruded. Whatever the aesthetics, computers are used to represent, design, fabricate and activate. Void, inc. benefits from and is defined by Mahmoodi's extensive and varied experience, and his dexterous use of computational technology.

Bobco Metals: Interior of building

The Bobco Metals Headquarters
Los Angeles

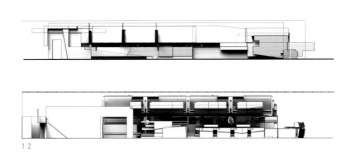

1 2

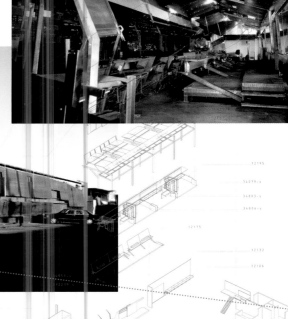

Bobco Metals is a self-described 'metals supermarket' that was renovated to address programmatic issues and develop a unique image. It was built in an existing 465-square-metre (5,000-square-foot) space originally erected in 1912 by the Hammond Lessner Co. as a power-generator house and later demolished and modernized with a steel-frame structure to serve as a storage warehouse. The aim was to convert this warehouse into a space with offices for three levels of operation. The space was layered to assemble these three functions with utmost transparency and immediacy while at the same time creating a visual cavern. Metal, quite naturally, was the basic building block, to the extent that 85 per cent of the structure was assembled with metal components. The owners have been struck by how design can affect the economics of a business.

4

6

5

1–2_Elevation / sections
3, 6_Interior of building
4_Exterior of building
5_Exploded axonometric

Ministry of Petroleum Headquarters
Tehran, Iran

This project for offices and related functions explored a compositional process that gained inspiration from fluid-dynamic models of oil flow; these forms were then translated into sectional building elements. The elements were deployed in relation to, and interacting with, each other. An analogy for this process is music software that allows the superimposition of several tracks to create a whole. The accommodation was reorganized to allow for rigid functions to form solid shapes in the rear of the building, transforming gradually to open out and flow into the public concourse.

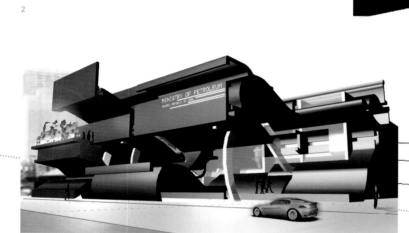

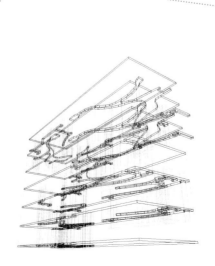

1_Exterior view
2_Sectional extrusion
3–5_Spatial flow diagrams

MUK Residence
Hollywood, California

12

A 465-square-metre (5,000-square-foot) luxury residence in the Hollywood Hills seeks inspiration from a steep hillside. The stark, rigid appearance creates a dialogue with the landscape, defining its as a man-made object. Client requests and needs become parameters for making design decisions and interweave seamlessly with formal and code-enforcement features. A multitude of design iterations allows the architects to optimize space, form and massing.

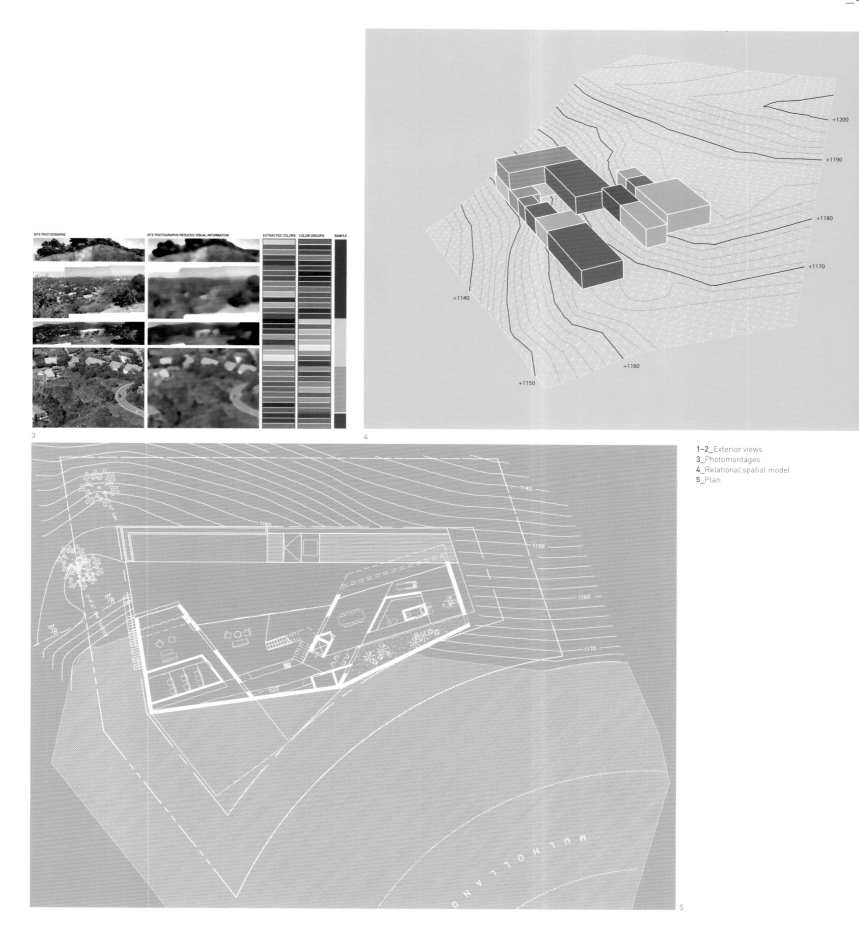

SITE PHOTOGRAPHS   SITE PHOTOGRAPHS REDUCED VISUAL INFORMATION   EXTRACTED COLORS   COLOR GROUPS   SAMPLE

3

4

+1200
+1190
+1180
+1170
+1140
+1160
+1150

1–2_Exterior views
3_Photomontages
4_Relational spatial model
5_Plan

5

MARCOSAND-MARJAN

LONDON

>

Marcosandmarjan is a studio based in London that combines the practice and teaching of architecture with experimental design research. Marcosandmarjan has a history more than a decade long that demonstrates a preoccupation with the dissolution of wall surfaces, with skins, skeins and pocket spaces. The practice revels in exploiting, distorting and blurring conventional thinking. Door becomes window, table becomes pocket, tube becomes vessel – all are hybridized and assimilated into Marcosandmarjan's architectural lexicon.

While the practice is undoubtedly fruity, it is simultaneously quite old-fashioned in its adherence to often overlooked notions of precedent, decoration, ritual and narrative. This and its interest in fungi, viruses, moulds and biotechnology can great a heady mix. While the architecture evidences a hedonistic hubris, both partners, Marcos Cruz and Marjan Colletti, earned PhDs with very rigorous and thorough theoretical arguments to back up their wayward aesthetic leanings. This makes Marcosandmarjan a practice to watch and one that will always surprise.

Garden of Vessels: Layout plan

Bai Jia Zhuang
Beijing

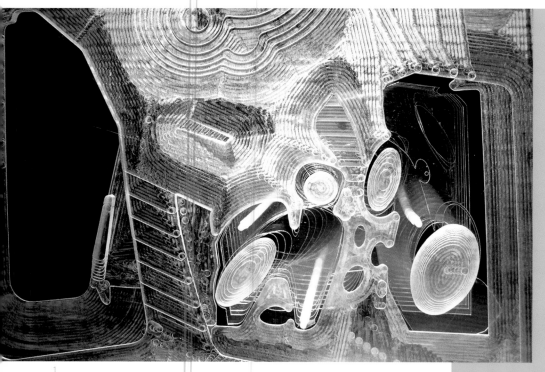

This proposed office and retail complex is situated on the eastern side of the busy Third Ring Road in Beijing. Positioned at the site's leading public edge, the building allows for the creation of a public garden at the back, from where the main access to the retail spaces can occur. The proposal's vertical organization is deliberately simple. The basement hosts vehicle parking, plant rooms and additional ancillary activities. The ground level merges the upper subterranean level and the lower above-ground level into a common public zone reserved for retail activities, while the remaining levels above are dedicated to residential / commercial (i.e. office) use. At roof level there is the opportunity to provide a unique, high-quality public space of terraces and restaurants.

At the lower public levels, the mass of the building dissipates among a cluster of volumes, supporting structures, routes and level variations. Here the proposal knits into the surrounding urban fabric, providing a circulation filter. The pace of movement is slowed, the intimacy is heightened, and the retail interface is maximized.

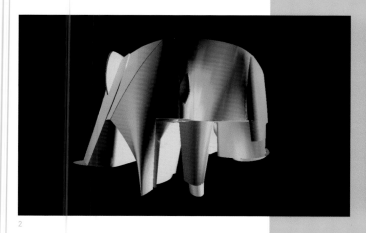

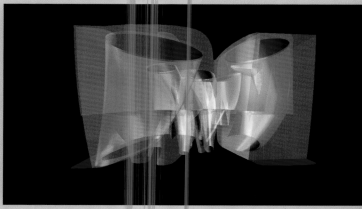

1

2

3

1_Roof plan
2–8_Vessel enclosure studies

Floating Vessel NGC
Istanbul

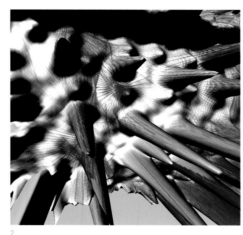

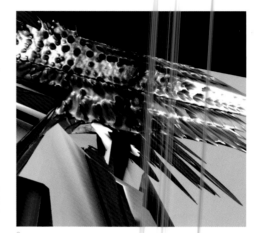

1

2

3

The Godet Club is located in the Beyoğlu district of Istanbul, an area with predominantly European-style nineteenth-century housing and the centre for entertainment and nightlife. The club is situated just off Istiklâl Caddesi, the city's main shopping street. The programmatic organization of the club into differentiated acoustic areas triggered the concept of a 'Floating Vessel', an enclosed chill-out lounge hovering over the noisy open areas of entrance, bar and dance floors. The transparent and informative façade is an interface that partly reveals the internal activities of the club to the outside.

The interior shows an 'inlucent' materiality: a translucent resin membrane incorporates the structure, technical appliances, robotic devices and audio-visual equipment, exposing itself as the visible 'vascular system' of the club. In the entrance floor, pressure-sensitive resin cushions change luminosity and colour saturation according to variable space occupation. On the dance floor, flexible flat screens are sound-responsive and linked to the Internet, while on the walls a series of monitor vessels reacts to the air quality, creating an ever-changeable pattern of biological matter.

6

1–4_Skin articulations
5_Structure
6_Laser-cut laminated model

45

New Tomihiro Museum of SHI-GA / Garden of Vessels
Azuma Village, Japan

> Vessels, skins and skeins are the grist of their mill, and nothing is what it seems.

To visit the New Tomihiro Museum of SHI-GA in Japan is to enter a reinterpreted landscape. The meandering route presents a process of discovery, a metaphorical life journey of the artist himself, Tomihiro. As one passes through, and between, numerous and varying exhibition 'vessels', the experience is one of incidences of confluence activity interspersed with moments of contemplation and intimacy. Travelling along suspended paths, the sensation of floating – parallel to artworks 'floating' against their neutral landscape – is communicated. Continuing beyond the museum's physical boundaries, paths provide connections to the forest above and the lake below. The possibility of a real encounter with nature is suggested. An internal garden, separating the exhibition spaces from the rest of the building, allows for the awareness of seasonal change: rain, snow and blossom falling 'within' the museum.

1_Vessels and roofscape
2–4_Montage of plans, models and perspectives
5_Overall structural view

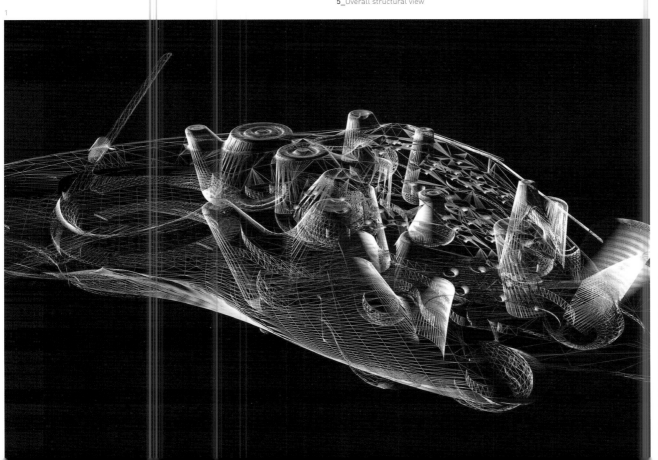

1

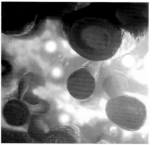

Lofting House
Lisbon

This proposal for a single-family house in the suburban area of Moita in Portugal was created on the occasion of the exhibition 'A Casa Portuguesa – Mudando a Arte de Habitar' at the Experimenta Design in Lisbon in 2005.

A simple division of programme was proposed. The public spaces would be spread out on the ground floor, while the private spaces would hover above in a series of 'vessels'.

1

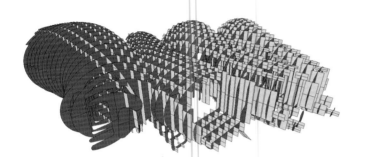
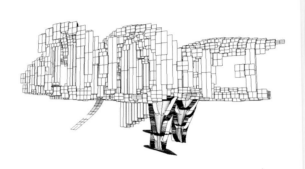
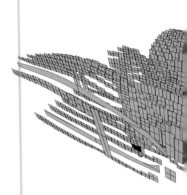

2

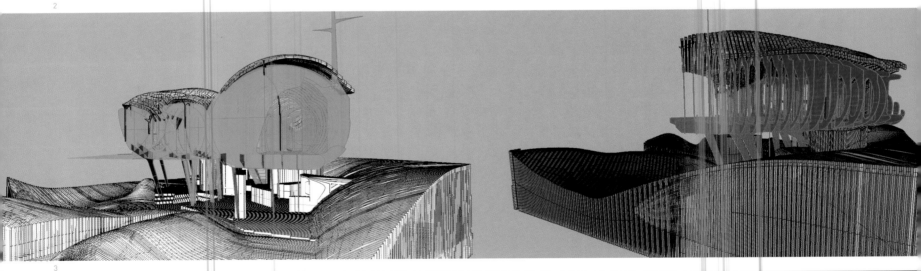

3

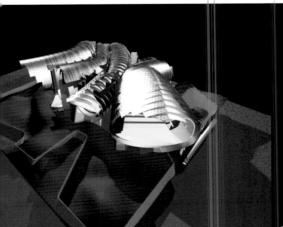
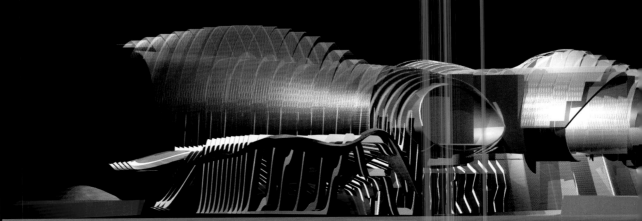

1_Structural studies
2_Piloti wireframes
3_Rendered views
4_Sectional perspective

4

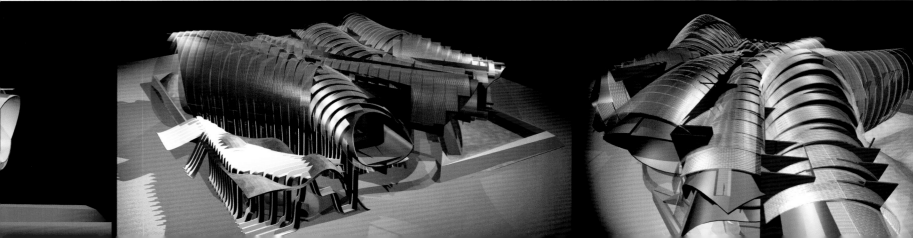

STUART MUNRO

LONDON
TOKYO

Of all the architects featured in this book, Munro's work is some of the most challenging and beautiful. He rejoices in finding compositional strategies that exploit non-orthogonal geometries, extreme juxtapositions and artful blur. His work has always been mixed-media and the computer only one of a multitude of technologies and processes that he employs. Munro is an exponent of creative play, happy accident and using technology in unintended ways, and this results in stunning images of architectures yet to be realized.

Trauma Furniture

Munro has been ahead of the architectural game for some time. His Virtual-Vital Parallax project dealt with an examination of the sorts of spaces that objects might inhabit, a synthesis between an actual location and a virtual one, each conditioning actions in the other. His Trauma Furniture also dealt with this synthetic virtual and actual space while imbuing furniture with an understanding of its position in the world. Further work, often inspired by Japanese iconography, idiosyncrasy and neon nights, utilizes a ghostly aesthetic. These apparitions are indications of the digital smearing itself across and within architectural spaces and memories.

Munro never demonstrates the myopia of many architects, seeing architectural potential in films, video, photography, graphic design, speed and tattoos.

Dee
Toronto

Each piece, shown at Gibsone Jessop Art Gallery in 2004,
described an imaginary section through a London house
that had disappeared, its garden and the River Fleet,
a river lost over time. The house was meant to have
belonged to the sixteenth-century alchemist John Dee.

1

1–4_House sections

2

3

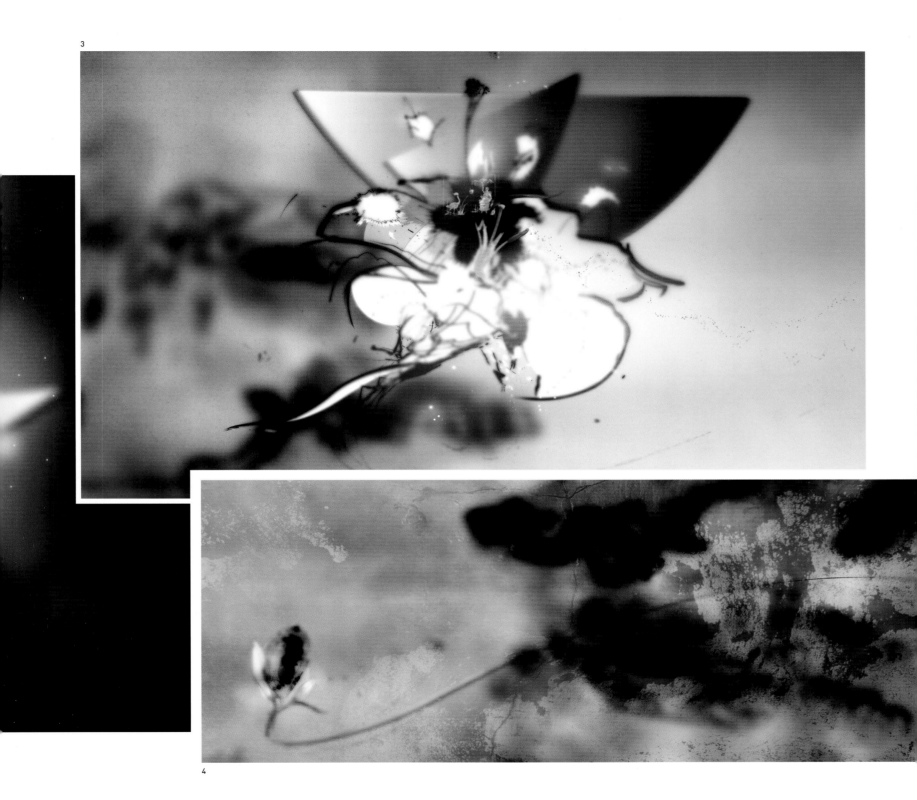

4

Virtual-Vital Parallax
London / Caspian Sea

1

Objects paranoid about their places in the visible world would run up and down overhead power lines at Finsbury Park in London. Dipping in and out of parts of the electromagnetic spectrum, a surge or deflection in electric current would cause the objects to overlay the qualities of another space on top of the Finsbury Park bus terminal. The rim of the Caspian Sea became the place that was peeled away and laid over this turbulent transport hub, an area that seemed to be in constant turmoil – buses, trains and subway transport all knotted their way through an equally chaotic social fog. The bus shelter, as the project became, needed to respond to an ever-fluctuating data landscape conditioned by the ecological conditions at the rim of the Caspian Sea, so it slowly, accordingly, wandered around its space.

2

3

4

1-4_Initial conceptual model

Trauma Furniture

This project consisted of creating furniture that took the weight of a user and distributed it along the edge of the infrared spectrum.

Non-specific furniture arranged itself in a room and adjusted to other furniture to give each piece a proxemic comfort zone. If a new piece of furniture was introduced, a rapid readjustment of space would occur.

Inspired in part by the essay 'AutoPlastic to Alloplastic' written by Mark Goulthorpe in the late 1990s, the idea of 'trauma' in a system was taken to mean a way for something to understand its place by actively pursuing 'pain' or 'incident' (like a chair balancing on its back legs about to fall). The carpet laid underneath each piece was its 'energy carpet', its way of 'feeling' and sensing.

1–2_Trauma Furniture with energy carpets

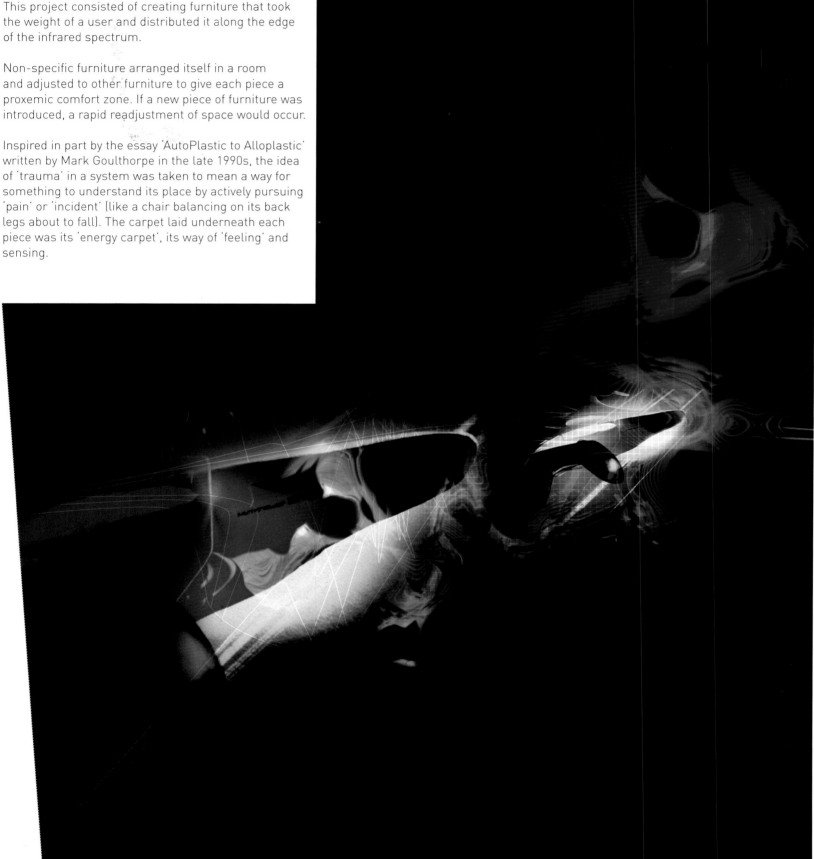

1

2

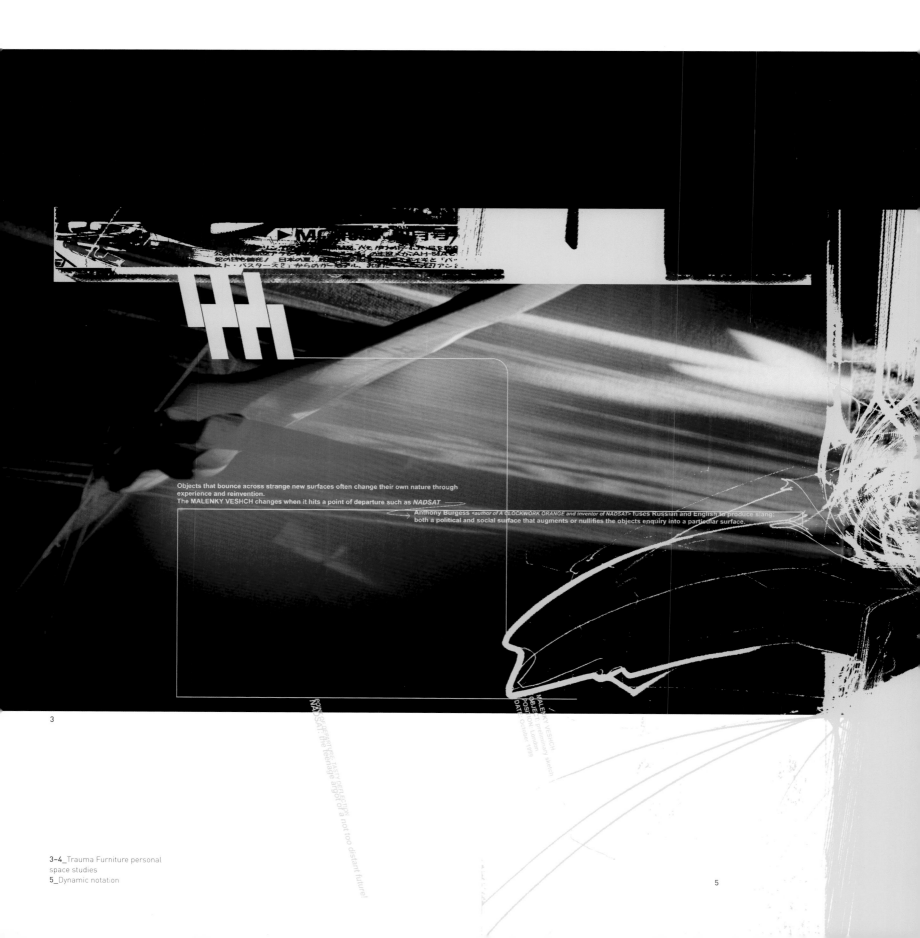

Objects that bounce across strange new surfaces often change their own nature through experience and reinvention.
The MALENKY VESHCH changes when it hits a point of departure such as *NADSAT*

Anthony Burgess <author of *A CLOCKWORK ORANGE* and inventor of *NADSAT*> fuses Russian and English to produce slang; both a political and social surface that augments or nullifies the objects enquiry into a particular surface.

3

3–4_Trauma Furniture personal
space studies
5_Dynamic notation

5

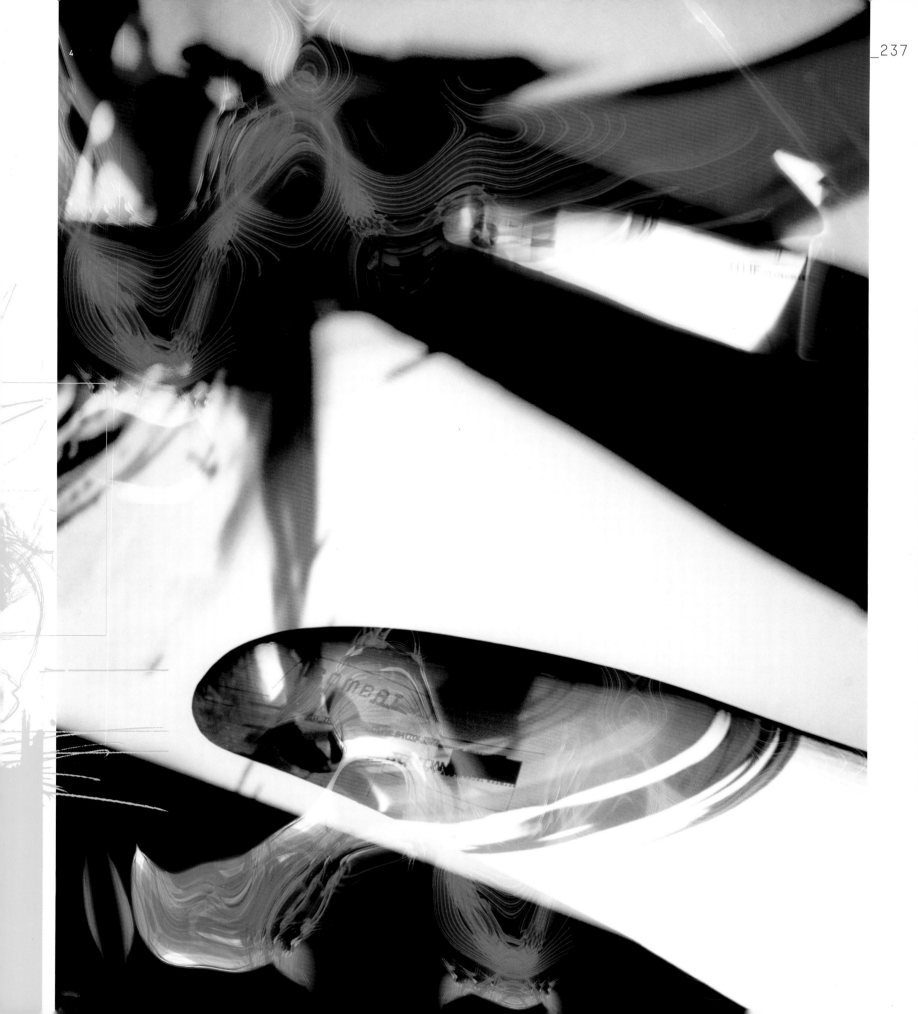

Osaka Urban Ideas Competition
Osaka, Japan

Made in collaboration with Shaun Murray and Ed Holloway, this entry for the Osaka Urban Ideas Competition in 2004 proposed uses for an area of land behind the main JR train station in Osaka, Japan.

The project took the simple premise of the game Paper, Scissors, Stone and embellished this with an attitude which was to not regenerate the land but to make it a sprawling urban sculptural oasis, a rich and ambitious scheme within one of the most densely inhabited cities in the world. Paper covers Stone, Scissors cut Paper, Stone kills Scissors.

osaka

1_Aerial perspective

> One of the most graphically
accomplished of architects
shows us vignettes of
exceptional grandeur.

Slamhounds
Rome

This is a model describing a building process for
a house on an island that takes its measurements
from Bramante's Tempietto in Rome and casts them
in shadow across the footings of a sculptural garden
belonging to the house. The model is photographed,
projected and re-photographed as a way of casting
its shadows across a new, unsuspecting surface.
The model was made as part of an extended project
by Neil Spiller and photographed in collaboration with
the graphic designer Vaughan Oliver.

1

2

1-4_Slamhound model

3

4

SHAUN MURRAY

Shaun Murray's projects are harbingers of a meaningful ecological (both mechanical and natural) audit of specific sites, also of the development of a series of tactics and protocols that can deliver to architects a full understanding of their sites and of the agents provocateurs, cybernetic systems, and disparate observers and drifters that influence and use them. Modern practice has failed to provide architects with these very necessary tools with which to create buildings that are fully in tune with the wide gamut of artificial and natural ecological conditions. For those of us interested in architecture for the cyberized, bio-machined inhabitants of the twenty-first century, Murray's research and propositions are beacons in a still-dark landscape of the future.

Murray has not only helped to develop this interesting and original approach to architecture and ecology (the subject of a PhD) but has also developed various methods of representing architecture. As with any architect who deals explicitly with the ravages of time, the choreography of sudden and not so sudden shifts in geography and geometry has to be charted. Thus Murray has needed to generate a unique draughting style that facilitates and explains his ideas.

Archulus: Interaction drawing

Archulus Flood Structure
Aldeburgh Coastline,
Suffolk, England

1

The coastline of Aldeburgh is a delicately balanced
interface between humans, sea and river. It is subject
to many geophysical processes. The spit and the river
are in constant flux; the coastline looses a metre
a year and will fail suddenly at some point, creating
a dangerous flood.

Archulus is the mechanism that will activate quickly
in the event of this landscape failure. When the flood
occurs, a harpoon mechanism will be fired out to sea,
skimming the surface of the water, then diving into
the seabed to act as an anchor. The tension will
build up on the leads, and the whole structure will
be shunted forwards, exposing a 'hyper-polder'.
A new landscape consisting of geo-textile membranes,
ripe for colonization, will be created in a few seconds,
stabilizing the coastline.

1_Site photo
2_Conceptual coastal installation

2

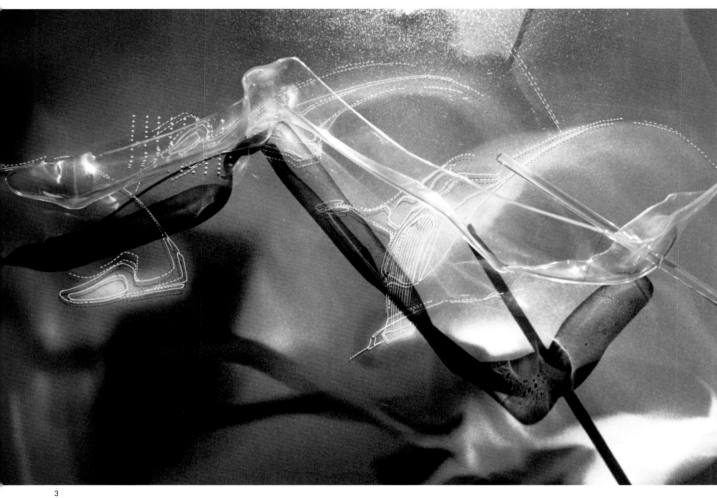

3

> Ecology, territory, and
swift and slow networking
create architectural
landscapes with a curious
beauty.

4

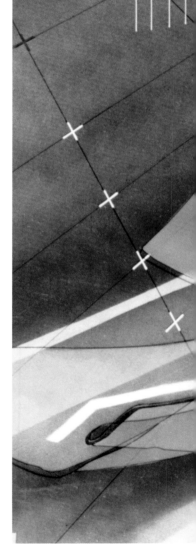

5

3_Archulus model
4_Harpoon detail
5_Archulus deployment

Camargue Condensations
France

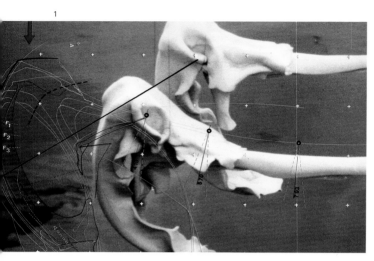

The Camargue, with its horses, the mistral, the Rhône river, the salt pans and the rugged inhabitants, is a romantic site to work within. This project is like some great prosthesis that allows the users / inhabitants to feel the ecological ripples of their immediate and also remote environs, like wired pond skaters.

The project deals with various phenomenological architectural conditions: mediation of the ground line, for example, is addressed with dune-like enclosures. The underworld of prehistoric cave art is penetrated by light cages, which illuminate yet also protect the art from the destabilizing glare of artificial light. A gaping calanque or fjord, which can flash-flood, has two small tusk-like buildings with a light-skirt inserted and strung above it. The floodwaters act like enlivening lifeblood. When soaked the light-skirt writhes like a fish with its head in a vice. Also a series of artful kites sup at the spiralling vortex of the mistral. The contextual integration of the pieces is established in this elemental way. On top of this is the spatial embroidery that flips scales, and links this to that, and makes each architectural piece a microcosm of the great whole. This, of course, is what we experience in our day-to-day life: the conical sections of vision are no longer conical; we can see far, wide, deep and all-engrossingly.

1_Camargue Calanque
installation pieces
2-3_Camargue Calanque
interaction trajectories

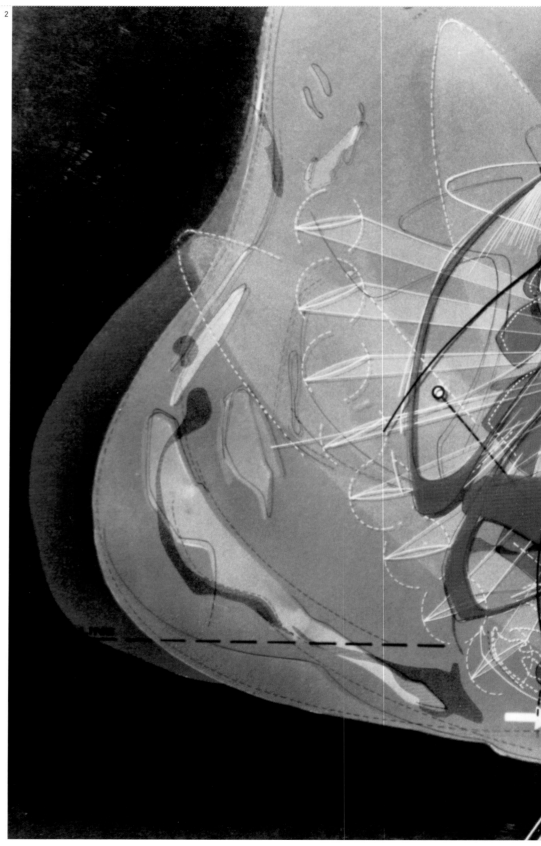

3

Information Polyp

The Information Polyp, linked via geo-satellite to
remote computers and driven by the vicissitudes of
the wind, would create a kind of alternative geography
of points and observations: a kind of weird Duchampian
'Stoppage' for the digital age, a mixed-reality yardstick
for the benchmarking of the Information Superhighway.

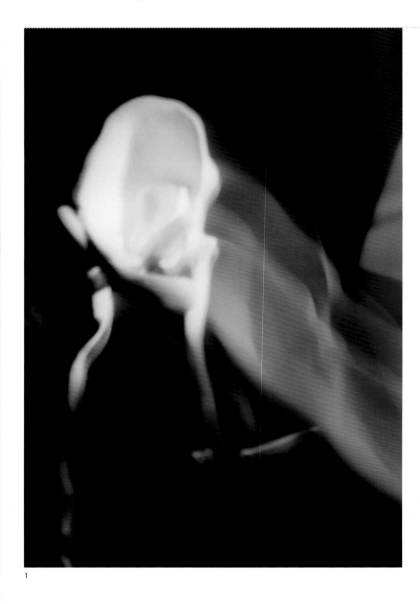

1

1-4_Information Polyp pathways,
sensors and model

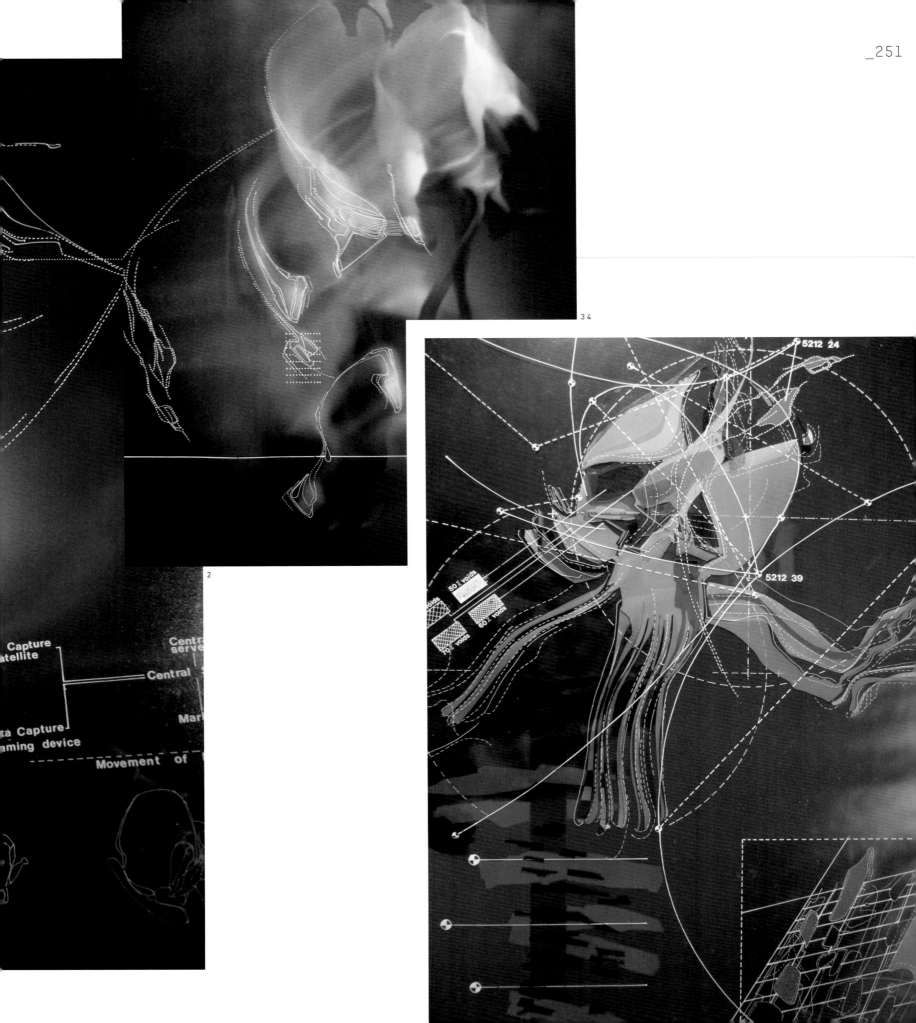

NAGA STUDIO ARCHITECTS

Tarek Naga founded Naga Studio in 1991 in Venice, California. The work is characterized by the use of exuberant form: spaces encircle, balconies jut, walls wrap and cosset. Naga Studio has developed an architectural lexicon that is open to sustainability, ecology and mythology, mixing them with pure architectural audacity. The practice bends both the traditional and the futuristic to its world-view.

Naga Studio's work is characterized by sweeping curves and multicoloured sketches that betray a looseness and a freedom of thought often missing from many contemporary architects' approaches. One of the downsides of the computer is that the fluidity of initial sketches and the playful rebus quality of their reading and rereading are often curtailed, even non-existent. Naga Studio's formal language is highly extrovert and powerful. It is undoubtedly a contemporary digital practice seeking to expand the envelope of it skills, but, intriguingly, it also gleans inspiration from older, more formal, historical ideas of enclosure and the organization of space.

CAIRO
LOS ANGELES

Phantom Limbs: General arrangement
perspective rendering

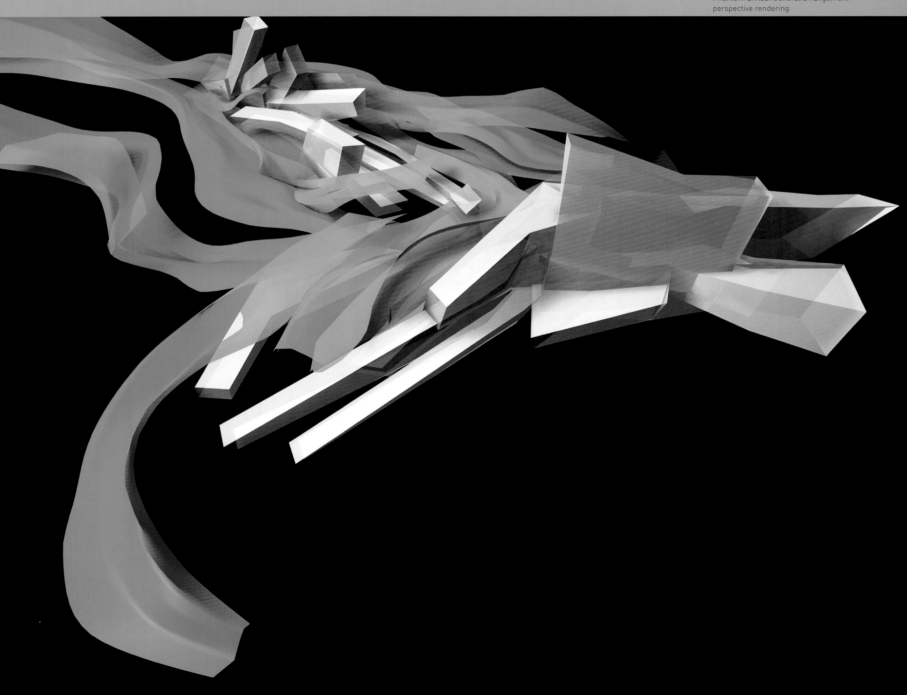

House of Emergent Suspensions
New Cairo

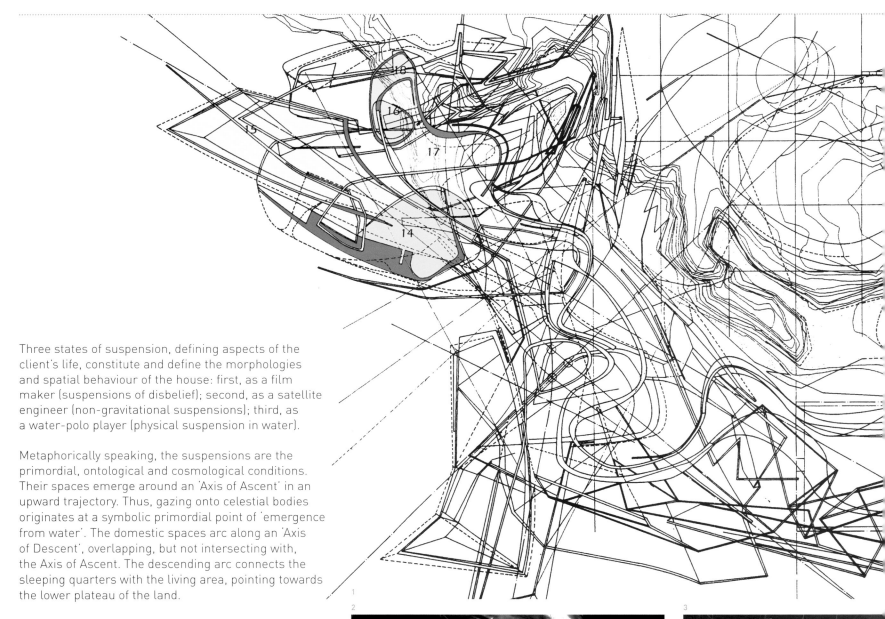

Three states of suspension, defining aspects of the client's life, constitute and define the morphologies and spatial behaviour of the house: first, as a film maker (suspensions of disbelief); second, as a satellite engineer (non-gravitational suspensions); third, as a water-polo player (physical suspension in water).

Metaphorically speaking, the suspensions are the primordial, ontological and cosmological conditions. Their spaces emerge around an 'Axis of Ascent' in an upward trajectory. Thus, gazing onto celestial bodies originates at a symbolic primordial point of 'emergence from water'. The domestic spaces arc along an 'Axis of Descent', overlapping, but not intersecting with, the Axis of Ascent. The descending arc connects the sleeping quarters with the living area, pointing towards the lower plateau of the land.

A vessel membrane contains and carries the house components. It is suspended on the hillside on one side (to provoke a sense of instability) while being cradled by continuous contours on the other (to evoke a sense of comfort and stability).

1-5_Spatial articulation and site configuration

> Naga's architecture has fields of intense
vortices and a vitality that has no precedent.

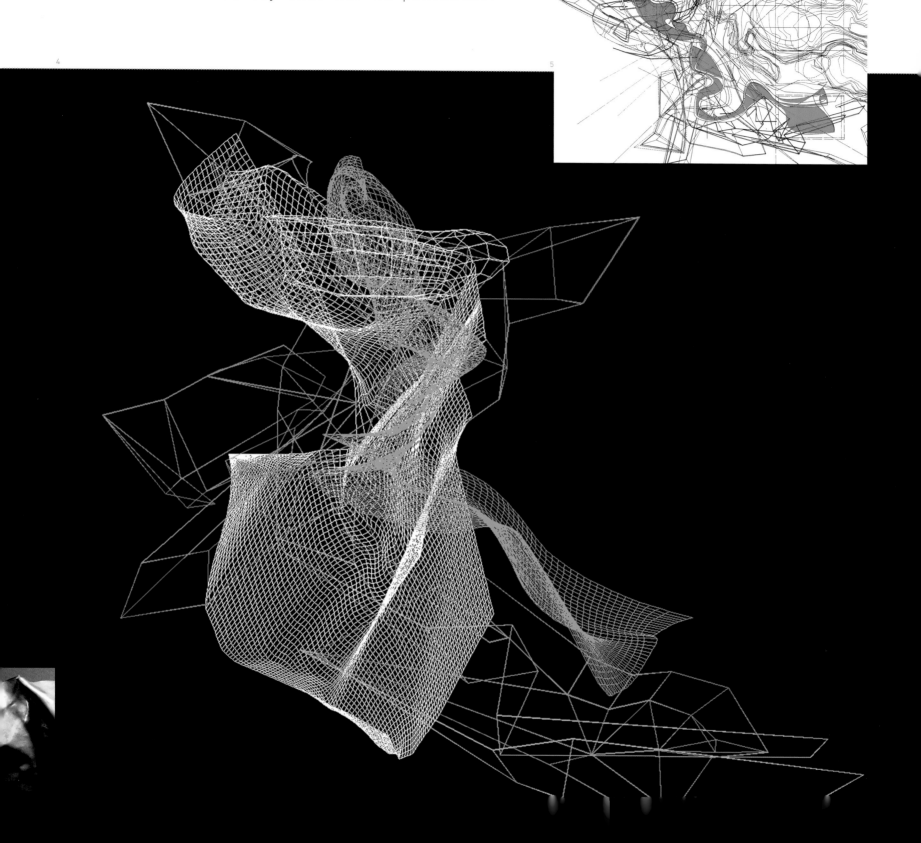

6 7 8 9 10

6–13_Conceptual
spatial flow

meditate

Spiritual

The Grand Egyptian Museum (GEM) Competition: Osiris Re-Membered Cairo

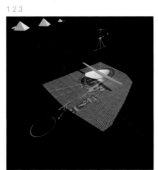

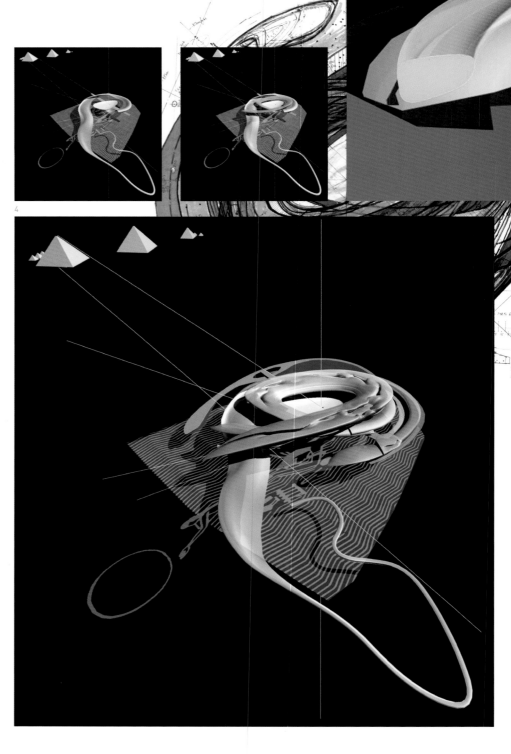

The nine periods of Egyptian history (Pre-Dynastic, Early Dynastic, Old Kingdom and so on) are chronologically sequenced as the membranes gradually coalesce into more complex folds. The five thematic routes are arranged in continuous braided flows, criss-crossing wherever a certain Theme / Route / Flow needs to merge, overlap or bypass another Route. This strategy is achieved through the employment of principles of viscosity and fluidity. For example, in the New Kingdom, where the collection of Tutankhamun is adjacent to the collection of objects from the Amarna period, the membranes split, allowing Akhenaten's collection to merge with The Religion Route to create Aten's Shift. At the same period, the Land-of-Egypt Route descends to a lower level to be in close proximity to the Man-and-Society Route. This strategy allows for maximum flexibility of hypertextual possibilities. Temporary exhibition zones and a virtual museum are also included, with the scheme climaxing at its centre with the display of royal mummies.

1-6_Conceptual sketch, conceptual models and evolving final form

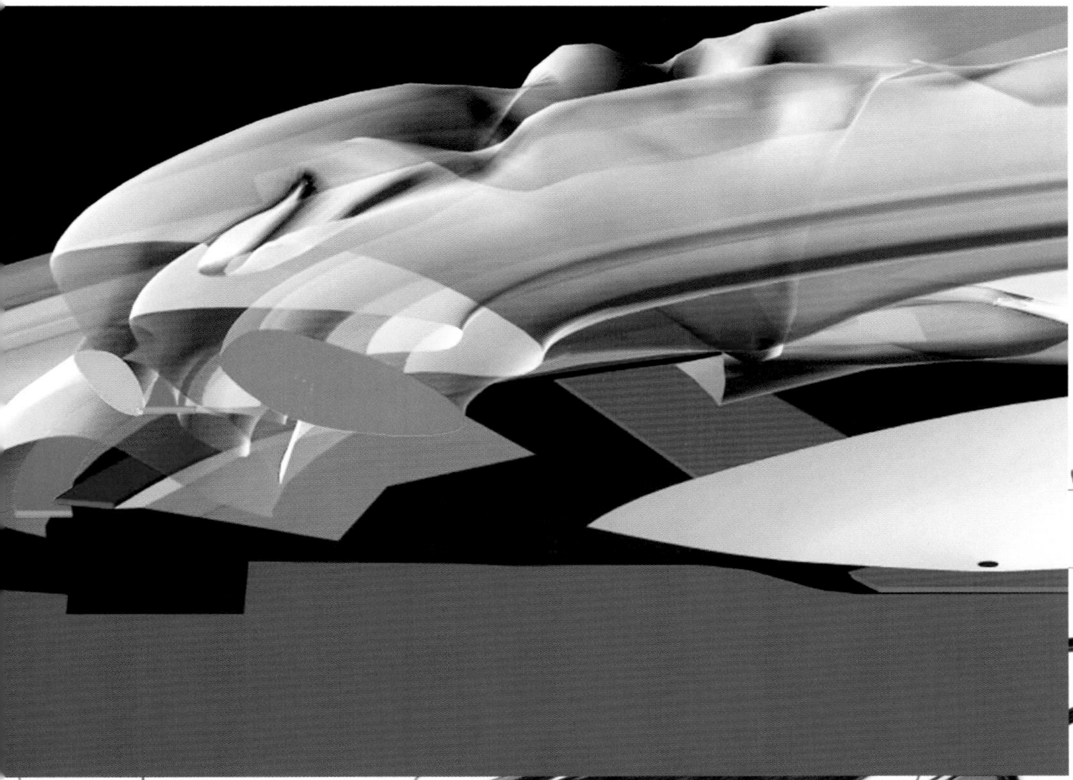

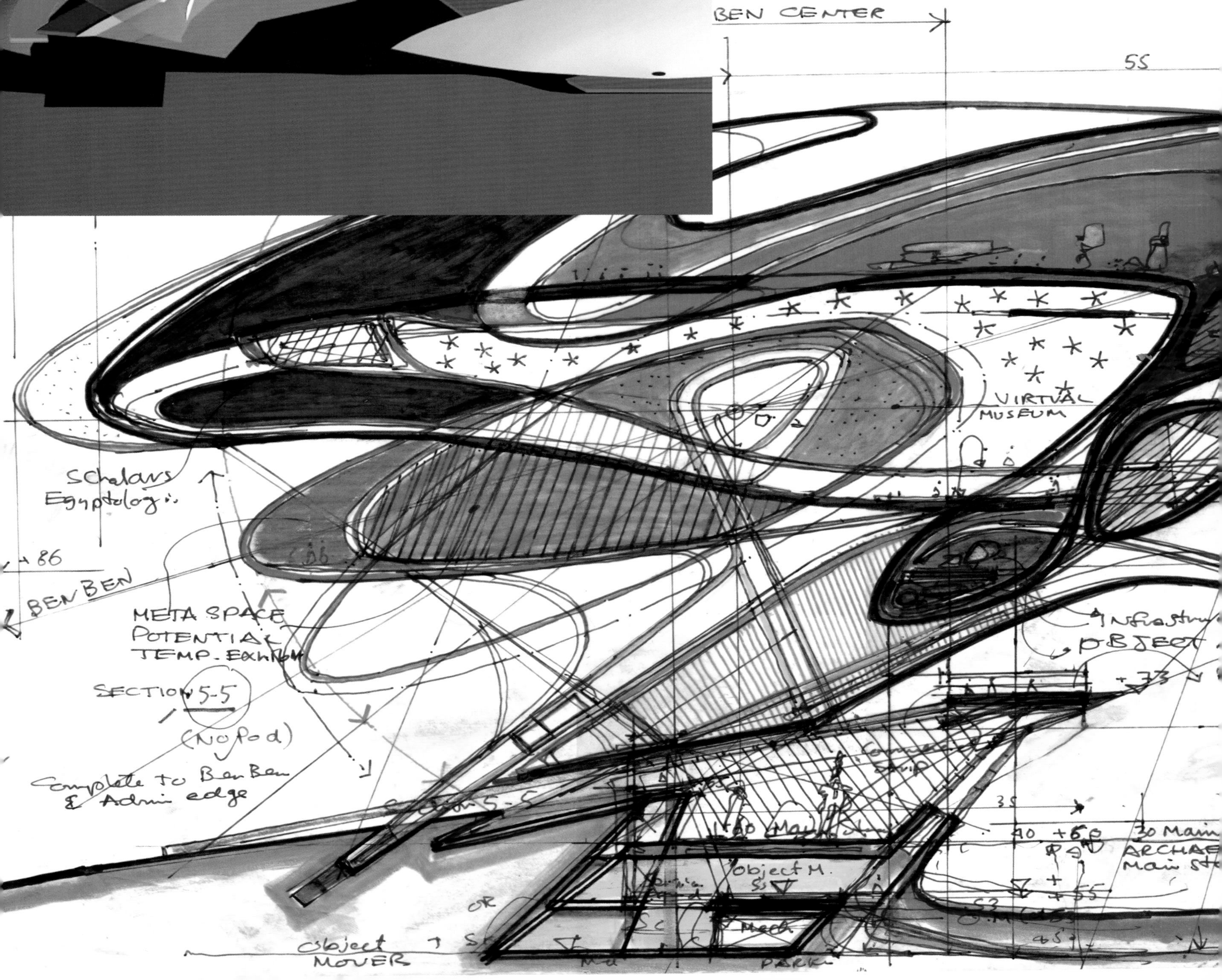

BEN CENTER

55

VIRTUAL
MUSEUM

Scholars
Egyptology.

+ 86

BEN BEN

META SPACE
POTENTIAL
TEMP. EXHIBM

SECTION 5-5

(NO Pod)

Complete to Ben Ben
& Admin edge

INFRASTRU
OBJECT

+ 73

35

+60   30 Main
       ARCHAE
       Main St

Object M.
SS

OR

+ 55

Mech.

Object   S
MOVER   PARK

Oqyana
Dubai

1

The Australia section of the 'World' project consisting of three hundred artificial islands, Oqyana is a mixed-use development with residential as the predominant component. It also includes several commercial, cultural and recreational facilities, as well as extensive marine facilities.

The Central Core is the heart of Oqyana's cultural and commercial activities. It is primarily defined by the landmark hotel, Aquarium and Amphitheatre. This area is flanked by the Core and Cove marinas, which differ in character and activities.

The architectural language is generated by means of several thrusting tectonic planes surrounding the Core marina. Between the positive volumes that house the Marina apartments, slices of negative open spaces are interchangeably located. This morphological language creates an atmosphere of dynamism that emphasizes the nature of the Central Core.

The inspiration for the architectural language emerged from a complex set of influences: Australia's aboriginal myths and dreamscape interwoven with concern for the environment and sustainable development. The marine nature of the project had a fundamental impact on its character. The Aquarium and Amphitheatre became the focal point of the composition, and the interlocking of the Aquarium with the hotel takes that experience to a more complex level formally, symbolically and commercially.

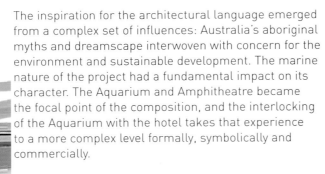

2

1_Formal experimentation
2_Terraforming
3_Final structural logic
4-5_Conceptual sketch

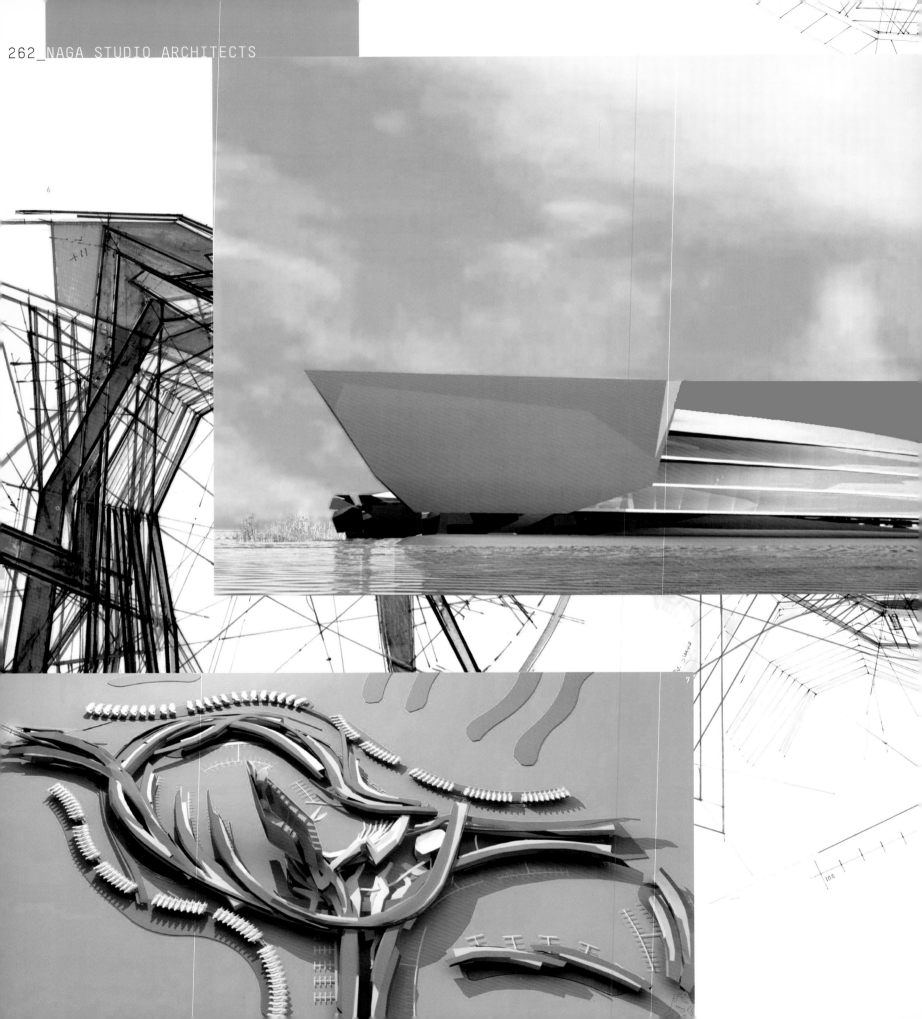

6–11_Final arrangement, section plans and models

Sharm Safari Gate
Sharm El Sheikh, Sinai, Egypt

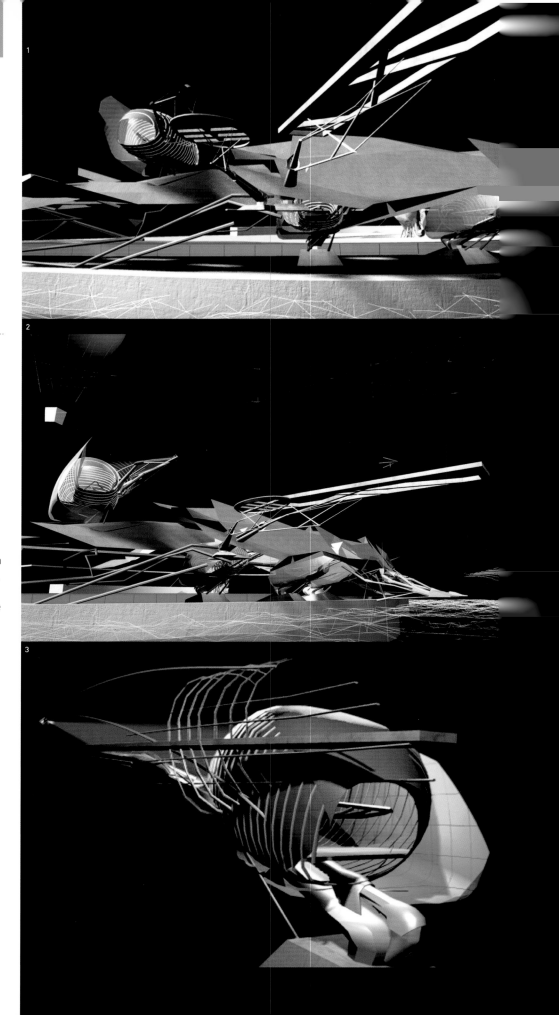

The Sinai desert is the quintessential condition of wilderness and nomadism. A facility designed for the exploration of such a rich locale has to take its clues from its natural and symbolic complexity. Mentally and physically, Sinai explorers cross from the realities and trappings of this century into the primordial wilderness of biblical time.

This concept became the basis for a narrative of five pods that, metaphorically, are themselves wanderers. In a search for the mystery of the place, they group and regroup, evolve and morph.

One of the pods metamorphosed into an 'evolved' entity that became their guide. A mysterious force in their path pulled them into the terrain at the base of the mountain. Their guide assumed a ritualistic position at the centre, becoming their beacon. A membrane that hovered above now shields them. Extended tentacles tenuously attach themselves down. In an act of defiance, the 'pod of flight' penetrates the shield and nestles above the folded plates.

A place for nomadic explorers is itself conceived by a nomadic myth. The architecture is imbued with the function that it is assumed to perform.

1-6_Computer model of space, structure and experience

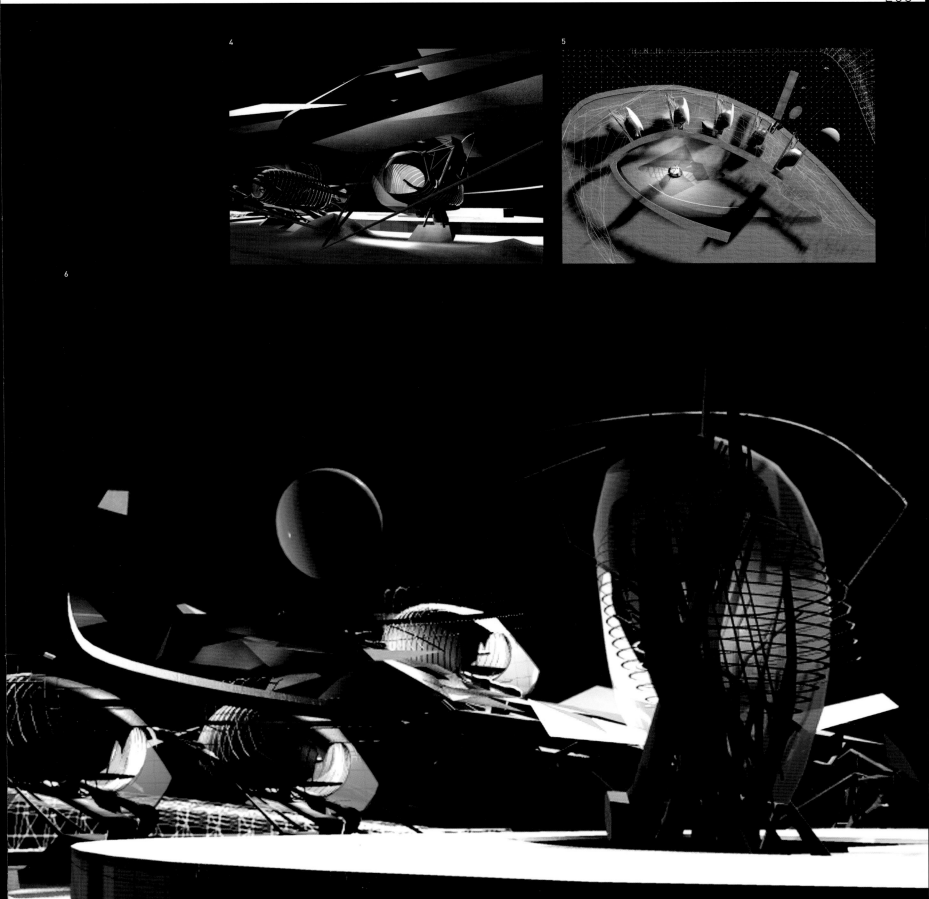

4

5

6

OCEAND

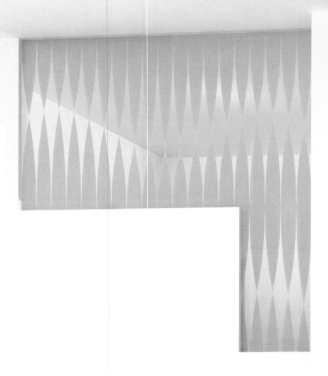

>

oceanD is a research-based design collaborative that originated in 1995 (as the multi-nodal design network OCEAN) and is currently based in London, New York and Boston. oceanD works in design areas ranging from product and material development to interiors, architecture and urbanism. The practice focus is the technological and conceptual transfer of computational techniques to new modes of materialization. It strives to embed design intelligence in its projects via the application of techniques such as mathematical scripting and material prototyping.

This synergy of disciplines facilitates the exploration and production of innovative forms, spaces, structures, materials and experiences. oceanD's work is slick; they often seem to be attempting the nearly impossible, trying to make seamless and invisible the transition from wall to floor. Their formal language speaks of designed mutability, of spatial morphology and of a search for the hybridization of both macro and micro programmatic and functional concerns. oceanD has been one of the most influential international practices advocating digital processes and techniques in recent years, and their aesthetic codes have infiltrated the visual language of many contemporary architects.

LONDON
BOSTON
NEW YORK
OSLO

Warner Penthouse: Interior

Warner Penthouse
London

The brief of this design commission is the remodelling of a once-converted penthouse loft in Farringdon, London. The clients collect Op Art paintings by Bridget Riley and others, and the organizational patterns are generated from similar mathematical arrangements, producing a range of optical effects on a three-dimensional stair, glass treatment, bespoke wallpaper and dynamic floor pattern. Significant structural works will be carried out to install the new stairway to the mezzanine, where an informal office will mix with living space.

1

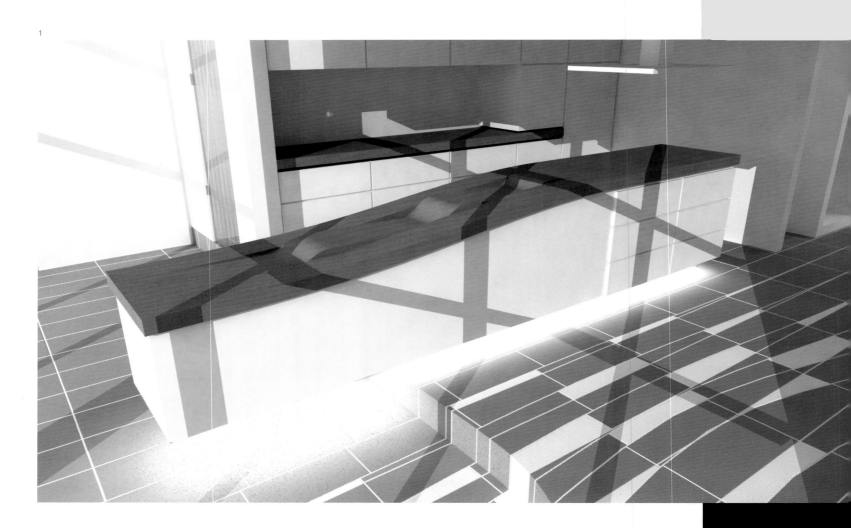

2

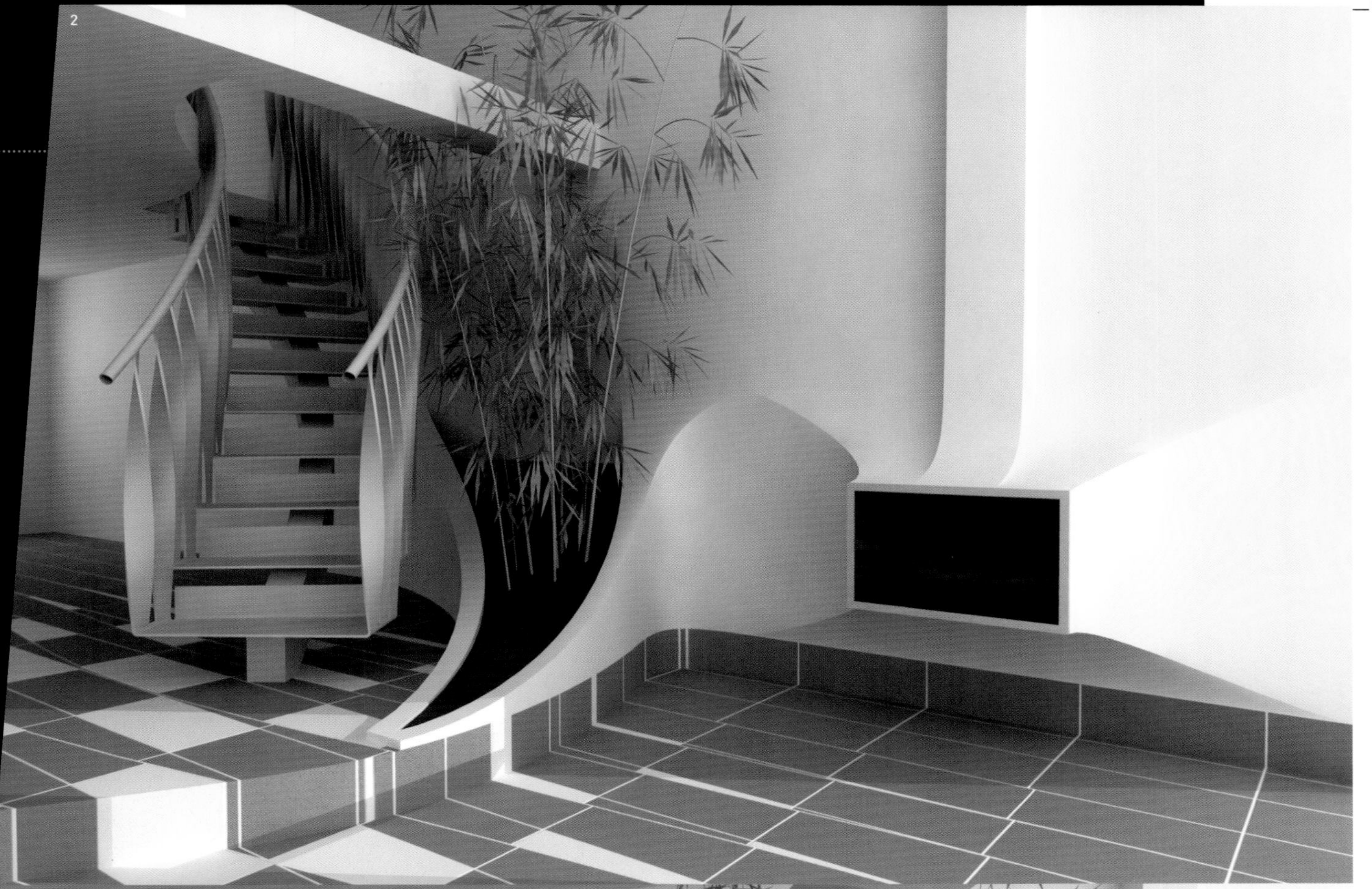

3

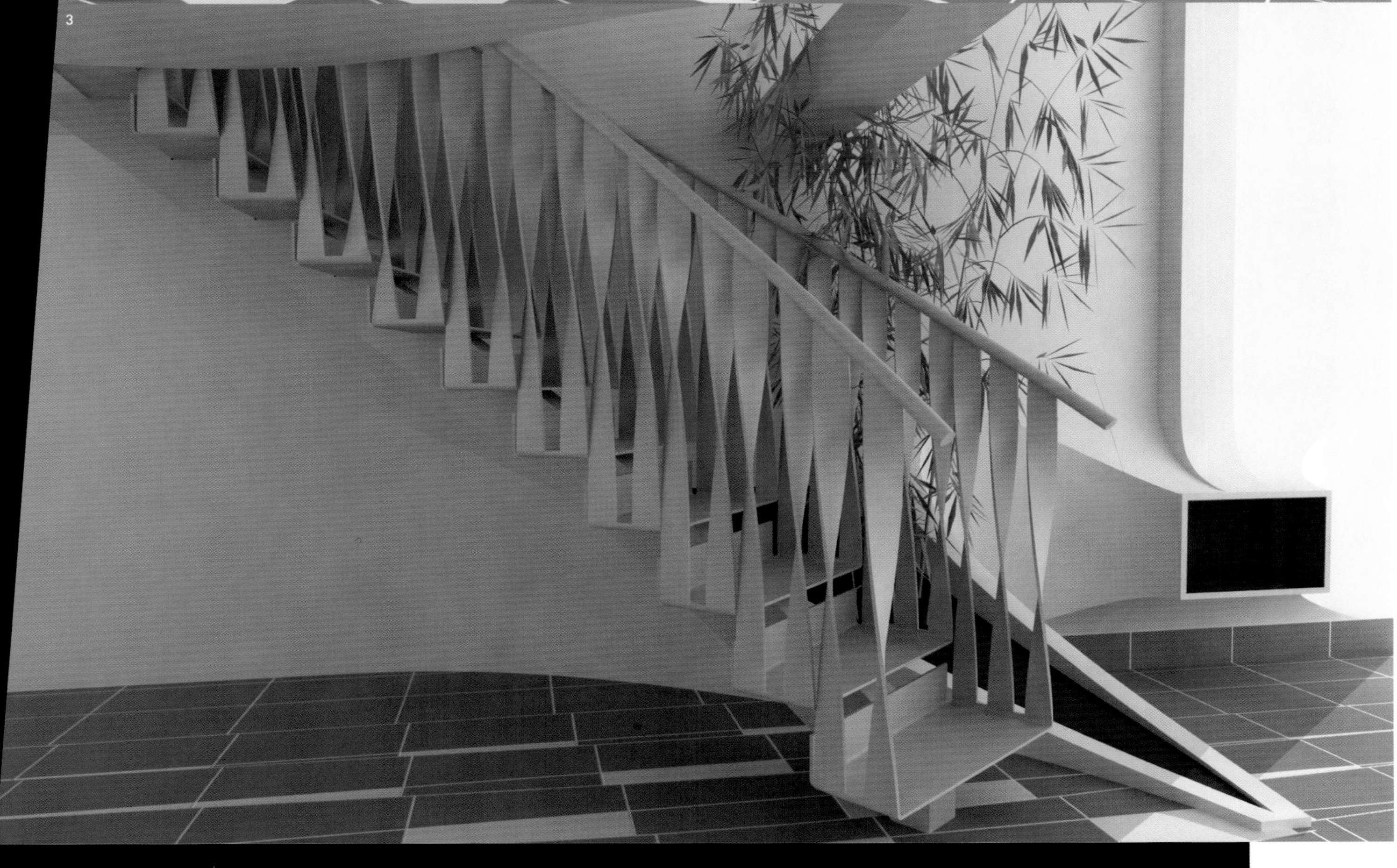

Rabin Peace Forum
Tel Aviv, Israel

A modulated series of eighteen looped object configurations is distributed along an open line, originating from the point where the Israeli politician Yitzak Rabin was assassinated in 1995. The objects grow and change in incremental gradients as a serial-event field, both within each object and across the range. A homogeneous parallel field is interrupted by the eighteen insertions, causing a transitional field of eighteen events. The objects increase in magnitude / size, each centred at a continuous and uniform oblique datum level that relates to the upper terrace. The modulation between each position and the preceding and subsequent positions will cause a topographical flow of convex and concave podia, while an irrigation topography interacts and responds as a geometric iteration of the range of objects, thus acting as a local re-orientation mechanism of pedestrian movement between each object. The upper terrace of the City Hall is linked with the datum level, reconfiguring the stairway with an integrated topography. The scheme deploys pools, aquatic and desert planting, seating, information and material surfaces within the directional field, in which up to 300,000 people can gather.

1

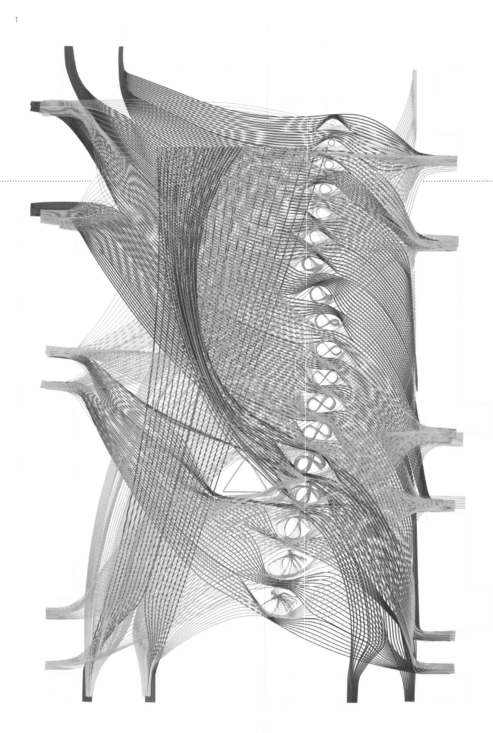

1_Plan and vectors
2-3_Topological forms

2

3

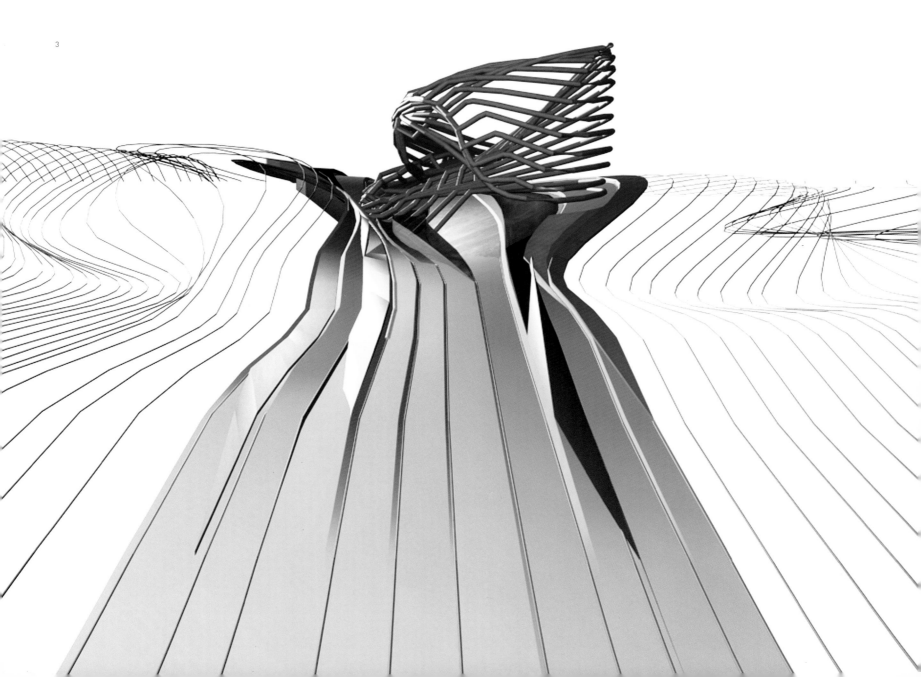

LJ House
London

This project is a conversion and extension of a 1970s late Modernist house located on a steep-sloped site, with proposed interior galleries overlooking an existing three-storey living space. A range of experiential effects was designed into this 1,000-square-metre (10,700-square-foot) house annex. A bridge with a gradient of 4 degrees spans the entry threshold and leads from the existing living space to a new pavilion to be used as a studio, children's play area and guesthouse. The subtle slope of the floor surface destabilizes the sense of grounding as one enters the annex. The external envelope opens to form graduated window openings, which are operable with heat-sensing gels and piezoelectric, photovoltaic effects. An integrated carbon-fibre stairway and balustrade connect the ground level with the sloped mezzanine. The walls are penetrated with non-standard window eyelids and spines of light that are actuated to glow with intensities in relation to the sensed proximity of the inhabiting body. The roof steelwork structure forms a morphing topography with a secondary structure of serially iterated timber joists. The ceiling is configured in response to the dramatic hillside site and the relation of the zigzag buttresses that link the existing house and support the annex.

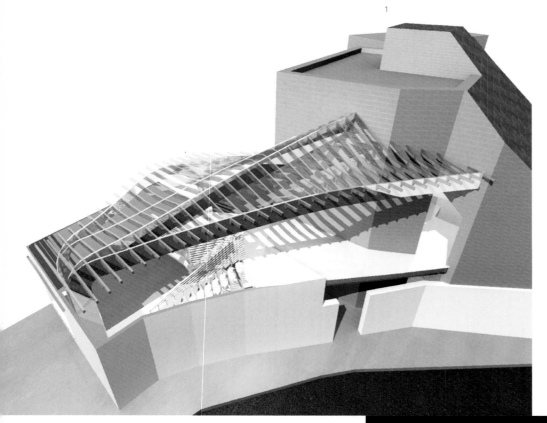

> oceanD is active in educating and creating discourse for the next generation of digital architects.

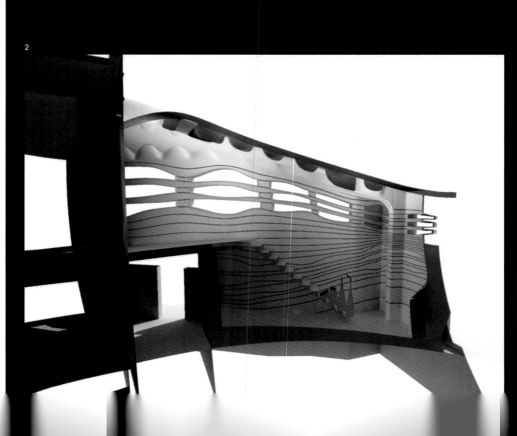

1_Roof structure
2_Section
3_Interior

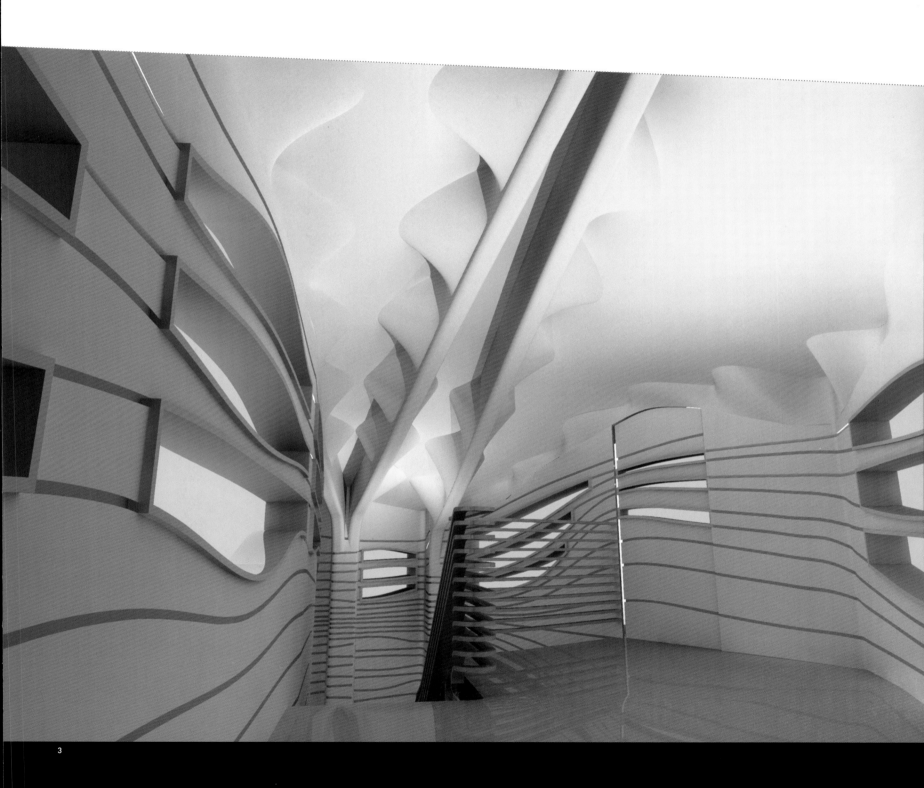

3

Ski Chalet
Chamonix, France

This project proposes to remodel the interior of a late Modernist ski-chalet flat on the slopes of Mont Blanc. All interior walls will be removed to open the 55-square-metre (590-square-foot) interior as a landscape of built-in furnishing elements, applying advanced computer-aided off-site manufacturing technologies. Intelligent and interactive lighting systems will be embedded in column and wall surfaces, and will also be linked to a seating area milled from soft polyurethane foam and coated with latex, recording the history of use in the flat in relation to lighting adjusted in real-time to conditions outdoors. Three-dimensional curved tectonics will be articulated in Corian, computer numerically controlled milling and traditional plasterwork.

1

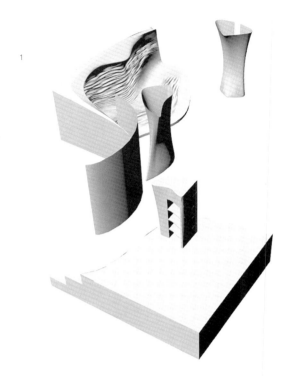

2

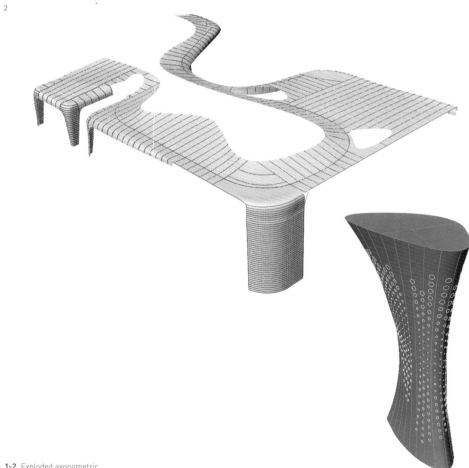

1-2_Exploded axonometric
3_Interior view

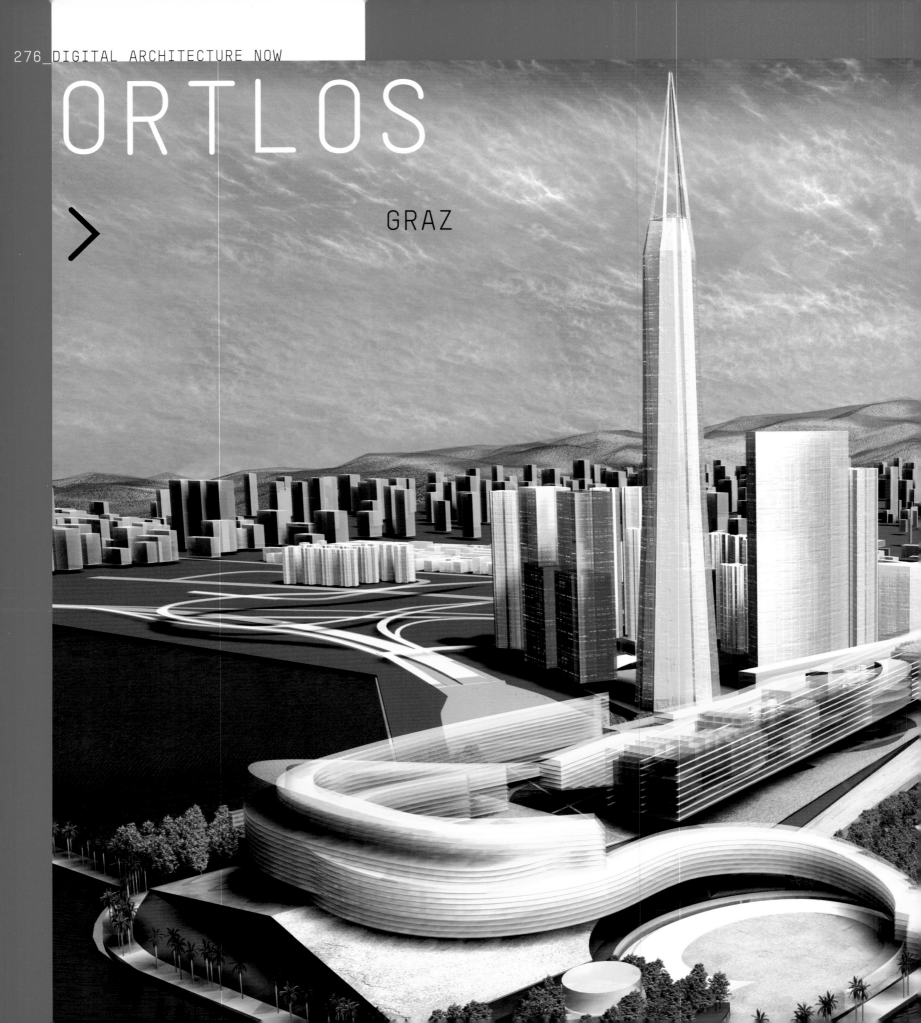

ORTLOS

GRAZ

ORTLOS is a kind of matrix, an infinite, constantly changeable field of the creative inputs who shape it. From a certain size on certain systems the first signs of self-organization show themselves; this has been the case with ORTLOS right from the beginning. ORTLOS sees itself as a virus, benign yet powerful. It has interfaces with the cyberspatial world, making clients / users gradually sink into this world whose laws correspond to a different logic. ORTLOS is an instrument for nomadic working methods. Its main preoccupations are experimental architecture and interface design.

Ortlos is German for 'placeless'. It is also the appropriate designation for a virtual office and discussion forum dealing with experimental architecture, urban planning, media theory, art installations and interface design. Architects, web designers, media theorists, media artists and information-technology specialists from around the world work together off-site, independent of a specific workplace. The conceptual and design process goes on in collaboration in a trans-local environment created out of a network of virtually combined workplaces. ORTLOS is also developing different types of collaborative software for designers. This software seeks to enable collaborators to excavate and share each other's references, preoccupations, sketches and favourite things. Interface design and architectural design blend in ORTLOS's world.

Hong Kong: Master-plan view

Urban Park
La Paz, Bolivia

The design intention follows the topographical gestures of the landscape with a geometric system of generated layers to make use of the panoramic qualities and levels of the site. The 'green grove of La Paz' will consist of a complex system of terraced wedges, a portfolio of landscape elements that suggest recreational potentials in groups as well as in peaceful isolation.

The project offers a high variability for spectacular views, walks, sports and play areas. A complex water-management system induces a new, poetic landscape approach as well as ecological improvement. The systematic use of vegetation will generate a specific character for the site, and areas of light and shadow will offer flexibility for multifunctional use.

12

> ORTLOS are not only fine architects but are also interested in the new working relationships of cyberspace.

1_Master plan
2_Urban Park structures

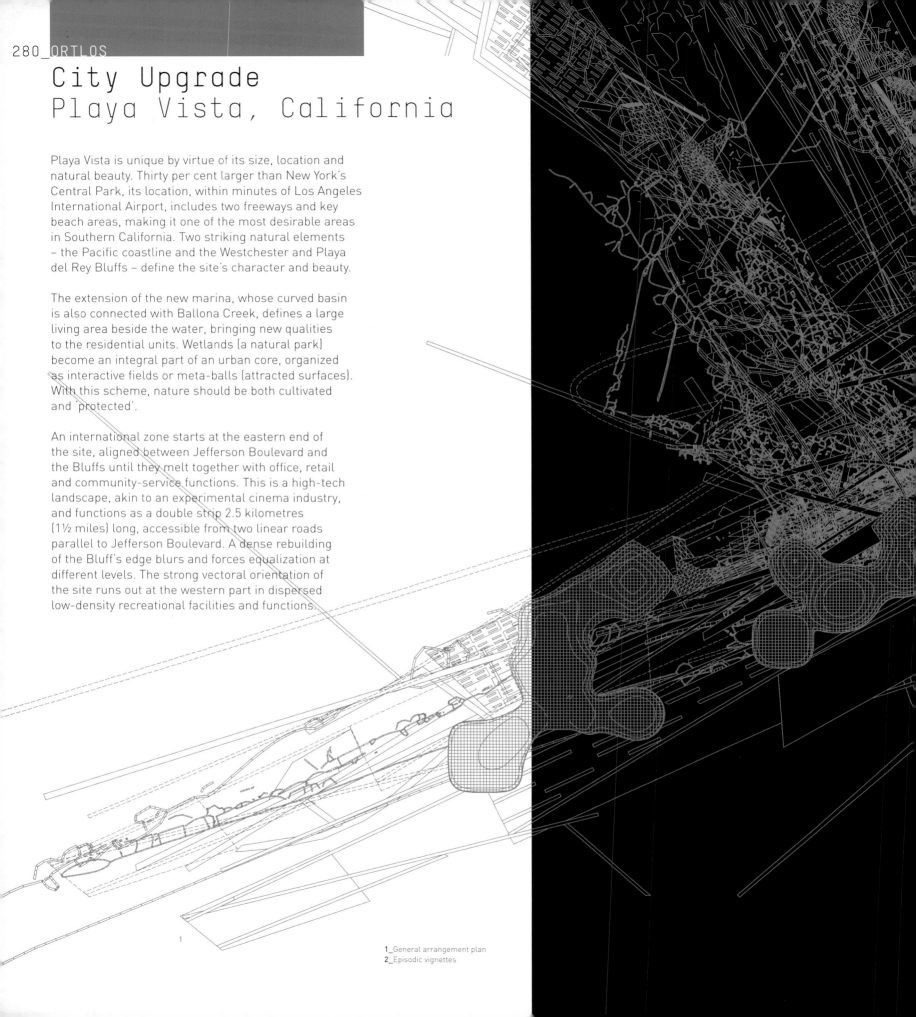

City Upgrade
Playa Vista, California

Playa Vista is unique by virtue of its size, location and natural beauty. Thirty per cent larger than New York's Central Park, its location, within minutes of Los Angeles International Airport, includes two freeways and key beach areas, making it one of the most desirable areas in Southern California. Two striking natural elements – the Pacific coastline and the Westchester and Playa del Rey Bluffs – define the site's character and beauty.

The extension of the new marina, whose curved basin is also connected with Ballona Creek, defines a large living area beside the water, bringing new qualities to the residential units. Wetlands (a natural park) become an integral part of an urban core, organized as interactive fields or meta-balls (attracted surfaces). With this scheme, nature should be both cultivated and 'protected'.

An international zone starts at the eastern end of the site, aligned between Jefferson Boulevard and the Bluffs until they melt together with office, retail and community-service functions. This is a high-tech landscape, akin to an experimental cinema industry, and functions as a double strip 2.5 kilometres (1½ miles) long, accessible from two linear roads parallel to Jefferson Boulevard. A dense rebuilding of the Bluff's edge blurs and forces equalization at different levels. The strong vectoral orientation of the site runs out at the western part in dispersed low-density recreational facilities and functions.

1

1_General arrangement plan
2_Episodic vignettes

Grand Egyptian Museum
Cairo

1

The project for the Grand Egyptian Museum attempts to present and visualize the country's great history rather than just to show the exhibits. The objects become more understandable when they can be viewed in the context of the everyday life of ancient civilizations (the highest level of education back then was received in the so-called 'houses of life'). The project's image is based on the tension between fluidity and materiality, dynamism and stasis, openness and closure.

There is no up or down. The building – like a city – surrounds us completely. The virtual structures are connected with each other at every conceivable angle. There is no horizon either; the mesh of building-like shapes stretches in all directions. Unlike the commercial spaces of the Internet, which have carefully enforced real-world rules such as horizon and perspective, the museum seems to have turned its back on petty Newtonian conventions.

2

1, 4_Views from within the complex
2_Overall elevational view
3_View at night

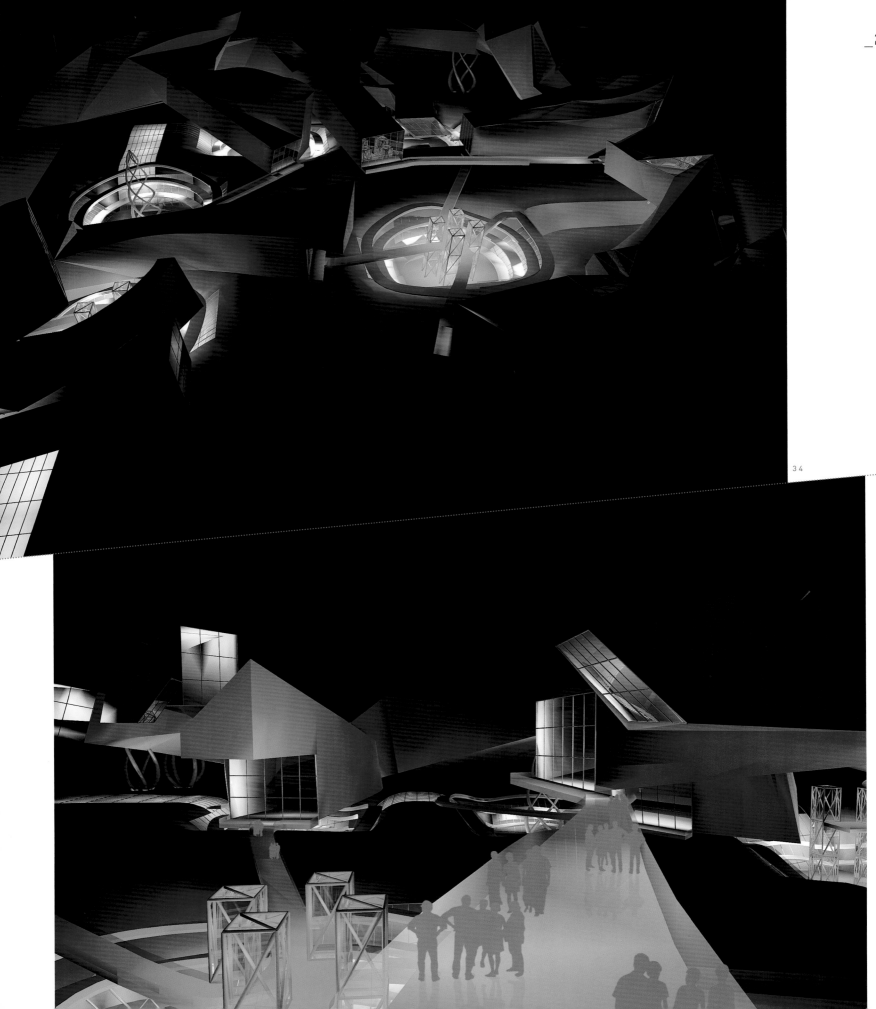

34

P-A-T-T-E-R-N-S >

LOS
ANGELES

P-A-T-T-E-R-N-S, founded by Marcelo Spina and Georgina Huljich, is a design, research and architectural practice based in Los Angeles that is known for its inventive approach. This approach fuses advanced digital techniques with an understanding of form and tectonics. The practice aims to create artificial, singular environments that operate in proximity to the systems and forces that influence and give rhythm to material life. Their work is formally innovative. Sometimes the architecture is hairy, sometimes muscular, sometimes light and ethereal.

This is a practice that should be better known to commissioners of buildings and attract wealthier clients. Their experimental approach always evolves a project and its aesthetics from first principles. That is to say the nature of the problem and the manner of its solution are not self-determined by a deracinated adherence to previous solutions and their pleasurable aesthetics but to an iterative experimentation of prototype. This is why P-A-T-T-E-R-N-S' work maintains its whiff of wonder and taste of originality. The partners have a wealth of academic experience, and this knowledge is put to work in the service of clients and product users. P-A-T-T-E-R-N-S are skilful artisans of the skin. The way their projects bob and weave, bump and grind and billow, illustrates that they are in control of every flare and frond.

Nodeul Island: Canopy structure

Nodeul Island Performing Arts Centre
Seoul, South Korea

This proposal can be described as an attempt to construct a holistic vision for this iconic site that promotes new spatial forms as a means of nurturing the continuing emergence and rehearsal of contemporary culture.

Rooted Flow proposes a rich augmentation of the vibrancy and dynamism of the Hangang River accentuated by the frenetic movement systems placed along its shores, the steadiness and diversity of a culturally unique programme, and the multiplicity of views from and towards the site.

The Nedoul Centre is organized by a branching structural lattice that adapts to the formal, programmatic and environmental needs of the project. The lattice system is made out of high-strength precast concrete elements. The structural design follows ideas that are common in biological systems in order to achieve minimum weight and energy use while maintaining maximum functional advantages.

Contrary to a conventional three-dimensional truss structure, this proposal suits the force paths within the system by using computer-aided structural-optimization techniques. The principal difference between a standard truss-like system and this biologically inspired one is that in nature the behaviour of bones and trees is optimized during evolutionary processes while in this proposal similar enhancements can be achieved using numerical solutions.

1

2

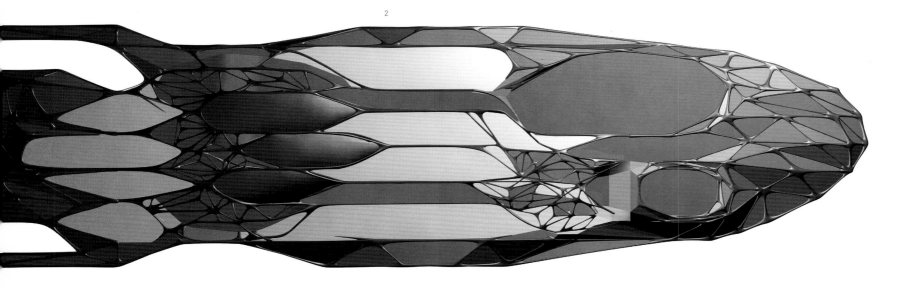

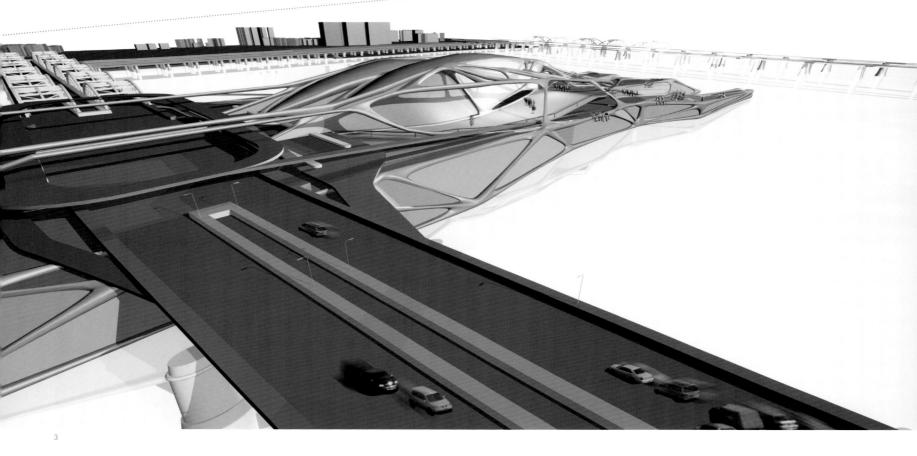

3

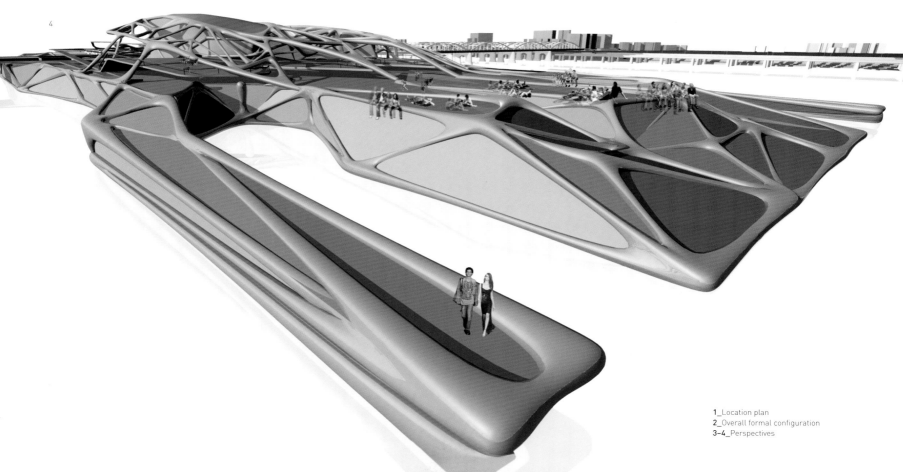

4

1_Location plan
2_Overall formal configuration
3–4_Perspectives

The Element
Rosario, Argentina

This residence can be described as an attempt to deal with the undifferentiated flatness of the pampas landscape. The project was conceived as a monolithic solid, a monochrome form punctuated by subtle inflections that establish a complex relationship among the different spaces while maintaining a sense of identity and privacy.

A supple concrete shell constitutes the body of the house. Problematic transitions are registered through folds and bends; punctuations in those transitions are effected through detached slits. These techniques, controlled by a structuring geometry governing the house's shape, imply a dexterous plasticity in its material. Folds and slits allow for luminosity, ventilation and views. Moreover, through their shape and disposition, they are means of emphasizing geometry while accentuating the topology of the shell.

Given that one of its clients is an agricultural engineer and landscape designer, the project offered the opportunity to incorporate a special activity: a small flower-forcing facility or greenhouse. Instead of isolating this feature, the greenhouse was situated in a continuous spatial sequence with the interior social spaces, swimming pool and solarium, thus integrating it and exploiting its dynamism.

The shell's warped surfaces will register experiences of different sorts – seeing, touching, smelling, hearing – and, through their proximity to distinct forms of flow, the unfolding of social and physical activity; the flow and sound of water and body movements in and around the pliant pool; and the textures and fragrances of flower species populating the greenhouse.

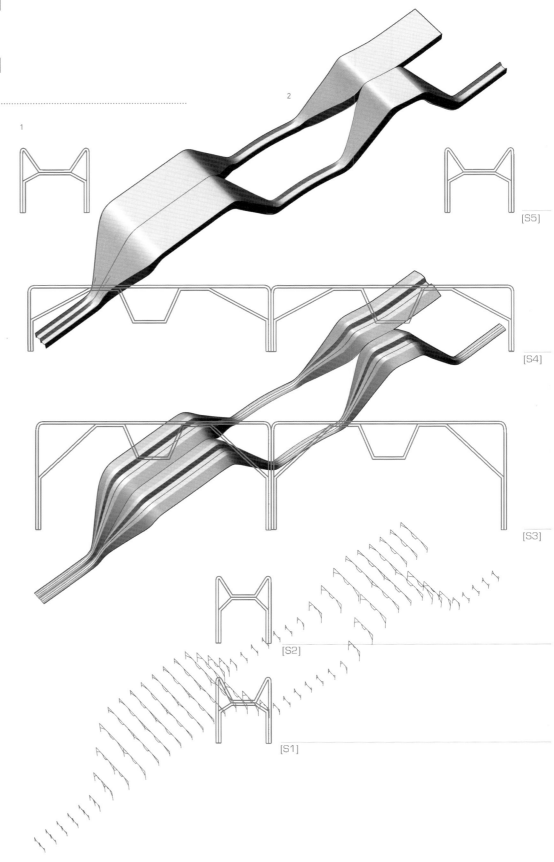

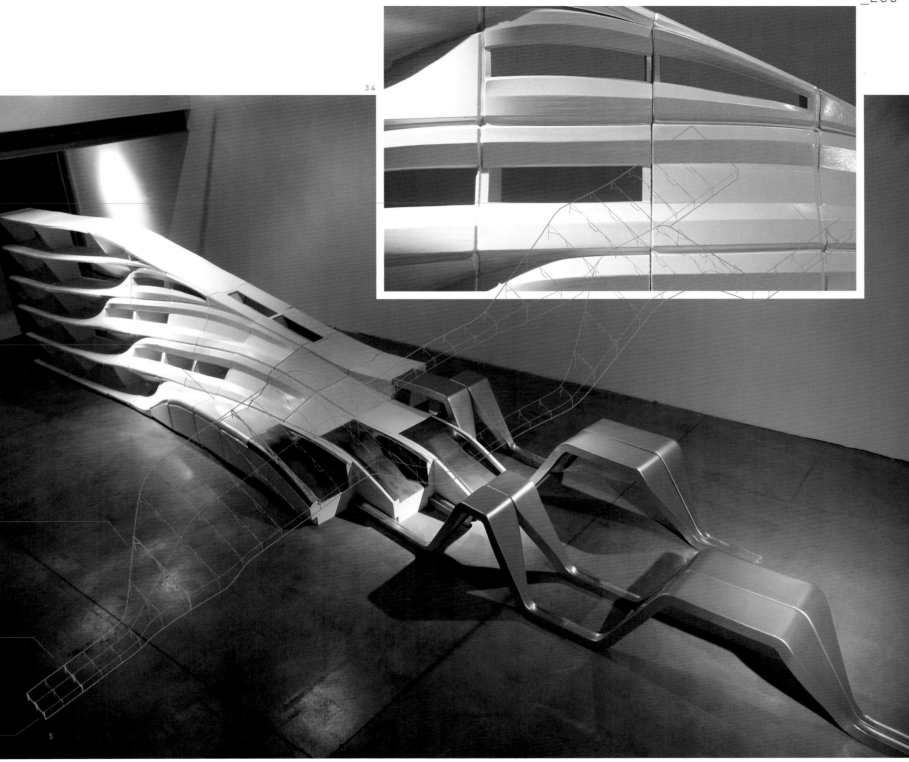

3 4

5

6

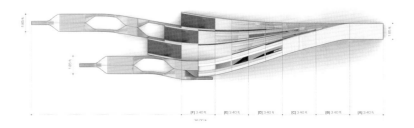

1–3_Element configuration and
deployment
4–6_Details and layout of final installation

UniBodies
New York

UniBodies is a collaboration between P-A-T-T-E-R-N-S and Makai Smith from the fabrication studio Kreysler & Associates. It is driven by P-A-T-T-E-R-N-S' ongoing research into shell structures and their impact on architectural form and tectonics along with the expertise of K&A in composites and digital fabrication.

Conceptually, UniBodies investigates the potential of composite shells in the production of small and intensive proto-architectures that challenge the implicit distinctions between skeleton and skin, modular and monolithic, smooth and porous, while pursuing an advanced degree of technological, formal and material invention.

Materially, UniBodies explores the plasticity of composites and unitized construction systems. Composites, or fibre-reinforced polymers, have the capacity to synthetically subsume systems, melding, fusing and embedding discrete components within single body-shells. Furthermore, composites imply an amalgamation of time and procedure. Based on a unique use of anisotropic components to assemble surfaces, each piece is made of a variable combination of fibre cloth, resin matrix and flexible core materials. UniBodies exploits the versatility of composites to produce artificial materials and intensive gradients. Variable degrees of translucency, viscosity and surface profile are integrally moulded and explored through pigmentation and filling of the resin.

> 'Vivacious and formally extravagant' is P-A-T-T-E-R-N-S calling card.

1

2

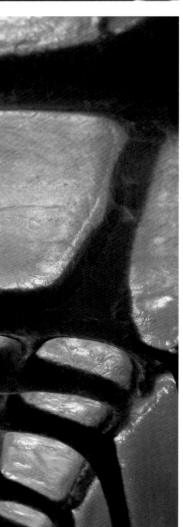

1–6_UniBodies: Details of fabrication,
skin and junctioning

Vertical Garden Competition Entry
MAK Center / Schindler House
Los Angeles

This proposal is an attempt to investigate the formal, spatial and atmospheric potential of a vertically sustainable garden in sync with the most advanced technology for plant growth. Its site is the famous Schindler House that was built in 1922.

The garden is composed of a branching network of PVC tubes. These tubes circulate and distribute water with a nutrient solution that nurtures aerial vegetation of different kinds. The section of the tubes diminishes as the trajectories they describe move up and away from the ground. The flow of water is induced by pumps. Water is distributed directly to the plants by pumping up from reservoirs or indirectly down by dripping from the upper branches.

The artificiality of plants growing directly on water, the modulation and scaling of them as they detach from the ground, the dynamism of the choreographed vegetation and its likely wind-induced oscillation, and the occasional forms of animal life negotiating temporary shelter within the garden all add up to an advanced ecosystem that both challenges and amplifies the assumed relationships between the architecture of the Schindler House and its surrounding 'natural' environment.

flowers

garden

patio

2

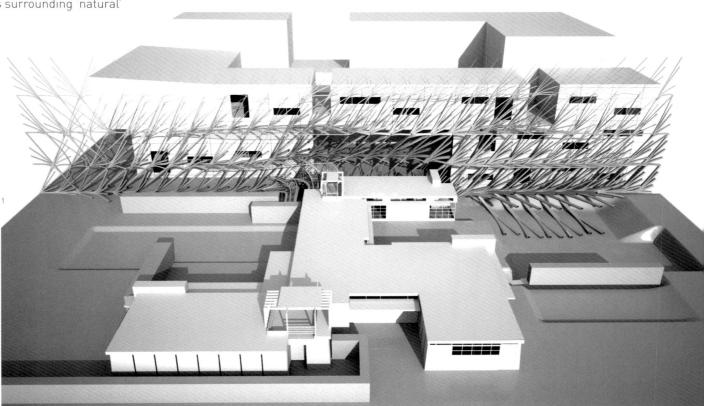

1_Overall view
2_Location plan
3_Branching structure
4_View from street

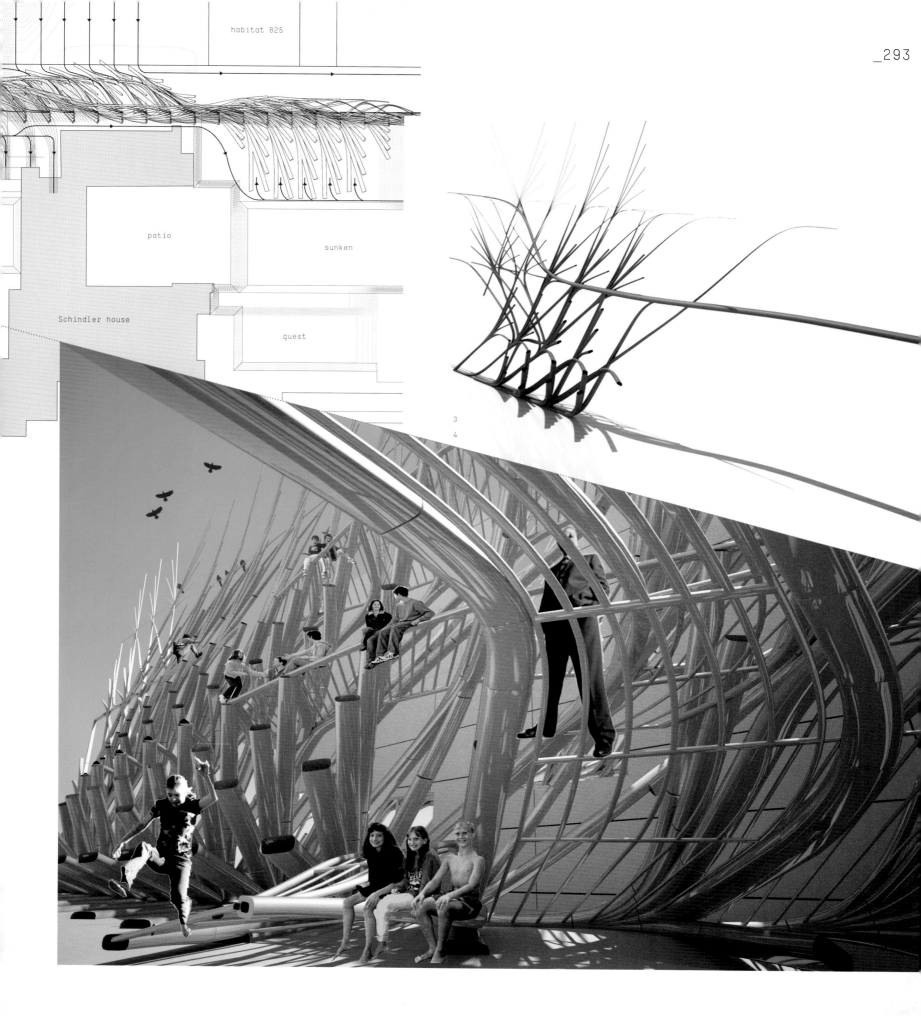

habitat 825

patio

sunken

Schindler house

guest

3
4

QUA'VIRARCH

> CHICAGO

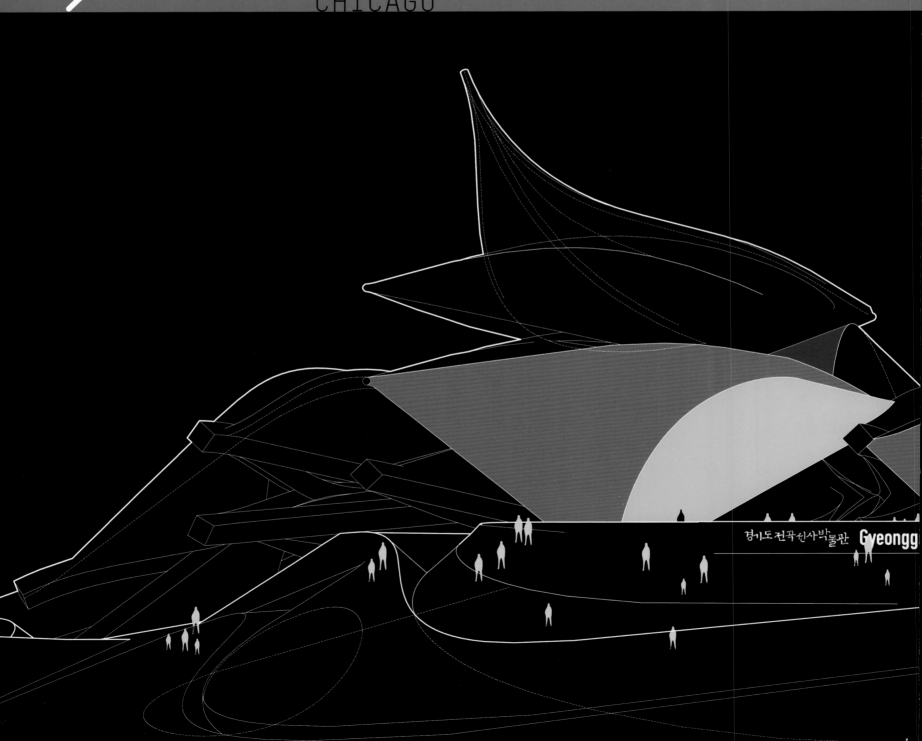

Qua'Virarch, founded in 2003 by Paul Priessner in Los Angeles and subsequently relocated to Chicago, is an award-winning practice committed to producing works of architecture, art and urban design that produce new feelings about the limits of atmosphere.

Qua'Virarch's preoccupations with ambience, situation and atmosphere are deployed at many scales. Aesthetically, their work has a sleek, braided quality that hybridizes and blends spaces, materials and junctions. One feels that the ground plane is drawn up into the work of the practice, one becoming the other.

Qua'Virarch's architecture is one of topological morphology, in a way a prototypical remodelling of the surface of the earth itself. One of the chief physical tactics of this remodelling is berming – pulling the earth over buildings – but the practice also berms ambiences. This architectural and spatial trope translates in the Qua'Virarch mind as a necessary rebellion against the normative legislation of architectural space and provokes an emotional response to its spaces that exceeds the rather flat and assertive good manners of traditional Modernism.

Gyeonggi-Do Jeongok Prehistory Museum: Diagrammatic section

Jeongok Prehistory Museum

The Czech Republic National Library Prague

The new National Library of the Czech Republic is envisaged as an extension of the surrounding terrain and cultural atmosphere, as a fibrous volume that emerges from itself, expanding onto the site, replicating itself numerous times (to produce the main volumes of the library) and ferociously changing from a soft and natural surface (terrain) into a strong and foreign material (building).

By creating a porous interior arrangement, with extra light atria and open floor plans, the library can be lit in large part by natural light. Even the sections located within the landscape and underground are illuminated by natural light from openings within the topography and the use of fibre-optic cable-supplied fixtures (in the lower levels) to provide authentic sunlight to the parking / warehouse levels. The thick exterior skeleton wall also allows for the natural maintenance of heating / cooling in the building by allowing for a slower heat-gain / loss cycle during the course of the day. The exterior gardens will provide a bouquet of visual complexity and excitement complementing the newness of the library itself.

1

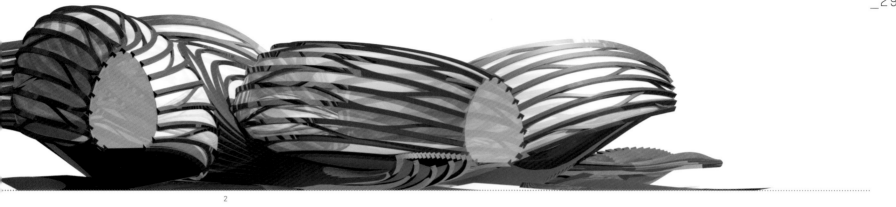

2

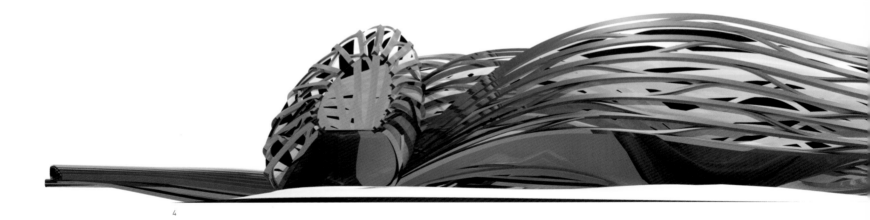

3

4

1_Site plan
2–5_Elevations

5

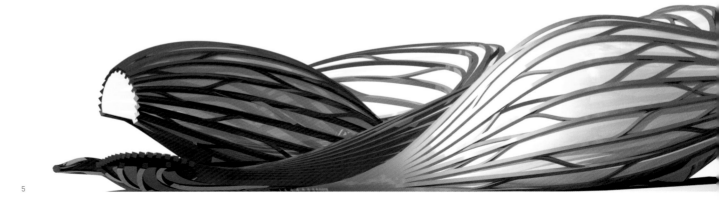

6–7_Form, structure and skin
8_Street elevation

6

7

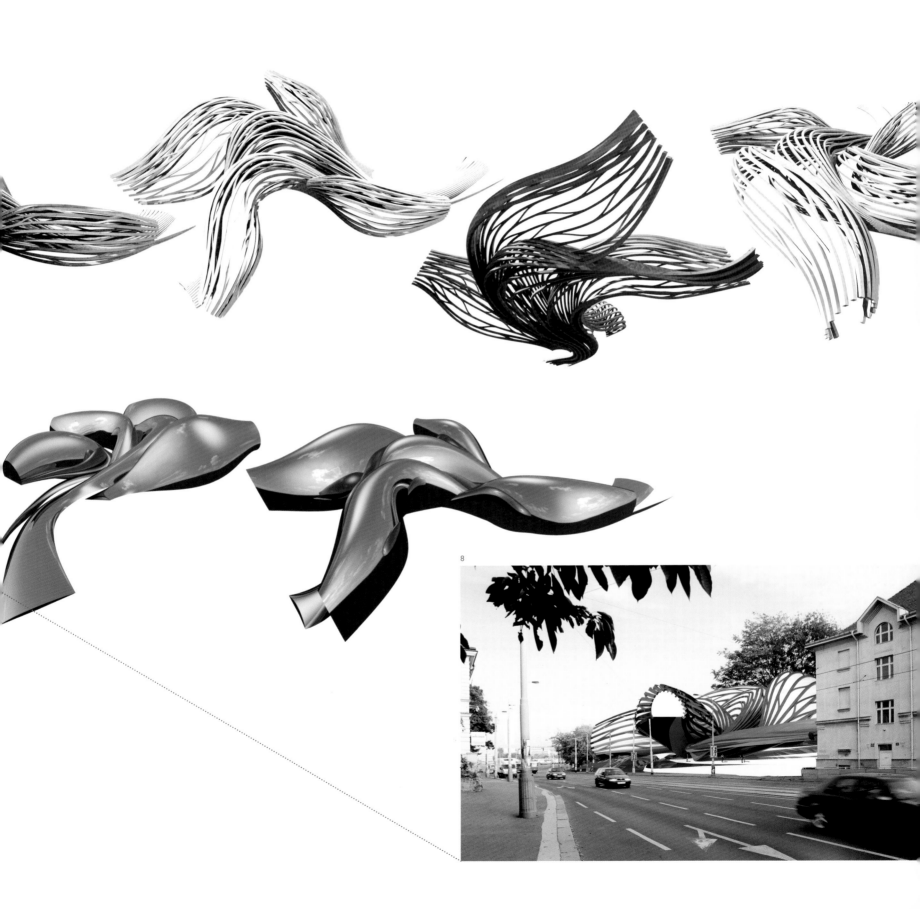

8

Gyeonggi-Do Jeongok Prehistory Museum
Jeongok Archaeological Site, South Korea

The design proposes an open, interconnected terracing of exhibition spaces. The exhibition rooms are separated by means of platform circulation, while visibility is constantly maintained.

The site is naturally steep, and so the design arose as the spatial continuation of the landscape and its organic metamorphosis into the building. The site negotiates between extremes in topography. This allows the landscape to appear uninterrupted by the project; it seems as if both site and building are beautiful confluences of natural forces.

The design concept is organized around an open and integrated platform interior. Every location within the museum is part of the continuous exhibition space, including the plant room, archival storage, curatorial restoration and basalt precipice. The levels are integrated via a network of elevators, walkways and stairs that creates continuity of circulation. Inside the museum entry, the park is extended to form the public spaces that become transition areas between the park and the exhibition on the floors above and below. Users access the building through gardens and four nubs containing the Common Zone: reception, exhibit halls and cafeteria.

1_Ground / building berming
2_Site and enclosure
3_Structural distortion diagram
4_Overall aerial rendering

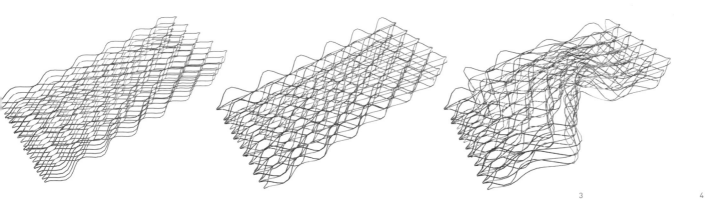

3   4

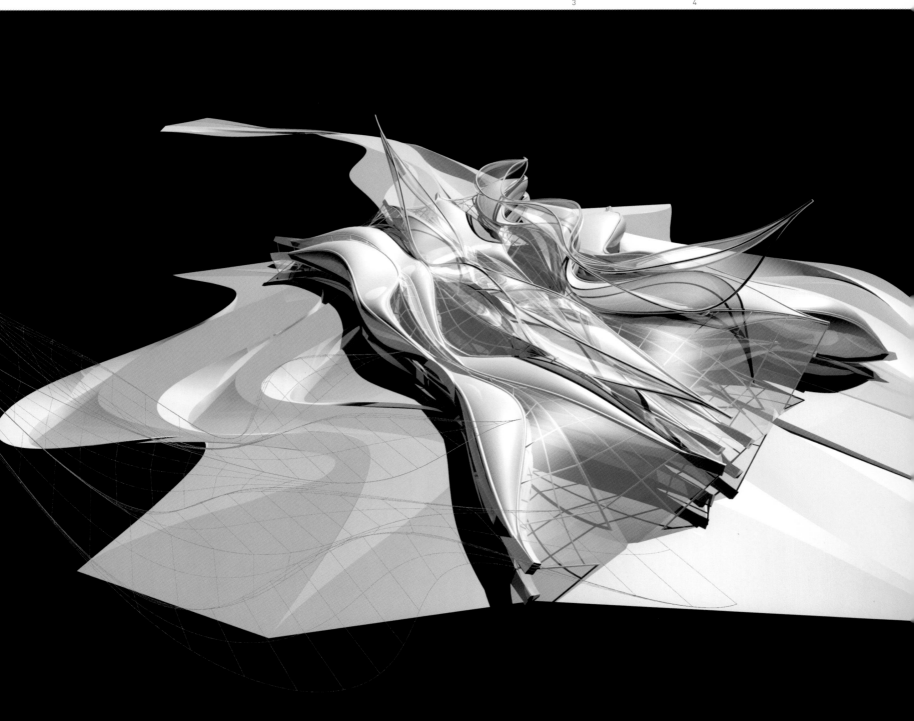

5

67

Southbank Planning Development
Cape Town

The Southbank Site urban organization is an aggressive proposal for a new artistic and cultural centre. The plan is for the development and transformation of an agricultural site into a world-class cultural community, complete with a central business district, high-end residential development, cultural facilities such as concert halls, museums and theatres, and leisure programmes, including a proposed facility to accommodate FIFA World Cup 2010 matches and tourist hotels. The site lies at the confluence of several important infrastructure links.

The project begins by tying together the basic infrastructure and urban context of the surrounding site. Lateral lines from topography and agricultural divisions are mutated across the site to become a major organizational force. Moving away from the grid model of planning large urban areas, this new diagram affords uniqueness to each building and area while still providing a movement diagram that facilitates intercommunication. The integration of these lateral connections with the main longitudinal axis creates a soft grid that forms the project's underlying framework. Unlike European or Asian models of city growth, the Southbank proposal provides a formalized system to establish a wild civic originality.

1   2

> Qua´Virarch have learned much
  from Eisenman and the previous
  generation. One project becomes
  a prototype for the next.

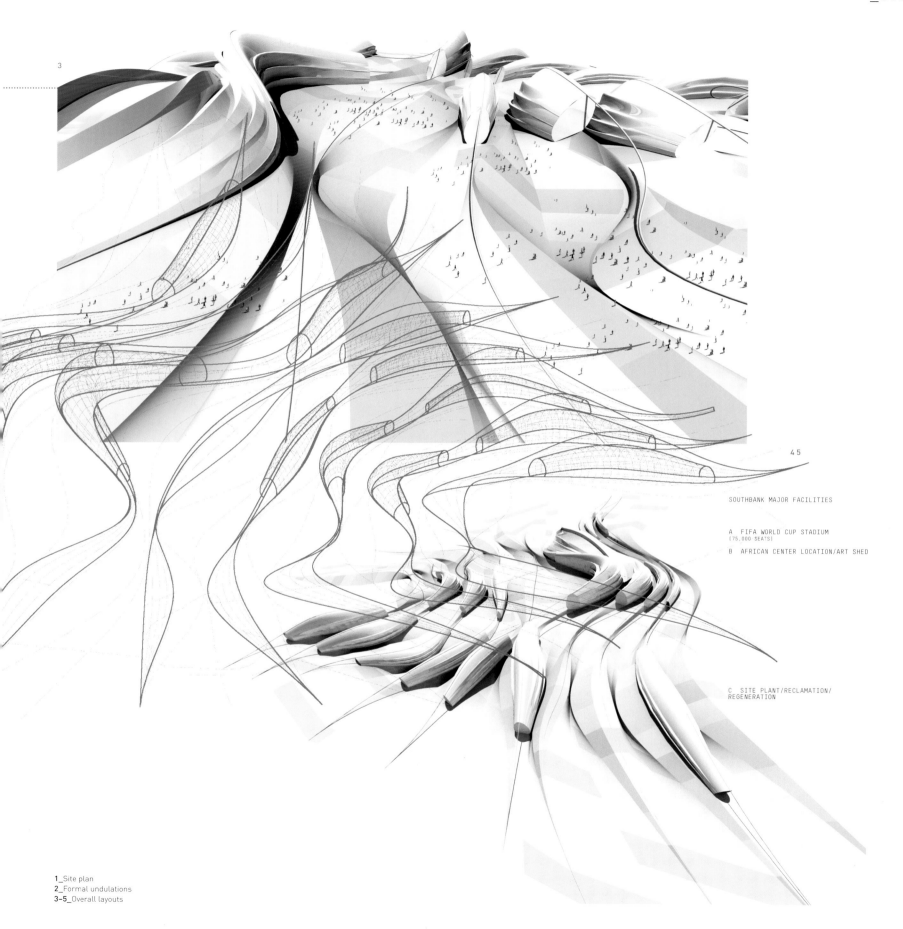

3

4 5

SOUTHBANK MAJOR FACILITIES

A   FIFA WORLD CUP STADIUM
    (75,000 SEATS)

B   AFRICAN CENTER LOCATION/ART SHED

C   SITE PLANT/RECLAMATION/
    REGENERATION

1_Site plan
2_Formal undulations
3–5_Overall layouts

LINDY ROY/
ROY CO.

NEW
YORK

ROY Co. was founded by Lindy Roy in New York in 2000. Undertaking projects of different sizes and scales in diverse places, ROY Co.'s approach relies on interpretations of site that are not limited to physical attributes but that also include informal social, cultural, technological and political insights.

An important trajectory here is the ability to explore and, in a productive sense, expose risk as a catalyst for design strategy. This broader understanding informs the design process and ultimately heightens the user's experience and perception. By going beyond geopolitical or cultural boundaries, ROY Co. exposes, draws from and explores ecological risk in all its manifestations.

While eco-tourism might be considered elitist, Roy Co. has used it innovatively to respond to social and cultural disconnection within regions in economic despair. Targeting two opposite audiences - prosperous tourists and impoverished residents - ROY Co.'s strategy explicitly deals with risk by balancing exploitation with exploration, and thus repackages sites as destinations where visitors are engaged as participants in the 'experience economy'.

In ROY Co.'s work, nature is objectified and even simulated to create a scenery of leisure. So ROY Co. utilizes digital-design methodologies to attempt to mitigate often deep-rooted social and economic problems with its architecture. Sometimes, in more wealthy commissions, the practice uses digital-architectural techniques to create buildings that luxuriate in the fold of a façade, the curve of a wall / floor junction and the pleat of a roof plane.

Okavango Delta Spa: Detail

Noah
New York

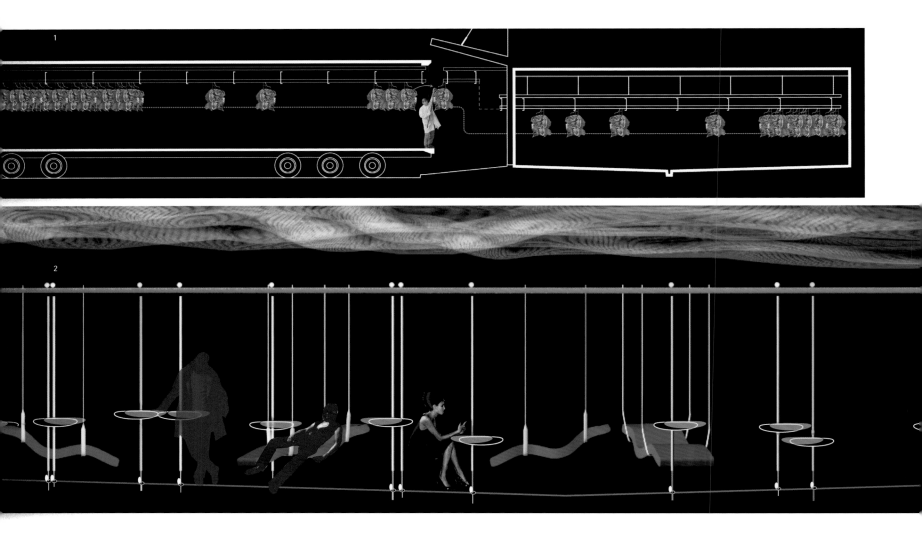

By reprogramming the overhead steel grid once used for transferring carcasses from refrigerated trucks into and around cutting rooms, this bar-lounge proposal preserves the once ubiquitous rail-and-switch infrastructure of Manhattan's Meatpacking District. The overhead steel grid of a now defunct cooler room suspends mobile, translucent-resin tables and red-leather chaises lounge. Adaptive and flexible, this proposal invites countless social settings, from long communal table configurations to cabaret-style intimacy, while leaving the original slope-to-drain floor untouched. Bundles of optical fibre – the material that wired the dot-com boom – is drawn up from the basement below and braided to form a light-leaking ceiling.

> Roy's work has an aesthetic all its own; the renders are quiet yet extraordinarily revealing of new dreams of human habitation and relaxation.

1–4_Bar-lounge layout, structure and form

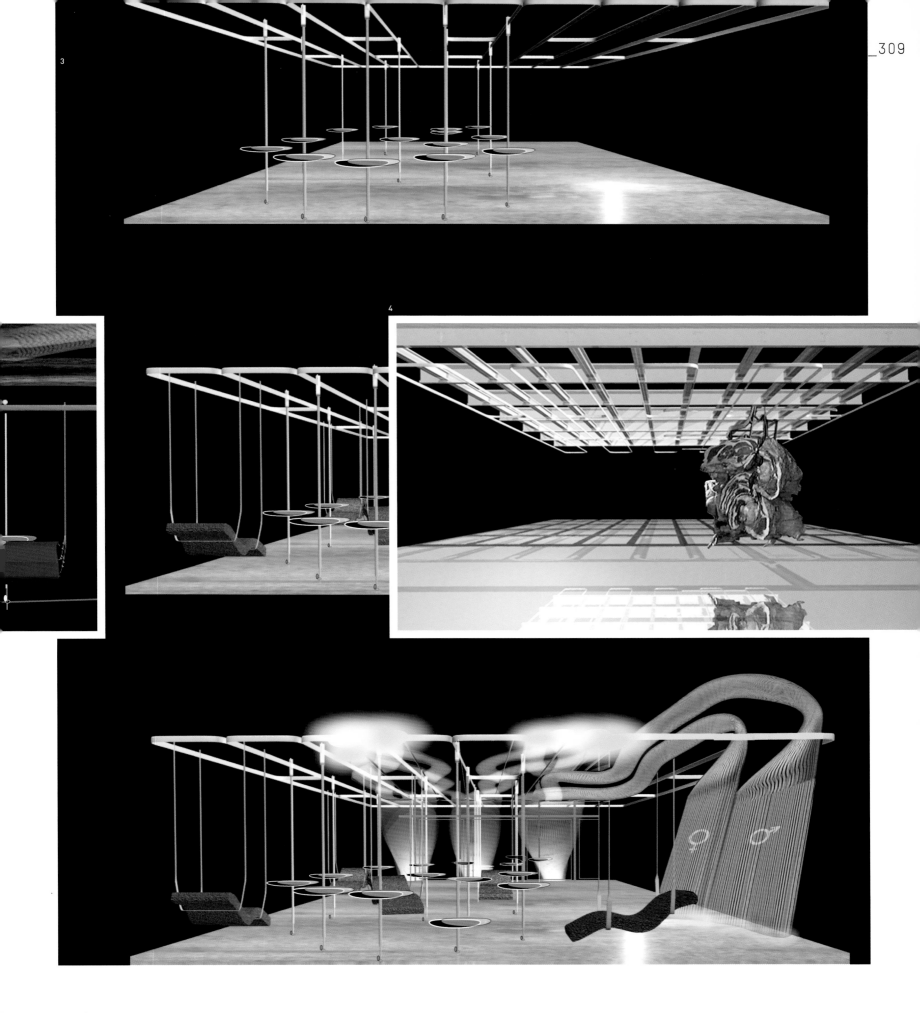

Okavango Delta Spa
Republic of Botswana

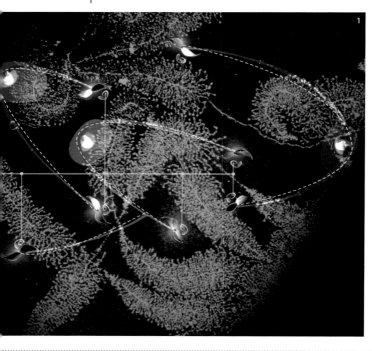

This spa, proposed for Botswana's Okavango Delta, introduces spartan luxury to an extreme wildlife experience. The Okavango Delta is a thin veneer of water covering 15,000 square kilometres (5,800 square miles) of the otherwise arid Kalahari Desert. Floodwaters from Angola replenish the region in winter. As the waters recede, fresh grazing land is exposed. Vast migratory herds of elephant, zebra and wildebeest follow the shifting pastures. The site can only be accessed by helicopter or small airplane. Seven thatch-roofed guest pods equipped with floating fibreglass spas are placed in natural clearings in papyrus beds; buoyant wood tracks weave through the papyrus connecting the pods. A sub-aquatic grid of pipes and pumps addresses stringent environmental criteria for waste disposal. Four mobile meditation pavilions and a crocodile-resistant lap pool, each powered by an outboard motor, manoeuvre through the channels and dock in the shade of extended roofs.

1_General arrangement plan
2_Detail
3_General arrangement

FLOATING LAP-POOL

UNIT #7

BAR+DINING

UNIT #1

LANDING

GENERATOR + WORKSHOP   LEECHFIELD   STORAGE   LAUNDRY KITCHEN

TAKE-OFF

UNIT #2

SOLAR PANELS

WINTER WIND

UNIT #5

UNIT #4   UNIT #3

UNIT #6

SPA

SUMMER WIND

MOBILE
MEDITATION PAVILLIONS

N

3

West Street Tower
New York

1

This speculative twenty-eight-storey residential tower formed part of the *New York Times Magazine*'s proposal for lower Manhattan post-9/11. Four grey ribbons reminiscent of the Westside Highway are extruded vertically and woven through the interior, generating interlocking duplex apartments of various sizes. The relocated highway tunnels below.

2

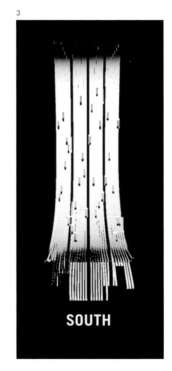

SOUTH

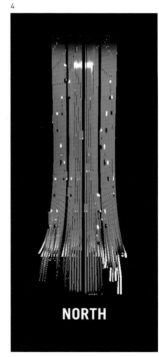

NORTH

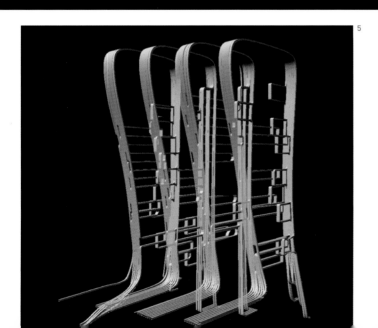

5

1_Overall tower view
2_Programmatic zoning diagram
3–5_Grey ribbon extrusions as façade

Wind River Lodge
Chugach Mountains, Alaska

Designed for Alaska Rendezvous Heli-ski Guides, the Wind River Lodge stands in southern Alaska's Chugach mountain range, a dramatic environment of inaccessible glacial ridges and peaks, some rising nearly 2,700 metres (9,000 feet). Serving as the base for an extreme-skiing operation, this complex comprises a hotel, heliport and control tower, bar, enclosed maintenance hangar and warehouse spaces.

Emerging from the landscape like a tanker trapped in the ice, the compound is defined by a continuous surface that wraps around a steel frame to form floors, walls and ceilings capable of bearing the weight of heavy snow. A series of concrete 'fins' supports the building, ensuring that it sits above the snow line. The twenty-six-room lodge, identified by its large, low-sloping roof, is economically designed as a cluster of prefabricated units. Built and then shipped to the site, the modular rooms are slotted into the hotel's folding structure. The lodge's south-facing elevation is sheathed in a series of galvanized sheet-metal louvres that provide solar protection as well as an appealing varied surface. The north-west façade, made entirely of glass, reflects the majestic landscape beyond.

1
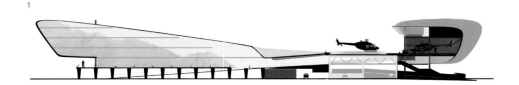

2

3

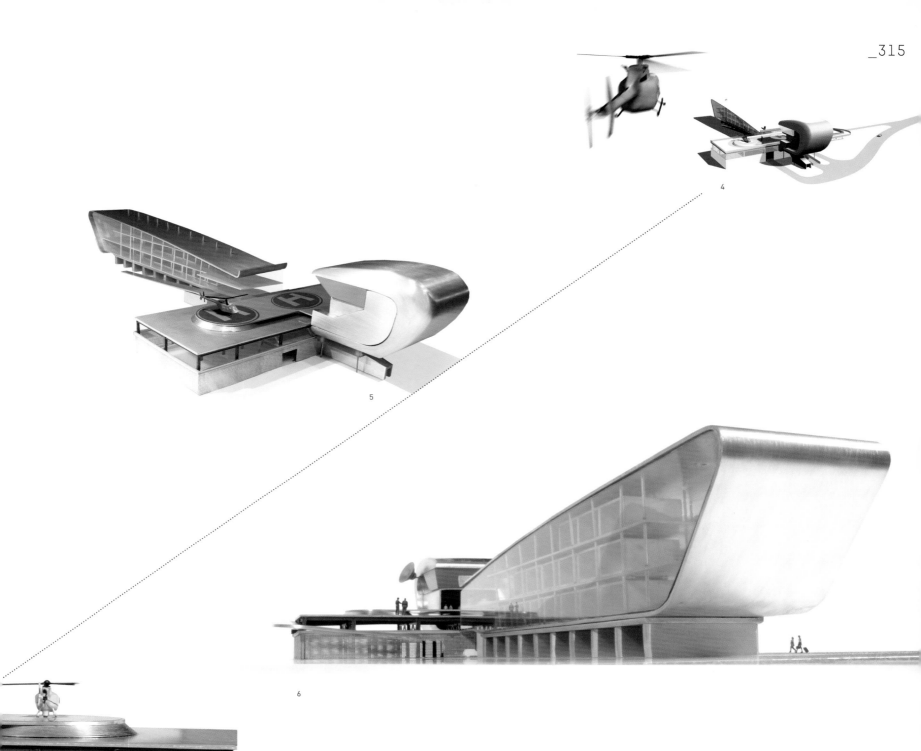

1–2_Elevations
3_Model
4_Aerial view
5_Perspective view
6_Aerial view

ENRIC RUIZ-GELI/ CLOUD9

BARCELONA
SAN PAOLO

>

Cloud9 is an architectural practice inspired by natural form – the ripples on a sandy beach, the leaves on a tree or the tree itself, or the fungus on the tree trunk. All of these inspirations are fed through the office and transmuted into buildings that seem to morph into their surroundings yet offer their inhabitants sublime space in which they can relax, work and observe. Enric Ruiz-Geli is the creative force at the helm of Cloud9, and one can see a little of his Catalan Surrealist predecessor Dalí in his work. Without digital technology it would be harder for a practice like Cloud9 to exist. Its biologically inspired formal language has to be created using CAM technology.

The double-curved forms and tendril-like structures all require the computer to plot nodal positions in three-dimensional space – a feat nigh on impossible with a drawing board and a calculator. Like only a few others in this book, Cloud9 often steps outside the good-taste aesthetics quickly establishing themselves on corporate clients' wish lists. Therefore their work can be visually arresting and sometimes otherworldly.

Villa Bio: Wall texture detail

Aviary
New Marine Zoo, Barcelona

The aviary, with its asymmetrical geometry, is laid out longitudinally in order to create longer flight paths. The main construction is a cable structure with two surfaces in the form of continuous stainless-steel mesh. The goal is to build a central tree-like structure, with hydroponic cultures, that could be used as a habitat for birds. The tree structure will serve as the habitat for nine species – stork, spoonbill, grey heron, cattle egret, little egret, night heron, glossy ibis, cormorant and sacred ibis (a total of more than two hundred birds) – and as a support for more than a hundred nests. The tree structure is an airport registering the birds' activities.

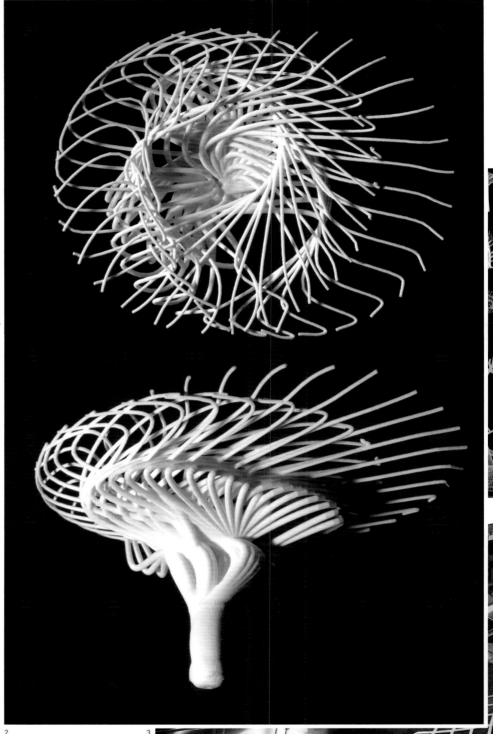

2

3

1

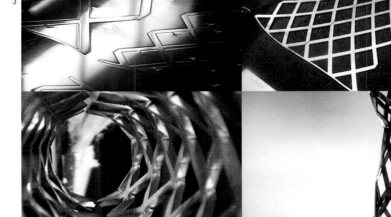

> The paradigms of the natural
  world combine to inspire
  work that is arresting
  and zoomorphic.

1_Overall drawing
2, 4_Structural model
3_Structural and spatial
experimentation montage
5_Overall elevations

Villa Bio
Llers, Girona,
Spain

Contemporary architecture is the platform upon which contemporary art and culture rest. Living on an exciting platform can itself become an art form: the art of living.

Cloud9 conceived this platform as a landscape of linear events. The landscape folds itself within the site and forms a growing spiral. The platform is a linear structure made of concrete of constant section in the shape of a 'C'. The longitudinal blind façades function as beams and create a 15-metre (50-foot) projection.

1

2

12

SERVO

>

LOS ANGELES
ZURICH
NEW YORK
STOCKHOLM

Established in the late 1990s, servo's office is distributed between Los Angeles, New York, Stockholm and Zurich. The practice does not hot-desk but hot-cities instead. Architects often brag about mileage travelled as a register of success, but usually these globetrotters are tethered to a rather large base where minions receive instructions like missals from an absent god. For servo there is no central hub, only the proliferation of consultants and collaborators. They speak not of discrete projects or oeuvres but of prototypes and mock-ups in which each commission is an experiment within a certain trajectory of design research.

servo has utilized the idea of networks as a platform for innovating the nature of practice and the nature of the objects of that practice, as the site for their designs, and as an organizational diagram for their work. Compositionally that work is nodal, often with invisible electronic tendrils that connect, feed back and observe. Much of the work is at small scale, with an exhibition installation here or there. But this networked way of creating space, often at intimate scales, is a microcosm for the much larger and more ambitious buildings, artefacts and products that servo will undoubtedly create in the future. Currently the work is sinuous, often transparent and alien-seeming.

The Genealogy of Speed installation

Dark Places
Santa Monica Museum of Art, Santa Monica, California

Integrating physical and virtual infrastructures, this exhibition concept operates less as a conventional display and lighting system than as a dynamic spatial instrument, absorbing, processing and integrating with the various levels of interaction between visitors in the gallery. Movement patterns, communication activity on the Internet, and other forms of physical and virtual use are monitored, or mapped, by a network of intelligent technologies embedded in the infrastructure's material surfaces. These use patterns are employed as inputs to generate new spatial effects through sound, lighting and image technologies. The system thereby indexes and materializes its users' activities by becoming an instrument of their individual and collective potential.

The system comprises eight 'strands', each of which comprises three basic components: the projector-vitrine, the partition and the counter. Each of these houses different display equipment and has different 'responsive' potentials. The embedded fibre-optic system 'listens' to the activity of the display field and pulses in response to interactions, producing more or less light in areas where there is more or less activity. This augments and makes visual the flow of both information (art) and audience. The fibre-optic system is a 'live diagram' documenting and supplementing spatial dynamics as they unfold over time.

1

1-4_Dark Places: Exhibition installation

The Genealogy of Speed is a private exhibition sponsored by Nike featuring thirty of the company's most technologically innovative shoes from its thirty-two-year history. The primary focus is to create a dynamic spatial catalogue of these shoes, exposing their individual design technology as well as specific performance criteria related to athletic records.

The exhibition infrastructure includes a display and a ceiling system. The display system comprises vertically oriented acrylic tubes, or stalactites, each of which contains a single shoe. The basic diagnostics of each shoe are sandblasted onto the tubes, collapsing a graphic informational environment related to content with the shoes themselves. An adjustable docking condition allows these stalactites to be removed for redistribution into one of three clusters. The result is a reconfigurable display system that allows material to be mixed and remixed according to different organizing principles such as colour or sole design.

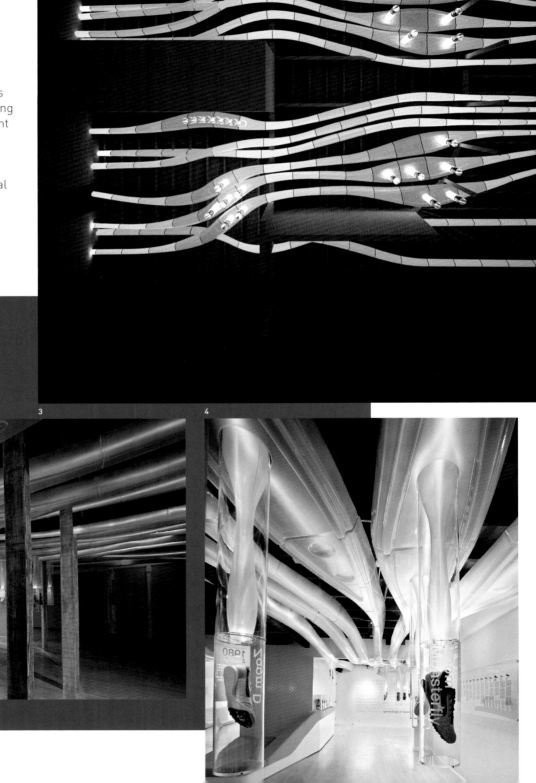

Spoorg
MAK Center at Schindler House,
Los Angeles

'Semi-porous operable organisms' takes its name from a primitive, usually unicellular, often environmentally resistant, dormant or reproductive body produced by plants and some microorganisms. These microorganisms are capable of developing either directly or indirectly after fusion with another spore, producing a new individual that is, in some cases, unlike the parent. In the context of this project, each spoorg cell is embedded with local intelligence, enabling it to communicate with other adjacent spoorgs. It is, to a specified degree, responsive to selected local and regional environmental changes.

The spoorg system is a cellular one that interfaces with the interior and exterior of glass building skins. It is essentially a demonstration project, exploring the potentially productive effects of integrating new material, geometric, sonic and photo-sensing technologies. The intelligence of the system is distributed (as opposed to being centralized) and based on wireless radio communication. Spoorg reacts to local as well as regional changes of light by generating various forms of ambient sonic output. The behaviour of each spoorg individually, and of the network of spoorgs collectively, evolves over time through the modulation of sound textures based on a series of algorithms.

Each spoorg cell is comprised of a thin-skin plastic shell with hollow regions for embedding microcontrollers, photo sensors, speaker elements and wireless radio-communications technology. The shells are manufactured through sintering and vacuum-casting. The local infrastructure combines wired and wireless technologies.

2

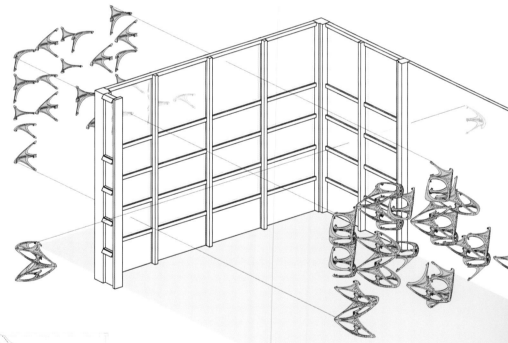

1

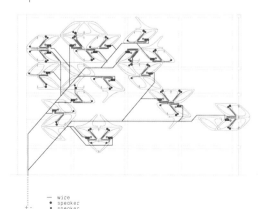

— wire
• speaker
• speaker
• sensor
■ PCB

⬡ RF signal

— wire
• speaker
• speaker
• sensor
■ PCB

1–6_Installation layout, diagramming, detailing and in-situ photographs

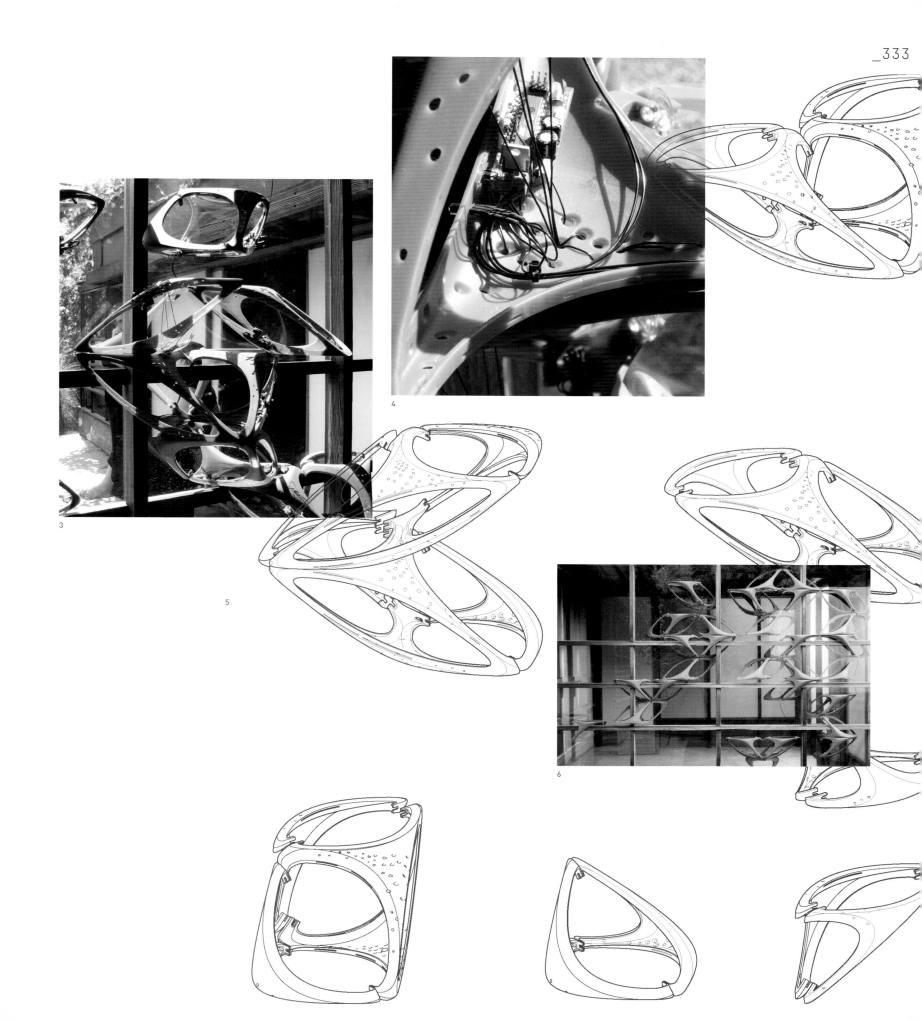

3

4

5

6

Thermocline
Wexner Center for the Arts, Columbus, Ohio

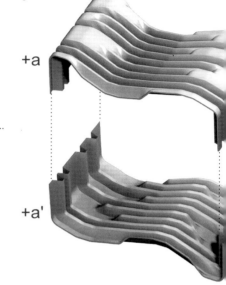

01 02

Thermocline upgrades the infrastructure of a conventional furniture unit, transforming its tactile interface into a multi-sensory user atmosphere. Responsive not only to physical but to virtual use, the vacuum-formed shells allow for multiple ergonomic positions while providing a vessel for the distribution of sound and light.

The architecture of Thermocline is a three-dimensional surface comprised of thermo-formed acrylic cells. Each cell's surface is corrugated to provide structural support for a variety of sitting and resting conditions. The corrugation patterns vary in density and organization, often exceeding their structural capacity so as to provide for the distribution of the system's virtual infrastructure on its lower surface. An LED lighting array and audio-speaker network are embedded in these corrugation channels and can be distributed in a variety of patterns and densities.

In 2003 Thermocline was upgraded in collaboration with two researchers from the Massachusetts Institute of Technology. The project was redeveloped to incorporate interactive technologies, including a network of motion and sound sensors. The Emonic Environment, Thermocline's virtual architecture, is an artificial neural network of sound, lighting and computing systems. An array of sound sensors collects residual conversation as well as other ambient sounds. This material is distributed to a central computer to be processed into new sound patterns which are then distributed into Thermocline's speaker network, ultimately triggering its LED lighting array. The result is a dynamic feedback loop between Thermocline and the space around it.

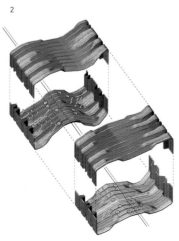

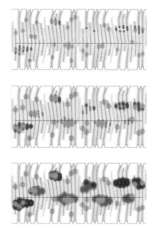

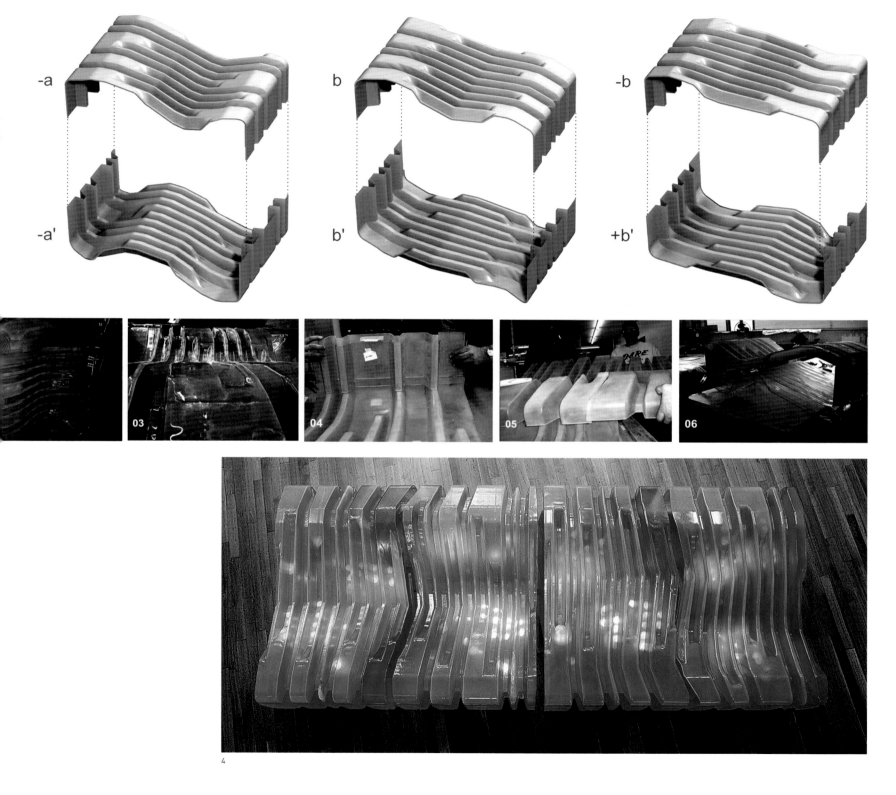

4

1–4_Exhibition layout, diagrams,
fabrication and formal junctioning

SIAL

MELBOURNE

>

The Spatial Information Architecture Laboratory (SIAL), the premier Southern Hemisphere research centre into digital architecture, is a facility for innovation in transdisciplinary design research and education at the Royal Melbourne Institute of Technology. Directed by Mark Burry, it embraces a broad range of investigative modes, involving both highly speculative and industry-linked projects. SIAL is concerned with the integration of technical, theoretical and social concerns as part of its innovative agenda. High-end computing, modelling and communication tools associated with disparate disciplines are combined with traditional production techniques. Researchers are engaged in a wide variety of projects that collaboratively disturb artificial distinctions between the physical and virtual, digital and analogue, scientific and artistic, instrumental and philosophical.

SIAL provides the opportunity to research new strategies for viewing and managing information in a spatial perspective. Instead of information technology constraining design decisions to two-dimensional abstractions, representations and models, the whole process is conducted from concept to realization 'in space' (the 'space' perhaps 'physical' for engineering and architectural applications, electronic for collaboration at a distance, and equally 'organizational' in creating new business structures).

Dynamic information facade

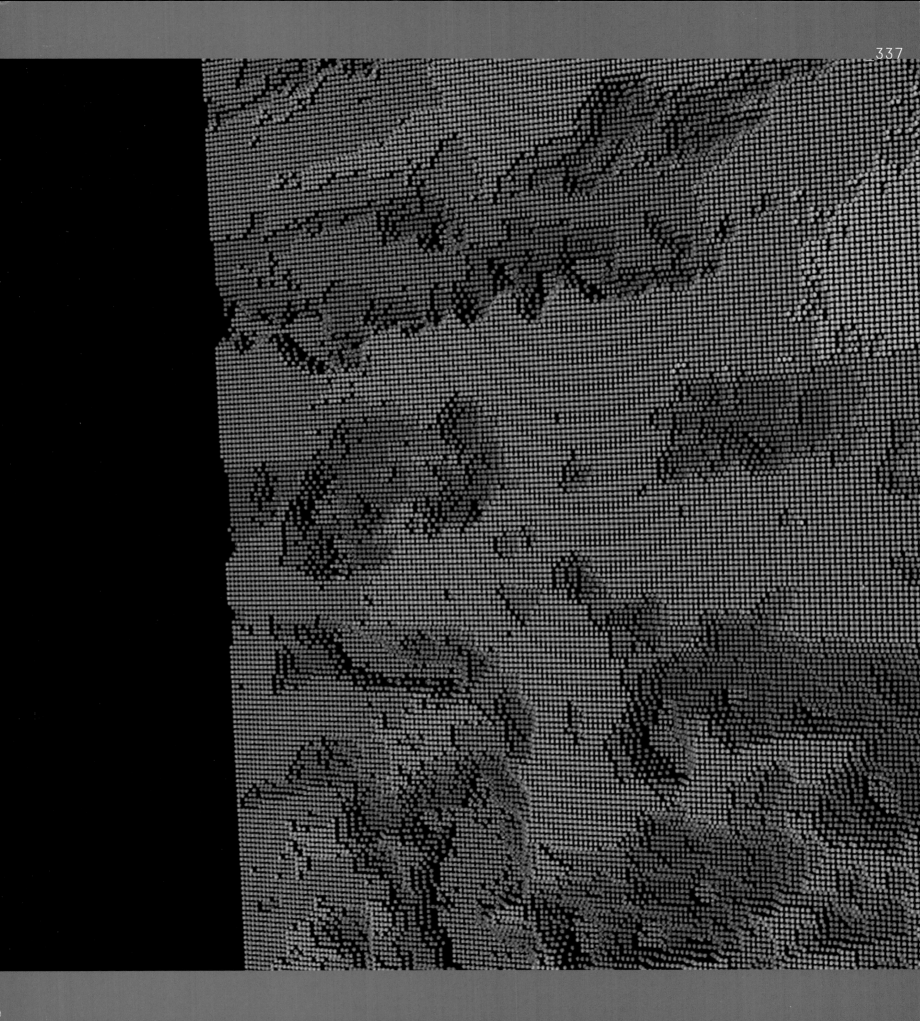

Spatial Dynamic Media System
Melbourne

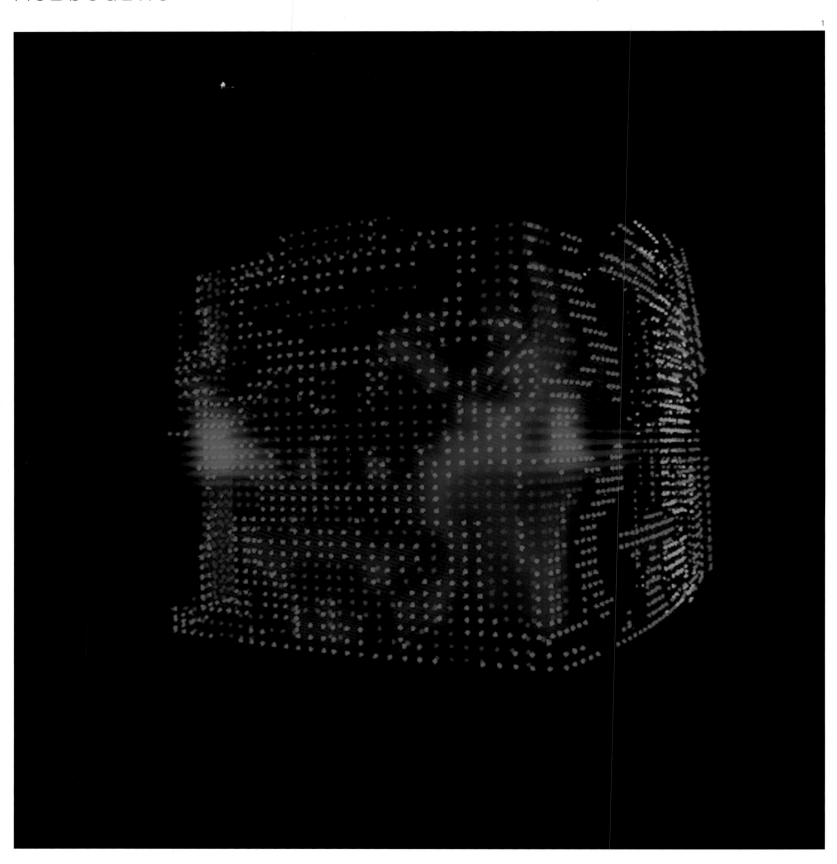

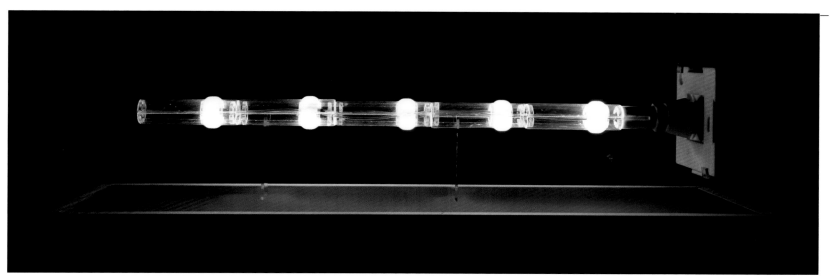

The core project has been the development of a system as an extension of existing media façades to allow the testing of the representation of information and ideas as 'form' within space that is constantly generated and regenerated as a result of fresh input. The hypothesis is that this real-time reconfiguration of space using light offers a variety of new perceptions ranging from information sharing to public art never experienced previously. An extensive body of evidence points to a growing scholarship around the details and impacts of media-façade technological developments and the content displayed on them. This project defines the boundaries of these shifts and enhanced content combinations limited to two dimensions. Also considered are the technical and media implications of extending conventional 2-D screens, currently limited to architectural cladding, into a 3-D matrix, thereby causing an alteration to spatial perception.

1–3_Media façade surface, detail and skin close-up

Informing Design Exploration
Melbourne

> The Australian equivalent of MIT's Media
> Lab blazes a trail into digital space and
> its structural opportunities.

1

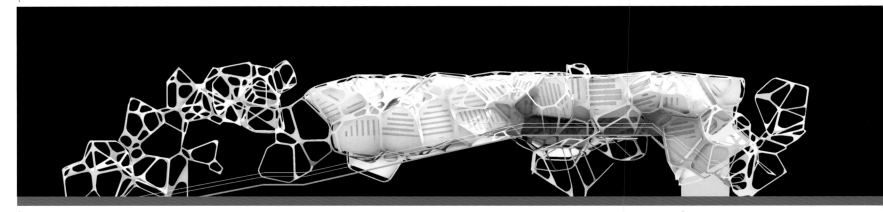

2

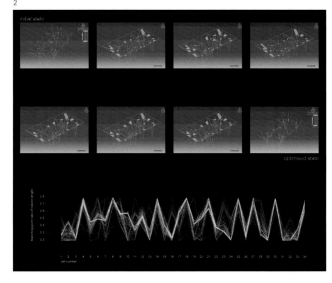

3

Increasingly, building complexity and the limits of time and budget are seen as requiring earlier interaction between architects and engineers, at a stage when design information is incomplete and relatively imprecise but the benefits of such interaction are greatest. Getting the engineers in early is something that is increasingly desired, perhaps even required, but the role they might play in enabling design exploration and the processes that support it are relatively undefined. This research aims to better understand how digital tools can enable early design exploration across domain boundaries. The research is being undertaken by an architect working within a consulting-engineering firm, and comprises live projects and research from within that practice. The hypothesis is that, during the early design phase, performance-based digital processes can short-circuit problems of translation within architect / engineer collaborations. However, their use challenges us to reassess the way in which we conceptualize the processes by which we share knowledge effectively across boundaries.

1–3_Early design interaction between
engineer and architect
4_Images identify the structure's
different zones

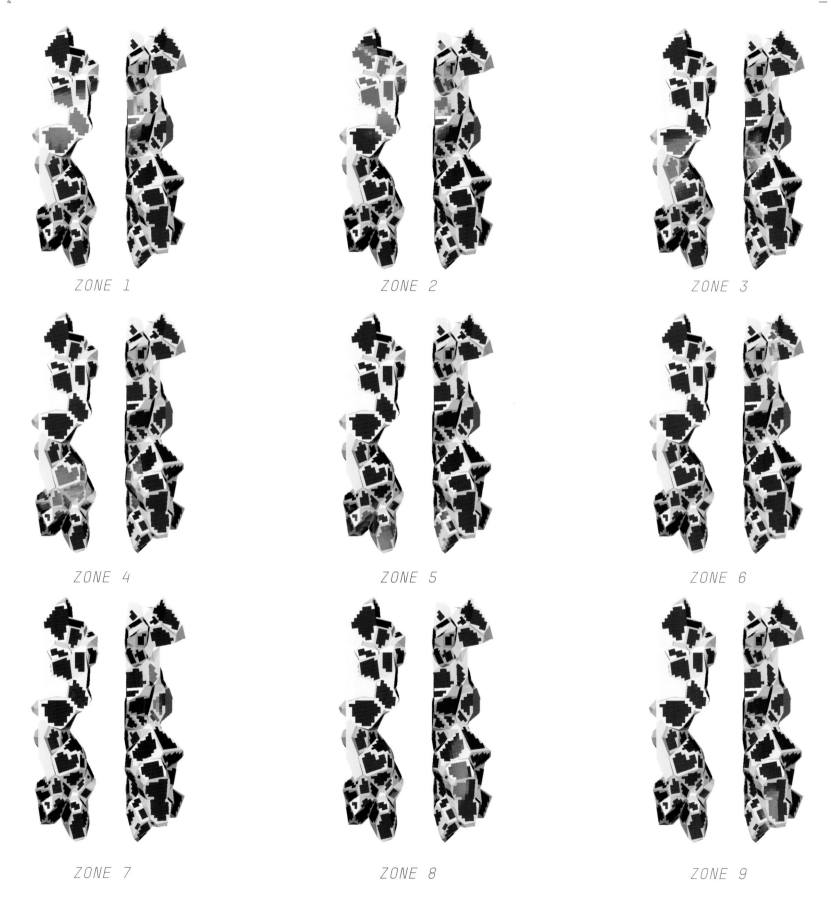

ZONE 1

ZONE 2

ZONE 3

ZONE 4

ZONE 5

ZONE 6

ZONE 7

ZONE 8

ZONE 9

Freefab – Concrete Rapid Manufacturing Melbourne

This research project addresses the most compelling of sustainability issues: the building industry and the way we build.

The construction industry is clearly in need of radical change. It consumes much of the world's resources and produces approximately 30 per cent of the world's waste. It is also the most inefficient of the world's high-capital industries. To compound the problem, buildings themselves are wasteful and inefficient. If the way we build can be fundamentally changed, huge gains could be made towards a sustainable future.

This research explores how a concrete rapid-manufacturing (RM) technique (under development) could be used in the construction industry. This technology, an offshoot of rapid prototyping and rapid manufacturing, is similar to that of 3-D printers, which lay down concrete in successive layers without the use of formwork. This technology has the potential to revolutionize the way we build by nesting concrete RM, CAD / CAM (including parametric modelling and optimization) and state-of-the-art fabrication technologies used by the construction and parallel industries.

The end product could negate the problems traditionally associated with the construction industry, such as large-scale repetition of elements and issues of tolerance and rework on site, while achieving dramatically higher quality and environmental performance.

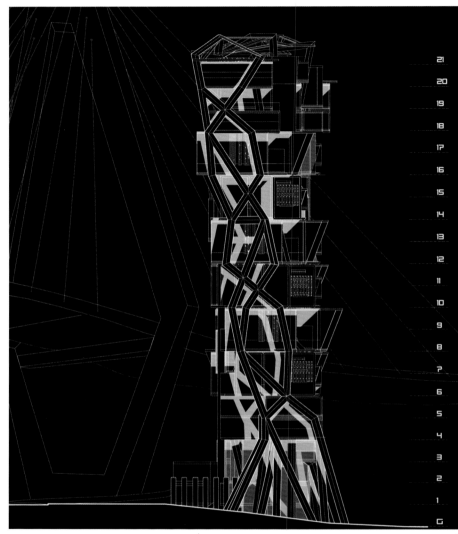

2

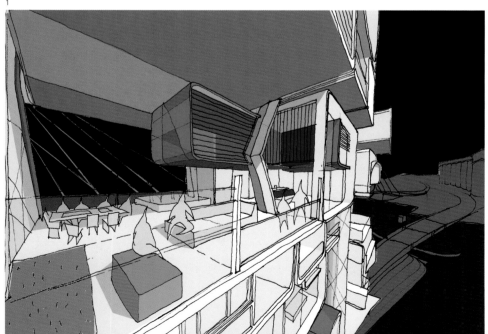

1

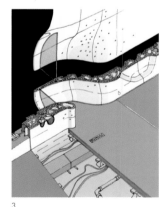

3

1–3_Concrete can be used as a material of rapid manufacture

Pavilion for New Architecture
Melbourne

This experimental structure was built for an architecture exhibition that proposed to capture the experiential quality of space, as opposed to the standard practice of presenting images of buildings on the wall. Using an integrated parametric process, a series of operations was undertaken on the honeycomb grid of a geodesic sphere, resulting in a cube of cells converging on a single point in space. To construct the piece, the cells were individually cut out of card, refolded and fixed to their adjacent cells. This structure was then suspended from the ceiling, allowing visitors to duck underneath and position their heads at the point of convergence. There only the edges were visible, and the piece appeared as a net. As depth dissolves, one senses that one is at the centre of an enormous system – Leonardo's Vitruvian Man in a galaxy of mid-twentieth-century geometry.

1–2_Cellular pavilion:
Overall and construction detail

SIXTEEN*
(MAKERS)
>

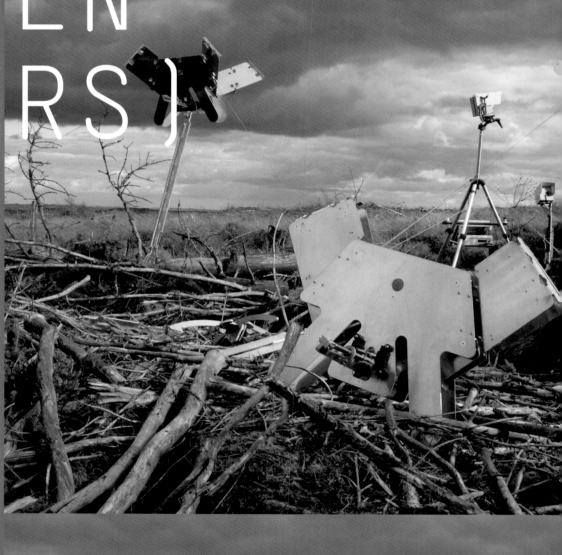

Kielder installation

LONDON

sixteen*(makers) is a group of four architects (Phil Ayres, Nick Callicott, Chris Leung and Bob Sheil), some engaged in professional practice, some in fabrication and some in research. The practice was formed in London in 1994 out of a shared ambition to sustain an experimental approach in the practice and development of architecture.

The work of the practice can best be described by the phrase 'Design through Making'. In recent years, while pursuing a broad set of teaching commitments at the Bartlett University College London, sixteen*(makers) has executed a number of projects in the field of responsive constructs and environments. The practice seeks direct engagement with a broad set of skills from drawing to making, where each affects the outcome of form and space.

For sixteen*(makers) sites are central to the development of all architectural projects. The practice regards access and occupation of architecture in progress as of equal importance to completed work. At the core of its approach is the gathering of information from which spatial and formal interventions are proposed.

sixteen*(makers) has a long history of creating work that asks questions of architecture and its users. The practice also synthesizes analogue workshop techniques with digital methodology, and it is in exploring this hybridized space of making that sixteen*(makers) comes into its own.

Blusher
Exhibition installation, London

Blusher was created in response to an invitation to participate in a year-long national touring exhibition across six venues entitled 'Making Buildings'. Unlike others in the show, sixteen*(makers) were commissioned to design and fabricate a new work specifically for the exhibition. The intervention could be reconfigured at each venue as a response to its specific spatial qualities. The project also explored how such a proposition might reflect, or act upon, the continually transforming and transient conditions of its context, including the presence and activity of exhibition visitors. Subsequently, the work was designed to explore spatial and temporal relationships between occupants and their environment. The focus was threefold: to explore variability and adaptability in the design and manufacture of architectonic components; to explore occupant behaviour in relation to alternate configurations of the assembly from venue to venue; and to investigate how such a system might act upon the variable behaviour of its occupants.

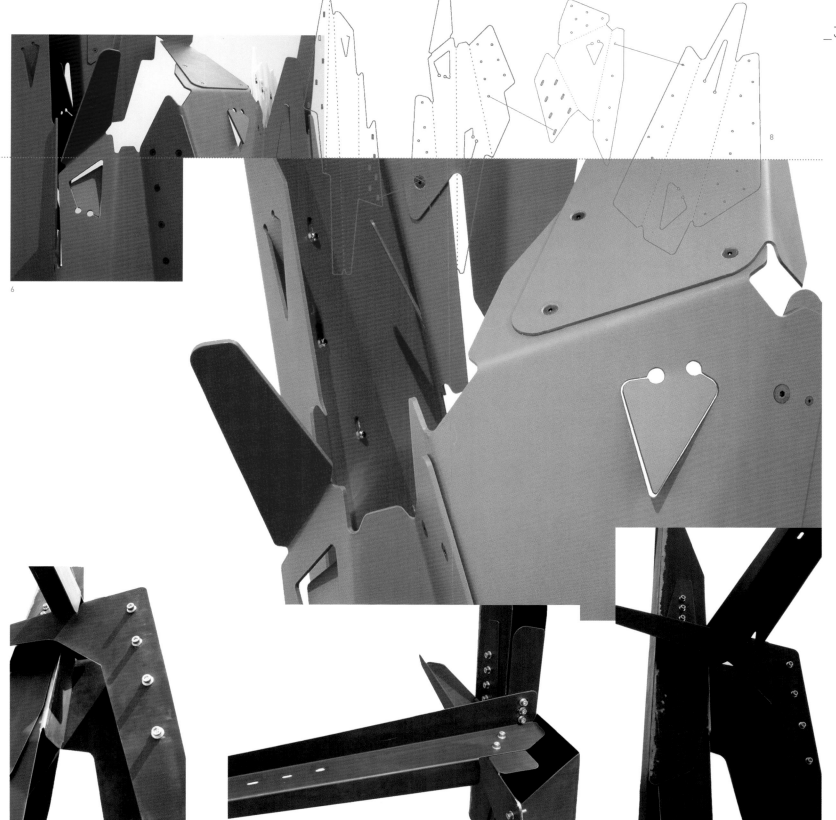

1–7_Blusher deployed in various contexts and configurations
8_Individual element arrangements

Kielder Residency
Kielder, UK

2

Bespoke surveying 'probes' were designed to act as dual monitors and responsive artefacts. The probes were installed on an approved test site chosen for its remoteness and variety. It was adjacent to a dense territory of trees, an area recently harvested and an area planted with saplings. The probes were designed to measure difference over time rather than the static characteristics of any given instance; powered by solar energy, they gathered and recorded 'micro-environmental data'. The probes were simultaneously and physically responsive to these changes, opening out when warm and sunny, closing down when cold and dark.

This aspect of the work generated three critical issues for design in relation to surveying methods. First, how do surveys become active tools in making design decisions? What is measured in a place will have a bearing on what is designed for that place. Second, how can micro-environmental conditions inform site selection? Different sites will induce different behaviours – for example, a site in constant shade will not be as animated as one that dips in and out of shade. Third, how can scope and variability in micro-environmental conditions drive passively activated responsive behaviour year round? The peaks and troughs of visitor numbers at this particular site correspond with seasonal variation. An architecture that responds to seasonal variation will be in synthesis with the same peaks and troughs.

1

1–5_Kielder interactive surveying installation

3

4

5

27 4:26PM

27 2:56PM

27 12:37PM

StaC
London

1

2

3

The advent of CAD / CAM reconfigured the relationship between representation and realization. What new strategies relating the 'making of information' to the 'making of things' does this reconfiguration permit, and how might these strategies exploit the implicit potential of CAD / CAM for the making of variety and difference?

A light-gathering conduit was constructed in an old observatory; the contraption was suspended by a neoprene gasket that allowed the conduit base to fully pivot within the instrument body. As local wind conditions drove the conduit, data gathered from an array of light-dependant resistors embedded within the hemispherical interior of the instrument body were analyzed to infer wind direction, wind intensity and ambient light level. An embedded microprocessor analyzed the data locally and in real time, converting environmental data into geometric instructions formatted as a command script. Running the script would construct a fully described 3-D model of an object with generic features attaining a specificity reflecting the conditions of the temporal snapshot. If desired, the object could then be directly manufactured using additive techniques similar to those used to construct the instrument body.

While the system was successful in that 'real-world' data could be fed back into the digital matrix to inform a 3-D representation in an automated manner, the resultant objects possessed a mute inertia. Prior objects lacked any possibility of feedback to subsequent ones. Without feedback informing the iteration, there was no indication of resultant objects exhibiting increasingly specific attributes over time.

1–6_StaC fabrication and details

5

4

> sixteen*(makers) combines
a familiarity with advanced
programming, a cybernetic
view of the world and a
compositional exactitude.

6

NEIL SPILLER

>

LONDON

Neil Spiller has pioneered research into the impact of advanced technology on architectural design and practice. His interests include nanotechnology, biotechnology, virtuality, media theory, contemporary architectural theory and history.

Spiller founded Neil Spiller Architects in 1993 in London, having gained a reputation as a visionary architect and free thinker. Currently he is engaged in a long-term research project that utilizes digital and biological technology to reinvent the age-old relationship between architecture and landscape. Spiller believes that the spatial notions of the Surrealists, arcane cosmologies and the Art of Memory are all up for re-evaluation in the face of the huge ontological changes taking place within architecture due to advances in technology.

Spiller aims to illustrate how contemporary architects are still only using a small proportion of the processes and techniques that are open to them. This, he believes, is because of how they have been taught and their adherence to fashionable aesthetic choices that identify them as members of a kind of hip digital coterie. Spiller's own world is full of vacillating objects, sensing mechanisms and poetic 'Pataphysical swerves.

Communicating Vessels: Gradiva Revolving and Catching sculpture

Bee Gates
Fordwich, Kent, England

If one attached an antenna to a bee's forehead and allowed a computer to record a short section of its flight pattern, the vectors could then be made to be the geometries of a kind of heavy-metal Art Nouveau gate, formed from foggy aerogel, only fleetingly there, billowing in the breeze like cigarette smoke slowly dispersing.

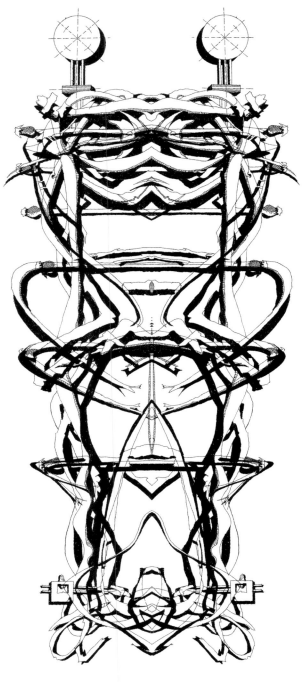

2

1_Bee Gate in context
2_Bee Gate configuration
3_Holey Hedge

Dee Trunks
Fordwich, Kent, England

The interiors of the various boxes enclose mechanical tableaux. Each box has two slightly inclined opposite sides. There is a small table in the centre. On the floor are some draught pistons, a cucumber, two De Chirico mannequins (one a dummy-headed pseudo-Classical plinth, the other a seated figure with what looks like a chess pawn for a head), an umbrella, some Swiftian academic gear-age, a ready-made bicycle wheel attached to a stool, a Duchampian voyeur's door, a shelf on which five artificial pairs of lips are perched, another shelf supporting an alembic and a turd-shaped mystery object (bread or a bandaged arm?). A Giacometti bird is imprisoned behind cool glass. Can I just see a little insect hugging the corner? Also on the table is a box with calf's-lungs rails beneath it. Mounted on a large Anglepoise is the 'Clinamen', inspired by Alfred Jarry's 'Painting Machine' of the same name.

Jarry's machine is a gyroscope that whirls at random through a 'Palace of Machines' vandalizing masterpieces by blowing a succession of primary colours ranged according to the tubes of its stomach. The Clinamen of this project also whirls, spraying paint from the tendrils of its anemone-like head. It is a maverick painting machine with no respect. It is activated when the box is sat upon and deactivated when the sitter stands up.

Also inside all the boxes are invisible computer-generated topologies that slither around, through and over the artefacts. The boxes are an editing engine and will mostly be used to develop new Surrealist poetry. The information topology can be re-coupled to other data sets when appropriate or when totally inappropriate.

1

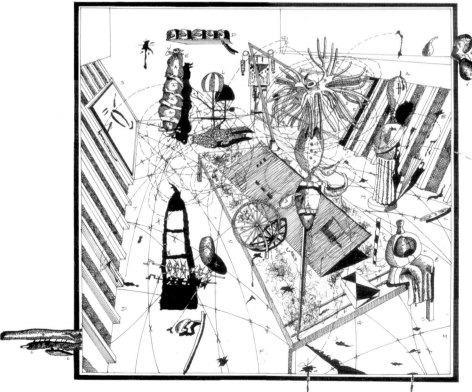

> Spiller reminds architects that there is much Surreal potential in digital technology.

1_Exterior on riverbank
2_Plan
3_Interior perspective

Velazquez Machine and Growing Vistas
Paris, Rome and Fordwich, Kent, England

At the heart of this project are two input machines: the Velazquez Machine, situated in the Orangerie in the Tuileries in Paris, and a not very smart measuring stick placed in and around Bramante's Tempietto in Rome. The Stick searches for discrepancies between the idealized and the theoretically repeatable but ultimately unobtainable dimensions of Classicism. The Velazquez Machine vibrates to activity on the Web, and fish decompose at its centre. All of these phenomena are recorded and transmitted back to the mother site in Fordwich and provide the driver data for Growing Vistas made of aerogel, meandering sculptures and digital chance. The formal quality of this work acts as a memory theatre and quotes from the history of art and virtuality.

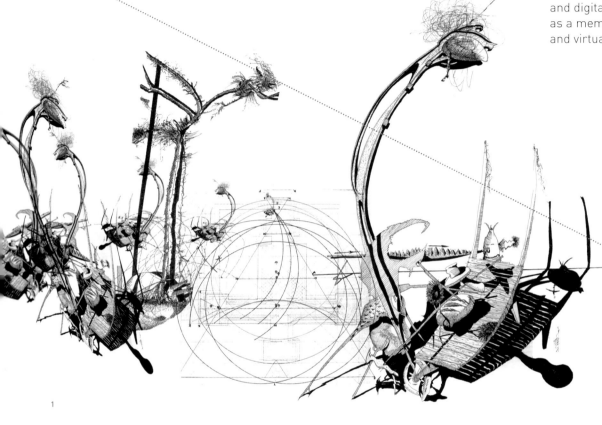

1

1_Growing Vista: Sculpture movement
2_Temple of Repose at source of vista
3_Communicating Vessels site plan
4_Island and vista growth plan

2

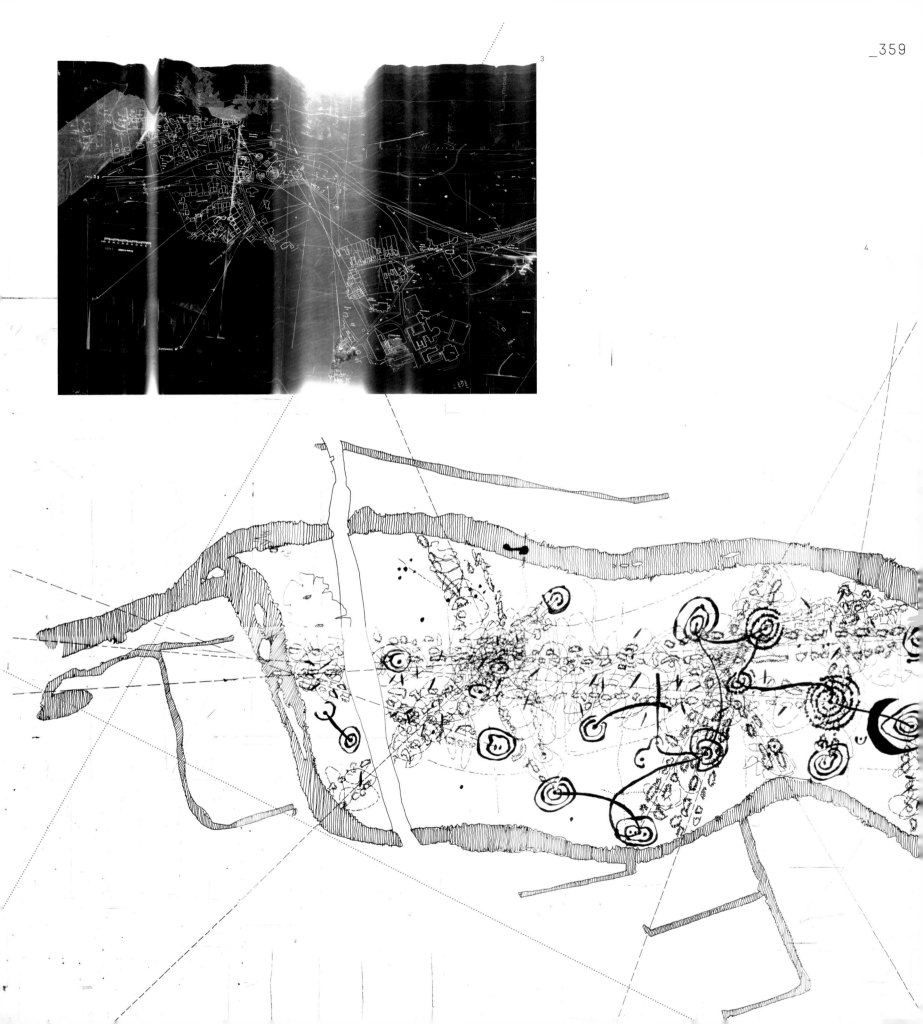

AFTERWORD

>

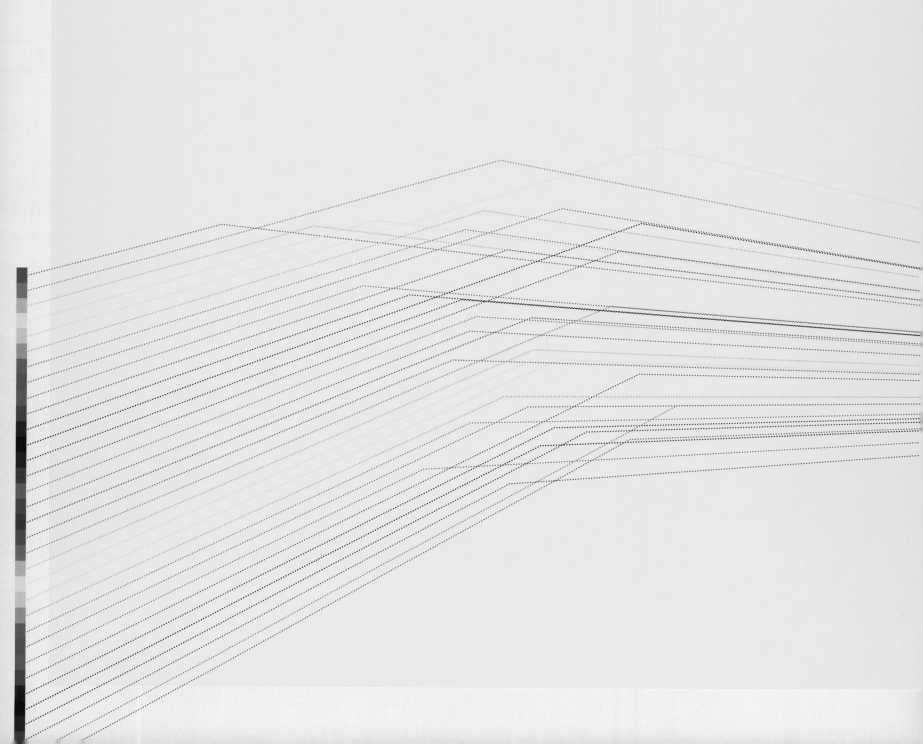

PLECTIC ARCHITECTURE: TOWARDS A THEORY OF THE POST-DIGITAL IN ARCHITECTURE

1

1–2_Christian Kerrigan
Harnessing the Growth Imperative

DEFINITIONS

First, it is important to stress that 'Post-Digital Architecture' is not architecture without a digital component. It is very much a synthesis of the virtual, the actual, the biological, the cyborgian, the augmented and the mixed. It is impossible, anymore, to talk of Digital Architecture as a binary opposite to normal, real-world architecture. Cyberspace has insinuated itself into our existence, at every scale and at every turn.

The physicist Murray Gell-Mann has defined 'Plectics' as

> the study of simplicity and complexity. It includes the various attempts to define complexity; the study of roles of simplicity and complexity and of classical and quantum information in the history of the universe, the physics of information; the study of non-linear dynamics, including chaos theory, strange attractors, and self-similarity in complex non-adaptive systems in physical science; and the study of complex adaptive systems, including prebiotic chemical evolution, biological evolution, the behaviour of individual organisms, the functioning of ecosystems, the operation of mammalian immune systems, learning and thinking, the evolution of human languages, the rise and fall of human cultures, the behavior of markets, and the operation of computers that are designed or programmed to evolve strategies – say, for playing chess, or solving problems.[i]

If we start to think of the architecture featured in this book as the first stirrings of a Plectic Post-Digital Architecture, then Gell-Mann's mid-1980s definition seems a suitably broad umbrella beneath which to situate it. Such terrain can include a variety of complex architectural subcultures that are all composed of differing degrees of the digital, the virtual, the biological and the nanotechnological without banishing more off-piste, often less fashionable investigations, propositions and researches. Above all, these architectures seek to simplify, amplify or facilitate and make visible the complex entanglement of contemporary space. The etymology of 'Plectics' speaks of braiding. Gell-Mann's description resonates with current architectural concerns:

> It is important, in my opinion, for the name to connect with both simplicity and complexity. What is most exciting about our work is that it illuminates the chain of connections between, on the one hand, the simple underlying laws that govern the behavior of all matter in the universe and, on the other hand, the complex fabric that we see around us, exhibiting diversity, individuality, and evolution. The interplay between simplicity and complexity is the heart of our subject. Likewise, if the parts of a complex system or the various aspects of a complex situation, all defined in advance, are studied carefully by experts on those parts or aspects and the results of their work are pooled, an adequate description of the whole system or situation does not usually emerge. The reason, of course, is that these parts or aspects are typically entangled with one another. We have to supplement the partial studies with a transdisciplinary 'crude look at the whole,' and practitioners of plectics often do just that.[ii]

It is this trans-disciplinarity and reflexivity that architects can often offer.

UNDERSTANDING THE ARCHITECTURAL DESIGN OF ARCHITECTURAL DESIGN

3

3_Massimo Minale
Rebooting Natural Ecologies:
Sound plates and algae
4_Lena Andersson
Mnemonics and the Ghost in the Machine:
Twinkles of movement on the periphery

4

Such an architecture must also address itself to the many epistemological unknowables in our world. Plectic Architecture cannot be developed as one would conduct a series of scientific experiments: objectively and sacrosanctly. First, we must establish an understanding of the activity of 'design' and the 'ontology of the designer'. Plectic Architecture can be nothing if not a second-order cybernetic system and its designers nothing if not epistemologically observing and acting conversational dynamos. Second-order cybernetics is relational; it never excludes the observer or the observer of the observer of a system. We must understand that everyone's world-view is different, and we construct our world-views by interacting and building, in short by having conversations with people, objects and ideas.

Language has a propensity for inaccuracy, for personalization, for misconstruing, for misreading and for relativity, and it is subjective. Scientists perceive themselves as fighting against this ontology and ask us to believe in objective and ubiquitous language to describe their allegedly ubiquitous knowledge. It is here that science's biggest error has been made, and it is here that poetry – through its acceptance of the ontology of language – has bloomed. Ranulph Glanville and his collaborators narrowed this problem down to the denial of the concept of 'I' in scientific reportage:

'To pretend that what is written is written without a writer seems to me to profoundly and intentionally misrepresent what is going on, at least as I understand it ... Rather, it is that the I needs not to be excluded, for to exclude it is to create an epistemology that we cannot sustain. Without the I there would be nothing to report and no one to report it.'[iii]

The practice of architectural design in the twentieth century was seduced by this impersonal way of documenting and describing science – denying the 'I'. Architectural discourse camouflages this lacuna with the myth of the hero-architect, visionary genius and beneficent form-giver. This approach has throughout the years fostered a Modernist mistrust of narrative, decoration, symbolism and anyone or anything seen to be 'self-indulgent' or of expressionist personality. This stripped-down architecture has been reductively honed to almost nothing – an ubiquitous plainness. All that distinguishes one building from another is the filmiest zone of cladding produced by a limited number of cladding manufacturers. One cannot preordain the way architecture is seen, observed and interacted with. The nuances that architecture delivers can only be personal and personally mnemonic to the observer / user – in short, a moveable feast, a radical constructivist mind-dependant reality, a nomadic science.

When I design, I make space by putting things together, creating void from mass and mass from void. When I put things together, I like them to do more than one job – to be multivalent. I might like an element to be structural and decorated, and change in position related to a predetermined algorithm, and that algorithm might be able to fluctuate in time, changing its criteria and optimization logistics. I might construct narratives about the whole or the pieces that allow me to develop deeper and more resonantly complex semiotics. I might like to take the view that my work is part of the 'Modernist Project' and that its functionalism includes its symbolic nuances. The conversation between my work and the user / viewer of it (and the ability or inability of the observer to understand and decode my intentions) should be able to evolve in all manner of associations and hierarchies, some considered by me and others not.

These internal (to me) and external (to me) conversations are all languages and metalanguages which are a rich broth of symbiotic interaction between me, my inspirations, my architectural lexicon and idiosyncrasies, my intent and the observers' / users' preoccupations, memories, and formal associations and intent. These systems are a-scalar universes of discourse. Cybernetically speaking, a universe of discourse denotes the entire set of ideas, notions and concepts that are potentially useable in a specific domain. Gordon Pask's Conversation Theory seeks to describe the parameters of conversations. A conversation is circular but not always verbal; it happens when one observes, and one can speak of conversations within conversations, of conversations with humans and also with machines, and our reflections on them define who we are. This is second-order cybernetics.

Design is a second-order cybernetic system; Pask was the first to stress the relevance of cybernetics to architectural design. Pask also introduced the notion that the architectural profession might start to use computers as surrogate assistants:

> **One final manoeuvre will indicate the flavour of a cybernetic theory. Let us turn the design paradigm in upon itself; let us apply it to the interaction between the designer and the system he designs, rather than the interaction between a system and the people who inhabit it. The glove fits, almost perfectly in the case when a designer uses a computer as his assistant. In other words, the relation 'controller / controlled entity' is preserved when these omnibus words are replaced by 'designer / system being designed' or by 'systematic environment / inhabitants' or by 'urban plan / city'. But notice the trick, the designer is controlling the construction of control systems and consequently design is control of control, i.e. the designer does much the same job as his system, but he operates at a higher level in the organisation hierarchy.[iv]**

All designers are different and feel that they have something original to bring to their world, solving problems in an original or idiosyncratic way. No two designers are the same, no two designs the same, no two sites and no two observers or users (and all change over time and have varying durations). These facts have led me to view the world as exceptional, as particular, as a series of cybernetic personal and conversational mnemonic events. My own design work within this blooming tapestry should do nothing more than exploit this systemic paradigm and create poetic moments in its interstices.

So Post-Digital Design must attempt to be immune to sophist arguments of style and good taste. It should rejoice in the particular and the 'I', whatever the 'I' is. (We must remember that objects are now becoming 'I' to a growing extent.)

Above all, Post-Digital Design is relativistic, operates on both a local and global level and is constructed from a genius loci that includes not just anthropomorphic site conditions but also deep ecological pathways, mnemonics, psycho-geography and narrative.

5_Melissa Clinch
Anamorphism and Hypertext

THE CONTINUA OF
ARCHITECTURAL COMPOSITION
AT THE BEGINNING OF THE
TWENTY-FIRST CENTURY

The experience of contemporary designers is one of positioning their work in relation to seven continua. These are:

SPACE

There is a continuum of space that stretches from 'treacle' space – standing in a field, no computer, no mobile phone, no connectivity whatsoever – to full-body immersion in cyberspace. Along the way between these two extremes are all manner of mixed and augmented spaces.

TECHNOLOGY

Like space, technology ranges from simple prosthetics (the stone axe) via the Victorian cog and cam, to the valve, capacitor, logic gate, integrated circuit, central processing unit, quantum computer, stem cell, nanobot and a million states and applications between and beyond.

NARRATIVE, SEMIOTICS AND PERFORMANCE

An architect or designer can choose whether their work operates along a continuum that ranges from minimal engagement in quotation or mnemonic nuance in relation to the history of culture or the contemporary world to embracing the multiplicity of the complex and emergent universes of discourse that we inhabit and engage with daily. A design might conjure up new conjunctions of semiotics as a way of re-reading them. It also might integrate itself with human and cultural memory, and it might be reflexive and performative (in real time or retrospectively).

CYBORGIAN GEOGRAPHY

A designer now can posit work that operates in all manner of mixed and augmented terrains subject to all manner of geomorphic and cyber-morphic factors and drivers.

SCOPIC REGIMES

Architecture can exist at all scales. Everything depends on the resolution of the scope one chooses to use – continents, oceans, cities, streets, rooms, carpets, micro-landscapes and medico-landscape are all part of this continuum.

SENSITIVITY

A designer might decide to make objects, spaces or buildings whose parts are sensitive and can pick up environmental variations or receive information. These sensors therefore can make objects and buildings that are influenced by events elsewhere or indeed are influential elsewhere.

TIME

Time is the most important of these continua. All the others can be time-dependent. Therefore designers can 'mix' the movement of their spaces, buildings and objects up and down the other six continua. So a design might oscillate the spaces within itself with varying elements of virtuality over time. A design might use different technologies at different times in its existence. A design might perform complex mnemonic tableaux at certain points in its life cycle. A design might demand of its occupants the use of a different lens with which to see other than anthropocentric phenomena or spaces. A design might coerce the occupant into being aware of environmental conditions in other locations that change. A design might change the sensitivity of objects over time, dulling them sometimes, making them hypersensitive at others.

6

In other words, it is the negotiation and understanding of these continua that will give us the opportunity mentally, physically and virtually to create Post-Digital Plectic Architecture. While the description of the continua is necessarily relatively simple, the manifestations of such architecture are extraordinary and infinite. It is important to illustrate some its spatial potential. It is also important to note that I have not included sustainable criteria in my continua for two reasons. Any design work done in the twenty-first century must be sustainable in some way. Also sustainability should be embedded in all seven continua. They cannot exist without issues of sustainability and indeed ethics.

For millennia the simple act of building has been in essence one of destruction or, at he very least, ecological truncation and rearticulation. Things and relationships are lost and others formed. A Post-Digital Plectic Architecture needs to buck the entropic trend and to be smart enough to comprehend and respond, if required, to the myriad of natural and artificial ecologies within which it sits. Architects also need to understand that architecture must be bedded into a landscape of ecology that far exceeds the boundaries of any specific site, country and continent, and it is in the spatial manipulation of the relationships in these ecologies that their architecture resides. Architects must understand, appreciate and design within the imperative of flora, fauna, machines and networks, and their architecture must be capable of husbanding the forces of biochemistry, virtuality, movement patterns, the seasonal and the diurnal, and even millennial perturbations, accommodating and rearticulating slow and abrupt phase-changes of sites and landscapes.

The following projects, a knot of positions utilizing the continua described above, are gleaned from work conducted by the AVATAR group at the Bartlett University College London and are presented as harbingers of the future.

6_Glen Tomlin
Nano Re: Creation: Nested painting

(i)   Murray Gell-Mann, 'Plectics', in John Brockman (ed.), *The Third Culture* (New York: Simon and Schuster, 1995)
(ii)   Murray Gell-Mann, 'Let's Call it Plectics', *Complexity*, 1/5 (1995/96).
(iii) R. Glanville, S. Sengupta and G. Forey, 'A(Cybernetic) Musing: Language and Science in the Language of Science', *Cybernetics and Human Knowing*, 5/4 (1998).
(iv) Gordon Pask, 'The Architectural Relevance of Cybernetics', *Architectural Design* (September, 1969).

MASSIMO MINALE

7
8

7–10_Massimo Minale
Soundplates seen from below water level.

REBOOTING NATURAL ECOLOGIES

Since the Industrial Revolution, bulk manufacturing processes have polluted and torn the delicate interrelationships of the natural world. Those natural relationships set in particular landscapes and geomorphic and economic conditions can create local rituals, cuisine and indigenous variations of animals and plants. Massimo Minale's project is situated in the Camargue and aims to optimize the indigenous fish populations. He does this by using four differently scaled sonic devices, each type employed in varying clusters to guide fish to various aquatic environments that suit the stages of their life cycles. The project has diurnal, seasonal and annual cycles and was inspired by Minale's earlier research into micro-sound. Under the skin of the musical note lies the realm of micro-sound, of sound particles lasting less than a tenth of a second. Recent technological advances have allowed us to probe and manipulate these pinpoints of sound, dissolving the traditional building blocks of music and, more importantly, architecture into a more fluid and supple medium. Whole sites, from the rasping drone of a car's exhaust to the flicker of a fly's wing, can be granulated down into points, pulses, lines and surfaces. Particle densities evaporate and mutate into one another, giving birth to fluid landscapes, spanning continents.

9

10

CHRISTIAN KERRIGAN

HARNESSING THE GROWTH IMPERATIVE

Christian Kerrigan's work is predicated on the fact that if one puts metal corsets around growing trees, it encourages timber to grow that has a higher density and therefore can be more effectively used to construct things. This extreme bonsai technique can utilize other technologies such as nanotechnology that can create within sections of trees a sort of Purist composition of objects growing and harvestable but as yet unseen. In short, the project harvests the growth imperative of trees, particularly a yew-tree copse (the subject of an extensive technical treatise), to grow a ship. This project was to have a two-hundred-year life span as the copse / ship / launching pier slowly grew. Kerrigan sought to understand and choreograph the effect that a radical brief change would have on his system. If he said that around year 150, the ship would become useless but he would need to harness the system to excavate an obelisk, how might this be achieved, using the partially formed ship's timbers? How would the system rearticulate itself? From a theoretical point of view, this project is about a synthesis of the natural and the artificial, and the potential of an architecture of parts that makes another architecture – an architecture before an architecture fuelled by the natural power of growth.

11

12

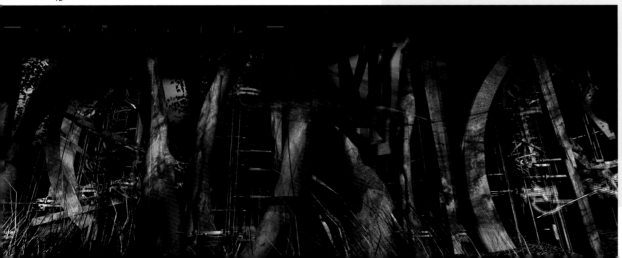

11–14_Christian Kerrigan
Harnessing the Growth Imperative:
Ship- and obelisk-construction machinery

13

14

15

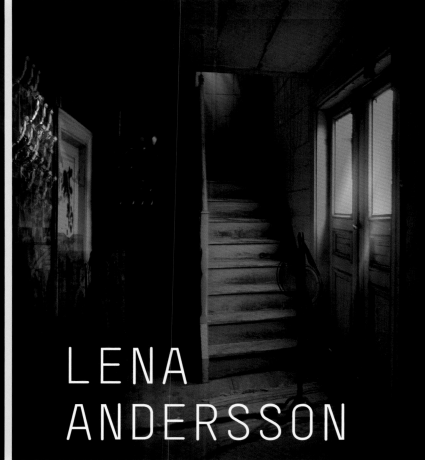

LENA ANDERSSON

MNEMONICS AND THE GHOST IN THE MACHINE

Lena Andersson's work attempts to create an architecture resonating with memory by utilizing the Renaissance Art of Memory and the second-order cybernetics of memory. It also utilizes a range of technology to create its allusions, ambiences and minute vibrations. Andersson's family owns a dilapidated house in Sweden that is now empty. But it has a rich and varied history as a farmhouse, a doctor's house and a grandmother's house. Andersson set about designing a series of small, very subtle architectures that hinted at past events and interactions. The pieces were composed of simple domestic utensils – spoons, bowls and bottles, pieces of a plough – and a doctor's ancient blood-transfusion unit. All the arrangements were given a little power by wind-catchers in the adjacent wood. This enabled them to subtly change position over long periods. These mnemonic micro-architectures exist in Rembrandtian shadow until they are occasionally highlighted by a redirected ray of the sun.

15–17_Lena Andersson
Mnemonics and the Ghost in the Machine:
House vignettes and memory events

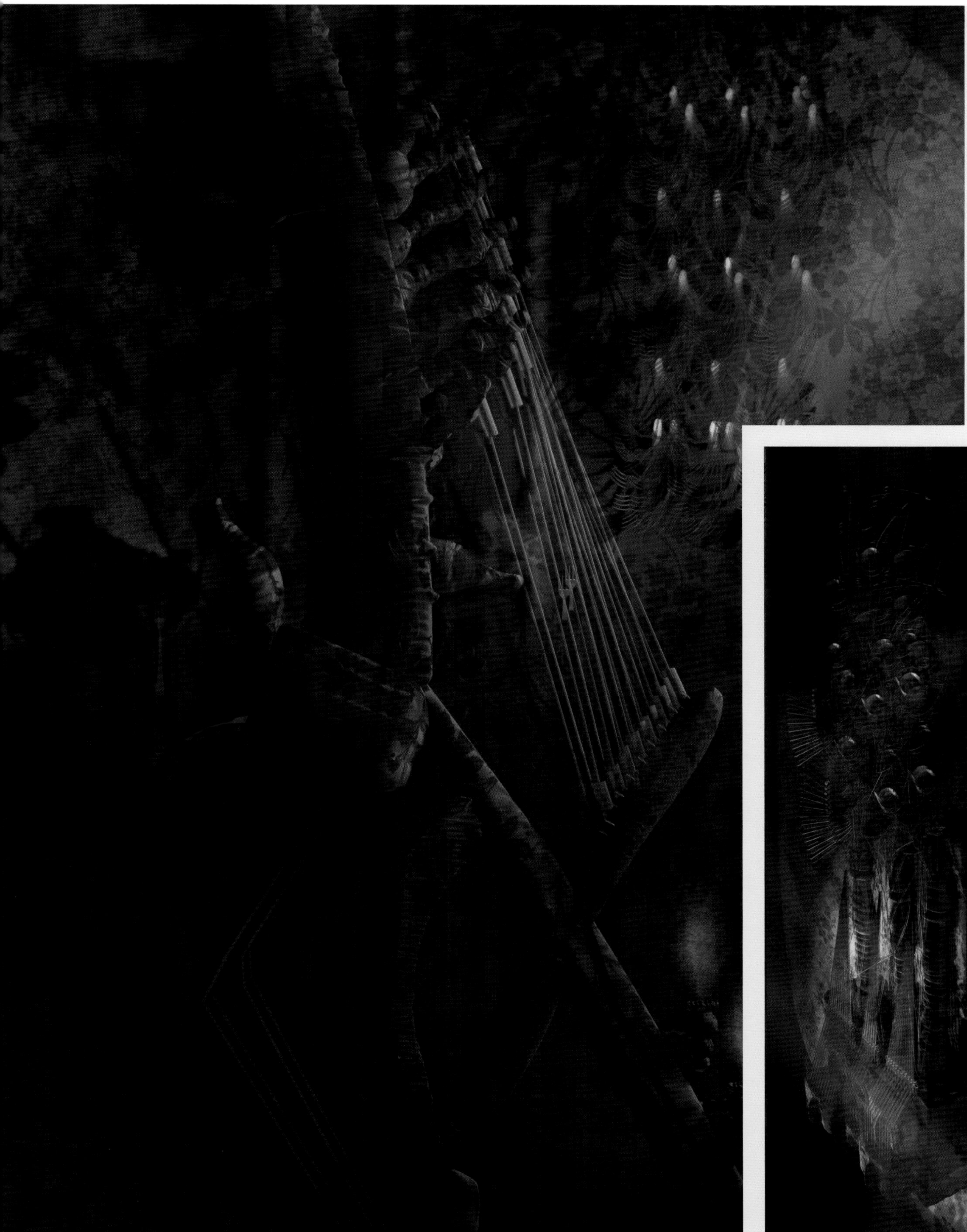

16

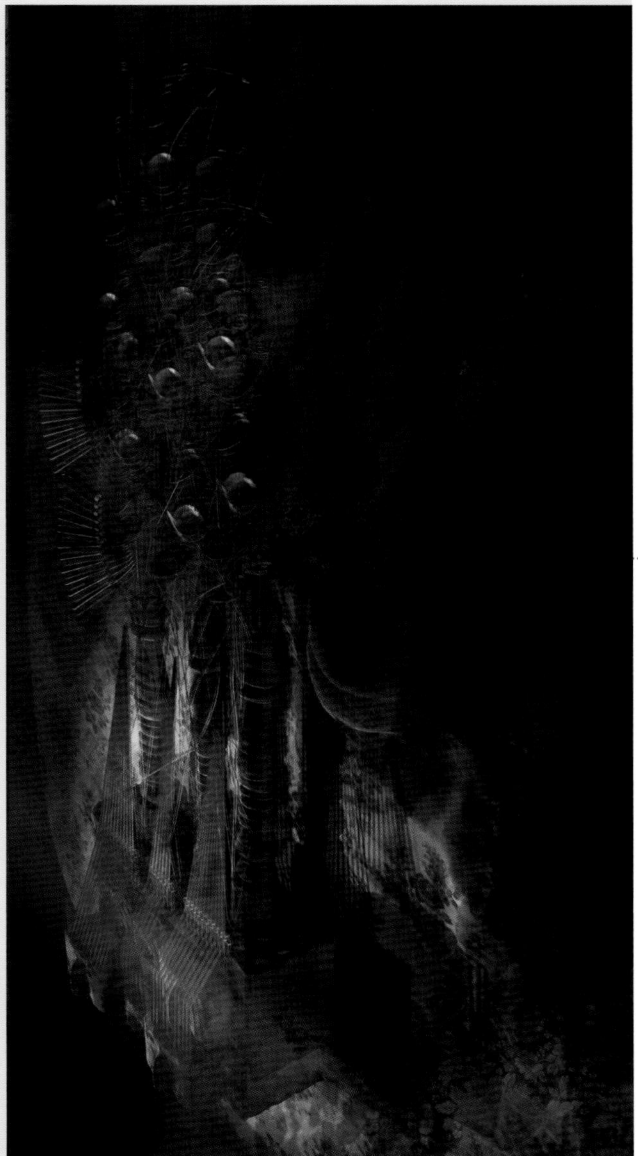

17

GLEN TOMLIN

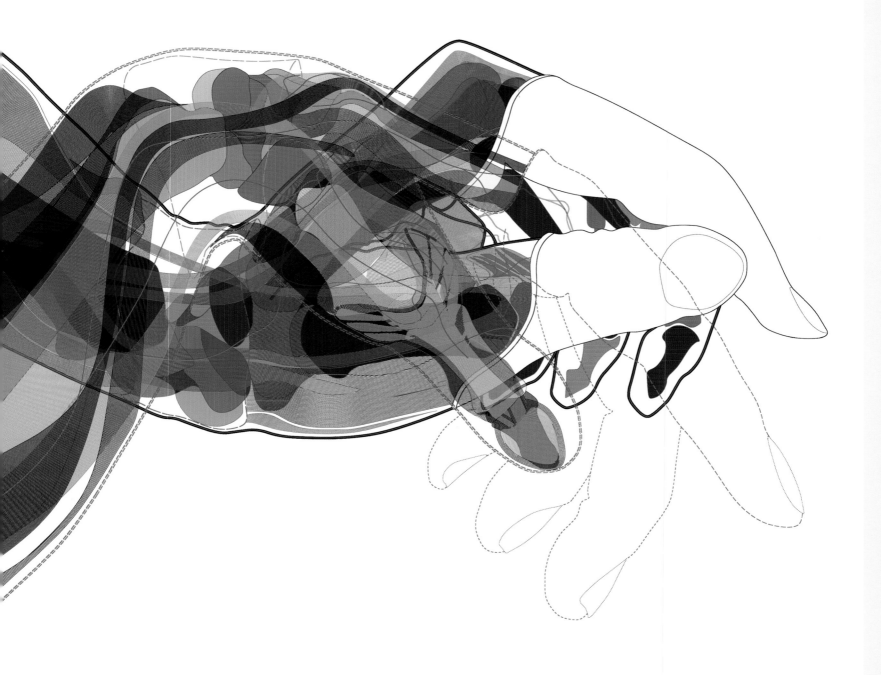

NANO RE:CREATION

Glen Tomlin's research was interested in the myriad vectors and spaces that are never seen or appreciated but that are generated as a side effect of the creation of a recognized masterpiece, in this case Picasso's *Les Demoiselles d'Avignon* (1909). To look at these, he utilized nanotechnological implants at an artist's wrists, elbows and shoulders. So as the work was in progress, three other nested 'paintings' were generated. Simultaneously such nanotechnological devices could act as preventative medical sensors, sensing the health of the user's bone marrow, blood constitution, muscle fibre and nervous system. The project, backed up by extensive technical and medical analysis, revealed a series of architectural spaces that could be provoked, interacted with or used to drive other architectures.

19 20 21 22

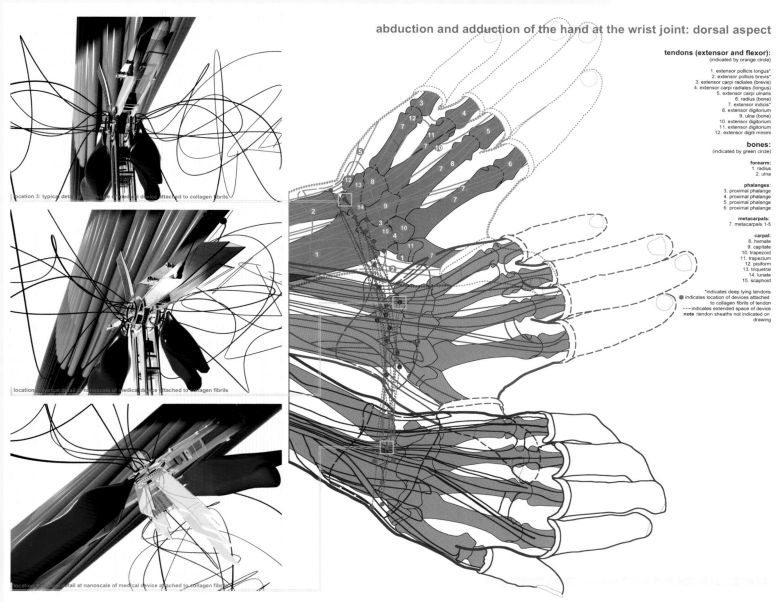

18–22_Glen Tomlin
Nano Re:Creation: Nanotechnological
medico-architectural drawing of wrist joint

MELISSA CLINCH

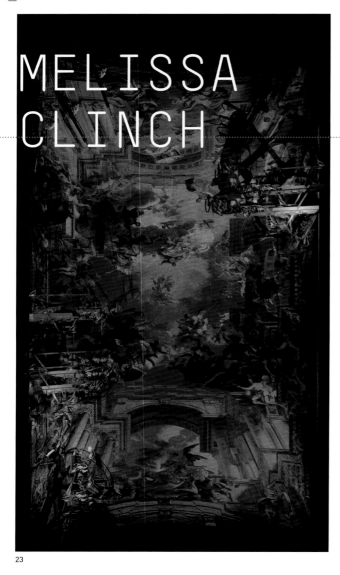

23

ANAMORPHISM AND HYPERTEXT

Melissa Clinch used ideas of architectural anamorphosis to create a series of spaces and semiotics that inhabit the Church of St Ignatius of Loyola in Rome. The church has an anamorphic painted ceiling and an extraordinary anamorphic painted dome. From certain positions in the nave, the dome looks perfectly real, while others reveal it for what it is: a distorted painted form. Clinch positioned three-dimensional forms within the church that create fluctuating spaces according to the dynamics of the observer. These spaces open and collapse as one moves and help the viewer to understand the science of anamorphic projection, and also the rituals and history of the church. These objects operate like four-dimensional hypertexts.

24

23–26_Melissa Clinch
Anamorphism and Hypertext: Objects
anamorphically morph at the Stations
of the Cross

25

26

JAMES CURTIS

27

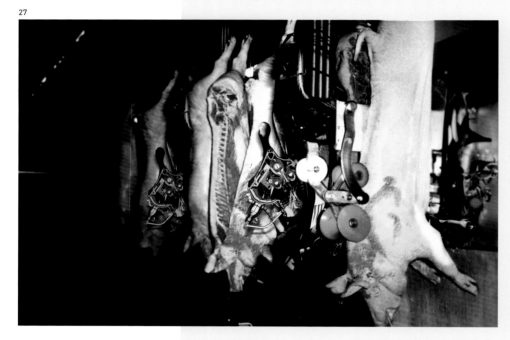

28

MEATY MYTHIC PERFORMANCE

Architecture has always to be considered as durational. It can be diurnal and seasonal, and a whole gamut of other temporal calibrations can and should be applied to it. James Curtis has taken inspiration from Louis Aragon's book *Paris peasant* (1926). After an evening's drinking, Aragon passes by a cane shop in one of Paris' arcades; he describes his vision of floating canes and sirens. Curtis has created an ecology of robotic devices that are dormant during the day and active during the night. They occupy a butcher's shop in London's Islington district and other locations associated with butchery throughout the city. At night the robots act out the myths of ancient Greece using butchers' shop-fronts as proscenium arches within which they can perform. This project, while it is polemic, shows that the contemporary architectural condition in relation to virtuality and digital space asks architects to question established demarcations between performing arts (set design, theatre generally, narrative and so on) and architecture. The hybridization of such forms of cultural output is fecund with possibility.

27–29_James Curtis
Meaty Mythic Performance:
Harpies and Meat

29

HARPIE CELEANO

.106

30

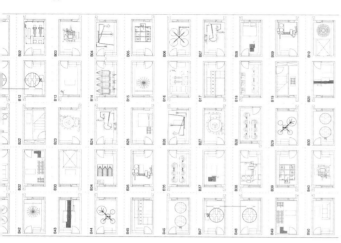

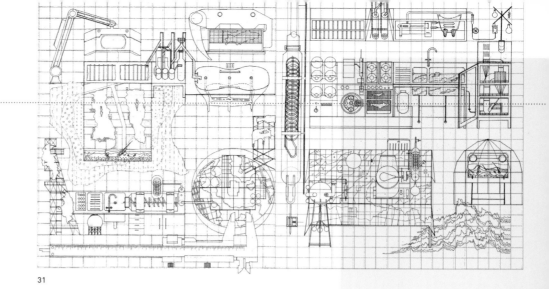

31

32

33

30–35_Sacha Leong
The Biotechnology of Breakfast

SACHA LEONG

THE BIOTECHNOLOGY OF BREAKFAST

Sacha Leong's polemical project focuses on the potential of bioengineering to become ubiquitous and everyday. His project is an artful mix of the scientific with the domestic. Leong explores a near architectural future in which the technologies of biochemistry will be as common and unremarkable as making breakfast. Breakfast, after all, is a biotechnological experiment practised time and time again. Leong then creates a lexicon of elements that can function as breakfast utensils and biotechnical laboratory equipment. The project culminates in a full-size installation and asks what is unusual anymore. Are we not indistinguishable from the advanced processes we manage to manipulate? What is normal for humanity now? Are we all not biotechnological engineers?

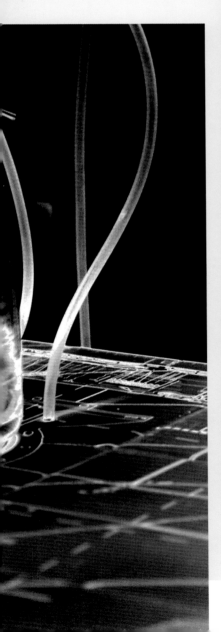

34

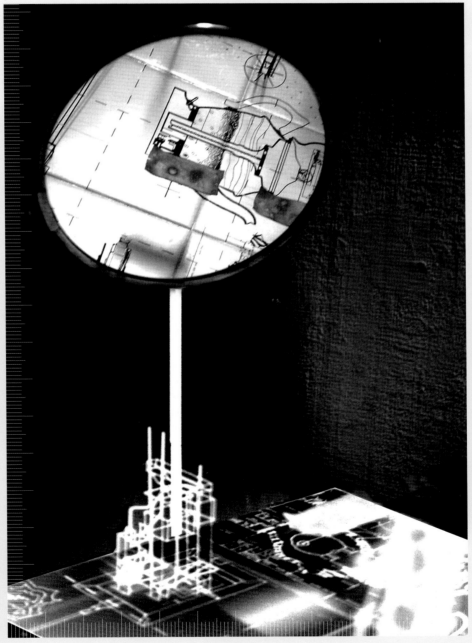

35

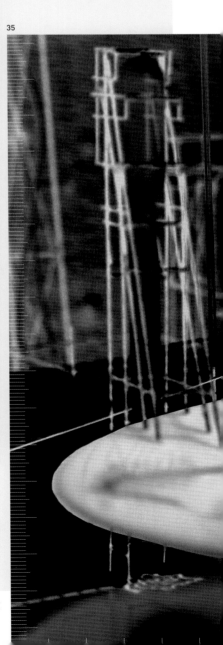

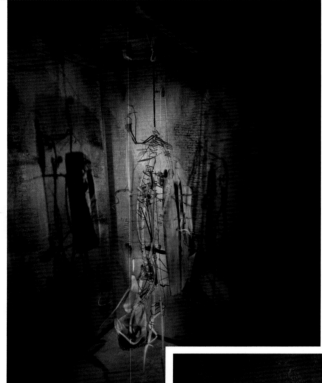

MARTHA MARKOPOULOU

THE SPACES OF LITERATURE

Martha Markopoulou's research project focuses on an inquiry into the possible relations between language and architecture; it is based on the novel *Salammbô* by Gustave Flaubert (1862). It explores how an architectural system could embody a novel's narrative and syntax, and how we could construct a physical reality out of this. The project is an attempt to conceive of architecture as the physical body of a 'fluid text'. It consists of a series of softly oscillating devices that translate in space and time the conditions found in the narrative concerning points of view and changes of direction, speed, perspective and scale. The barbaric aesthetic aims to reveal the exotic beauty that exists in Salammbô's literary world.

37

36

36–38_Martha Markopoulou
The Spaces of Literature

38

SOURCES

AMID* architecture

Cristina Díaz Moreno and Efrén García Grinda have been associate professors of Architecture at Escuela Técnica Superior de Arquitectura de Madrid since 2000 and associate professors of Architectural Design at Escuela Superior de Arte y Arquitectura since 1999. They have lectured in many international schools of architecture, including Columbia University in New York, Harvard University in Cambridge, MA and the Bartlett University College London, as well as at schools and colleges throughout Spain. Their work and articles have been widely published in international periodicals including *Bauwelt*, *Quaderns* and *Ottagono*. A book about their work from 1995 to 2005 was published as Design Document Series No. 13 (2005).

Lena Andersson

Lena Andersson studied Architecture at the Bartlett University College London; her thesis was concerned with cybernetics and mnemonics. Subsequently she formed her own practice in Sweden.

Asymptote Architecture

As well as buildings, Asymptote has been involved in innovative exhibition, multimedia and graphic-design projects. Clients for exhibition and graphic design have included the Solomon R. Guggenheim Museum in New York, the Venice Biennale and the Ministry of Public Works in Madrid. Asymptote has also received acclaim for several of their art-scaled projects, which range from large public works to smaller gallery installations. Their work has been featured in numerous publications, including *Time*, *Newsweek*

and *Esquire*, and is held in major museum collections worldwide. In 2000 partner Hani Rashid co-represented the US at the American Pavilion at the Venice Biennale, and in 2004 he and partner Lise Anne Couture were designated the architects of the 9th International Architecture Exhibition at the Venice Biennale. Rashid and Couture have taught at MIT, Yale and Harvard universities in the US as well as in Europe; both are currently on the faculty of the Columbia University Graduate School of Architecture in New York.

Philip Beesley

Philip Beesley is an experimental architect and sculptor based in Toronto who focuses on public buildings and visual art. He is a professor at the School of Architecture and co-director of the Integrated Centre for Visualization, Design and Manufacturing, a high-performance computer centre at the University of Waterloo. His creative work has been recognized by national awards including a Governor-General's Award, two Dora Mavor Moore awards and the Prix de Rome for Architecture (Canada). His built works include the York University Student Centre, the provincial Legislature at Queen's Park, and a series of theatres and community facilities. Beesley has been a member of a number of art and performance collaboratives.

Melissa Clinch

Melissa Clinch studied Architecture at the University of Liverpool and then at the Bartlett University College London, graduating with a commendation. She currently works with Foster and Partners.

Preston Scott Cohen

Preston Scott Cohen's most renowned project to date is the Tel Aviv Museum of Art, which is scheduled to open in 2010. He is also known for the Goodman House in Dutchess County, New York (2004); the Torus House in Columbia County, New York (2000); and his competition proposal for the Eyebeam Museum of Technology, New York (2001). He is the Gerald M. McCue Professor of Architecture and director of the Master in Architecture programme at Harvard University Graduate School of Design. He was the Frank Gehry International Chair at the University of Toronto (2004) and the Perloff Professor at UCLA (2002), having previously held faculty positions at Princeton University, Rhode Island School of Design and Ohio State University.

Contemporary Architectural Practice (CAP)

Ali Rahim is a member of the Permanent Design faculty at the University of Pennsylvania in Philadelphia, as well as Louis I. Kahn Visiting Professor at Yale University; in 2006 he was visiting professor at Harvard University. Hina Jamelle is a member of the Design faculty at the University of Pennsylvania. The work of CAP has received extensive press attention. The two principals were selected for inclusion in *10x10_2* (2005) and in *Architectural Record*'s 'Design Vanguard 2004' as one of eleven practices worldwide 'building the future of architecture'. Their work was also on show at the Tel Aviv Museum of Art in 2008. Past exhibition venues include Essen in Germany, the Museum of Modern Art in New

York, the first Architectural Biennale in Beijing and RIBA in London.

James Curtis

James Curtis studied for a postgraduate architectural diploma at the Bartlett University College London. His work has been widely published, and he has had much success in architectural competitions, in particular the 2004–5 B& Q Shop of the Future Competition, which he won with a colleague. He has worked with the Richard Rogers Partnership in London.

Hernan Diaz Alonso / Xefirotarch

Hernan Diaz Alonso and his architectural office, Xefirotarch, are based in Los Angeles. Diaz Alonso is currently studio professor at SCI-Arc in Los Angeles, studio professor at Columbia University's Graduate School of Architecture, Planning and Preservation, and visiting professor at the Universität für angewandte Kurst in Vienna. He has architecture degrees from the National University of Rosario and from Columbia. Before setting up Xefirotarch, Alonso worked with Enric Miralles and Peter Eisenman. He has lectured and been published and exhibited internationally.

Dennis Dollens / Exodesic

Denis Dollens's office Exodesic is based in Santa Fe and Barcelona. Dollens has taught and lectured internationally, most consecutively in Alberto T. Estevez's Genetic Architectures programme at the Universitat Internacional de Catalunya and in collaboration with Ignasi Pérez Arnal's programme at Barcelona's ELISAVA design school; Dollens is an associate professor at both institutions.

He has worked as an editor, film maker and art director, and has been published and exhibited internationally. In 2006 he produced a small comic book featuring his work entitled *Pangolin's Guide to Biometric and Digital Architecture*.

Ammar Eloueini /AEDS

Ammar Eloueini studied architecture at the Ecole d'Architecture de Paris-Villemin in 1994 and graduated with an MS in Advanced Architectural Design from Columbia University in 1996. In 1997 he established Digit-all Studio, an award-winning firm in architecture, product and digital media with offices in the US and Europe. The firm's projects challenge traditional design processes and respond to contemporary architectural and urban conditions. In 2001, Eloueini was awarded the prestigious Nouveaux Albums des Jeunes Architectes, the French Institute of Architects' highest recognition for architects under thirty-five. In 2005 and 2006, the firm's in-store designs for Issey Miyake in Berlin and Paris received an award from the Chicago Chapter of the American Institute of Architects. The firm's designs have been featured in solo and group exhibitions, and published worldwide. Currently Eloueini is an associate professor at Tulane University in New Orleans and a visiting professor at the California College of the Arts in San Francisco. He has been a contributing editor to *TENbyTEN* since 2004.

EMERGENT

Tom Wiscombe is an architect based in Los Angeles. In 1999, he founded EMERGENT, a platform for researching issues of materiality, technology and systems through built form. EMERGENT won second place in the international competition for the Seoul Performing Arts Center in 2005 and is currently involved in several other international competitions. Its work was showcased in a solo show at the UCLA Architecture Gallery entitled 'Notes on Micromultiplicity' in 2005. Other exhibitions have included the 2006 Beijing Biennale, the 2006 London Biennale, and 'Glamour: Fabricating Affluence' at the San Francisco Museum of Modern Art in 2004. EMERGENT's work is part of the permanent collections of the FRAC Centre in Paris, as well as of the Museum of Modern Art in New York. Awards have included the Architectural League of New York Young Architects Award and the New York Engineering Excellence Platinum Award (both 2004). The work has been extensively published, notably in *Vogue*, *Architectural Record*, *Architectural Digest* and *A+U*. Wiscombe has taught Design and Technology in the US and Austria, and is currently teaching in the postgraduate programme at SCI-Arc in Los Angeles.

Evan Douglis Studio

Evan Douglis studied architecture in London prior to receiving a Bachelor's degree in architecture at The Cooper Union in New York and a Master's from Harvard University. Douglis is currently chair of the Undergraduate School of Architecture at Pratt Institute in New York. Prior to this he was on the faculty at Columbia University, director of Columbia's Architecture Galleries and a visiting professor at The Cooper Union. In 1999, the Architectural League of New York recognized him as an 'Emerging Voice' in architecture. He received a New York Foundation for the Arts Fellowship in Architecture and Environmental Structures in 2002. Douglis was selected as a participant and exhibitor in the 2004 ARCHILAB International Conference in Orléans in France. In 2006, he received a Design Merit Award in the Far Eastern International Digital Architectural Design Award competition, was a finalist nominee for the James Beard Foundation Restaurant Design Awards, and received the ACADIA Award for Emerging Digital Practice. His work has been published internationally.

Thom Faulders / BEIGE ARCHITECTURE AND DESIGN

Recent awards received by Thom Faulders / BEIGE ARCHITECTURE AND DESIGN include an Honorable Mention Award from the 2005 Possible Futures: Miami+Beach Bienal competition. In 2004, he received a Society for Environmental Graphic Design Honor Award. In tandem with running his architectural practice, Faulders teaches at California College of the Arts in San Francisco as an assistant professor in Architecture. He has taught at the University of California at Berkeley and the Royal Institute of Technology in Stockholm, Sweden. Early in his career, Faulders worked for Cristiano Toraldo di Francia, one of the founding members of the conceptual theorist group Superstudio in Florence, Italy. He received his advanced diploma in architecture from the Cranbrook Academy of Art in Michigan, and has been published and exhibited widely.

Mark Goulthorpe / dECOi

Mark Goulthorpe was educated in England and the US, and apprenticed professionally for four years with Richard Meier. Later he was invited as digital-design consultant to Foster & Partners in London. In 1991 he established the dECOi atelier to undertake a series of architectural competitions, largely theoretically biased. These resulted in numerous accolades, thus establishing the studio's reputation for design work suggestive of new possibilities for architecture and architectural praxis. The rubric 'dECOi' was intended to allow for the possibility of collaboration, which has latterly become essential to any digitally networked creative enterprise. dECOi's portfolio ranges from pure design and artwork through interior design to architecture and urbanism, and at every scale its work has received acclaim. It has been awarded numerous commissions for artworks / sculptures, and has taken on a number of architectural projects. The atelier has been involved with numerous publications, international lectures and conferences, and frequent guest professorships, including a design unit at the Architectural Association in London. Based in Paris and Boston, dECOi has developed a supple working practice to bring its skill to bear in an international arena. It has represented France three times at the Venice Biennale. Goulthorpe himself took a professorship at Massachusetts Institute of Technology in 2003. Several books about dECOi's work are forthcoming.

Greg Lynn FORM

Greg Lynn FORM is a critical component of the international discussion and development of digital architecture. Lynn has published six books on architectural design with a digital component. In 2002 he became a professor at the Universität für angewandte Kunst in Vienna, and for the last several years he has been a studio professor at UCLA as well as Davenport Professor at Yale University. Greg Lynn FORM has been published in design magazines as well as newspapers and exhibited worldwide.

Usman Haque / Haque Design + Research

Usman Haque has created responsive environments, interactive installations, digital-interface devices and choreographed performances. He has been an invited researcher at the Interaction Design Institute in Ivrea and artist-in-residence at the International Academy of Media Arts and Sciences in Japan, and has also worked in the US, the UK and Malaysia. As well as directing the work of Haque Design + Research, he has been a teacher and member of the Interactive Architecture Workshop at the Bartlett University College London. He is a recipient of a Wellcome Trust Sciart Award; a grant from the Daniel Langlois Foundation for Art, Science and Technology; the Swiss Creation Prize; the Japan Media Arts Festival Excellence Prize and the Asia Digital Art Award Grand Prize. His work has been exhibited internationally.

Jerry Tate Architects

Before establishing his own practice in 2007, Jerry Tate worked on various high-profile projects for Grimshaw Architects, including in-depth involvement as a project architect on the Eden Project in Cornwall in the UK. His experience on projects focusing on environmental sustainability runs alongside an understanding of large-scale transport-infrastructure schemes. This breadth of experience is coupled with an academic interest in new forms of computer-aided design tools.

J. Mayer H.

Jürgen Mayer H. is the founder and principal of the cross-disciplinairy studio that bears his name. He studied at the University of Stuttgart, The Cooper Union in New York and Princeton University. His work has been published and exhibited worldwide, and is part of numerous collections including the Museum of Modern Art in New York. National and international awards include the Mies van der Rohe Award, Emerging Architect Special Mention (2003) and a Holcim Award (2005). Mayer has taught at Princeton, the Universität der Künste in Berlin, Harvard University and the Architectural Association in London, and is currently teaching at Columbia University.

Christian Kerrigan

Christian Kerrigan initially studied Architectural Technology at Dublin's Bolton Street College, moving on to Edinburgh and Kansas before graduating from the Bartlett University College London. He works on stage-set designs for Mark Fisher.

Tobias Klein

Tobias Klein studied architecture in London and has worked with Coop Himmelb(l)au in Vienna. He has taught at the Royal College of Art and South Bank University in London. In 2007 his work won the *Architects Journal* 'best newcomer' prize at the Royal Academy in London.

KOL / MAC LLC

KOL/MAC LLC is a professional architecture and design firm established in 1988 and based in New York. Operating internationally, the firm is opening a second office in Istanbul. The firm's principal, Sulan Kolatan, is of Turkish origin and was educated in Turkey, Germany and the US. Its director, William MacDonald, is American and was educated in England, Germany and the US. The work produced by KOL / MAC LLC is in the permanent collections the CNAC Georges Pompidou in Paris, the Museum of Modern Art in New York and the Deutsches Architektur Museum in Frankfurt. KOL / MAC LLC is frequently featured in the international media.

Sacha Leong

Sacha Leong has worked with FAT Architects, having graduated with a degree in Architectural Design from the Bartlett University College London.

Arshia Mahmoodi / Void, inc.

Arshia Mahmoodi received his Master's degree in Architecture and Urban Design from Shahid Beheshti University in Tehran in 1997. In Iran he worked with Bahram Shirdel and Jeffrey Kipnis as project architect for the Imam Khomeini International Airport and other projects. In the US, he was the principal architect in Michele Saee's studio for two years, winning two major competitions for the firm. In 2003, with his partner Reza Bagherzadeh, Mahmoodi launched null. lab, an architectural design, research and implementation firm. Mahmoodi's work has been published in the US, Iran, Italy, Dubai, South Korea and Japan. He is currently the principal of Void, inc., a collaboration with Axel Schmitzberger of Hostcell.

Marcosandmarjan

Marjan Colletti studied in Innsbruck and London. He is currently lecturer in Architecture at the Bartlett University College London, visiting professor at the University of Innsbruck, and a guest lecturer at the University of Westminster in London. The print collection of his work entitled *2&1/2D Twoandahalf Dimensionality* was published in 2006. Marcos Cruz, a lecturer in Architecture at the Bartlett, studied in Barcelona, Porto and London. In 2000 he was part of the design team for the Kunsthaus Graz competition with Peter Cook and Colin Fournier, winning First Prize. In 2003 he served as a co-commissioner to the Austrian Ministry of Education for the restructuring of Viennese architecture schools. Marcosandmarjan's student and professional work has been widely published and exhibited. The firm has had approximately fifty exhibitions in Europe, Brazil and Asia, including at the Venice Architectural Biennale in 2004 and 2006.

Martha Markopoulou

Martha Markopoulou graduated in Architectural Design from the Bartlett University College London.

Massimo Minale

Massimo Minale studied at the undergraduate level at the University of Cambridge and graduated with distinction from the Bartlett University College London. He then worked for the Richard Rogers Partnership, subsequently becoming managing director of Minale and Minale in London.

Stuart Munro

Stuart Munro is a freelance architectural designer, webmaster, film maker and graphic designer. His took his undergraduate degree at Kingston University in London and finished his MArch at the Bartlett University College London in 2000. He has been a teaching fellow on the MArch Architectural Design AVATAR programme at the Bartlett, where he often collaborates with Neil Spiller and the graphic designer Vaughan Oliver. Munro has practised in London and Tokyo. His work has been published in *Blueprint*, *Architectural Design* and *Archis*, to name but a few, and has been exhibited at the ICA in London, as well as in New York, Berlin, Canada and Tokyo.

Shaun Murray

Shaun Murray studied at Bartlett University College London in the late 1990s. He has been unit master of the interactive web-based course at the Royal Institute of Technology School of Architecture in Stockholm and visiting professor at the Arkitektur- og designhøgskolen in Oslo. He has co-taught a diploma unit and is currently a teaching fellow on the MArch Architectural Design AVATAR programme at the Bartlett. His work has been published internationally, including in a solo monograph, *Disturbing Territories* (2006).

Naga Studio Architects

Naga Studio Architects was founded in 1991 by Tarek Naga, a qualified architect in the UK, the US and Egypt. Naga studied at Ain Shams University in Cairo and the University of Minnesota, and was a doctoral candidate at the University of Pennsylvania. Naga Studio Architects works internationally and has been exhibited and published frequently.

oceanD

oceanD has directors in four cities. Tom Verebes (London) studied architecture at McGill University in Canada, LoPSiA in France and the Architectural Association in London, where he has taught as course master in the Design Research Lab since 1997. He was a visiting and guest professor in 2003–5 at the Staatliche Akademie der Bildenden Künste in Stuttgart. Prior to co-founding oceanD, Verebes was a partner in IDP Hong Kong. He has lectured and taught in Europe, North America, the Middle East and Asia. Robert Elfer, AIA (Boston), who also studied at McGill, is a licensed architect in the US and Canada. He has practised architecture since 1992, most notably in Paris with Francis Soler, as well as in Jakarta, Hong Kong and Boston. He currently teaches at Boston Architectural College. Kevin Cespedes (Boston) studied at the University of Miami School of Architecture and then at the Design Research Laboratory at the Architectural Association in London, where he earned a Master's degree in Architecture and Urbanism. He worked in the office of Zaha Hadid prior to joining Wallace Floyd in Boston. He has been a guest critic and taught in various institutions in Boston and Cambridge. M. Wade H. Stevens, AIA (New York) is a graduate of the Massachusetts Institute of Technology School of Architecture and the Harvard Graduate School of Design. Since 1993, he has built projects as varied as aquariums, laboratories and courthouses.

ORTLOS

Ivan Redi and Andrea Redi are principals of ORTLOS architects in Graz, founded in 2000 as a network of interdisciplinary partners. With their strong commitment to working online, ORTLOS has focused on expanding classic architectural tasks by simulating virtual environments to be applied to future realities and by using cutting-edge computer technologies. Their work has been published and exhibited worldwide, including at the Venice Biennale in 2000. They are currently teaching at Graz University of Technology and lecture around the world. In collaboration with the graphic designer David Carson, ORTLOS has recently published *ORTLOS :: Architecture of the NetWORKS*, which illustrates works from 2000 to 2003, as well as more recent projects.

P-A-T-T-E-R-N-S

Marcelo Spina holds a professional degree from the National University of Rosario and a Master's degree in Architecture from Columbia

University, where he was the recipient of the William Kinne Fellowship and the Honor Award for Excellence in Design. He has been on the Design faculty at SCI-Arc in Los Angeles since 2001, and has been a visiting professor at a number of institutions including Harvard University. Previous teaching positions included the National University of Rosario and Universidad Torcuato Di Tella in Buenos Aires. Georgina Huljich also holds a professional degree from the National University of Rosario as well as a Master's degree in Architecture from UCLA, where she was the recipient of several design awards. She has worked at the Solomon R. Guggenheim Museum in New York and as a project designer at Morphosis in Los Angeles. As the co-principal of fl-oz, Huljich was named one of the six winning entries for the 21st.Century Park Competition organized by the Graham Foundation in Chicago; she also designed the exhibition 'Pass Through' at the University of Southern California in Los Angeles. She participated in the Beyond Media '05 Script Show in Florence with her video installation *Fairy_Tails*, a collaboration with the video artist Gaby Hamburg. Huljich is currently a member of the Design faculty in the Department of Architecture at UCLA.

Qua'Virarch

Paul Preissner studied for his MArch at the Graduate School of Architecture, Planning and Preservation of Columbia University in New York from 1998 to 2000. He was the founding partner of Qua'Virarch in Chicago in 2003. Previously he had worked for Eisenman

Architects in New York; Skidmore, Owings and Merrill in Chicago; and Philip Johnson / Alan Ritchie Architects in New York. Preissner has had numerous academic appointments, including posts at the University of Illinois at Chicago, University of Nebraska at Lincoln and SCI-Arc in Los Angeles. His work has been exhibited and published widely.

Lindy Roy / ROY Co.

Lindy Roy moved to New York after receiving a BArch from the University of Cape Town in 1985. She went on to receive an MArch from Columbia University in 1990 and taught at Rice University, Princeton University, Columbia and The Cooper Union. In 2000 she founded ROY Co. in New York City's Meatpacking District, where her studio remains. Roy's work has been published internationally, and examples are included in the permanent collections of both the San Francisco Museum of Modern Art and the Museum of Modern Art in New York.

Enric Ruiz-Geli / Cloud9

Cloud9 was formed in 1997 by Enric Ruiz-Geli and has offices in Barcelona and São Paulo. Ruiz-Geli is an architect at the Escola Tècnica Superior d'Arquitectura de Barcelona. He has been a visiting visual artist at the Zentrum für Kunst und Medientechnologie Karlsruhe, associate set designer for Robert Wilson's *Danton's Tod* at the Salzburger Festspiele, and curator of the Spanish Pavilion of the Venice Biennale of Architecture. Ruiz-Geli has won numerous awards, including First Prize in the 2G Contest for the new Fundació Mies van der Rohe (1998).

servo

servo's principals are Marcelyn Gow, Ulrika Karlsson and Chris Perry. servo's work increasingly seems to map the organization of their practice. Early projects operated at the interface between bodies – human or architectural – but were themselves relatively discrete devices. Beginning with Lattice Archipelogics, these objects have increasingly given way to discrete component systems knitted together into a network field. These are not so much installations as a *projective urbanism* where the territories of the city, like the firm's own organization, are defined by software firewalls and signal strength, with traditional notions of public space displaced by proprietary Wi-Fi hotspots. Recent exhibitions have included 'Metamorph' at the 2004 Venice Architecture Biennale, and 'Glamour: Fashion, Industrial Design, Architecture' at the San Francisco Museum of Modern Art in 2005; recent publications include *10x10_2* (2005).

SIAL

SIAL exploits developing resources in high-end computing and software with the Internet to forge connections that transcend the typical barriers to interdisciplinary work. As a facility its distinctiveness comes from working with a wide range of software and hardware, and a clear association with all areas of design in the university combined with social and cultural studies. Internationally it is one of a small number of established schools; within Australia it is quite unique. Five main points characterize the unique features of SIAL: international expertise

in Parametric Design; programming as a core aspect of design teaching; unique experience in pure and applied research; unparalleled abilities in the representation of information and ideas; and a suite of electro-acoustic studios

sixteen*(makers)

Founded in London in 1994, sixteen*(makers) includes Phil Ayres, Nick Callicott, Chris Leung and Bob Sheil, all of whom studied at the Bartlett University College London and have subsequently taught there. Sheil is diploma director and diploma unit master of Unit 23. Ayres is a diploma unit master in Unit 14 and is engaged in PhD research in Copenhagen. Callicott was formally director of Computing at the Bartlett and is now director of Ehlert Engineering in Germany. Leung is an architect, programmer and technical tutor at the Bartlett and the University of Westminster in London. All four have extensive experience in practice. Their work has been lectured on, exhibited and published internationally.

Neil Spiller

Neil Spiller graduated from Thames Polytechnic London in 1986. He is author of *Digital Dreams – Architecture and the New Alchemic Technologies* (1998) and co- or guest editor of special issues of *Architectural Design*. He is co-editor with Peter Cook of *The Power of Contemporary Architecture* (1999) and *Paradox of Contemporary Architecture* (2001). His monograph *Maverick Deviations* was published in 2000 and his book *Lost Architecture*, about

projects of the last two decades of the twentieth century, in 2001. His history of twentieth-century visionary architecture was published in 2006. Spiller is professor of Architecture and Digital Theory and a practising architect. He is the MArch Architectural Design AVATAR course director, director of AVATAR and vice dean at the Bartlett University College London. He was the 2002 John and Magda McHale Research Fellow at the State University of New York at Buffalo. Spiller lectures around the world, and his work has been exhibited and published internationally.

Glen Tomlin

Glen Tomlin studied Architecture at Nottingham University and then graduated with distinction from the Bartlett University College London. He is currently working with Foster and Partners in London.

AMID* architecture

8th Spanish Architecture Biennale Exhibition (2005)
Architects: AMID* (Cristina Díaz Moreno, Efrén García Grinda, Nerea Calvillo)
Collaborators: Jaime Bartolomé Yllera, Alessandro Cariello
Production: Empty S.L.
Administrative Building and Town Hall (2004)
Architects: AMID* (Cristina Díaz Moreno, Efrén García Grinda)
Collaborators: Luis Cabrejas, Íñigo González-Haba, Jorge Martín Sainz de los Terreros, Hsiao-Tien Hung, Javier González Muñoz, David Marsinyach, Isabel Caballero, Javier López-Soldado
Structure: Schlaich Bergermann und Partner
Landscaping: Teresa Galí Izard
Forms of Energy: La Biennale di Venezia (2002)
Architects: cero9 (Cristina Díaz Moreno, Efrén García Grinda)
Collaborators: Luis Cabrejas, Íñigo González-Haba, Aritz González
The Magic Mountain: Ecosystem Mask for Ames Thermal Power Station (2002)
Architects: cero9 (Cristina Díaz Moreno, Efrén García Grinda)
Collaborators: Dries van de Velde, Íñigo González-Haba, Miguel Paredes

Asymptote Architecture

Alessi Flagship Store (2005–6)
Client: Alessi US Shops
Principal Architects: Hani Rashid, Lise Anne Couture
Project Architects: Jill Leckner, Stella Lee, David Lessard
Design Team: Carsten Laursen, Karen Lee, Jong Kouk Kim, Erick Carcamo, Asako Hiraoka-Sperry
Assistants: Jenny Chow, Ruben Useche, Salvador Lopez,
Natalia Ibañez Lario, Carlo Kessler, Marcia Akermann, Peter Heller
Structural Engineer: Robert Silman Associates; Nat Oppenheimer, Partner
MEP Engineer: Kam Chiu Associates
Lighting Consultant: Tillotson Design Associates; Suzan Tillotson, Partner
Contractor: Fountainhead Construction
Auditorium Beukenhof (2004)
Client: Beukenhof Foundation
Principal Architects: Hani Rashid, Lise Anne Couture
Project Architect: Eric Goldberg
Assistant Architect: Asako Hiraoka-Sperry
Design Team: Claudia Cipriani, Clarissa Lenz, Simon Nageli, Charlotte Schmidt-Jensen
Budapest Bank Tower (2006–9)
Client: Orco Property Group
Architects: Hani Rashid, Lise Anne Couture
Local Architect: Pozitan Architects
MEP and Structural Engineer: Arup
Façade Consultant: Front, Inc.
Carlos Miele Flagship Store (2002–3)
Client: Carlos Miele
Principal Architects: Hani Rashid, Lise Anne Couture
Project Architect: Jill Leckner
Project Team: Noboru Ota, John Cleater, Peter Horner, Cathy Jones
Assistants: Micheal Levy Bajar, Janghwan Cheon, Teresa Cheung, Mary Ellen Cooper, Shinichiro Himematsu, Michael Huang, Lamia Jallad, Ana Sa, Markus Schnierle, Yasmin Shahamiri
Engineers: Kam Chiu, PE; Andre Tomas Chaszar, PE
Lighting Design: Focus Lighting Inc.
A/V Consultant: Ben Greenfield
Contractor: Vanguard Construction & Development
Fabricator: 555 International

Contemporary Architectural Practice (CAP)

Migrating Coastlines: Residential Tower (2006)
Directors: Ali Rahim, Hina Jamelle
Project Team: Jeroen van Ameijde, Dejan Liu
Assistants: Kevin Sperry, Dejan Liu
Reebok Flagship Store (2005)
Directors: Ali Rahim, Hina Jamelle
Project Team: Jeroen van Ameijde, Dejan Liu
Assistant: Kevin Sperry
Residence for a Fashion Designer (2002)
Design Director: Ali Rahim
Project Team: Yu-Chuan Chang, Hale Everets, Nathaniel Hadley
Assistants: Ben Stough, Beatrice Witzgall, Jeroen van Ameijde, Dejan Liu

Hernan Diaz Alonso / Xefirotarch

BCA Competition (2006)
Principal in Charge: Hernan Diaz Alonso
Project Designer: Joshua M. Taron
Project Team: Chikara Inamura, Ben Toam, Mirai Morita, Brian De Luna
Project Text: Benjamin H. Bratton, Hernan Diaz-Alonso, Joshua M. Taron
Busan Metropolitan City (2003)
Principal in Charge: Hernan Diaz Alonso
Digital Visualization: Xefirotvisual
Image Savant: Richard 'Doc' Baily
Design Team: Drura Parrish, Mark Nagis, Bryan Flaig, Laura Fehlberg, Timothy Rash II, Kevin Sperry, Asako Hiraoka
Exhibition Team: Drura Parrish, Mark Nagis, Bryan Flaig, Laura Fehlberg
Structure: Bruce Danziger -

Ove Arup, LA
Consultant Associate: Peter Zellner
Maison Seroussi: 'Seingemer'
Principal: Hernan Diaz Alonso
Project Architect: Joshua Taron
Project Team: Brian De Luna
Job Captains: Marcus Friesl, Robert Cha, Sanjay Sukie, Josh Sprinkling
Animation: Erick Carcamo

Ammar Eloueini / AEDS

***California* Set Design**
(2003)
Client: John Jasperse Co.
Choreography: John Jasperse
Original Music: Jonathan Bepler
Performers: Steven Fetherhuff, Eleanor Hullihan, John Jasperse
Lighting Design: John Jasperse, Joe Levasseur
Me Boutique, Issey Miyake
(2006)
Client: Issey Miyake
Light Consultant: Philippe Almon
This project received the AIA (American Institute of Architects) Chicago Chapter: Divine Detail Design Excellence Award (2006)
Pleats Please, Issey Miyake
(2004)
Client: Issey Miyake
This project received the AIA (American Institute of Architects) Chicago Chapter: Interior Architecture and Divine Detail Design Excellence Awards (2005)

EMERGENT

Cell House (2006)
Principal: Tom Wiscombe
Project Team: Takeshi Masuyama, Alina Grobe
Paris Courthouse (TGI) (2006)
Principal: Tom Wiscombe
Project Team: Kevin Regalado, Bjorn Dyvik, Alina Grobe
Stockholm City Library (2006)

Principal: Tom Wiscombe
Project Team: Josh Sprinkling, Can Sucuoglu, Alina Grobe, Justin Botros

Thom Faulders / BEIGE ARCHITECTURE AND DESIGN

AirSpace (2006–7)
Thom Faulders, with Proces 2 (San Francisco) and Studio M (Japan)
BEIGE Design Project Team: Patrick Flynn, Jessica Kmetovic, Tomohiko Sakai, Agnessa Torodova-Dowell
Screen Design: Thom Faulders, with Sean Ahlquist / Proces 2 (San Francisco) and Hajime Masubuchi / Studio M (Tokyo)
Building Design: Hajime Masubuchi / Studio M
Chromogenic Dwelling (2005)
Design: Thom Faulders / BEIGE Design
Project Team: Jessica Kmetovic, Agnessa Torodova-Dowell, Joyce Hsu
Model Photography: Peter Honig
MOCA@LBC (2004)
Design: Thom Faulders
Design Team: Noah Sherburn, Young-chae Lee
Mute Room (2001)
Design: Thom Faulders
Design Team: Hajime Masubuchi, Lara Kaufman, Sherman Warren
Installation: CCA Institute
Sponsored by the CAA Institute at the California College of the Arts, San Francisco

Greg Lynn FORM

BLOB WALL©
Design: Greg Lynn FORM (Jackilin Bloom, Adam Fure, Chris Kabatsi, Daniel Norell)
Fabrication and Robotic Technology: Froech Design US (Andreas Froech, Jeff McKibban)

Exclusively available through PANELITE
Flatware (2004–present)
Design: Greg Lynn FORM (Brittney Hart, Jackilin Bloom, Adam Fure, Chris Kabatsi, Andreas Krainer, Helen Lee, Elena Manferdini)
Slavin House (2004–7)
Clients: Sylvia Lavin, Greg Lynn
Design Team: Jackilin Bloom, Chris Kabatsi, Florencia Pita, Deborah Chiu, Martin Sobota
Structural Engineers: Bollinger and Grohmann GmbH; Thorton Thomasetti Group
Vitra Ravioli Chair (2003–7)
Client: Vitra
Design: Greg Lynn FORM (Chris Kabatsi, Jackilin Bloom, Brittney Hart, Adam Fure, Brian Ha, Elena Manferdini, Deborah Chiu, Shannon Loew)

Usman Haque / Haque Design + Research

Open Burble
Architect: Usman Haque
Algorithmist and Chromodynamicist: Rolf Pixley
Detail Designers: Kei Hasegawa, Fred Guttfield
B2B Network, Balloon Hardware Design: Seth Garlock
Logistics: Susan Haque
Field Overseer: Ai Hasegawa

Jerry Tate Architects

New Orleans Neighbourhood Community Centre and Hurricane Shelter (2006)
Client: Project New Orleans, African-American Museum, New Orleans
Sorrento Bathing Platform (2007)
Project Partner: Dan Clark
Swiss-Army Wall Project (2001–2)
Structural Engineer: Price and Myers
Main Contractor: WS Butcher

J. Mayer H.

BMW Event and Delivery Centre (2001)
Danfoss Universe, Master Plan – Curiosity.Centre / Food. Factory (2005–7)
Project Team: Jürgen Mayer H., Marcus Blum, Thorsten Blatter, Andre Santer, Alessandra Raponi
Architect on Site: Hallen & Nordby
Technical Consultants: Carl Bro
Model: Werk5
Metropol Parasol (2005–7)
Clients: Ayuntamiento de Sevilla and SACYR
Project Team: Jürgen Mayer H., Andre Santer, Marta Ramírez Iglesias, Jan-Christoph Stockebrand, Marcus Blum, Ana Alonso de la Varga, Paul Angelier, Hans Schneider, Thorsten Blatter, Wilko Hoffmann, Claudia Marcinowski, Sebastian Finckh, Alessandra Raponi, Olivier Jacques, Nai Huei Wang
Competition Team: Jürgen Mayer H., Dominik Schwarzer, Wilko Hoffmann, Ingmar Schmidt, Jan-Christoph Stockebrand, Julia Neitzel, Klaus Küppers, Georg Schmidthals, Daria Trovato
Management Consultant: Dirk Blomeyer
Technical Consultant for Competition (2nd Phase) and Multidisciplinary Engineers for Realization: ARUP GmbH
Technical Support for Plants – Competition (2nd Phase): Coqui-Malachowska-Coqui with Thomas Waldau
Translation of Competition Text: Carmen Diez
Plexi-Model: Werk 5
Timber Model: Finnforest Merk
New National Library of the Czech Republic (2006)
Project Team: Jürgen Mayer H., Jonathan Busse, Hans-Juergen Wetlesen, Christoph

Emenlauer, Paul Angelier, Marcus Blum, Alessandra Raponi

KOL / MAC LLC

MUTEN Galataport, Coastal Urban Development
Client / Sponsor: Garanti Bank / Garanti Galeri
Design Principals: Sulan Kolatan, William MacDonald
Senior Designer: Robert Cervellione
Consultant: Arup AGU
Fifty-Storey Office Building and Shopping Centre
Design Principals: Sulan Kolatan, William MacDonald
Senior Designer: Robert Cervellione
Mixed-Use High-Rise and Highway Infrastructure
Design Principals: Sulan Kolatan, William MacDonald
Senior Designer: Phillis Wong
Project Manager: Michael Huang
Museum Campus Comprising an Archaeological Research Institute, Visitors' Centre, Offices and Parks
Client: Farouk Hosny, Minister of Culture, Arab Republic of Egypt
Design Principals: Sulan Kolatan, William MacDonald
Project Architect: Julian Palacio
Project Manager: Y. Suatanto
Urban Redevelopment of Former Brewery
Client / Sponsor: Carlsberg
Design Principals: Sulan Kolatan, William Mac Donald
Senior Designer: Robert Cervellione

Arshia Mahmoodi / Void, inc.

The Bobco Metals Headquarters (2004)
Architect: Arshia, Reza (null.lab)
Structural Engineers: David C. Weiss / Farzin Rahbar

Team: Afshin Rohani, Elizabeth Marley, Wuttichai Piyasowan, Jennille Amerman, Yaron Naim
Ministry of Petroleum Headquarters (2005)
Client: Ministry of Petroleum, Islamic Republic of Iran
Architect: Arshia
MUK Residence (In process)
Client: Dr Kwan Kim
Architects: Arshia, Axel Schmitzberger (Republic Architecture)
Team: Spencer Brennan, Miguel Gonzalez, Felix Monasakanian, Efren Soriano, Edwin Liu
Structural Engineer: Amir Pirbadian

Naga Studio Architects

House of Emergent Suspensions (1999–2000)
Client: Kal Naga
Architect: Tarek Naga
Project Team: Nathan Kim, Brian Holland
Sharm Safari Gate (2004–5)
Client: Sanafir-Sharm Development Company

oceanD

LJ House (2002–3)
Tom Verebes, Dirk Anderson, Felix Robbins, Jasmina Jugovic
Structural Consultants: Arups BG4; Bob Lang
Rabin Peace Forum (2001)
Felix Robbins, Tom Verebes, George Liaropoulos-Legendre, Cynthia Morales, Sarah Quinn, Wade Stevens, Robert Elfer, Kevin Cespedes
Ski Chalet (2003–5)
Client: Gustavo Mana
oceanD (London): Tom Verebes, Yael Harel-Gilad, Robert Neumayr, Abraham Gordon, Boyan Tzvetkov, Meiko Nibashima, Jay Chayhun, Lionel Sacks-Monsky, Eva Krane; (Boston): Robert Elfer, Kevin Cespedes; (New York) Wade Stevens

P-A-T-T-E-R-N-S

The Element (2005)
SITE: SCI-Arc Gallery, Los Angeles, temporary site installation
Principals in Charge: Marcelo Spina, Georgina Huljich; En Jang, James Vincent, Robert Johnson
Nodeul Island Performing Arts Centre (2005)
Client: Seoul Metropolitan Government / International Ideas Competition
Principals in Charge: Marcelo Spina, Georgina Huljich; En Jang, Ben Toam, Naoko Miyano, James Vincent
Unibodies (2006)
SITE: Artists Space, New York, temporary site installation
Project Team: Marcelo Spina, Georgina Huljich
Project Architect: Seyavash Zohoori
Project Designers: Marcus Friesl, Jooyoung Chun
Assistants: James Vincent, Noriaki Hanaoka, Lionel Lambourn, Duly Lee
Kreysler & Associates: Bill Kreysler, Makai Smith, Scott Van Note, Joshua Zabel, Jesus Ambriz-Villasenor, Miguel Ambriz-Villasenor, Jesus Flores

Qua'Virarch

The Czech Republic National Library (2006)
Client: Czech Republic
Project Team: Paul Preissner, AIA (Principal in Charge), Katherine Monachos, Nick Poulos, Patrick Baudin
Gyeonggi-Do Jeongok Prehistory Museum (2006)
Client: Gyeonngi Prefecture
Project Team: Paul Preissner, AIA (Principal in Charge), Matthew Utley
Southbank Planning Development (2006)
Client: Spier Properties

Project Team: Paul Preissner, AIA (Principal in Charge), Jason Chernak, Katherine Monachos

Enric Ruiz-Geli / Cloud9

Aviary (2002–7)
Clients: City of Barcelona, BSM, BCN Regional, BCN Zoo
Villa Bio (2006)
Client: Fontecha Family

servo

Dark Places (2006)
Client: Santa Monica Museum of Art
Curation: David Erdman, Marcelyn Gow, Ulrika Karlsson, Chris Perry
Interactive Design: Joshua Decter
Interactive Design / Installation: Casey Reas
Installation Foreman: Richard Haga
CNC Milling and Fabrication: Aria Group
Vacuum Forming: Warner Brothers Construction
Fibre-optic Design / Installation: Glass Illuminations Inc.
A/V Consultation and Specification: Charles M Salter Assoc.
The Genealogy of Speed (2004)
Client: Nike
servo in collaboration with Stephen Kinder Design Partnership and Karen Kimmel
Architecture and Lighting: servo (David Erdman, Marcelyn Gow, Ulrika Karlsson, Chris Perry)
Design Team: Julianna Morais (Project Architect), Mike Mangiagli, Jason McCann, Jeremy Whitener, Shlomi Kagan
Curation: Jenelle Porter with SKDP / Karen Kimmel
Apparel and Event Design: Karen Kimmel
Environmental Graphics: SKDP (Graham Hill, John Kieselhorst,

Jenelle Porter, Conny Purtill)
Installation Consultants: Tomas Osinski Design (Critter Pierce)
Fabrication Consultants: CNC Milling (Foam Moulds)
Vacuum Forming: Warner Brothers Construction
Sandblasting: Pierose Productions; Solter Plastics
Fibre-optic Lighting Consultants: Robert Morais, Vladimir Rubtsov, Glass Illuminations Inc.
Spoorg (2006)
Installation Design: David Erdman, Marcelyn Gow, Ulrika Karlsson, Chris Perry
Design Team: Ulrika Karlsson, Marcelyn Gow, Erik Hökby
Electronic and Algorithmic Design: Pablo Miranda, Åsmund Gamlesæter
Sound Design: Leif Jordansson, Martin Q. Larsson
Special Thanks: Jonas Barre, Sue Huang
With Generous Support from Konstnärsnämnden, Sveriges Bildkonstnärsfond, Stiftelsen Framtidens Kultur, BSK arkitekter, White, Wingårdhs, Royal Institute of Technology (KTH), Atmel Norway AS
Installation for 'Gen(h)ome' exhibition, MAK Center for Art and Architecture, Los Angeles
Thermocline (2002–3)
servo in collaboration with Perry Hall (2002) and MIT Media Lab (2003)
Prototype Design: servo (David Erdman, Marcelyn Gow, Ulrika Karlsson, Chris Perry)
Design Team: Anne Barakat, Rafael Cardenas, Leonore Daum, Jeff McKibbin, Julianna Morais
Sound Design (2002): Perry Hall
Responsive Lighting and Sound Design (2003): MIT Media Lab (Winslow Burleson, Paul Nemirovsky)
Design Team: Assaf Biderman, Rebecca Luger-Guillaume,

Michael Lew
Fabrication Consultants: Kintz Plastics
Lighting Consultants: Norlux Corporation, RSL Lighting, Inc.
Special thanks: Jeffrey Kipnis, Annetta Massie (Wexner Center for the Arts), Centre Pompidou, Council for the Arts at MIT, Robert Morais, Gio Tomasi, Steve Vornsand, Dan Walczyk
Multi-media furniture prototype commissioned by Wexner Center for the Arts for 'Mood River' exhibition (2002); responsive system upgraded for 'Non-Standard Architectures' exhibition, Centre Pompidou, Paris (2003)

sixteen*(makers)

Blusher (2001)
Authors: R. Sheil, P. Ayres, N. Callicot, C. Leung
Curator: Prof. Greg Votolato
Created for 'Making Buildings' exhibition (New Art Gallery Walsall; Crafts Council Gallery, London; Centre North East, Middlesborough; Turnpike Gallery, Leigh; Aberystwyth Arts Centre; Brighton University); re-exhibited at Entwistle Gallery, London (2002); Bartlett University College London (2005)

Neil Spiller

Bee Gates (2001)
Architect: Neil Spiller, Fordwich, Kent, England
Dee Trunks (2003–4)
Architect: Neil Spiller, Fordwich, Kent, England
Velazquez Machine (2002) **and Growing Vistas** (2002–8)
Architect: Neil Spiller, Paris, Rome, Fordwich, Kent, England

Image Credits

Asymptote
All images Asymptote: Hani Rashid + Lise Anne Couture except Alessi Flagship Store (Elizabeth Felicella); Carlos Miele Flagship Store (Paul Warchol)

Ammar Eloueini / AEDS
Me Boutique, Issey Miyake, Photography: Gitty Darugar, Nomoto Masafumi; MU Chair, Photography: Nathan Kirkman; Pleats Please, Issey Miyake, Photography: Christian Richters

Thom Faulders / BEIGE ARCHITECTURE AND DESIGN
Page 127, illustration #6 Photography: Kevin Dwarka

J. Mayer H.
Photography: Uwe Walter

Arshia Mahmoodi / Void, inc.
Photography: Tara Wujcik and Barbara Runcie; Fotoworks; null.lab

Ortlos
Photography: Nathan Kirkman
All images © ORTLOS architects – www.ortlos.com

3-D knitting
Digital and fabrication techniques and processes that allow architects to create three-dimensional surfaces.

Biomimetic practice
The application of methods and systems found in nature to the study and design of engineering systems and modern technology.

CAD
Computer-Aided Design

CAM
Computer-Aided Manufacture

Capacitance sensor
The capacitance of an object is its capacity to store electricity. A capacitance sensor records an object's change in capacitance or its electrical inertia.

Cellular tectonics
Composite forms and surfaces that are created from the same module element or formed from morphing cellular pieces.

Computer numerically controlled machine
A machine that is manipulated by a computer or a series of microprocessors.

Deposition-printing technology
A technology that allows three-dimensional virtual computer models to be 'printed' into reality as rapid prototype models; this is done in layers using starch or resin.

Distributed-system paradigm
A distributed system is a network that is dispersed geographically yet communicates with itself.

Dynamic-modelling software
Computer software that is capable of measuring and illustrating dynamic shifts in vectors, loads and turbulence within and around architectural propositions.

Emergence
Emergence is the phenomenon that results in large groups of organisms and organizations not found in the individual unit's make-up. Examples include all types of animal swarming. Many complex systems both natural and artificial exhibit emergence. It is believed that emergence is fundamental to nature in all its forms.

Five-axis rapid prototyping milling
A state-of-the-art rapid-prototyping process that can mill objects in a machine which can hone material from all angles in one process.

Generative component
Generative Components is a model-oriented CAD environment which combines direct interactive manipulation design with visual and traditional programming techniques.

Hyperlink
A hyperlink is a navigational element within a text. The fundamental way in which people navigate around the World-Wide Web, it is otherwise known as a 'hot button'.

Hypersurface
A hypersurface is a building skin or element that screens / projects information.

Material prototyping
The prototypical exploration of new hybridized building materials.

Mathematical scripting
Computer programming that allows the programmer to describe worlds with mathematical objects.

Morphogenesis
The study of how physical and mathematical constraints inhibit cell growth.

Nanotechnology
The fabrication and sometimes the self-replication of devices at the scale of a nanometre; the manipulation of matter at the atomic level.

Parametrics
The use by architects of computer programs that allow them to put parameters of spaces or objects into their computer models. So when a dimension of a space is changed, its other dimensions adjust accordingly to maintain the programmed parameter (often the area or numbers of seats in an auditorium).

Patch dynamics
Patches are areas of landscape or population that appear different from their surroundings; patch dynamics map their metamorphosis over time.

Productive-interference system
Systems can be designed to interfere architecturally with each other. Such systems can be choreographed to benefit a particular architectural condition or many of them.

Rapid manufacturing / rapid prototyping
Rapid manufacturing or prototyping is an additive fabrication technique for making solid objects by the sequential delivery of energy and / or material to specified points in space to fabricate the whole.

Rotational moulding
A casting technique that quickly rotates moulds so the casting material penetrates all areas of them.

Router CNC Machine
A computer controlled groove and hole-making machine.

Shape-memory alloy-wire actuator
Shape-memory materials are those that 'remember' a predefined shape at rest or when activated. These materials can be formed into wires and used as switches or agents of deformation of other structures.

Sintering
A manufacturing process that makes objects from powdered raw material by heating them – for example ceramics.

Tessellating geometry
The family of regular and irregular tiles that can cover a surface without gaps.

Topological design
Topology is a fundamental way of characterizing forms. It classifies objects according to the number of holes in them or the types of twists of material that makes them up.

X-Frog-plant simulation
A software program that mimics biological growth patterns within computer models.

Abu Dhabi 62
Adamatzky, Andrew 158
Alaska 314
Aldeburgh 244
Alessi, Alberto 29
Ames 18
AMID* architecture 16–25, *16–25*
    8th Spanish Architecture Biennale Exhibition 20, *20–21*
    Administrative Building and Town Hall 24, *24–5*
    Forms of Energy: La Biennale di Venezia 22, *22–3*
    The Magic Mountain: Ecosystem Mask for Ames Thermal
    Power Station *16–19*, 18
Andersson, Lena *365*, 374, *374–5*
Angola 310
Aragon, Louis 380
Architectural Association (London) 10, 129
Argentina 288
Arizona 84
Ascona 174
Asymptote Architecture 2–4, 26–35, *26–35*
    Alessi Flagship Store *28–9*, 29
    Auditorium Beukenhof 30, *30–31*
    Budapest Bank Tower *32–3*, 33
    Carlos Miele Flagship Store 34, *34–5*
    Guggenheim Guadalajara *2–4*, *26–7*
Australia 338, 342, 343
AVATAR 369
Ayres, Phil 345
Azuma Village 224
Barcelona 82, 318
Bartlett University College London 12, 369
Beesley, Philip 36–49, *36–49*
    Cybele 38, *38–9*
    Implant Matrix *36–7*, 40, *40–41*
    Orgone Reef 42, *42–3*
    Orpheus Filter *44–5*, 45
    Reflexive Membranes 46, *46–9*
Beijing 202, 220
Benedikt, Michael 12
Berlin 93, 173
Beukenhof (Netherlands) 30
Bolivia 278
Boston 72, 266
Bramante 358
Budapest 32, 33
Building Centre (London) 42
Burry, Mark *12*, 13, 336
Busan 76
Cairo 206, 258, 282
California 50, 102, 122, 124, 126, 142, 148, 214, 216, 252, 280, 292,
    328, 330, 332
Callicott, Nick 345
Camargue 248
Cambridge (Canada) 46
Cambridge (Massachusetts) 45, 50, 56
Canada 40, 46, 230

Cape Town 304
cero9 17
Chamonix 274
Chareau, Pierre 134
Chicago 93, 293
China 50, 52, 202, 220
Clinch, Melissa *367*, 378, *378–9*
Cohen, Preston Scott 50–59, *50–59*
    Nanjing University Student Centre 52, *52–3*
    Taiyuan Museum of Art *50–51*, 56, *56–9*
    Tel Aviv Museum of Art 54, *54–5*
Colletti, Marjan 218
Columbus (Ohio) 334
Contemporary Architectural Practice (CAP) *1*, 60–69, *60–69*
    Commercial High-Rise 64, *64–5*
    Migrating Coastlines: Residential Tower *60–61*, 62, *62–3*
    Reebok Flagship Store *66–7*, 67
    Residence for a Fashion Designer *1*, 68, *68–9*
Coop Himmelb(l)au 100
Copenhagen 198
Couture, Lise Anne 26
Cruz, Marcos 218
Cuba 192
Curtis, James 380, *380–81*
Czech Republic 182, 296
Daniel Langlois Foundation for Art and Technology (Montreal) 45
Davis, Robert 158
Dee, John 230
Denmark 178, 198
Dollens, Dennis / Exodesic *80–89*, 81–9
    Digitally Grown Botanic Tower for Barcelona – #2 82, *82–3*
    Digitally Grown Botanic Tower #3 – (Arizona / Arcosanti):
        Homage to Arcosanti *80–81*, 84, *84–5*
    Exodesic / Digitally Grown Trusses, Connectors and Towers
        (Part 1) 86, *86–9*
Diaz Alonso, Hernan / Xefirotarch 70–79, *70–79*
    Art Hotel *70–71*
    BCA Competition 72, *72–5*
    Busan Metropolitan City 76, *76–7*
    Maison Seroussi: 'Seingemer' *78–9*, 79
Díaz Moreno, Cristina 17
Dubai 62, 64, 162, 260
Egypt 206, 254, 258, 264, 282
Eisenmann, Peter 304
Eloueini, Ammar / AEDS 90–99, *90–99*
    California Set Design 96, *96–7*
    CoReFab#71 92, *92*
    Me Boutique, Issey Miyake 94, *94–5*
    MU Chair 98, *98–9*
    Pleats Please, Issey Miyake, Galeries Lafayette 93, *93*
EMERGENT 100–109, *100–109*
    Cell House 102, *102–3*
    Paris Courthouse *100–101*, 104, *104–7*
    Stockholm City Library *108–9*, 109
Empuriabrava 322
England 68, 129, 244

Evan Douglis Studio 110–17, *110–17*
    Auto Braids / Auto Breeding – Jean Prouvé Display-scape 112, *112–13*
    Heliocopes – Media-scape Installation *110–11*, 114, *114–15*, *400*
    REptile – Haku Japanese Restaurant *116–17*, 117
Faulders, Thom / Beige Architecture and Design 118–27, *118–27*
    AirSpace *118–19*, 120, *120–21*
    Chromogenic Dwelling 122, *122–3*
    MOCA@LBC 124, *124–5*
    Mute Room 126, *126–7*
Flaubert, Gustave 384
Florida 11
Fordwich 354, 356, 358
France 78, 92, 94, 96, 104, 114, 132, 248, 274, 358
Frazer, John and Julia 11, 12, 13
Freyssinet, Eugène 104
García Grinda, Efrén 17
Gaudí, Antoní *12, 13*, 191
Gell-Mann, Murray 365
Germany 93, 96, 176
Giacometti, Alberto 356
Gibson, William 11
Glanville, Ranulph 365
Goulthorpe, Mark / dECOi Architects 128–39, *128–39*, 234
    Hyposurface *128–31*, 130
    Miran Galerie 132, *132–3*
    MV2 Apartments 134, *134–5*
    Paramorph 2: Bankside Towertop Penthouse 136, *136–9*
Graves, Michael 29
Greg Lynn FORM 140–51, *140–51*
    5900 Wilshire Blvd Restaurant and Trellis Pavilion 142, *142–3*
    BLOB WALL© 144, *144–5*
    Flatware 146, *146–7*
    Slavin House 148, *148–9*
    Vitra Ravioli Chair *140–41*, 150, *150–51*
Haque, Usman / Haque Design + Research 152–9, *152–9*
    Evolving Sonic Environment 158, *158–9*
    Floatables 154, *154*
    Open Burble *152–3*, 155
    Sky Ear 156, *156–7*
Havana 192
Hebb, Donald 158
Holloway, Ed 238
Hollywood 216
Houston 61
Huljich, Georgina 285
Hungary 32
Institute of Contemporary Arts (London) 10
Iowa 18
Iran 215
Israel 54, 270
Istanbul 204, 210, 222
Italy 168, 240, 358
J. Mayer H. 172–89, *172–89*
    ADA1 *172–3*

BMW Event and Delivery Centre 176, *176–7*
Danfoss Universe, Master Plan – Curiosity.Centre / Food. Factory 178, *178–81*
Metropol Parasol 186, *186–9*
New National Library of the Czech Republic *182–5*, 184
Seasonscape – Ascona Lakefront Pier *174–5*, 175
Jamelle, Hina 61
Japan 120, 224, 238
Jarry, Alfred 356
Jasperse, John 96
Jeongok Archaeological Site 300
Jerry Tate Architects 160–71, *160–71*
    Dubai Waterfront Hotel *160–61*, 162, *162–5*
    New Orleans Neighbourhood Community Centre and Hurricane Shelter *166–7*, 167
    Sorrento Bathing Platform 168, *168–9*
    Swiss-Army Wall Project 170, *170–71*
Kalahari Desert 310
Kerrigan, Christian *362–3*, 372, *372–3*
Kielder 348
Klein, Tobias 190–95, *190–95*
    Synthetic Syncretism 192, *192–5*
KOL/MAC LLC 196–211, *196–211*
    Fifty-Storey Office Building and Shopping Centre 210, *210–11*
    Mixed-Use High-Rise and Highway Infrastructure 202, *202–3*
    Museum Campus Comprising an Archaeological Research Institute, Visitors' Centre, Offices and Parks 206, *206–9*
    MUTEN Galataport / Coastal Urban Development 204, *204–5*
    Urban Redevelopment of Former Brewery *196–7*, 198, *198–201*
Lalín 24
La Paz 278
Leong, Sacha *382–3*, 383
Leung, Chris 345
Lisbon 226
Llers (Girona) 320
London 68, 129, 136, 170, 218, 232, 266, 268, 272, 346, 350, 352, 380
Los Angeles 13, 70, 100, 102, 142, 214, 285, 292, 295, 327, 332
Louisiana 166
Lynn, Greg 13
Madrid 17
Mahmoodi, Arshia / Void inc. 212–17, *212–17*
    The Bobco Metals Headquarters 214, *214*
    Ministry of Petroleum Headquarters 215, *215*
    MUK Residence 216, *216–17*
MAK Center 292
Marcosandmarjan 218–27, *218–27*
    Bai Jia Zhuang 220, *220–21*
    Floating Vessel NGC 222, *222–3*
    Lofting House 226, *226–7*
    New Tomihiro Museum of SHI-GA / Garden of Vessels *218–19*, 224, *224–5*
Markopoulou, Martha 384, *384–5*
Massachusetts 45, 50, 56, 72
Massachusetts Institute of Technology (Cambridge) 11, 45
    Media Lab 45, 340
Meier, Richard 129

Melbourne 338, 342, 343
Mendelsohn, Eric 54
Mendini, Alessandro 29
Minale, Massimo *364, 370–71*, 371
Mitchell, Bill 13
Miyake, Issey 93, 94
Montreal 45
Munich 176
Munro, Stuart 228–41, *228–41*
   Dee 230, *230–31*
   Osaka Urban Ideas Competition 238, *238–9*
   Slamhounds 240, *240–41*
   Trauma Furniture *228–9*, 234, *234–7*
   Virtual-Vital Parallax 232, *232–3*
Murray, Shaun 238, 242–51, *242–51*
   Archulus Flood Structure *242–7*, 244
   Carmargue Condensations 248, *248–9*
   Information Polyp 250, *250–51*
Naga, Tarek 252
Naga Studio Architects 252–65, *252–65*
   The Grand Egyptian Museum (GEM) Competition:
     Osiris Re-Membered 258, *258–9*
   House of Emergent Suspensions 254, *254–7*
   Oqyana 260, *260–63*
   Phantom Limbs *252–3*
   Sharm Safari Gate 264, *264–5*
Nanjing 52
Nanjing University 52
Negroponte, Nicholas 11
Netherlands 30
New Cairo 254
New Orleans 166, 167
New York 26, 28, 61, 110, 112, 129, 134, 266, 280, 290, 307, 308, 312,
   327
Niewenhuys, Constant 10
   New Babylon 10
Nordborg 178
Nouvel, Jean 93
Novak, Marcos *8–9*, 10, 12, 13
   AlloSpace 13
   AlloSphere 13
   Eversion information landscapes *8–9*, 13
   Transarchitecture 13
null.lab 213
oceanD 266–75, *266–75*
   LJ House 272, *272–3*
   Rabin Peace Forum 270, *270–71*
   Ski Chalet 274, *274–5*
   Warner Penthouse *266–7*, 268, *268–9*
Ohio 334
Oliver, Vaughan 240
Oosterhuis, Kas 13
Orléans 114
ORTLOS 276–83, *276–83*
   City Upgrade 280, *280–81*
   Grand Egyptian Museum 282, *282–3*

Hong Kong *276–7*
   Urban Park 278, *278–9*
Osaka 238
Paris 78, 92, 94, 104, 129, 132, 358, 380
Pask, Gordon 10, *10*, 11, 158, 366
P-A-T-T-E-R-N-S 284–93, *284–93*
   The Element 288, *288–9*
   Nodeul Island Performing Arts Centre 284–7, 286
   Unibodies 290, *290–91*
   Vertical Garden Competition Entry 292, *292–3*
Pearce, Martin 13
Picasso, Pablo 377
Playa del Rey 280
Playa Vista 280
Portugal 226
Prague 182, 296
Price, Cedric 10, 11
   Fun Palace 10
   Generator 11
Priessner, Paul 295
Prouvé, Jean 112
Qua'Virarch 294–305, *294–305*
   The Czech Republic National Library 296, *296–9*
   Gyeonggi-Do Jeongok Prehistory Museum *294–5*, 300,
     300–303
   Southbank Planning Development 304, *304–5*
Rabin, Yitzak 270
Rahim, Ali 61
Rashid, Hani 26, 29
Rastogi, Manit *10*
Republic of Botswana 310
Riley, Bridget 268
Rome 240, 358, 378
Rosario 288
Rossi, Aldo 29
Roy, Lindy / ROY Co. 306–15, *306–15*
   Noah 308, *308–9*
   Okavango Delta Spa *306–7*, 310, *310–11*
   West Street Tower *312–13*
   Wind River Lodge 314, *314–15*
Royal British Architects Pavilion (Birmingham) 42
Royal Melbourne Institute of Technology 336
Ruiz-Geli, Enric / Cloud9 316–25, *316–25*
   Aviary 318, *318–19*
   Villa Bio *316–17*, 320, *320–21*
   Villa Nurbs 322, *322–5*
San Francisco 119, 122, 126
Santa Monica 13, 328
Seoul 286
servo 326–35, *326–35*
   Dark Places 328, *328–9*
   The Genealogy of Speed *326–7*, 330, *330–31*
   Spoorg 332, *332–3*
   Thermocline 334, *334–5*
Seville 186
Shanghai 67

Sheil, Bob 345
SIAL 336–43, *336–43*
        Freefab - Concrete Rapid Manufacturing 342, *342*
        Informing Design Exploration 340, *340–41*
        Pavilion for New Architecture 343, *343*
        Spatial Dynamic Media System *338–9*, 339
Sinai 264
sixteen*(makers) *12*, 344–51, *344–51*
        Blusher 346, *346–7*
        Hot Desk (with Neil Spiller) *12*
        Kielder Residency *344–5*, 348, *348–9*
        StaC 350, *350–51*
Smith, Makai 290
Soleri, Paolo 84
Sonoma 124
Sorrento 168
South Africa 304
South Korea 76, 286, 300
Spain 17, 24, 82, 186, 318, 320, 322
Spiller, Neil *12, 13*, 240, 352–9, *352–9*
        Bee Gates 354, *354–5*
        Communicating Vessels *352–3*
        Dee Trunks 356, *356–7*
        Hot Desk (with sixteen*(makers)) *12*
        Mediatheque *12*
        Velazquez Machine and Growing Vistas 358, *358–9*
Spina, Marcelo 285
Spuybroek, Lars 13
Stockholm 108, 327
Suffolk 244
Sweden 108, 374
Switzerland 174
Tehran 215
Tel Aviv 54, 270
Texas 61
Tokyo 120
Tomlin, Glen *368–9, 376–7*, 377
Toronto 40, 230
Turing, Alan 9
Turkey 204, 210, 222
UK 136, 170, 268, 272, 346, 348, 350, 354, 356, 358
United Arab Emirates 62, 64, 162, 260
University of Waterloo (Canada) 38
US 96, 129
Venice (California) 148, 252, 330
Venice (Italy) 22
Wiscombe, Tom 100
Zurich 327